AF597947

LOVE STORIES

ART, PASSION & TRAGEDY

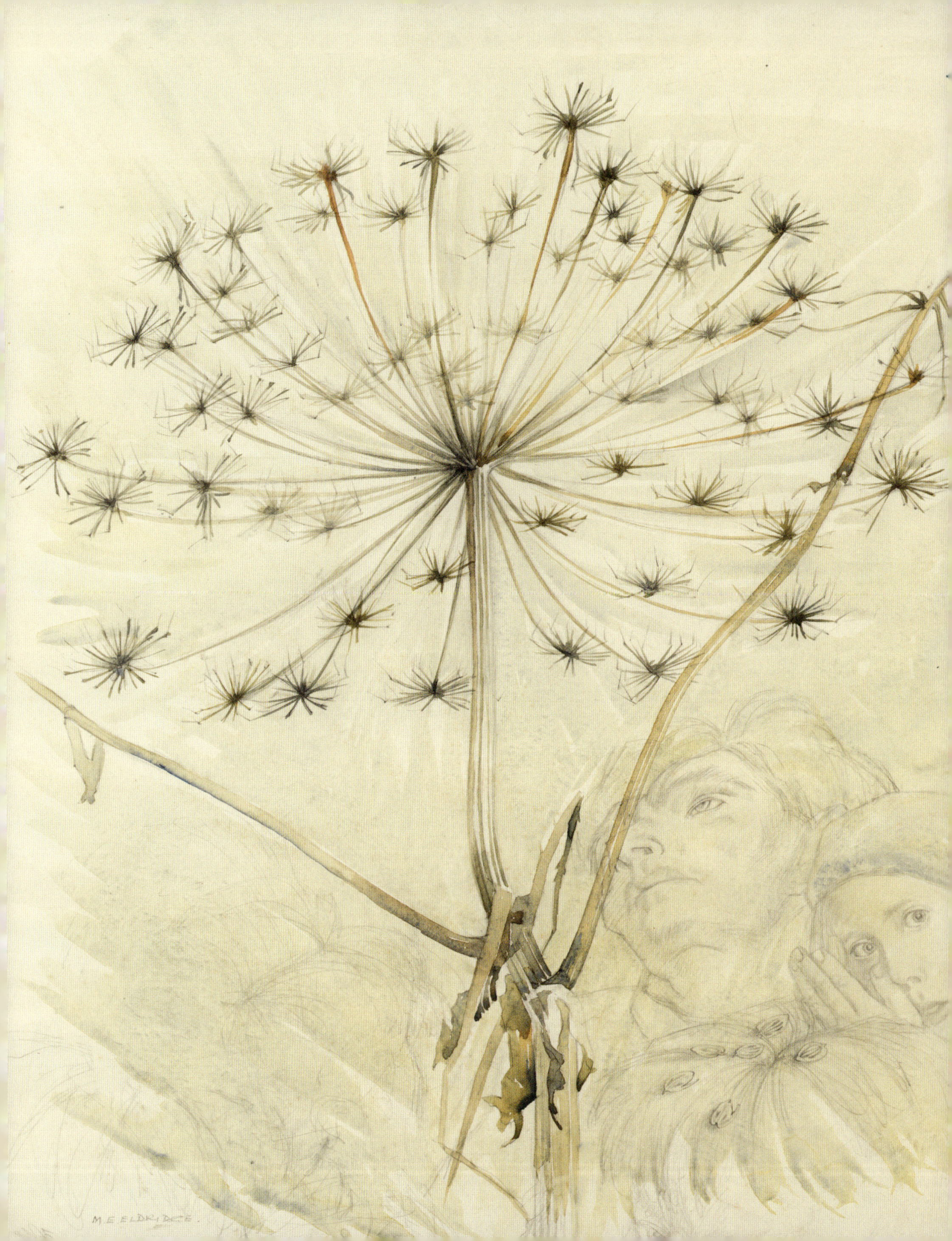
M E ELDRIDGE

LOVE STORIES

ART, PASSION & TRAGEDY

EDITED BY
LUCY PELTZ
&
LOUISE STEWART

NATIONAL PORTRAIT GALLERY, LONDON

CONTENTS

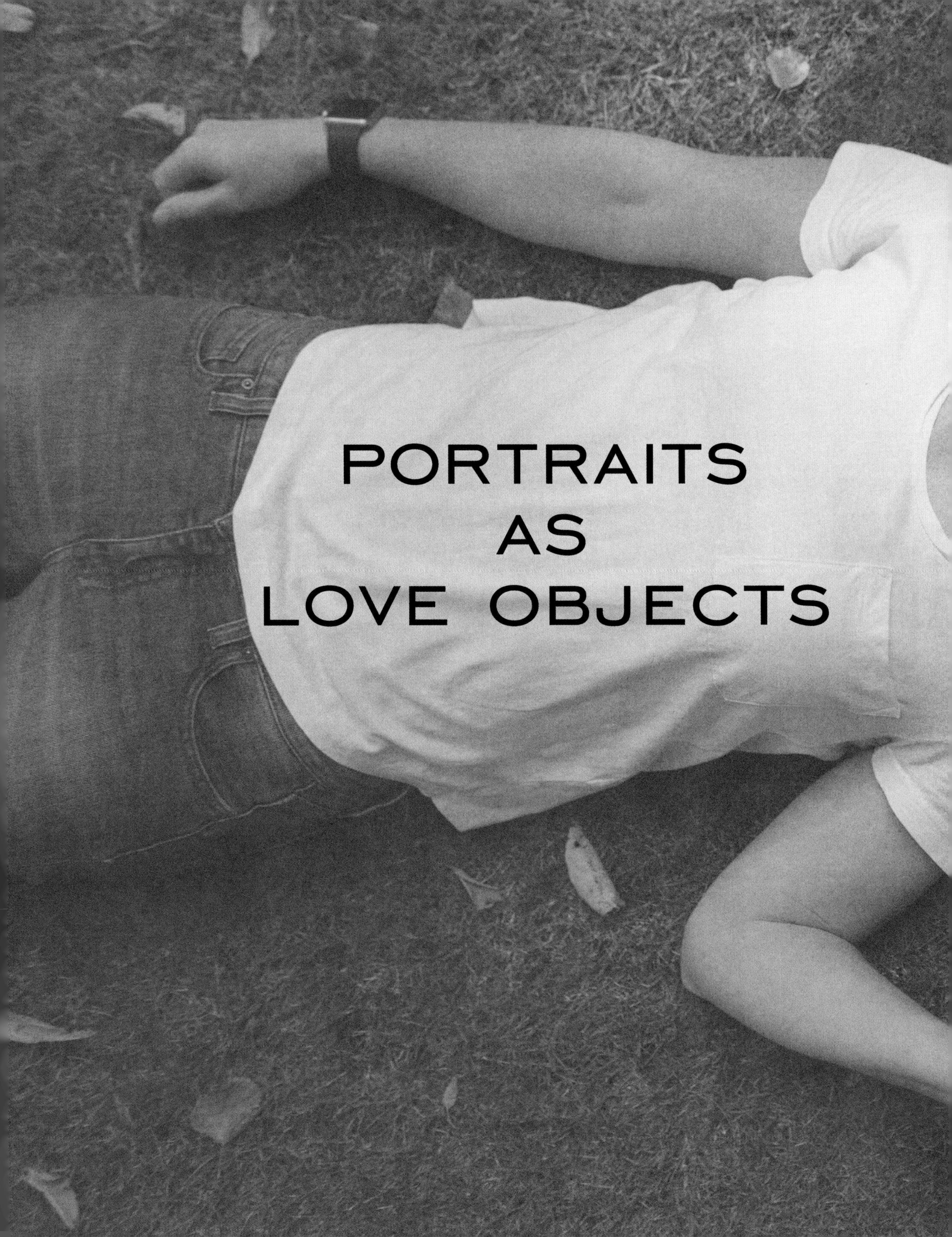

PORTRAITS AS LOVE OBJECTS

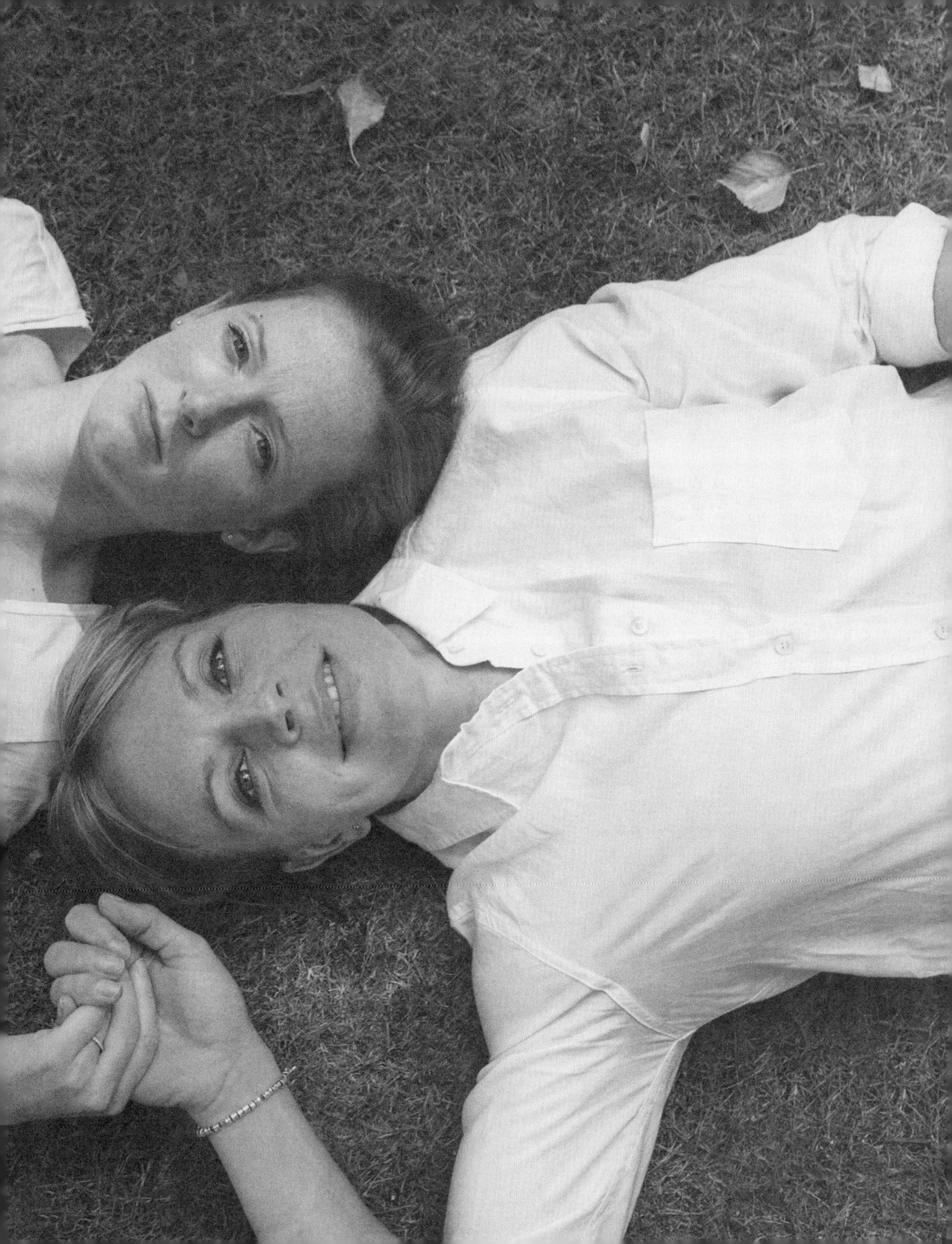

LOUISE STEWART

PORTRAITS AS LOVE OBJECTS

CHANGING IDEAS: LOVE & LITERATURE

Love Stories explores the relationship between portraiture and romantic love in Britain from the Tudor period to the present day. This relationship has been evident throughout the history of Western art, as is made clear by the ancient Roman historian Pliny the Elder's explanation of the origins of painting. In Pliny's account, a maiden from Corinth traced the outline of her lover's shadow as a way of keeping him present although he was leaving for battle. Pliny's story neatly encapsulates the relationship between love and portraiture, with the portrait acting as substitute for the lover during his absence. Pliny's account fascinated British artists and writers in the eighteenth century. One of several representations of this story is by Joseph Wright of Derby, who completed his depiction of the maiden and her lover in 1784 (fig.1). As well as providing a romantic explanation for the origin of painting, which undoubtedly appealed to artists, the ubiquity of the story is indicative of a wider contemporary interest in this tale of love, loss and art, and of society's preoccupation with love stories more generally.

Love is widely recognised as an essential element of the human condition. It has had huge cultural impact, but remains notoriously elusive and difficult to define. Society's ideas and expectations about love are subject to historical change and have shifted over time. This is made clear in texts produced since the sixteenth century, when the subject of love came under scrutiny in a variety of literary genres: from love poetry expressing an idealised vision of romance to medical texts outlining the perceived dangers of love or popular novels which shaped expectations of romantic relationships. The changes and continuities in ideas about love in Britain revealed in these texts provide an important context for the exploration of portraits as love objects and help us understand their role in romantic relationships.

Although love is elusive and changeable, it is ultimately characterised by the deep affection of one person for another, often arising from physical desire. With its tales of knights yearning after beautiful yet unattainable ladies, the medieval tradition of courtly love has been a powerful force in shaping

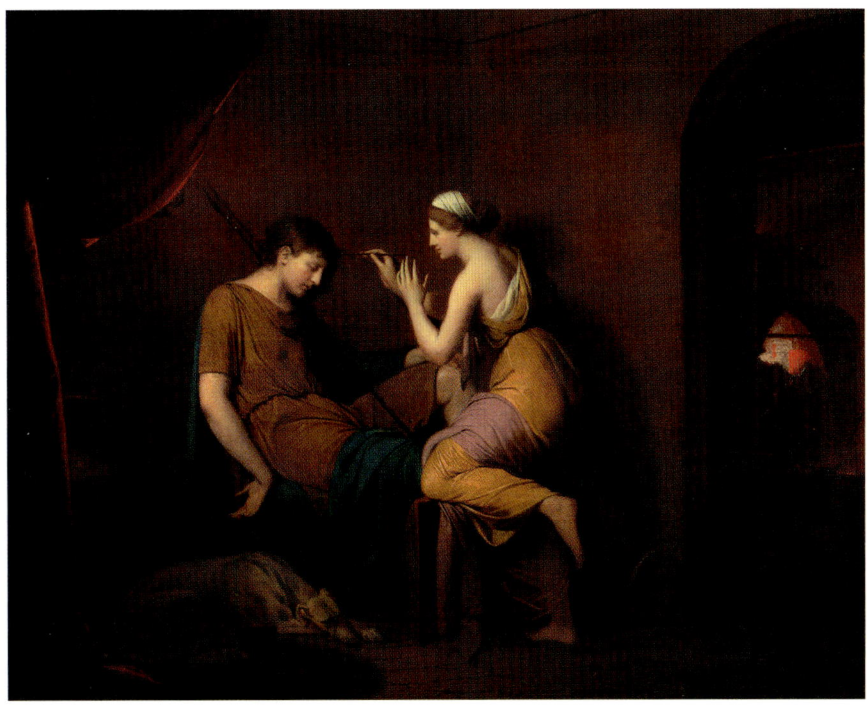

Fig.1 *The Corinthian Maid*, 1782–4
Joseph Wright of Derby
Oil on canvas, 1063 × 1308mm
National Gallery of Art, Washington, Paul Mellon Collection

Western understanding of romantic love between men and women. The genre was underpinned by historically specific codes of behaviour that included chivalry, honour, courtesy and loyalty and required the male lover to complete heroic feats for the sake of the lady who was the object of his desire. Love in this mode was a powerful influence at the court of Elizabeth I, where male courtiers competed for the queen's affections, with the likes of Sir Walter Ralegh and Sir Philip Sidney producing love poetry in praise of Elizabeth, casting her in the role of the unattainable lady of courtly romance. In 1587, Ralegh addressed Elizabeth as 'my princess, My world's joy and my true fantasy's mistress'.[1] Popular literature, letters, diaries and material artefacts show that romantic love has been both a cultural preoccupation and an important aspect of the lives of people across the social scale in Britain since the middle ages. In sixteenth and seventeenth-century Britain, themes of romantic love were expressed in popular ballads and plays which, as in Shakespeare's *Romeo and Juliet* (*c.*1591–5), often dealt with the tension between passionate, romantic love and society's expectations of familial duty. At the same time, the role of romantic love in a well-lived life was debated in medical texts, advice books and moral treatises. These texts interpret romantic love in myriad ways: as a healthy emotion which underpinned successful marriage, as an inherently destructive passion or even as a physical or mental illness. Robert Burton's *Anatomy of Melancholy* (1621) and Jacques Ferrand's *Erotomania* (1640) detail the causes and symptoms and propose cures for 'love or erotique melancholy'.[2] The idea of the melancholic lover is epitomised in a portrait of one of the most talented love poets of his age, John Donne, represented in the guise of a melancholic lover, dressed in black and brooding in shadows (fig.2). The portrait was made while Donne was in his twenties, a time of intense creativity when he produced much of his love poetry, often dealing with themes of forbidden love and physical longing. The portrait is inscribed, 'O Lady, lighten our darkness', which is a reworking of a psalm and suggests that the painting may have been produced for a lover.

According to Ferrand's *Erotomania*, the only complete cure for love melancholy was marriage. Ideas about marriage were subject to much debate and generated a great deal of literature, including advice books and treatises. John Evelyn's portrait (fig.3) was made to accompany his *Instructions Oeconomique*, a manuscript treatise on marriage which stresses the importance of a wife's obedience to her husband. This private treatise was sent with the portrait to his wife Mary in 1648, shortly after their marriage.

For much of the period explored here, marriage was the norm. In the sixteenth and seventeenth centuries between 80 and 90 per cent of people who survived to adulthood got married. England was a Christian country in which the official and widely accepted view, at the time, was that marriage was a 'holy estate' belonging to God and should be celebrated in church. 'The Form of Solemnization of Marriage' in the *Book of Common Prayer* of 1559, the established form of worship in the English church, makes the reasons for marriage clear.[3] It reflected the relationship of Christ with the Church.

> It was ordained for the procreation of children to be brought up in the fear and nurture of the Lord, and praise of God. Secondly, it was ordained for a remedy against sin, and to avoid fornication, that such persons as have not the gift of continency might marry, and keep themselves undefiled members of Christ's body. Thirdly, for the mutual society, help, and comfort, that the one ought to have of the other, both in prosperity and adversity.[4]

The marital union was therefore positioned as the ideal state for the expression of love.

Until at least the eighteenth century in Britain, marriages were usually, to some extent, arranged by a couple's parents because of considerations such as the consolidation of property and status. Despite this, the ideal marriage as defined in 'conduct books' was invariably founded on mutual affection. The expectation was that affection should be fostered through a period of courtship, during which love tokens and letters could be exchanged. The love which grew

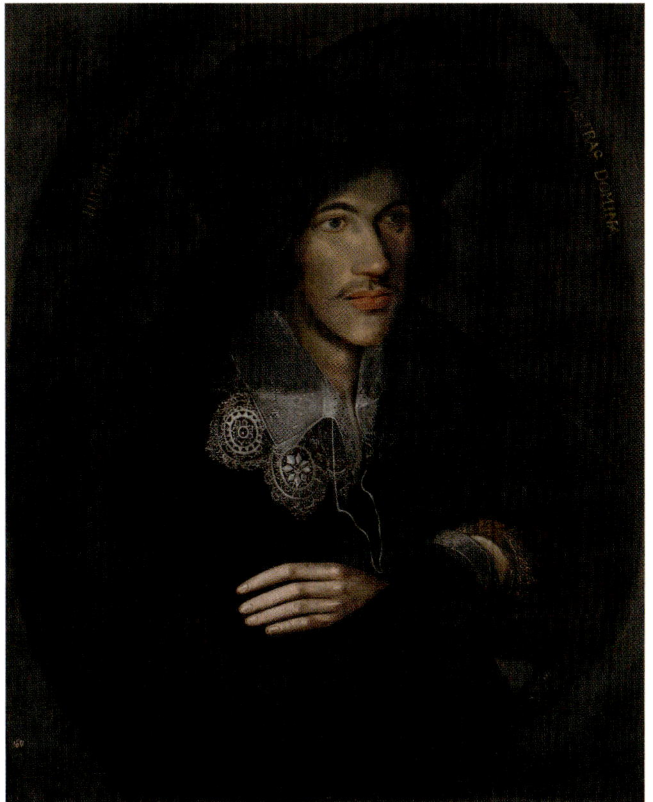

Fig.2 *John Donne, c.*1595
Unknown English artist
Oil on panel, 771 × 625mm
National Portrait Gallery, London

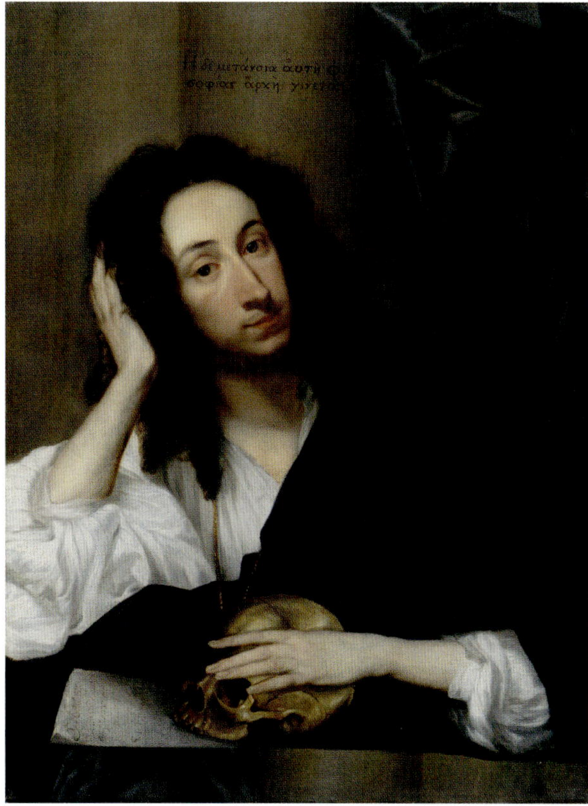

Fig.3 *John Evelyn, c.*1648–56
Robert Walker
Oil on canvas, 879 × 641mm
National Portrait Gallery, London

between the couple gave rise to both husband and wife fulfilling their marital roles within this hierarchical relationship, as codified in the Church of England marriage rite: to cherish and protect and love and obey, respectively.

In 1753, 'Lord Hardwicke's Marriage Act' saw parliament take control of the legal definition of marriage. This had previously been left to church courts, which recognised marriages as valid so long as a couple stated their intent to marry in front of witnesses. Hardwicke's act by contrast stipulated that valid marriages had to take place in a formal ceremony in an Anglican church following the calling of banns (with exemptions for Quakers and Jews), as a public declaration of the forthcoming wedding, or the purchase of a marriage licence. Marriages could only be made at certain times, on certain days, and the couple had to be over twenty-one or have the consent of their guardians. Additionally, at this time, marriage was practically indissoluble: until the passing of the Divorce Act (1857) any couple wanting a divorce required an individual act of parliament. The indissolubility of marriage and its inherent inequality, with women expected to obey their husbands and, legally speaking, ceasing to

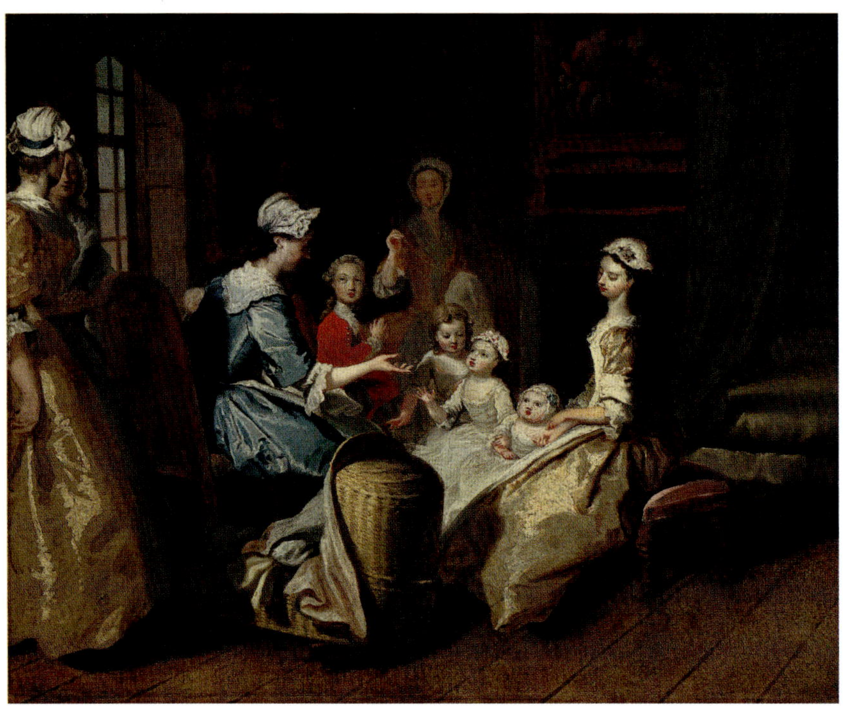

Fig.4 *Pamela Tells a Nursery Tale*, c.1744
Joseph Highmore
Oil on canvas, 628 × 760mm
The Fitzwilliam Museum, Cambridge

exist as separate individuals after marriage, meant that some couples decided not to marry. Mary Wollstonecraft and William Godwin were two radical thinkers and activists who, as a couple, objected to marriage as it stood in the late eighteenth century. Godwin felt that it was irrational to promise to feel the same way for ever while Wollstonecraft wanted marriage reformed due to its inherent inequality that made women vulnerable to abuse of all kinds.[5] In 1797 Wollstonecraft discovered that she was pregnant. The pair married reluctantly in order to avoid a scandal that would forever affect the life of their child to be. Other couples were prevented from marrying by a lack of financial resource, or difficulties in obtaining divorces.[6]

In the mid-eighteenth century, just as Hardwicke's Marriage Act sought to tighten the legal definition of marriage, in the wider cultural sphere an interest in 'companionate marriage' emphasised that a loving relationship should be the basis of virtue and duty.[7] This evolution coincided with a new focus on finding fulfilment and meaning in individual emotional experiences that was being expressed in philosophy and literature. This ideal has been linked to the emergence of the romantic novel as a new genre which, for the first time, presented a narrative through the eyes of a single, central character, and often dealt with desire, love and longing alongside questions of morality, social status and faith.[8] The first romantic novel was Samuel Richardson's *Pamela* (1740). The work is constructed as a series of personal letters detailing an often licentious tale of the virtue and reward of the eponymous servant girl Pamela who is exploited and sexually assaulted by the rakish (and entitled) master of the house. Pamela, however, through her modesty, god-fearing behaviour and steadfastness, brings about a reform in her master's character and ends up as the contented wife and lady of the house surrounded by their healthy and happy infants (fig.4).

As a literary form, the popular novel emerged in tandem with a culture of 'sensibility' that it also helped to disseminate. Associated with gentility and elite social status, sensibility entailed a heightened receptiveness to one's feelings and to the beauty of nature. The ability to feel passionate, romantic love was therefore considered to be a mark of refinement and was expressed in the increasingly fashionable practice of sending love letters.[9]

This emphasis on companionship and the possibility of achieving personal happiness through a romantic relationship remained an important theme in ideas about love throughout the nineteenth century. The romantic novel continued to be hugely popular, with works by writers such as Jane Austen and the Brontë sisters avidly consumed by an increasingly literate public. This has been considered by some historians to have changed expectations of love and marriage. Young women in particular now sought romantic passion rather than the mutual affection underpinned by duty for which their counterparts in earlier centuries are characterised as having hoped.[10] This period also saw the roles assigned to each marriage partner crystallize further, with the ideal woman conceived as the 'angel in the house' dedicated to serving her husband and children.[11] This female role model was firmly associated with the domestic sphere, where she raised the couple's offspring and maintained the home as a welcoming haven for the husband. He, meanwhile, supported the family in the world of work and engaged with politics and society as an active citizen.[12]

In the late nineteenth century and into the twentieth, traditional ideas of identity, family and marriage were increasingly being questioned in the wake of industrialisation, urbanisation, campaigns for women's rights and the First and Second World Wars. During the 1960s and 1970s the Women's Liberation movement gained momentum in Britain, with magazines such as *Spare Rib* and authors including Kate Millett and Germaine Greer calling for equal opportunities for women and undermining the idea that feminine identity inevitably involved marriage and maternity. A decline in the numbers of people practising formal religion, the 'sexual revolution' of the 1960s and the increased availability of contraception was liberating for some and meant that romantic love and sex could more openly co-exist alongside (or apart from) conventional ideals of marriage and family life for a wider cross-section of society than ever before. In tandem with this, an ever-growing emphasis on personal happiness

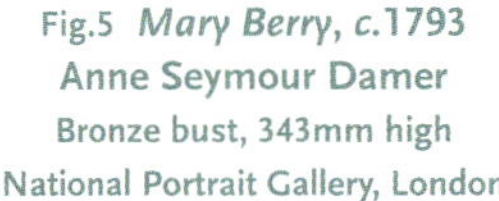

Fig.5 *Mary Berry*, *c.*1793
Anne Seymour Damer
Bronze bust, 343mm high
National Portrait Gallery, London

above duty led to romantic love being increasingly understood as a means to personal fulfilment and identity.[13] In the early twentieth century, brave individuals openly resisted traditional gender roles and ideas about relationships. The publication of works such as Radclyffe Hall's *The Well of Loneliness* (1928), which caused controversy with its candid portrayal of a lesbian relationship and Virginia Woolf's *Orlando* (1928), which features a poet who changes sex as its main character, and was dedicated to Woolf's lover Vita Sackville West, are indicative of these changing ideas. In the same year, D.H. Lawrence's *Lady Chatterley's Lover*, which deals with love across class divisions and includes explicit sexual descriptions, was published privately in Italy. An unexpurgated version was not published in Britain until 1960 after the publishers, Penguin, had been prosecuted and found not guilty under the Obscene Publications Act.

In 1967, the Sexual Offences Act partially decriminalised sex between men, first made a criminal offence under Henry VIII in 1533. Sex between women, on the other hand, was never criminalised. For many Victorians, including the queen herself, lesbian relationships were either inconceivable or were not seen to threaten the patriarchal status quo and therefore were not considered to require legislation. Sex, of course, is not the only facet of a loving relationship, nor can we always establish if a physically intimate dimension was critical to any couple. Nevertheless, there are many examples of queer women in history, devoting themselves to each other and providing powerful literary and artistic evidence of their bond, as was the case with the sculptor Anne Seymour Damer who is recognised as being in love with the author Mary Berry (fig.5) in the late eighteenth century.[14]

In 2004, the Civil Partnership Act made it possible for same-sex couples to enter into legally binding relationships in England, Scotland and Wales, while the Marriage (Same-Sex Couples) Act (2013) granted them marriage equality. Following a 2019 court ruling opposite-sex couples in the UK were granted the right to enter civil partnerships, giving those who do not wish to be married the opportunity to have their relationship legally recognised, all changes which reflect widespread public acceptance of love in all its forms.

In the UK today, a spectrum of love from romance to more explicit sexual desire is a key focus for artistic and cultural production. The ubiquity of romantic literature and 'rom coms' in film, alongside TV shows focused on dating and mating such as *Love Island,* position the attainment of sexual or romantic love as a key achievement in life, in a way that is very different from historic perspectives of love as the conduit to holy office or duty. Meanwhile, the global interest in the recent 'fairytale' weddings of members of the royal family indicate that interest in love stories continues to thrive. Set against these changing ideas, from notions of romantic love as a dangerous illness in the sixteenth century, to today's celebration of love as one means of finding fulfilment in life, the examples in this volume ultimately reveal love, in all its guises, as a constant and defining element of human experience.

LOVE TOKENS & COURTSHIP

The portraits discussed here are testament to the changing ideas about love outlined above. Many also functioned as love objects at different stages of relationships and across the social spectrum from the Tudor period until today. Portraits have been used as love tokens exchanged during courtships, have symbolised and celebrated marriage and shared lives, and have served as memorials to lost loves. Taken together, these examples demonstrate that portraits not only record the appearance of loved ones, but also play an active role in fostering love and cementing relationships; they have agency and can affect, rather than merely reflect, reality.

In October 1505, a portrait of the widowed English king, Henry VII, was completed by a Netherlandish artist working at the English court (fig.6). This impressive image was made to be sent to the court of Savoy, where the Duchess Margaret was considering Henry as a possible third husband. In this period, royal couples might not meet until their wedding day with love expected to grow afterwards, if at all. It was believed that a painted portrait could provide not only a record of a person's appearance but also, through the use of pose, props and clothing, give an insight into their social status and virtue. This made portraiture an effective means of judging a person's desirability as a potential husband or wife. Here, the rich textiles, including a gown of crimson cloth-of-gold trimmed with ermine, are appropriate to Henry's status as king and suggestive of extreme wealth. He also wears the chain of the Golden Fleece,

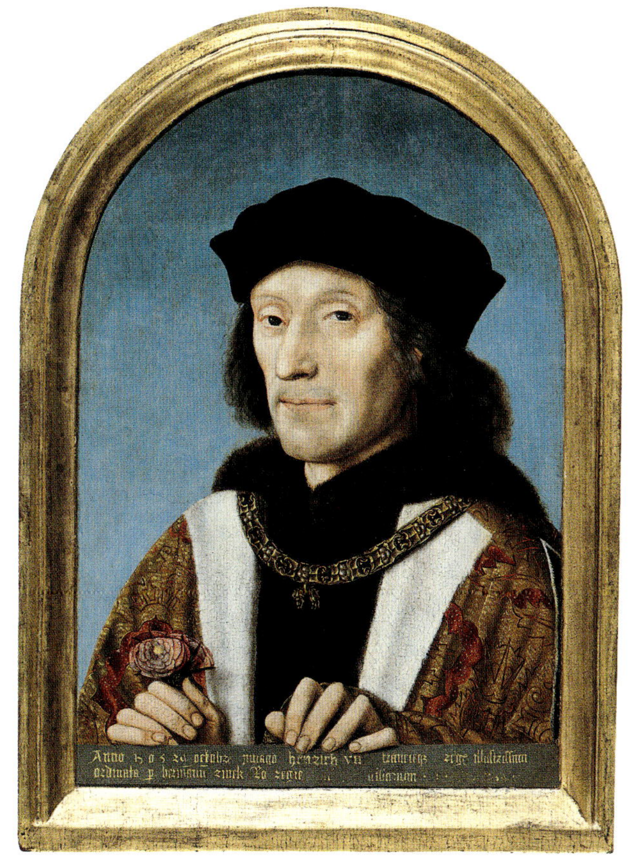

Fig.6 *King Henry VII*, 1505
Unknown Netherlandish artist
Oil on panel, 425 × 305mm
National Portrait Gallery, London

a chivalric order to which he was elected in 1491. Although Margaret ultimately declined Henry's offer of marriage, she kept his image in her possession until her death. Today, it is the earliest painted portrait in the collection of the National Portrait Gallery, London. Small and portable, Henry's likeness is typical of the portraits made to be exchanged between the glittering courts of renaissance Europe, facilitating marriage negotiations between their powerful ruling dynasties. Created at the moment when portrait painting was developing in Britain, this resonant object marks the beginning of an artistic tradition in which portraiture is closely bound up with marriage, desire and romantic love.

In 1527, King Henry VIII was obsessed with a woman who was not his wife and who refused to become his mistress. This woman, whom he had been pursuing for over a year, and who would go on to become his second queen, was Anne Boleyn.

A series of Henry's love letters to Anne, dating from 1527–8, shed light on his state of mind at the time. In them he describes his 'great agony', professes his love for Anne and begs her to become his mistress. Some of these letters were sent with gifts, including a miniature portrait of the king set into a bracelet which, unfortunately, has not survived. In the accompanying letter, Henry wrote:

> MY MISTRESS & FRIEND, my heart and I surrender ourselves into your hands, beseeching you to hold us commended to your favour, and that by absence your affection to us may not be lessened.... seeing that I cannot be personally present with you, I now send you the nearest thing I can to that, namely, my picture set in a bracelet, with the whole of the device, which you already know, wishing myself in their place, if it should please you.[15]

The same series of letters indicates, albeit fleetingly, that Anne reciprocated by sending Henry a jewel which has also not survived. According to descriptions, this was in the form of a ship in a storm bearing a female figure; as such it functioned as a form of psychological portrait depicting a storm-tossed woman, in turmoil, that served as a symbolic representation of Anne's state of mind.[16]

The giving of portrait jewels was part of a long-established tradition of exchanging love tokens as an element in the courtship process. Such gifts were small, intimate objects generally given to a woman by a male suitor. Legal records show that the offering of love tokens was common across the

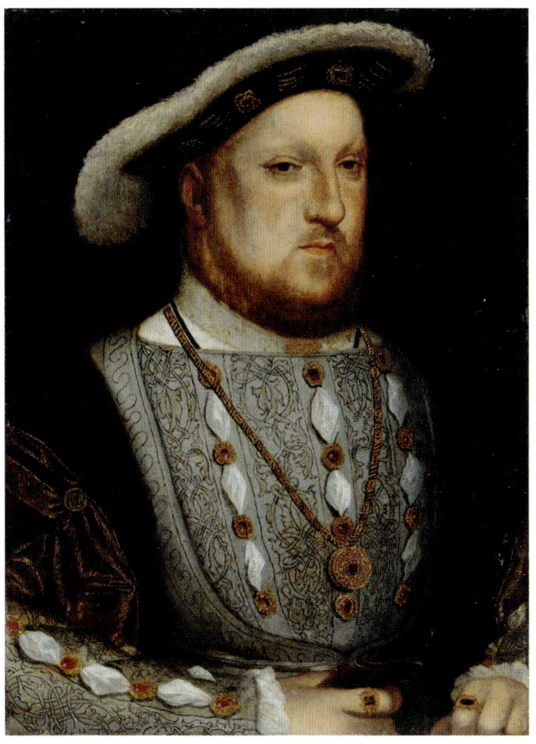

Fig.7 *King Henry VIII*, probably 17th century, based on a work of 1536
After Hans Holbein the Younger
Oil on copper, 279 × 200mm
National Portrait Gallery, London

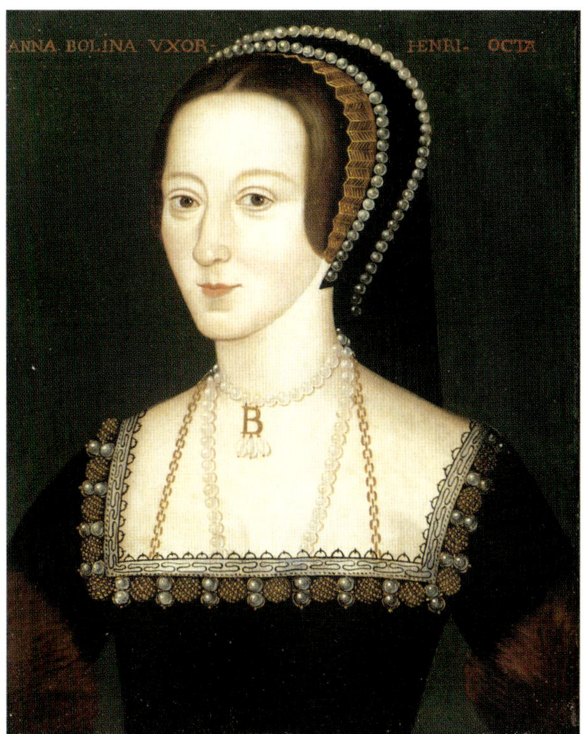

Fig.8 *Anne Boleyn*, late 16th century, based on a work of *c.*1533–6
Unknown English artist
Oil on panel, 543 × 416mm
National Portrait Gallery, London

social spectrum. Rings were most common but brooches, ribbons, gloves and handkerchiefs were also popular. As these offerings were intended to forge or deepen a connection between two people their acceptance was highly significant. It placed an obligation on the receiver and could even be considered as proof that a marriage had taken place.[17]

Henry and Anne's tokens were exchanged at a crucial juncture in their relationship; Henry was trying to secure Anne as his mistress and was clearly concerned that his absence might cause her 'affection to be ... lessened', undermining his ambition to win her over. It is significant that Henry and Anne chose to exchange representations of themselves rather than any of the more common types of love gift, at this key turning point (figs 7 and 8). The portrait, as an image of the absent lover, acted as a substitute, keeping them present and imbuing the love token with the power to evoke loving feelings in the viewer. Indeed, Henry's letter indicates that it is precisely this function he hoped the portrait would fulfil, being the 'nearest thing' to his physical presence. Ultimately, Anne was not willing to become Henry's mistress, despite this exchange of letters and portraits. However, it was around this time that the king decided to seek a divorce from his first wife, Catherine of Aragon, in order to pursue marriage to Anne.[18]

The giving of portraits by both Henry VII and Henry VIII occurred at moments of heightened anxiety about the future of their relationships and their dynasty. This indicates that love tokens in the form of portraits could be intended to catalyse events, move romantic relationships forward and create binding commitments. They shared these aims with portrait objects that were exchanged as love tokens lower down the social scale, from silhouettes to decorated dress accessories and coins.

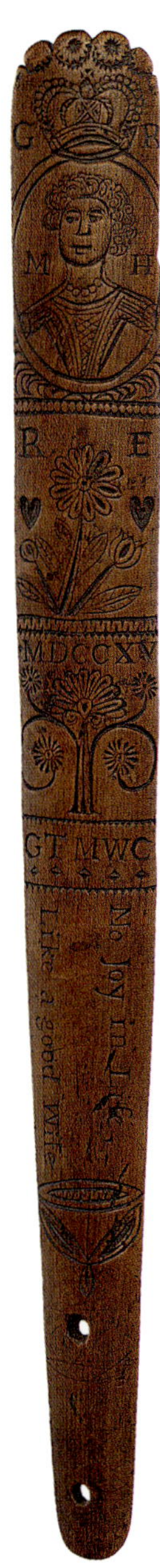

Fig.9 ***Busk**, c.*1715
Unknown maker
Beech
Bryan Collection, USA

Stay busks, which were worn close to the body to stiffen the stays (corset) at the front of a woman's bodice, were a common form of courtship token that often incorporated portrait images, as seen in the example illustrated (fig.9).[19] When given as love tokens they could be carved by the giver with symbols including love hearts, initials and rhymes. In some cases they also featured small compartments which contained keepsakes, such as locks of hair or lovers' notes.[20] Worn in internal pockets, and secreted next to the body, busks were very intimate, even erotic objects that have been interpreted as symbols of masculine possession and are highly evocative of the sexual act.[21] Like miniatures, they were intended to foster love and memory and help in the development of romantic relationships. Some surviving examples urge the recipient to remember the love of the person who gave them the busk, while the symbolism of the carving in the object illustrated suggests that it was part of a marriage proposal.[22] It bears a representation of a woman, presumably meant to be a depiction of the recipient, as love tokens were usually given to women by men. This contrasts with the practice of male lovers giving portraits of themselves to their intended, as discussed above.[23] It seems likely that the portrait here was carved as an act of devotion by the giver, perhaps to demonstrate his intimate knowledge of his loved one. The portrait is surmounted by a crown and the initials 'GR' for King George I. Also incorporated are the initials of the couple between whom the busk was exchanged: 'MH' and 'RE'. The busk is decorated with flowers, hearts and a quotation derived from the apocryphal book of Ecclesiastes, 'No joy in life like a good wife' (9:9). The crown and royal initials along with a biblical quotation invoke a triad of institutional authorities that provide a context or function for the busk, while the portrait and initials mitigate any ambiguity about who was involved in the interaction. This is particularly significant given that prior to 1753, marriages could be effected by the exchange of promises without the direct involvement of church or state, although such unions were often disputed later. In such cases, love tokens were sometimes used in court as evidence that a marriage had taken place and was valid.[24] All of this supports the idea of this busk as an element in a marriage proposal; its acceptance could have indicated assent and the iconography, the initials and the portrait would have helped to make the promise of marriage binding. In this context, the portrait may be read, like the miniature portraits discussed above, as a means of advancing the romantic relationship at a critical turning point.

The wooden stay busk was a popular, domestically-produced love token. Another form of intimate keepsake made to foster memories of loved ones were coins which were rubbed down to form flat surfaces onto which romantic symbols, sentimental rhymes and portrait images could be inscribed.[25] Hundreds of surviving examples in museum and private collections are testament to how widespread this practice was during the eighteenth and nineteenth centuries. These tokens were passed between lovers to mark key life events, including impending separation. A number of poignant examples were left behind by convicts who were transported from Britain to penal colonies in the New World, particularly Australia.[26] They often bear names and dates along with symbols such as hearts, Cupid's arrows and images of happy couples strolling together or toasting their happiness. A typical example is dated 1829 and carries the initials 'TR' (fig.10). It shows a couple standing by a table laid with a carafe and wine glasses. Images representing lovers enjoying a favoured pastime are likely to have evoked shared experience, making the tokens more potent in fostering memory and eliciting longing for the missing lover. The survival of loops on some examples suggest that, like miniatures, these engraved coins were not only handled and gazed at but also worn on the body.[27] The text inscribed on the reverse of this token and signed 'T Rea' reads:

Fig.10 ***Token engraved with stippled image***, 1829
Unknown artist
Lead, 36mm diameter
National Museum of Australia, Canberra

> when this you see / remember me / and ber me in / your mind / let all the world / say What they / Will. dont Prove / to me un / kind 1829

Clearly the verse was intended to keep the absent lover in the memory of the recipient, presumably in the hope that they would remain faithful until a possible return. This, however, was unlikely. Sentences varied from two years to life, but in practice most convicts never returned to Britain or saw their loved ones again.[28]

SHARED LIVES

While the convict tokens speak of relationships unexpectedly curtailed, until relatively recently in Britain a serious courtship between a man and a woman was expected to culminate in a wedding.[29] Resulting in a formal union, marriage was a major rite of passage which was transformative for the people involved,

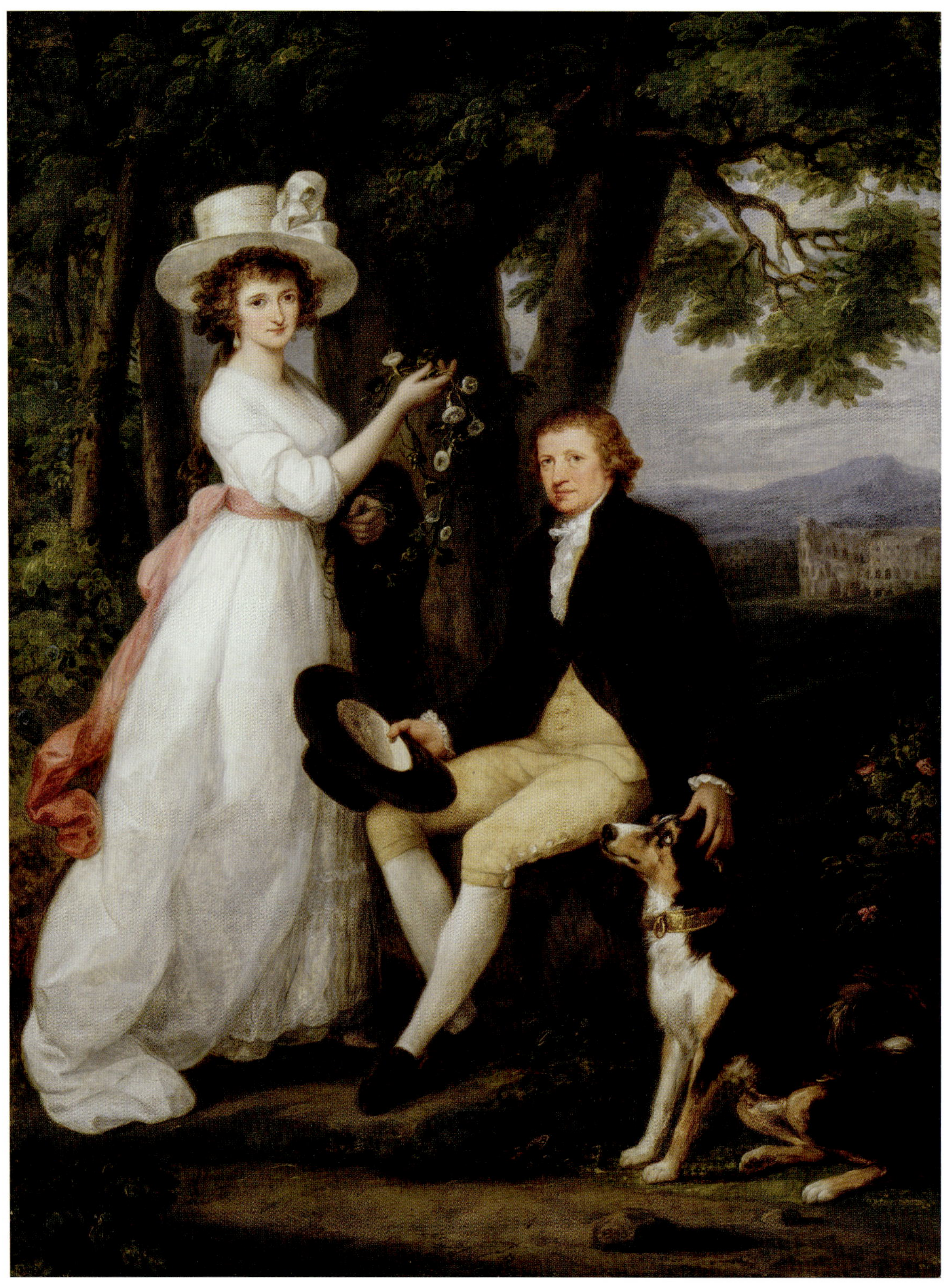

Fig.11 *Anna Maria Jenkins and her Uncle, Thomas Jenkins*, 1790
Angelica Kauffmann
Oil on canvas, 1295 × 946mm
National Portrait Gallery, London

particularly the woman. As a wife, she was expected to bear children as well as be responsible for the everyday running of the household under her husband's command. In turn, the man found his own authority enhanced as head of a household. Because of this, marital status was regarded as an important aspect both of personal identity and coming of age, until well into the twentieth century.

As we have seen, portraits could play an important role in bringing marriage about. Small-scale images were exchanged as love tokens, and more imposing oil portraits might form part of royal marriage negotiations. The practice continued into the eighteenth century, as seen in Angelica Kauffman's portrait of Anna Maria Jenkins and her uncle Thomas, which was intended to promote Anna Maria as an eligible young woman on the marriage market (fig.11). The rural setting, albeit with distant view of the Colosseum, her white dress and the flowers she holds all signify Anna Maria's beauty and purity. As Jenkins was an art dealer and banker in Rome, the portrait may have hung in a space typically frequented by his male friends, colleagues and even clients in the hope that an appropriate gentleman might ask after the attractive girl posed with their host. In a gesture seemingly welcoming potential suitors, her uncle takes off his hat and pats the dog, a symbol of loyalty, whose collar reads 'Jenkins'.

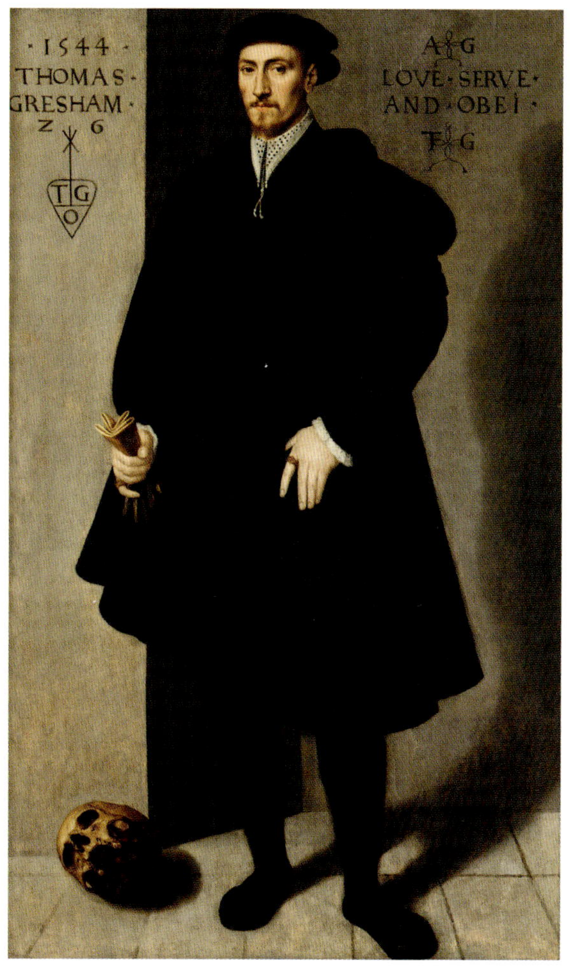

Fig.12 *Thomas Gresham, aged 26,* 1544
Unknown Flemish artist
Oil on panel, 1800 × 1070mm
Mercers' Company, London

Portraits have a long history of recording, symbolising and celebrating marriage itself as well as recording married couples at various moments in their life together. On occasion, portraits that celebrate marriage have been highly innovative. One such example is a portrait of the merchant Sir Thomas Gresham, made to commemorate his marriage to Anne Fernely in 1544 (fig.12). This is a surprising, even audacious work. Prior to this painting, the full-length format in England was associated purely with portraits of rulers – kings, queens and members of their families. Gresham, as the painting indicates, was not even a nobleman, but a young, ambitious merchant trader. He is expensively dressed in black, while a skull, a reminder of mortality and the necessity for Christian humility, rests by his right foot. To the left of his head, where we might

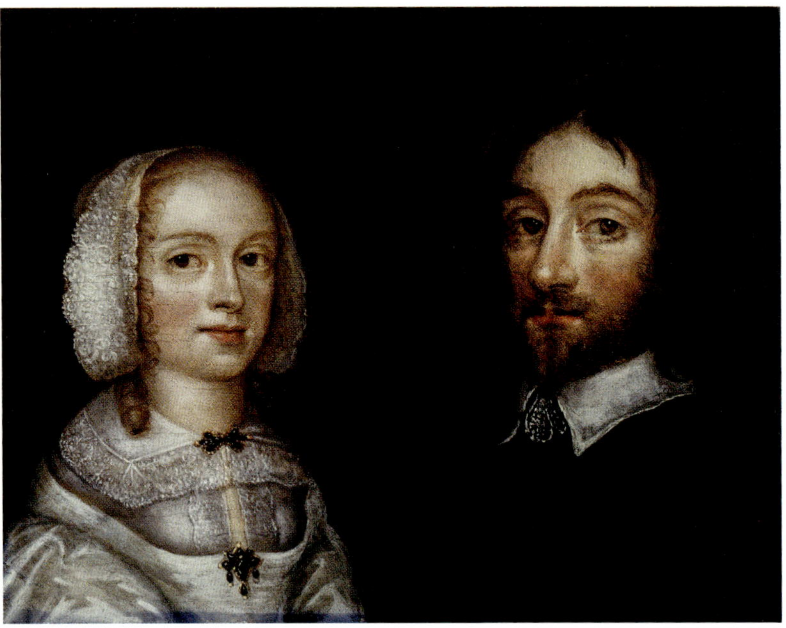

Fig.13 *Dorothy, Lady Browne and Sir Thomas Browne*, c.1641–50
Attributed to Joan Carlile
Oil on panel, 184 × 229mm
National Portrait Gallery, London

expect to find a heraldic coat of arms, is Gresham's merchant's mark, which would have been used to designate his goods and property as well as serving as his cypher on official documents. The inscription also bears his name, the year and his age when the portrait was painted: 26. To the sitter's right are the initials of his wife, with the instruction: 'LOVE, SERVE AND OBEI TG'. Derived from the marriage service, they speak of the duties of a virtuous wife towards her husband.

Impressive in its size, composition and iconography, Gresham's portrait is likely to have been displayed in his home where it would have conveyed his status and authority. It may have been intended as a gift for his wife, and is revealing about the roles expected of marriage partners in sixteenth-century England. Anne was clearly expected to be subordinate to Gresham and defined by her obedience to him and her servitude. The portrait may have been intended to preside over their home during Gresham's frequent absences in the Low Countries on business, functioning as a reminder to Anne of her wifely duties. For the contemporary viewer, it would also have highlighted both Thomas and Anne's virtues in light of the sixteenth-century understanding of marriage as a hierarchical relationship dedicated to the good of the entire household.

Apparently represented on a more equal footing are the prosperous physician and author Thomas Browne and his wife Dorothy (fig.13). They were married in 1641 and painted at some point before 1650 in a work attributed to Joan Carlisle, one of the first professional female portraitists in England.[30] Dorothy was described by Thomas' biographer as being 'of such a symmetrical proportion to her Worthy Husband both by the Graces of her Body and Mind, that they seemed to come together by a kind of Natural Magnetism'.[31] In this portrait they are both dressed in relative sobriety, demonstrating restraint and modesty, although Dorothy wears lace and jewels which indicate their wealth. Their poses, turned slightly towards each other, create an impression of intimacy that is emphasised by the relatively small scale of the painting. It measures just 18 × 23cm (7 × 9in) and is likely to have been hung in their home. This was particularly significant at a time when the marriage contract was considered to be the foundation of an ordered society. With its emphasis on love, loyalty and obedience on the part of the wife and good government on the part of the husband, a successful marriage provided a model for the relationship between ruler and subject and domestic harmony was understood as the basis of national harmony.[32] Located within the home, portraits like this one would have provided a daily reminder of the marriage contract and the vows and duties it entailed.[33]

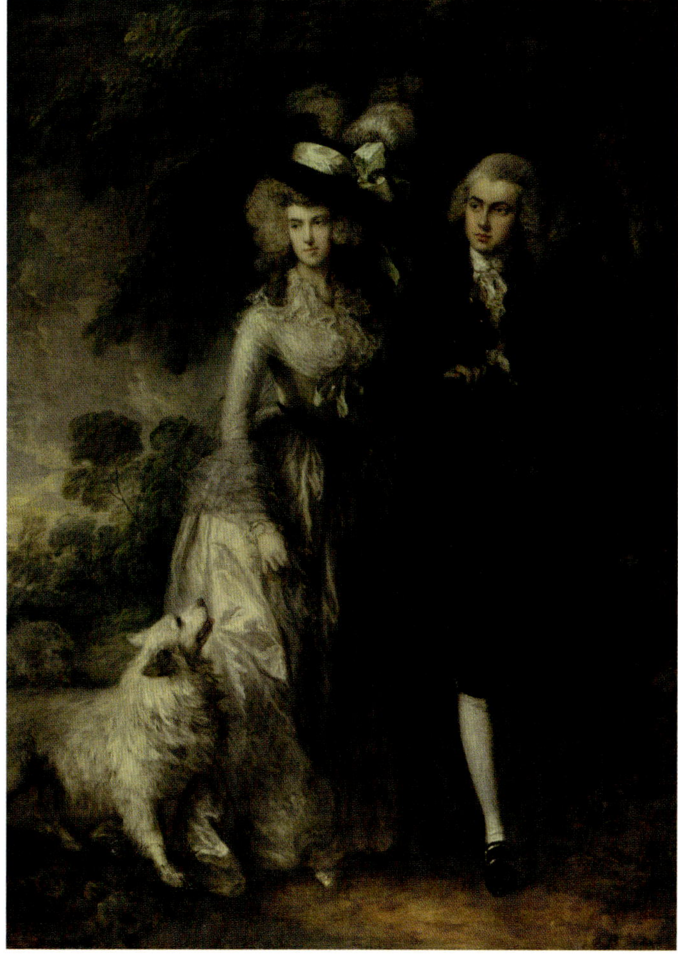

Fig.14 *Mr and Mrs William Hallett ('The Morning Walk')*, 1785
Thomas Gainsborough
Oil on canvas, 2362 × 1791mm
National Gallery, London

A later portrait of a couple, Thomas Gainsborough's *Mr and Mrs William Hallett ('The Morning Walk')* (1785) (fig.14) was painted when the cult of sensibility was at its height and expresses late eighteenth-century ideas about companionate marriage. It shows the young couple strolling in a summer landscape with their dog, also serving as a symbol of their devotion. Both sitters were aged twenty-one when the painting was completed in 1785 to celebrate their forthcoming marriage. They wear fashionable clothing, possibly their wedding outfits.[34] The portrait points to their refined appreciation for

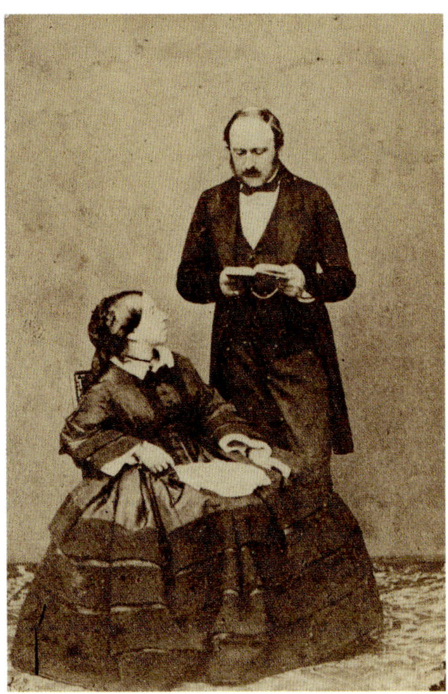

Fig.15 *Queen Victoria and Prince Albert*, May 1860
John Jabez Edwin Mayall
Albumen *carte-de-visite*, 84 × 55mm
National Portrait Gallery, London

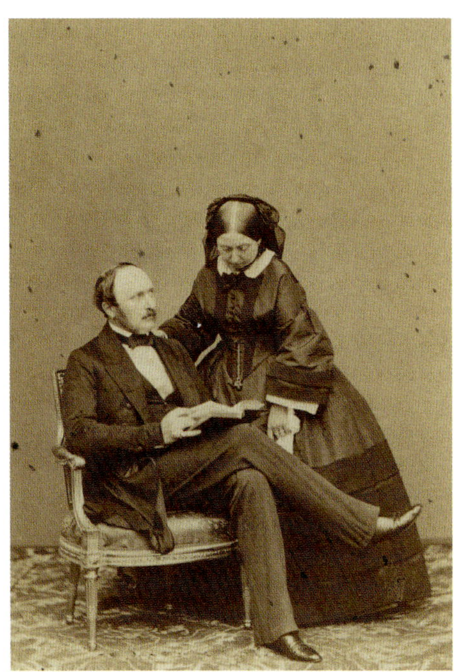

Fig.16 *Queen Victoria and Prince Albert*, May 1860
John Jabez Edwin Mayall
Albumen *carte-de-visite*, 87 × 58mm
National Portrait Gallery, London

nature through its setting and the pair's discerning gazes, directed towards landscape invisible to the viewer. Their affectionately linked arms and the studied informality of their poses contribute to Gainsborough's visual celebration of the ideal of companionate marriage characterised by shared interests and the deep emotional connection associated with 'sensibility' and refinement. In this case, life reflected art, as Hallett's will, written in 1834, stated that he had lived with Elizabeth 'most happily for 48 years, as it was impossible to do otherwise with such a woman'. His will also shows the importance of this portrait to the family, as it was singled out as a bequest to the couple's eldest daughter.[35]

Victorian notions of the ideal relationship between man and woman were promoted in photographic portraits of Queen Victoria and Prince Albert that were published as *cartes-de-visites* and purchased cheaply by the public (figs 15 and 16). These images present Victoria and Albert as the archetypal Victorian husband and wife and have been credited with greatly enhancing their popularity. They are dressed not in the finery associated with the court, but as an ordinary, middle-class couple. He, engrossed in a book, is fulfilled through intellectual pursuits while his devoted wife appears to look to him for guidance or stands to minister to his needs. This arrangement leaves the viewer in no doubt that in spite of the reversal of gender roles between the queen and her consort in public, their private relationship was underpinned by their fulfilment of conventional roles entailing wifely subordination and masculine authority.[36]

At the same time, and into the twentieth century, creative couples were finding fulfilment through partnerships that straddled the boundaries between personal and professional life. This is typified in Joseph Southall's 1911 self-portrait with his wife Anna Elizabeth, known as Bessie (fig.17). The pair were leading proponents of the Arts and Crafts movement in the Midlands, of which working partnerships between men and women were an important aspect. The Southalls were married in 1903 and spent their honeymoon in Southwold, Suffolk. They returned there regularly throughout their marriage and its beach provides the setting for this double portrait. The painting has the title *The Agate* and central to the image is Bessie's act of passing an agate to Joseph, their almost-touching hands conveying their intimate connection. Agates and other gemstones can often be found washed up on the beach at Southwold, but the stone depicted here is of further significance in that it symbolises the collaborative artistic relationship between the couple. Agate stones were central to Bessie's practice in gilding the frames for Joseph's paintings, using the stones to burnish their golden surfaces. The couple's collaboration is also reflected in the painting's composition, which gives them both equal space and importance. As is typical of marriage portraits, Joseph's will indicates that the image was kept as a treasured possession within the marital home.[37]

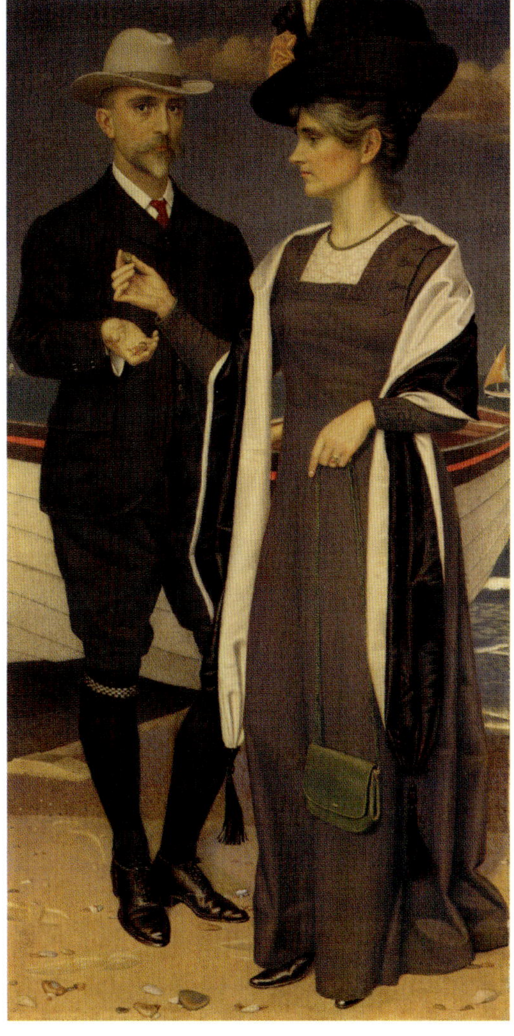

Fig.17 ***Joseph and Anna Elizabeth Southall ('The Agate')*, 1911**
Joseph Edward Southall
Egg tempera on linen, 1003 × 503mm
National Portrait Gallery, London

The double format of the marriage portrait has also been used by couples who were unable to get married. Kenneth Green's 1943 portrait of the singer Peter Pears and the composer Benjamin Britten bears testament to a personal and creative relationship which spanned many years (fig.18). Pears and Britten first became lovers in 1939. Their commitment to one another continued until Britten's death in 1976 and their artistic collaboration resulted in one of the most celebrated voice and piano duos of the twentieth century. Their double portrait shows Britten leaning against Pears in a gesture too intimate to

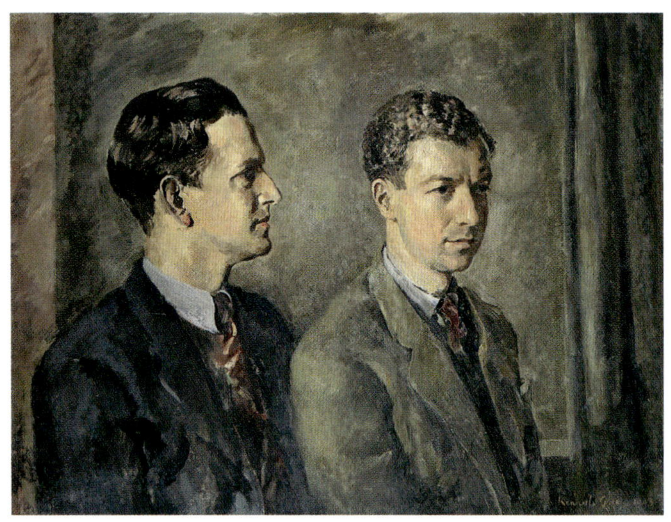

Fig.18 *Peter Pears and Benjamin Britten*, 1943
Kenneth Green
Oil on canvas, 715 × 969mm
National Portrait Gallery, London

suggest colleagues or friends. It consciously – and courageously – uses the conventions of marriage portraiture to celebrate their commitment at a time when gay men could face a lifetime in prison for being in a same-sex relationship.

Graham Hughes' portrait of Helen and Kate Richardson-Walsh was made in a very different climate with regards to attitudes to same-sex relationships. Helen Richardson and Kate Walsh married in a civil ceremony in 2013. Both play women's hockey for Team GB and at the 2016 Rio Olympics they became the first married British couple to win Olympic gold together since 1920, with their achievement fêted in the press. Hughes' photograph was taken just days after their Olympic victory (fig.19). The couple's similar clothing and the intimacy of their clasped hands speak of a deep partnership. The personal relationship between two very public figures is also evident in a double portrait of the Labour politicians Neil and Glenys Kinnock which was commissioned by the National Portrait Gallery (fig.20). Aiming to depict their marriage as well as their politics, the artist Andrew Tift

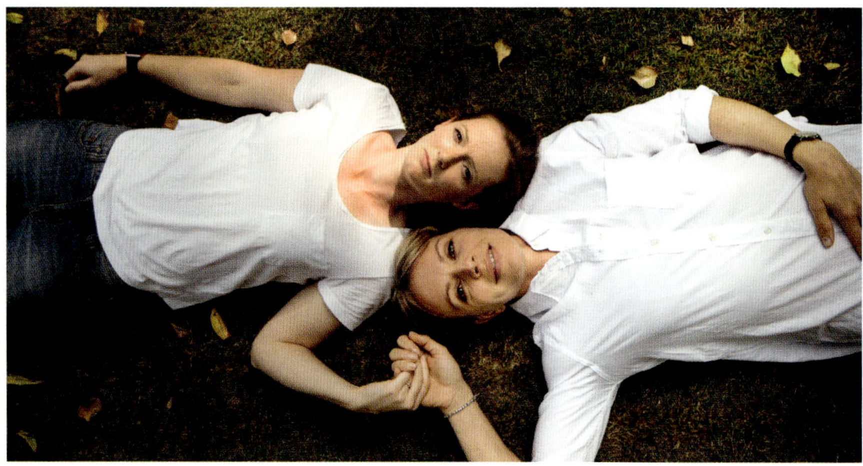

Fig.19 *Helen and Kate Richardson-Walsh*, 30 August 2016
Graham Hughes
Chromogenic print, 268 × 485mm
National Portrait Gallery, London

set the portrait in their home near Cardiff in Wales. The pair are surrounded by objects which have a personal significance for them. Figures of their heroes, Nelson Mandela and post-war Labour Minister Aneurin Bevan, jostle for space with gifts given to each other, including the teapots on the fireplace which were a Christmas present from Neil to Glenys. The photographs in the background depict their parents, children and grandchildren, highlighting the importance of family in their lives. The artist stated that he hoped the portrait would resemble 'a celebrity-style spread from *Hello* or *OK!* Magazine'.[38] The sense of an intimate glimpse into the couple's private life certainly mirrors the 'at home' features in celebrity magazines, although the portrait's emphasis on personally significant objects contrasts with the celebrity magazine's presentation of their subjects' homes as glossy status symbols. Here, the home is, in Neil Kinnock's words, a 'cocoon that we have built for ourselves over a third of a century'.[39] The painting therefore celebrates their love and a life lived together.

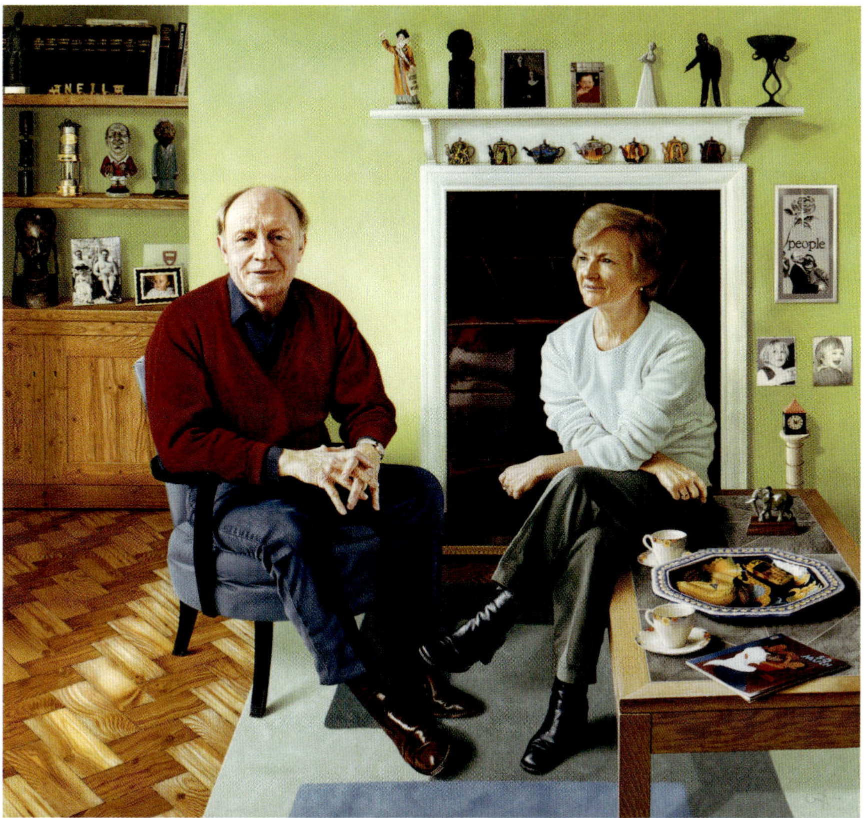

Fig.20 ***Neil and Glenys Kinnock*, 2001**
Andrew Tift
Acrylic on canvas, 1330 × 1386mm
National Portrait Gallery, London

Whether displayed within the domestic interior or depicting it, the portraits discussed here identify the home as the space in which a marriage is played out but also as a canvas for the expression of a shared identity and a couple's commitment to one another. In considering portraiture produced in connection with mourning, it is clear that this is a commitment which can endure beyond the death of a partner.

LOVE & LOSS

It has long been recognised that one of the key functions of portraiture is the remembrance of the dead. Renaissance thinkers including the Italian humanist Leon Battista Alberti and the Portuguese artist and author Francisco de Hollanda wrote of the portrait's capacity to retain a living presence and thus comfort the living.[40] These ideas are reflected in a number of portraits of Frances Howard, one of the great beauties of the late Elizabethan and Jacobean courts, who had an eventful romantic life. Left a penniless orphan following the death of her parents, she married a wealthy merchant when she was only thirteen and after his death in 1599 was besieged by suitors. They included Sir George Rodney, who made her the subject of an elegy describing her as 'sweet poison ... infectious jewel ... a lady that is fair and cruel'.[41] She responded with a poem in which she critiqued the conventions of wooing and explained that she was promised to another. On receiving this, Rodney committed suicide.[42]

According to a seventeenth-century account of her life, during her second, unhappy marriage to Edward Seymour, Earl of Hertford, she was 'courted' by Ludovic Stuart, Duke of Lennox, who visited her wearing 'odd disguises', the details of which are sadly lost to history.[43] Seymour died in 1621 and Lady Frances married Stuart in secret just weeks later. This seems to have been the happiest of her three marriages, but it was to be short-lived. Stuart, by now Duke of Lennox and Richmond, died in 1624. Frances outlived him by fifteen years and never remarried. During her widowhood she commissioned several portraits of herself from leading artists. Cornelius Johnson showed her wearing white, the colour associated with purity and the later stages of mourning. In this portrait she is surrounded by a number of objects which refer to her status as a duchess, the rank she attained through her final marriage (fig.21). Here, as in many of her other portraits, she wears a heart-shaped miniature of her late husband Ludovic Stuart pinned to her breast above her own heart. This cherished object survives today in the collections of the National Portrait Gallery (fig.22). Perhaps originally given as a love token, in Frances' portraits it functions as testament to her ongoing love for her husband and the devotion appropriate to a virtuous widow. Portraiture was frequently used to present a woman in the guise of the ideal widow, which was an important aspect of

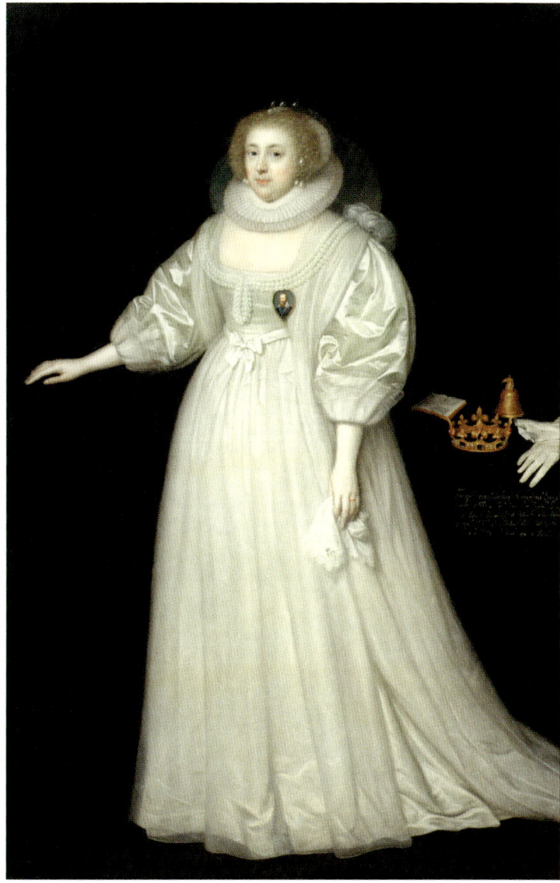

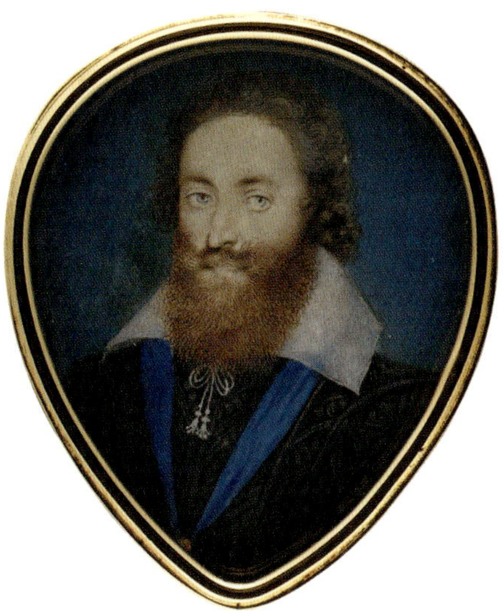

Fig.21 *Frances Howard, Duchess of Richmond and Lennox*, 1635
Cornelius Johnson
Oil on canvas, 2108 × 1346mm
Gilcrease Museum, Tulsa, Oklahoma

Fig.22 *Ludovic Stuart, 1st Duke of Richmond and 2nd Duke of Lennox*, *c.*1605
Isaac Oliver
Watercolour and bodycolour on vellum, 57 × 44mm
National Portrait Gallery, London

female identity and propriety in the early modern period. As men were not judged by the same standards, portraits of grieving widowers are more rare. Some men, such as Kenelm Digby, did commission portraits of themselves in mourning, and they also used portraiture to commemorate lost loved ones.[44] Digby commissioned Sir Antony van Dyck to make a portrait of his wife on her deathbed, which he kept by his bed for the rest of his life. Similarly, William Godwin treasured a portrait of his wife, Mary Wollstonecraft which was made shortly before her death in childbirth (see p.66). Godwin was too traumatised to attend his wife's funeral, and wrote to a friend, 'I have not the least expectation that I can now ever know happiness again.'[45] In the following years, he was devoted to his wife's memory, publishing *Memoirs* of her life in 1798. It is clear that Godwin was well aware of the memorialising function of portraiture, describing his own likeness by James Northcote as 'the principal memorandum of my corporal existence that will remain after my death' (see p.66).[46] Opie's portrait of Wollstonecraft hung above the fireplace in his study until Godwin's own death, a memorial to her and the fleeting years of happiness shared by two of the Enlightenment's leading thinkers.

The use of the portrait to conjure the presence of a dead partner reached its height in the Victorian era, with its elaborate mourning rituals.[47] In this, Queen Victoria herself provided the ultimate example, descending into deep and prolonged mourning following the death of her husband, Prince Albert, in 1861. Victoria's journals, kept throughout their marriage, are testament to the intensity of her feelings for Albert: she revelled in his beauty and their happiness, describing her wedding night as 'bliss beyond belief', and the couple went on to have nine children.[48] Fine art, including portraiture, was at the very heart of Victoria and Albert's relationship with many of their happiest times spent collecting, viewing and discussing art. They exchanged numerous portraits during their courtship and marriage, often giving these as presents on birthdays, wedding anniversaries and at Christmas.[49] They include a sensuous private portrait of Victoria with her hair loosely styled which the queen commissioned as a gift for Albert's twenty-fourth birthday (fig.23). Immediately following his death in December 1861, images of Albert became an important means of memorialisation. At Christmas that year the men of the Royal Household were given black-bordered photographs of the prince, while the women received lockets bearing his portrait.[50] Popular prints showing Albert's deathbed circulated among the public, and Victoria commissioned the Albert Memorial in Kensington Gardens, a most magnificent public portrait statue. Portraits also played an important role in Victoria's private mourning. Following his death, the queen slept with a cast of Albert's hand within touching distance and his painted portrait hung above her bed.[51] This, and another portrait to the side, can be seen in an image of the queen on her deathbed taken forty years later (fig.24). Albert's portrait and the cast of his hand may have provided the grief-stricken queen with a consoling sense of her dead husband's presence. It is this ability of portraits to mitigate absence which has led to them playing an important role in many love stories. It is clear that portraits have long been associated with a quasi-magical ability to capture the sitter and elicit feelings of love in the eyes of the beholder. As such, they do not merely reflect reality, but have the ability to affect the course of love, even sustaining it beyond the grave. More than passive likenesses, as Samuel Johnson observed in 1758, portraiture can be 'employed in diffusing friendship, in reviving tenderness, in quickening the affections of the absent, and continuing the presence of the dead'.[52]

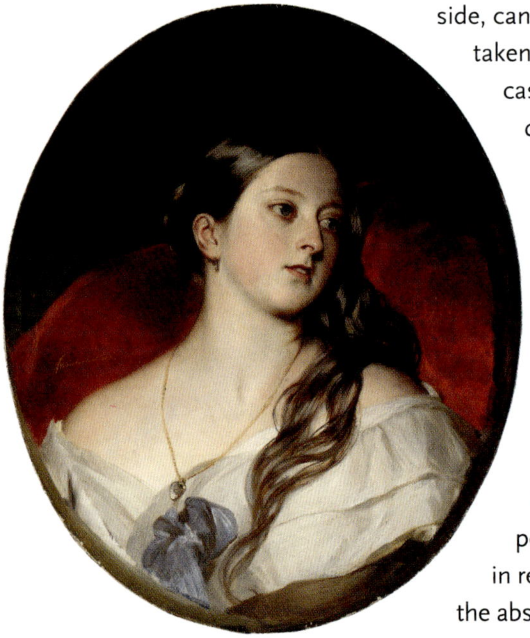

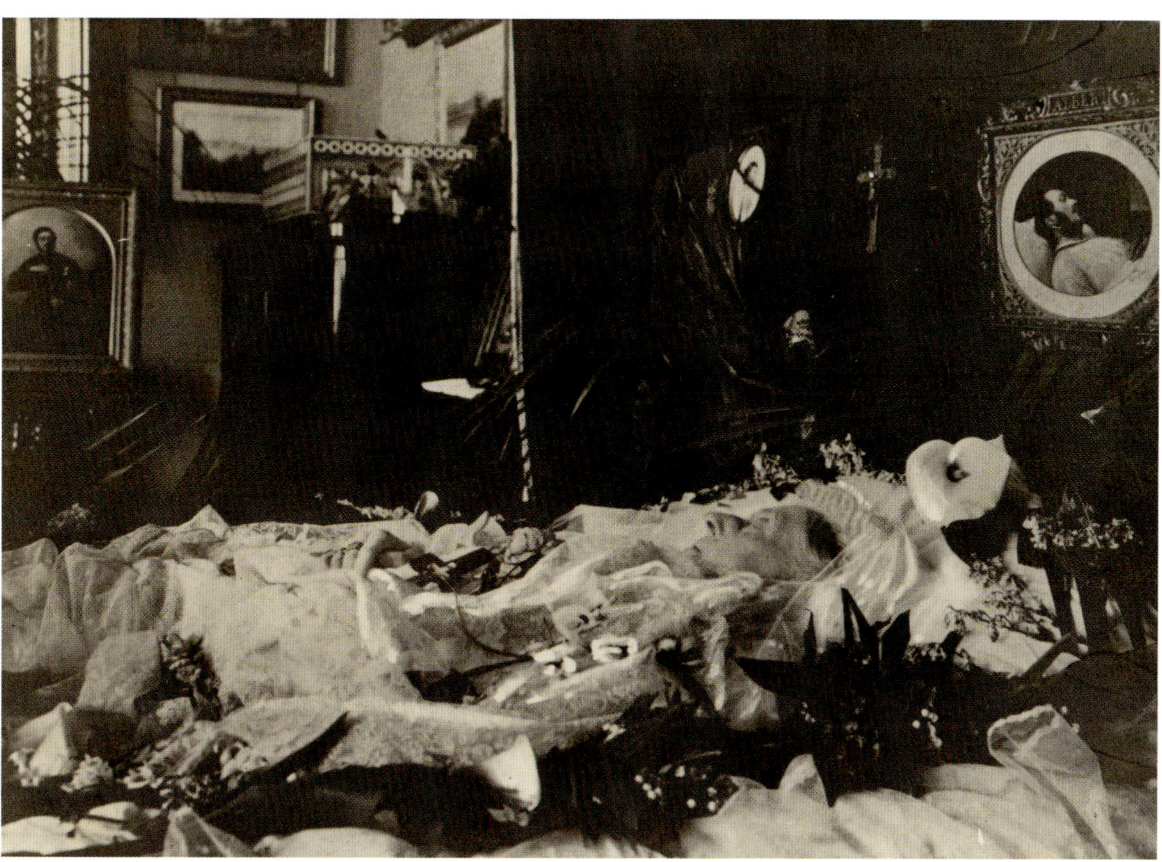

Fig.24 *Queen Victoria on her Deathbed*, 1901
Possibly by Sir Hubert von Herkomer
Gelatin silver print, 169 × 232mm
National Portrait Gallery, London

OPPOSITE
Fig.23 *Queen Victoria*, 1843
Franz Xaver Winterhalter
Oil on canvas, 648 × 533mm
The Royal Collection/ HM Queen Elizabeth II

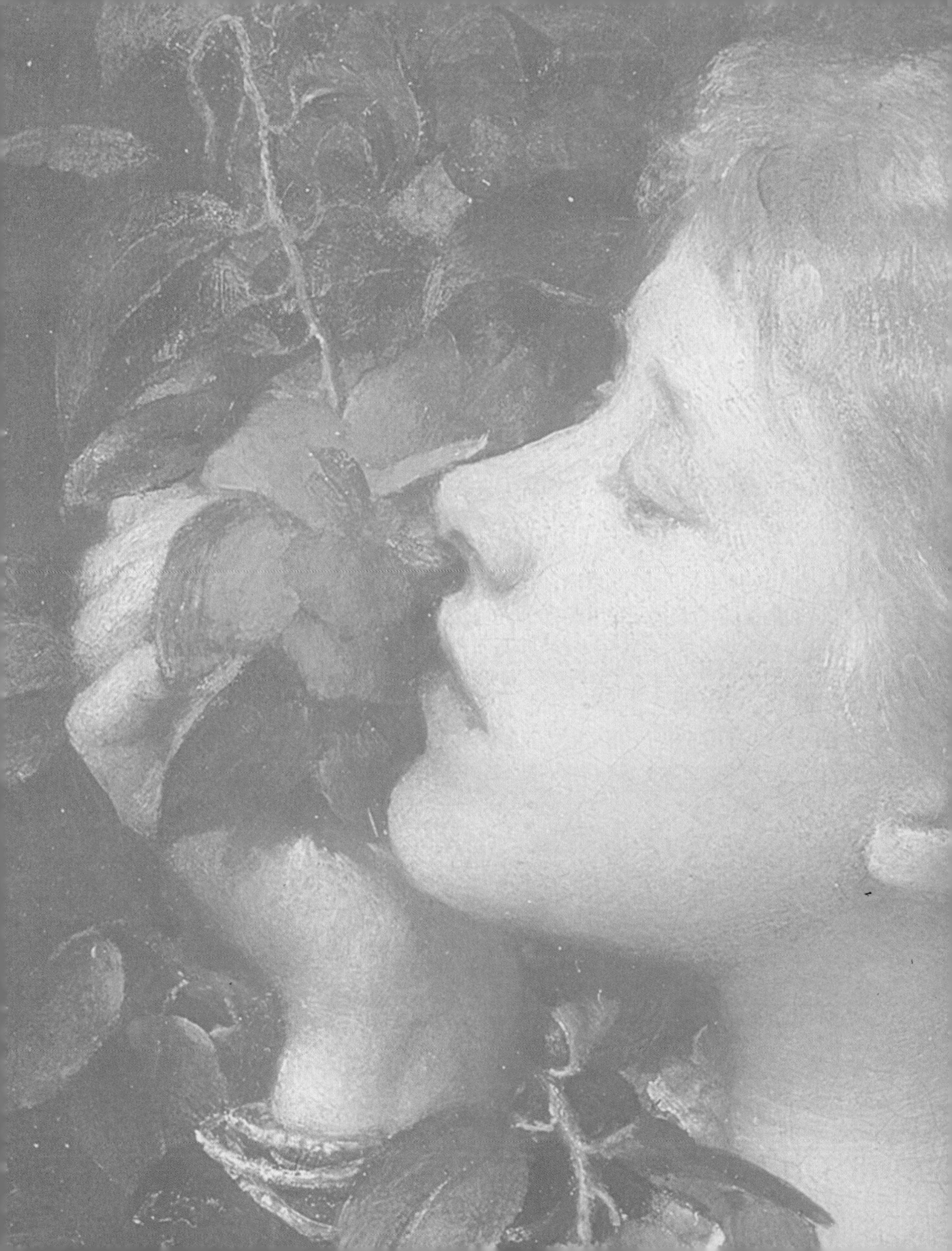

OBSESSED WITH THE MUSE

LOUISE STEWART

OBSESSED WITH THE MUSE

The relationship between artist and muse has been an important theme throughout the history of British portraiture. A beautiful and usually unattainable woman who sparks inspiration in the male artist, the traditional idea of the muse derives from the ancient Greek muses. In Greek mythology, the Muses are a group of goddesses who inspired achievement in the various branches of the arts they represent. When transposed to the context of portraiture, the trope of the muse was long understood as a beautiful, passive woman with whom the male artist becomes obsessed. An object of desire, the muse is repeatedly depicted by the artist, sparking great creative achievement in his quest for total comprehension and possession. However, as becomes clear through the stories of artists and their muses found in this section, the reality is often much more complex. Artists' relationships with their muses have involved collaboration, cool-headed commercial transactions and playfulness and both men and women have performed the role of creative muse for artists making portraits. The idea of the 'muse' has also been consciously adopted and manipulated by both artists and sitters to promulgate celebrity and to challenge traditional ideas about the role of men and women in artistic production.

Taken at face value, the relationship between George Romney (fig.1) and Emma Hamilton (fig.2) would appear to conform to the traditional artist–muse pairing. One of the leading portraitists of his day, in 1782 Romney was engaged to make a series of portraits of the aristocrat Charles Greville's beautiful mistress Emma Hart as a commercial venture focused ultimately on the print market. The artist was captivated by Emma's beauty, charm and intelligence, which later saw her marry Sir William Hamilton, British Ambassador in Naples, and become the mistress of Admiral Lord Nelson (see pp.150–5). Over the following nine years, Romney depicted Emma hundreds of times, as herself but also in character as Nature, a spinstress and as classical figures including Medea, Circe, the nymph Thetis and a bacchante (fig.2). In a portrait of Emma now in the National Portrait Gallery's collection (p.151), her simple white dress evokes the classical past: as well as evoking the ancient idea of the

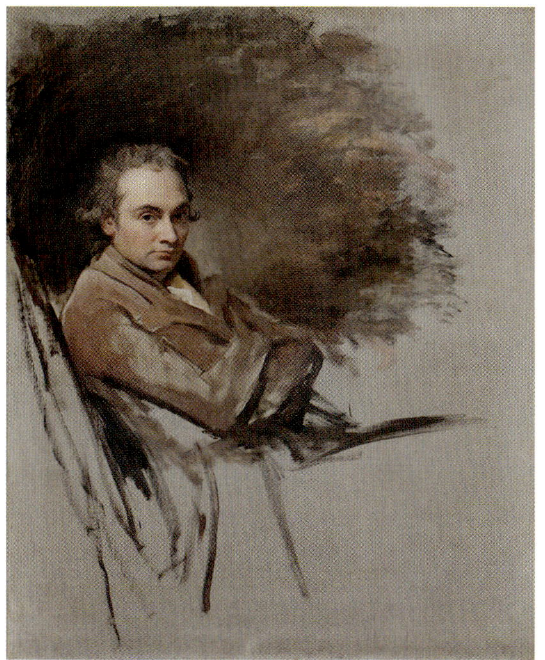

Fig.1 *Self-Portrait*, 1784
George Romney
Oil on canvas, 1257 × 991mm
National Portrait Gallery, London

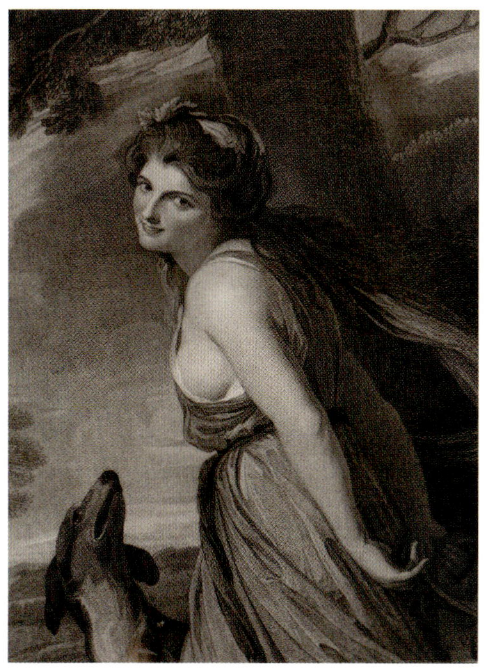

Fig.2 *Emma Hamilton as a Bacchante*, 1797
Charles Knight after George Romney
Stipple engraving, 286 × 206mm
National Portrait Gallery, London

muse, the classical themes seen in Romney's portraits of Emma were highly fashionable and appealed to connoisseurs and collectors. After her move to Naples in 1786, Emma exploited her skills as a model and an actress in her 'attitudes', a set of choreographed poses in which her performance evoked ancient mythical and historical characters (fig.2). As a result of the set of engravings and a stellar list of guests that included the philosopher Goethe, her 'attitudes' and her portraiture made her a celebrity. By the early 1790s, Emma was famous throughout Europe and she went on to be painted by Joshua Reynolds, Élisabeth Vigée Le Brun, Thomas Lawrence and Angelica Kauffman. It is telling that Romney's portraits enhanced the celebrity of both artist and sitter and that through these the talented and astute Emma can be viewed as Romney's collaborator, undermining the idea of the muse as passive foil for the artist.

Over a century before Emma and Romney met, Barbara Villiers, Duchess of Cleveland, had also used her relationship with an artist to enhance her celebrity. Beautiful, famous and scandalous, Cleveland was mistress to King Charles II and was depicted numerous times by Peter Lely, the leading portrait painter working in England in the 1660s. Like Hamilton, Cleveland took up a range of characters in her portraits, including Mary Magdalene, St Catherine, and, perhaps most audaciously, as the Madonna herself, with the king's

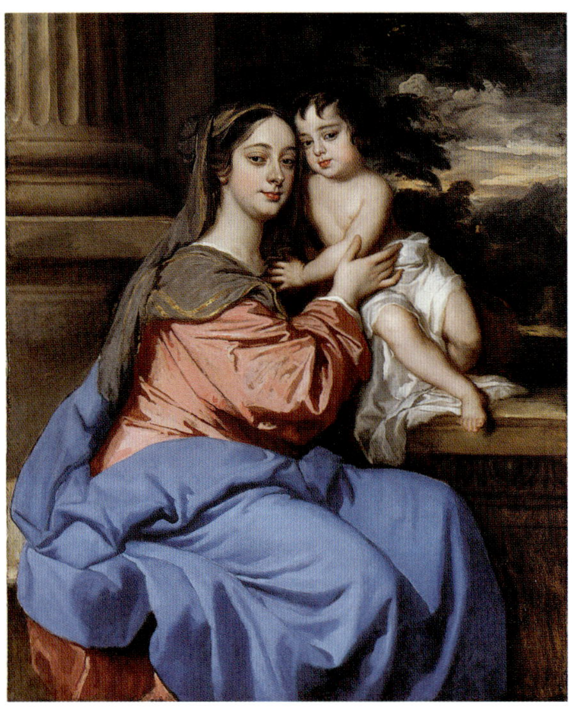

Fig.3 ***Barbara Villiers, Duchess of Cleveland with her Son, probably Charles FitzRoy, as the Virgin and Child*, c.1664**
Sir Peter Lely
Oil on canvas, 1247 × 1020mm
National Portrait Gallery, London

illegitimate son held aloft in the role of the Christ child (fig.3). The creative partnership between Lely and Cleveland ended with her move to France in 1676, but her influence on his work continued. Lely's version of ideal female beauty was based on Cleveland's features and in particular, her distinctive heavy-lidded, 'sleepy' eyes. Evidence of this look in many of Lely's portraits led one contemporary to comment that the artist 'put something of Cleveland's face as her Languishing Eyes into every one Picture'.[1] Lely, for his part, reportedly claimed 'that it was beyond the compass of art to give this lady her due, as to her sweetness and exquisite beauty'.[2] This comment, however, belies a relationship that was about much more than an artist's admiration for a beautiful woman. It is not clear who instigated the artistic relationship between Lely and Cleveland, but it is likely to have been motivated by a range of complex commercial and political factors. One of the first celebrities in the modern sense, Cleveland may have wished to use Lely's images of her, and engravings based on them which could be purchased by the public, to enhance her status at court and her prominence in society. While individual courtiers might have commissioned images of the king's mistress as a means to access royal favour, Lely's own reputation was enhanced by depicting a sitter with such close links to the throne. Again, the relationship between artist and muse is revealed to be complex and multifaceted, and underpinned by ambition as much as obsession.

Famous beauties have continued to be represented by leading artists, and the development of photography has led to the increasing ubiquity of portraits as objects of desire. Like Hamilton and Cleveland, the actress Audrey Hepburn was depicted by many of the leading artists of her age in numerous guises. Hundreds of thousands of photographs of Hepburn featured in newspapers and magazines in the middle of the twentieth-century, representing her as the characters she portrayed in films, as a paragon of beauty or as an icon of ideal femininity. Angus McBean's photographs of Hepburn from 1950 formed the foundation of her public image. In that year, he produced a portrait of her which was used in a widely disseminated skin cream advertisement and this image, taken just a month later, provides a similarly idealised image of Hepburn as a flawless beauty (fig.4). The repetition of her image in triplicate is typical of

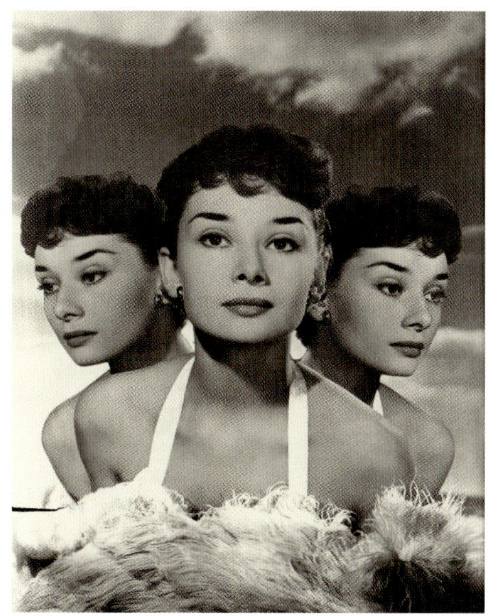

Fig.4 *Audrey Hepburn*, November 1950
Angus McBean
Modern gelatin silver print, 445 × 300mm
National Portrait Gallery, London

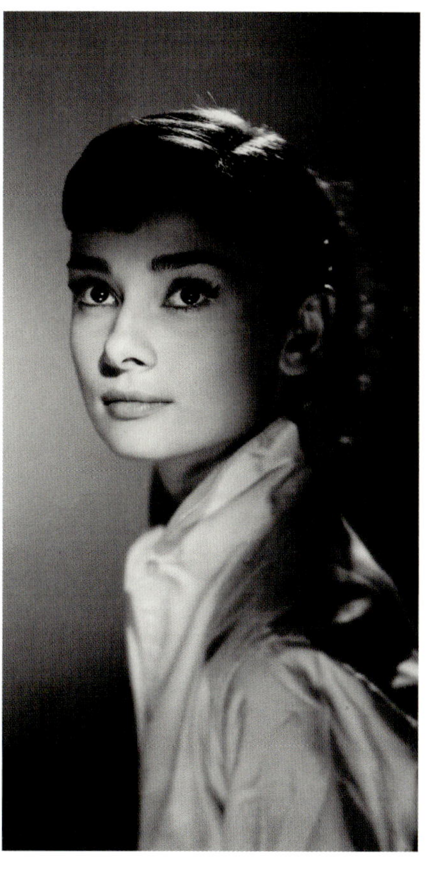

Fig.5 *Audrey Hepburn, during the filming of War and Peace*, 1956
Jack Cardiff
Inkjet print, 960 × 480mm
National Portrait Gallery, London

McBean's surrealist approach to photography but also suggests the way in which photographic portraits of Hepburn were seemingly endlessly reproduced in the media. It is clear that Hepburn was aware of the power of photography in constructing her public image; *Illustrated* magazine reported that 'She will not hesitate to advise a photographer about her best, and worst, camera angles, and which of his photographs he should publish, or destroy.'[3] When her career was beginning to take off in the 1950s, the role of women in society was a subject of debate and redefinition. Through her public image, Hepburn promoted herself as a new and alternative form of femininity; youthful, carefree and optimistic. This is captured in Jack Cardiff's 1956 image of the actress (fig.5). Taken during the filming of *War and Peace*, it gives no hint of period drama: instead it represents Hepburn dressed in a characteristically modern, casual style and through the use of dramatic lighting it evokes a hopeful atmosphere in a post-war Britain. Like Hamilton and Cleveland, Hepburn should be considered as a collaborator, crafting her own public identity and celebrity by appropriating the conventions of the muse as an ideal beauty, an icon of femininity and as an unattainable object of desire for the now-widespread audiences for her photographic portraits that were published and

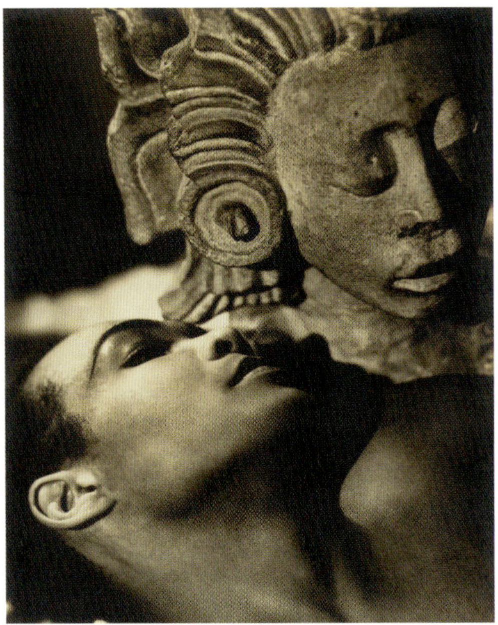

Fig.6 ***Berto Pasuka*, c.1946**
Angus McBean
Gelatin silver print, 140 × 103mm
National Portrait Gallery, London

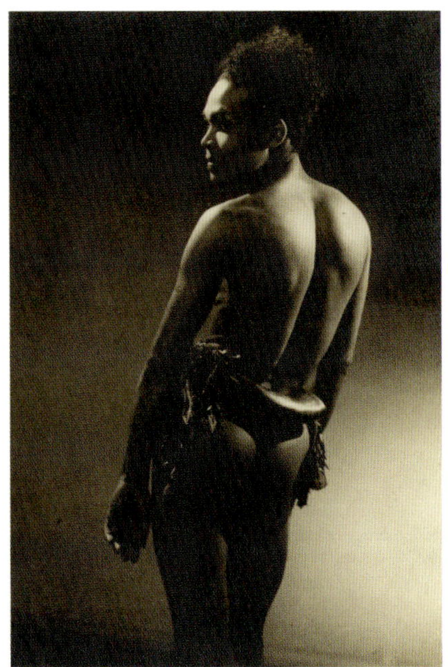

Fig.7 ***Berto Pasuka*, c.1946**
Angus McBean
Gelatin silver print, 148 × 97mm
National Portrait Gallery, London

available. Shortly before he created his iconic images of Audrey Hepburn, Angus McBean portrayed Berto Pasuka in the role of the muse (figs 6 and 7), making a number of dramatically lit portraits of the dancer and choreographer in 1946–7. The inclusion of a sculpture in one of the images of Pasuka seems to consciously refer to the act of depiction and to place the dancer's features on a par with the exoticizing sculptural image. McBean makes reference to Pasuka's own creative practice by depicting him seemingly in motion and in costume for performance. With their sensual lighting and carefully judged nudity, McBean's images are imbued with the eroticism often associated with portraits of the muse. These photographs, depicting a gay, black man, taken by a photographer who was also a gay man, provide a powerful vision of both ideal beauty and the persona of the muse as black, queer and creative.

The Australian-born performance artist Leigh Bowery became one of several muses of the painter Lucian Freud, following their meeting in 1988. Bowery was an iconic figure on the underground club scene who expressed himself through his elaborate fetishistic, carnivalesque costumes and masks. With his costumes and performance Bowery used his body to construct an identity through which he could express aspects of his personality. Bowery sat regularly for Freud over a four-year period until he died suddenly from AIDS in 1994. In numerous portraits, Freud depicted the performer naked and unmasked; he was fascinated by Bowery's body, which he treated as a sculptural object, stating 'I found him

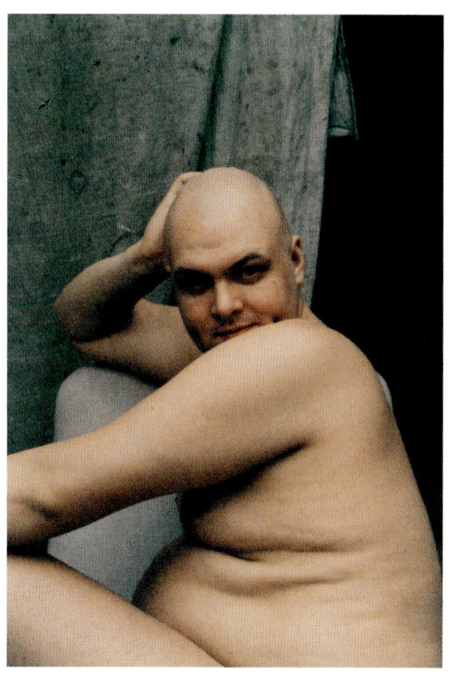

Fig.8 *Leigh Bowery*, 1992
Bruce Bernard
Chromogenic print, 498 × 330mm
National Portrait Gallery, London

perfectly beautiful.'[4] Their relationship provides another example of an artist–muse partnership founded not on sexual desire but, in this case, aesthetic appreciation and, at least for Bowery, personal and psychological exploration. The photograph shown here captures Bowery during a sitting for Freud (fig.8).

Female artists have also consciously explored and expanded the idea of the muse in portraits of men. Sam Taylor-Johnson's video portrait of David Beckham sleeping, for example, represents the footballer unclothed and vulnerable (fig.9). Offered up to the viewer as an object of desire, Beckham seems to belong to a long line of artists' muses. As is the case in all of the examples discussed here, however, the reality is more complicated. This portrait was commissioned for the National Portrait Gallery, London and was therefore the product of a professional transaction rather than an artist's obsession. Nevertheless, in portraying Beckham in a way that invites the viewer to gaze upon him voyeuristically, and even to imagine sleeping next to him, Taylor-Johnson appears to knowingly refer to his 'sex symbol' media image at the time the portrait was made. This resulted in a time-based portrait that is at once startlingly intimate and surprisingly playful.

The idea of the artist's muse is one that has long haunted British portraiture. No relationships between artists and sitters conform precisely to the traditional notion of the muse, and the creation of a portrait is just as likely to be motivated by financial, political or social factors as obsessive love. Nevertheless, the notion of an individual who inspires great artistic achievement through becoming an object of fascination and desire is compelling. It is a role that sitters have knowingly performed in the successful creation of their public persona, while the artistic conventions associated with the depiction of the muse have provided a rich seam of inspiration for artists in the creation of portraits across several centuries.

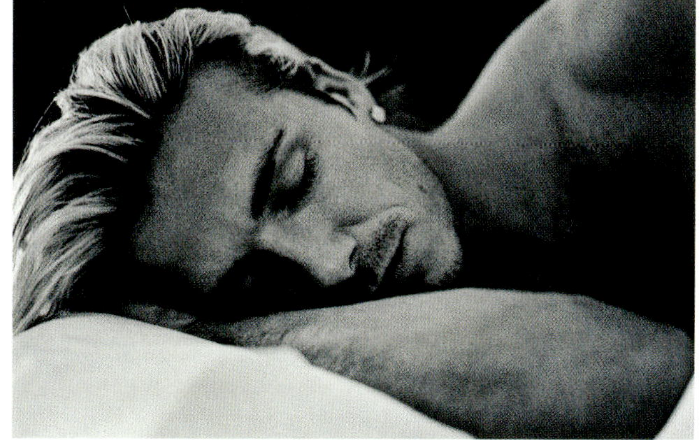

Fig.9 *David Beckham ('David')*, 2004
Sam Taylor-Johnson
Digital video displayed on plasma screen
National Portrait Gallery, London

ALISON SMITH

Ellen Terry & George Frederic Watts

The marriage of the high-minded artist G.F. Watts to the vivacious young actress Ellen Terry was a topic of gossip during their lifetime and has been the stuff of fiction ever since. Terry's own brief account of it in her biography, *The Story of My Life* (1908), is generous given that neither the marriage nor the separation were of her making. At the time they first met, Watts, a middle-aged painter of lofty but obscure allegories, was firmly established as a permanent house-guest at Little Holland House in Kensington, where legend has it that he came to stay for three days and stayed thirty years. This was the bohemian home of Sara and Thoby Prinsep who played host to many of the great artists and writers of the day. It was here that in 1863 Watts was introduced to the actresses Kate and Ellen Terry and took a particular liking to Ellen who was then performing in Tom Taylor's play *Our American Cousin* at the Haymarket. Watts' feelings for Ellen come across in his unfinished double portrait of the Terry sisters in which he delights in her auburn hair and tender expression (fig.2). In the self-portrait Watts is said to have given Ellen around this time he presents himself as a rather chivalric figure (fig.3): indeed he later admitted that he married her to rescue her from 'the dangers and temptations of the stage' and to give her an education.[1] Wavering between adoption and marriage he decided the latter was the safer course, believing she was too old to be his child and ignoring the fact – which he later admitted – that at sixteen she was probably too young to be engaged. Ellen was equally naïve, apparently fearing she had become pregnant upon receiving

Fig.1 *Ellen Terry ('Choosing')*, 1864
George Frederic Watts
Oil on strawboard, 472 × 352mm
National Portrait Gallery, London

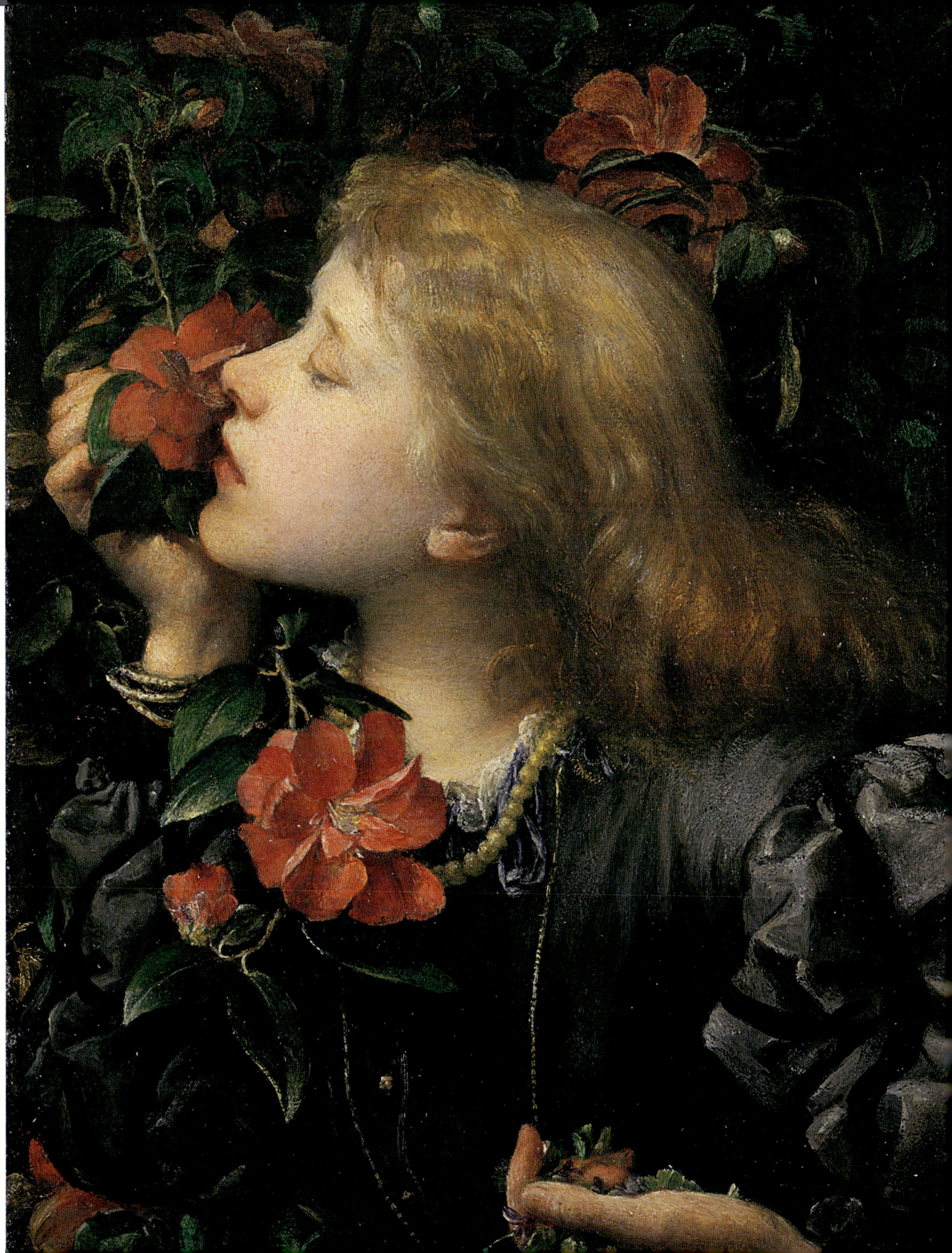

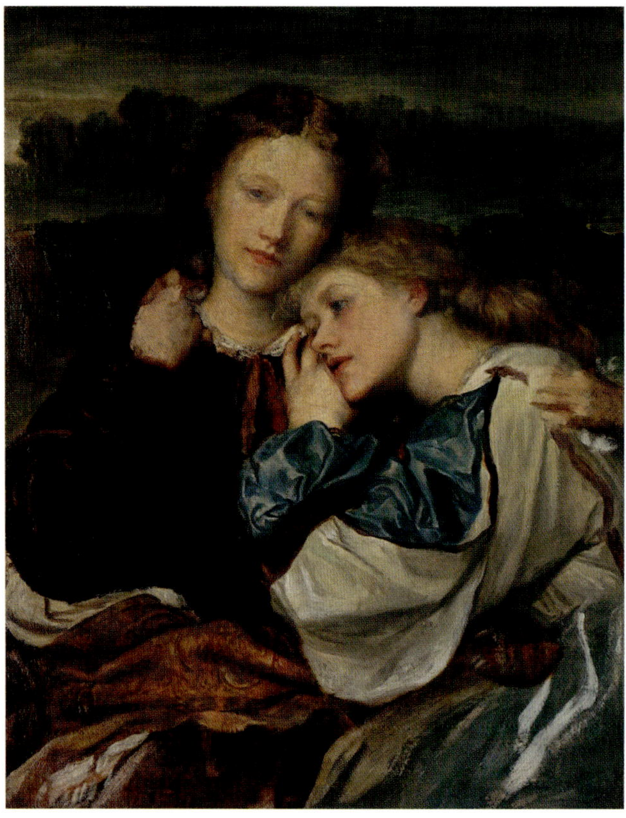

Fig.2 *The Sisters Kate and Ellen Terry*, 1863
George Frederic Watts
Oil on canvas, 875 × 648mm
Eastnor Castle Collection, Herefordshire

her first kiss. The marriage followed on 20 February 1864: he was aged forty-seven, she just a week short of her seventeenth birthday. At this point Ellen abandoned her professional life to serve as Watts' muse at Little Holland House where she was widely regarded as something of a curiosity by the socially and intellectually elite company that assembled there.

Choosing was painted during the first few months of the marriage and shows Ellen, wearing her brown silk wedding-dress, turning away from the modest, sweet-smelling violets in her hand towards a brilliant but scentless camellia (fig.1). The 'choice' may be emblematic of the challenges she faced in trying to conform to Watts' expectations, or of his own quest for the unattainable. Needless to say, such a high-spirited girl found it impossible to settle down to the role expected of a Victorian wife and by early 1865 their incompatibility had become obvious to all. A deed of separation was drawn up and signed by both parties leaving Ellen free to return to the stage, with a great career ahead of her.

On a chance meeting years later Terry forgave Watts and this led to a divorce enabling both to marry again: he to Mary Fraser Tytler in 1886, she (after eloping with William Godwin) to Charles Kelly in 1877 and, following their separation, to James Carew in 1907. In 1882 Watts presented Terry with *Choosing* which remained in her possession until her death, the 'favourite of all the portraits painted of her'.[2]

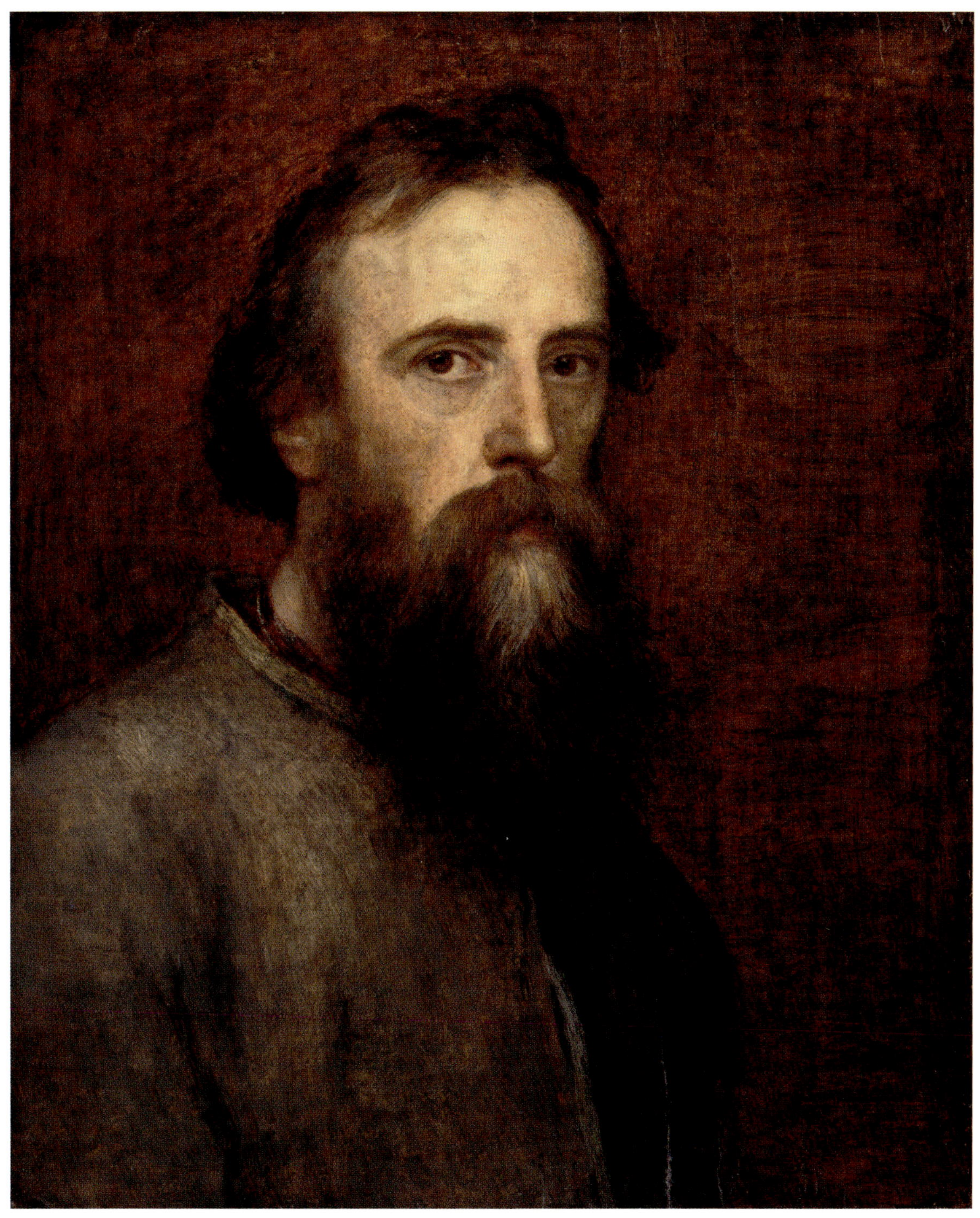

Fig.3 *Self-Portrait, c.*1860
George Frederic Watts
Oil on panel, 610 × 502mm
National Portrait Gallery, London

SARAH MOULDEN

The Bloomsbury Group

On Thursday evenings from 1905, the two sisters Vanessa and Virginia Stephen, a budding artist and a novelist respectively, hosted gatherings of like-minded writers, artists and critics at their home in Gordon Square in the Bloomsbury area of London. Called 'at homes', these meetings provided a tolerant and friendly forum for a number of avant-garde creatives to discuss big ideas, from the status of art or reformist politics, to love, sex and experimental modes of living – issues largely at odds with their strict Victorian upbringings. Dynamic friendships, creative partnerships, open marriages and polyamorous relationships quickly formed between the members who came to be known as the Bloomsbury Group (fig.1).

A number of portraits of individuals associated with the group form a compelling set at the National Portrait Gallery. Together, these portraits bear witness to an intricate web of intimate connections that were central to Bloomsbury's social, artistic and sexual identity, and which knitted the group together for decades to come.

A central member of the group was the artist Duncan Grant (fig.2) who promoted an open attitude to sexuality. His love life was principally played out in homosexual relationships, including with his cousin Lytton Strachey (fig.7) who introduced him to other Bloomsburyites, including the economist John Maynard Keynes, Adrian Stephen, the younger brother of Vanessa Bell and Virginia Woolf, the writer-publisher David Garnett, and the mountaineer George Leigh Mallory.

Grant's portrait of Mallory (fig.3), made not long after the 26-year-old had climbed Mont Blanc, reverberates with same-sex desire. Painted at Grant's Brunswick Square studio in 1912, it shows Mallory naked from the waist up, his arms

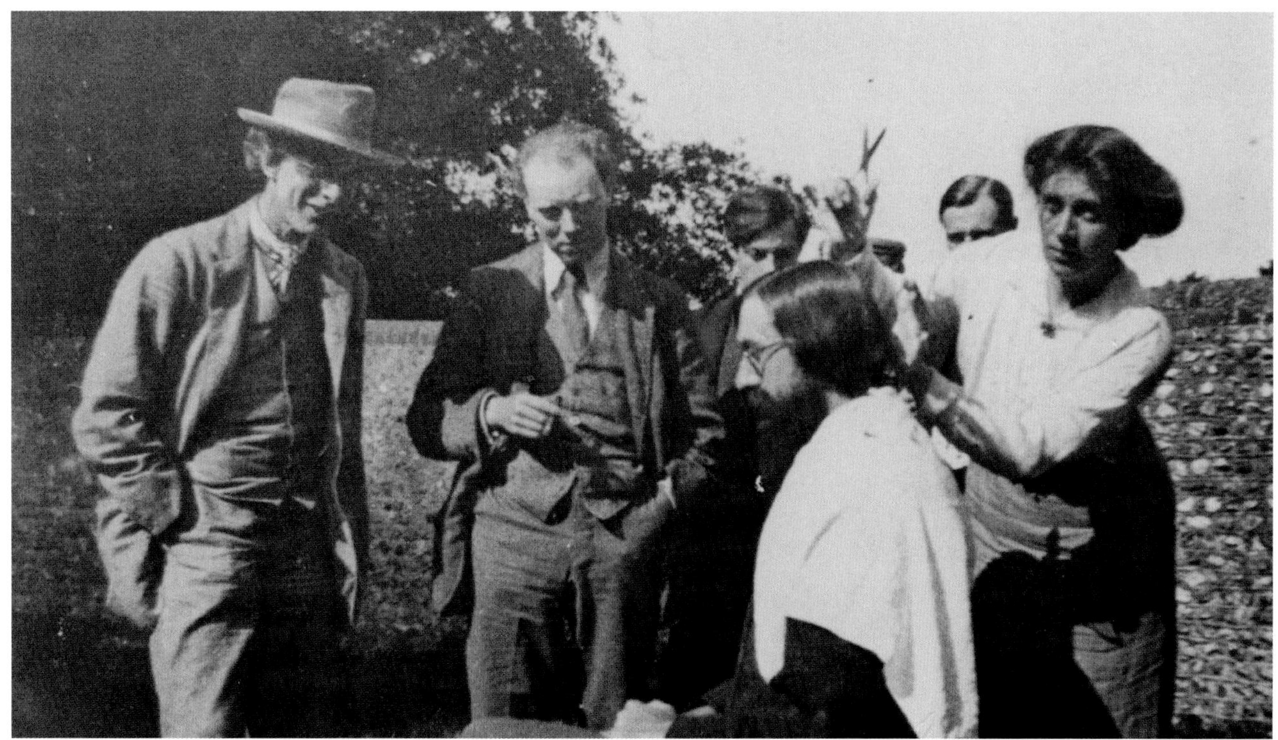

Fig.1 *Roger Fry, Clive Bell, Duncan Grant, Lytton Strachey, Saxon Arnold Sydney-Turner and Vanessa Bell, c.*1916
Unknown photographer
Gelatin silver copy print, 75 × 126mm
National Portrait Gallery, London

vulnerably encircling his knees and with a wry smile on his brooding, dark-featured face. His thick neck might claim the compositional centre of the portrait, but our gaze is quickly distracted by his lean, muscular arm and his delicately delineated nipple. Its precise rendering marks it out for special attention amidst the thicker daubs of paint, an early technique that Grant dubbed his 'leopard' style. The artist described Mallory as 'a beautiful creature who was perfectly willing to sit for me' and he became Grant's muse for a time, posing for a series of completely nude portraits around the same date.[1]

Alongside his affairs with men, Grant maintained a forty-year relationship with the artist Vanessa Bell who remained in an open marriage with the art critic Clive Bell. In 1918, Vanessa gave birth to Grant's daughter, Angelica, and they set up home together at Charleston farmhouse in Sussex. Grant's male lovers often lived there too, as did Clive who remained on friendly terms with Vanessa and brought up Angelica as his own child alongside their two sons. Vanessa's sexual relationship with Grant is believed to have ceased before Angelica's birth, but the two continued to live and travel together and support each other creatively, domestically and emotionally.

This kind of close, relaxed companionship is captured in Grant's portrait of Bell (fig.6) stretched out on a red sofa on a summer's day in the Garden Room at Charleston. Like Mallory, Vanessa does not engage with the viewer. Yet here she is presented as a different kind of muse: her comparative distance, blank stare and blurred features, together with her self-assured pose and fully-clothed state, render her less an object of desire than a crucial

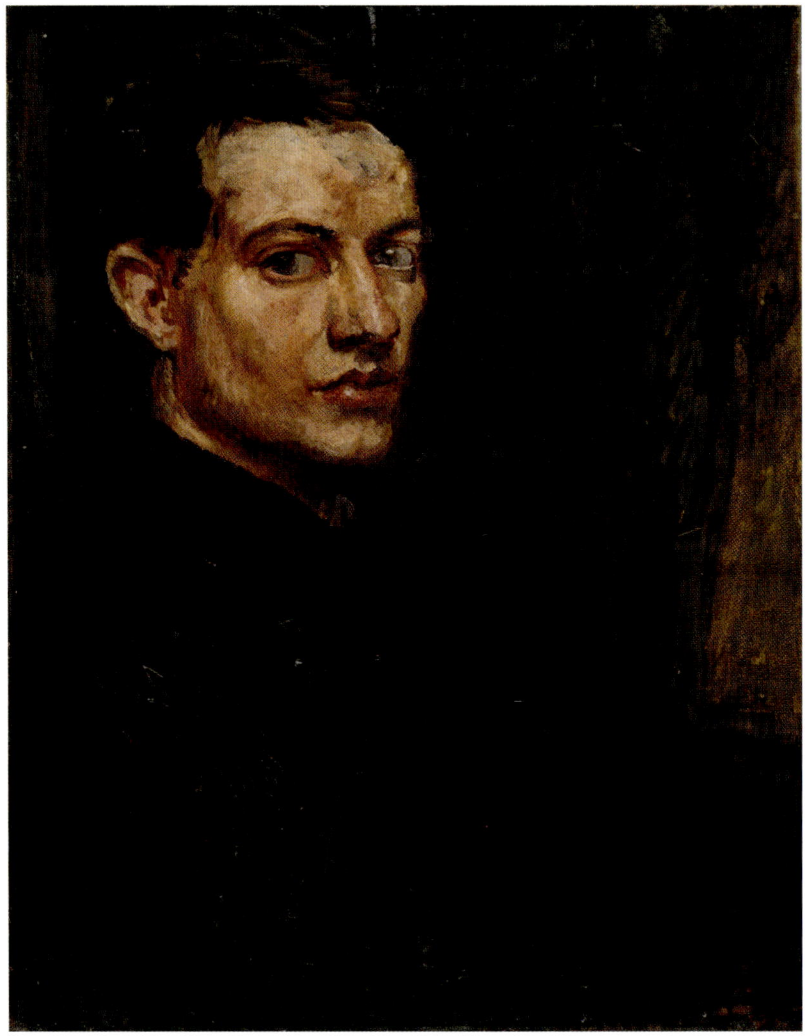

Fig.2 *Self-Portrait*, *c.*1909
Duncan Grant
Oil on canvas, 543 × 419mm
National Portrait Gallery, London

part of the brightly-coloured and patterned surroundings that she and Grant had created at Charleston. The dazzling palette showcases Grant's adoption of a Post-Impressionist style advocated by fellow Bloomsbury member Roger Fry in his exhibitions of 1910 and 1912–13 and his radical writings on art, which were taking the British art world by storm. Bell was similarly experimenting with bold colour and simplified form in her own painting. By treating her in this way, Grant acknowledges one of the shared interests that helped bond their unconventional relationship.

Vanessa's younger sister Virginia Woolf (fig.4) also inhabited a sexually-experimental identity – what she herself called 'diverse'.[2] Its diversity was

OPPOSITE
Fig.3 *George Leigh Mallory*, 1912
Duncan Grant
Oil on panel, 775 × 530mm
National Portrait Gallery, London

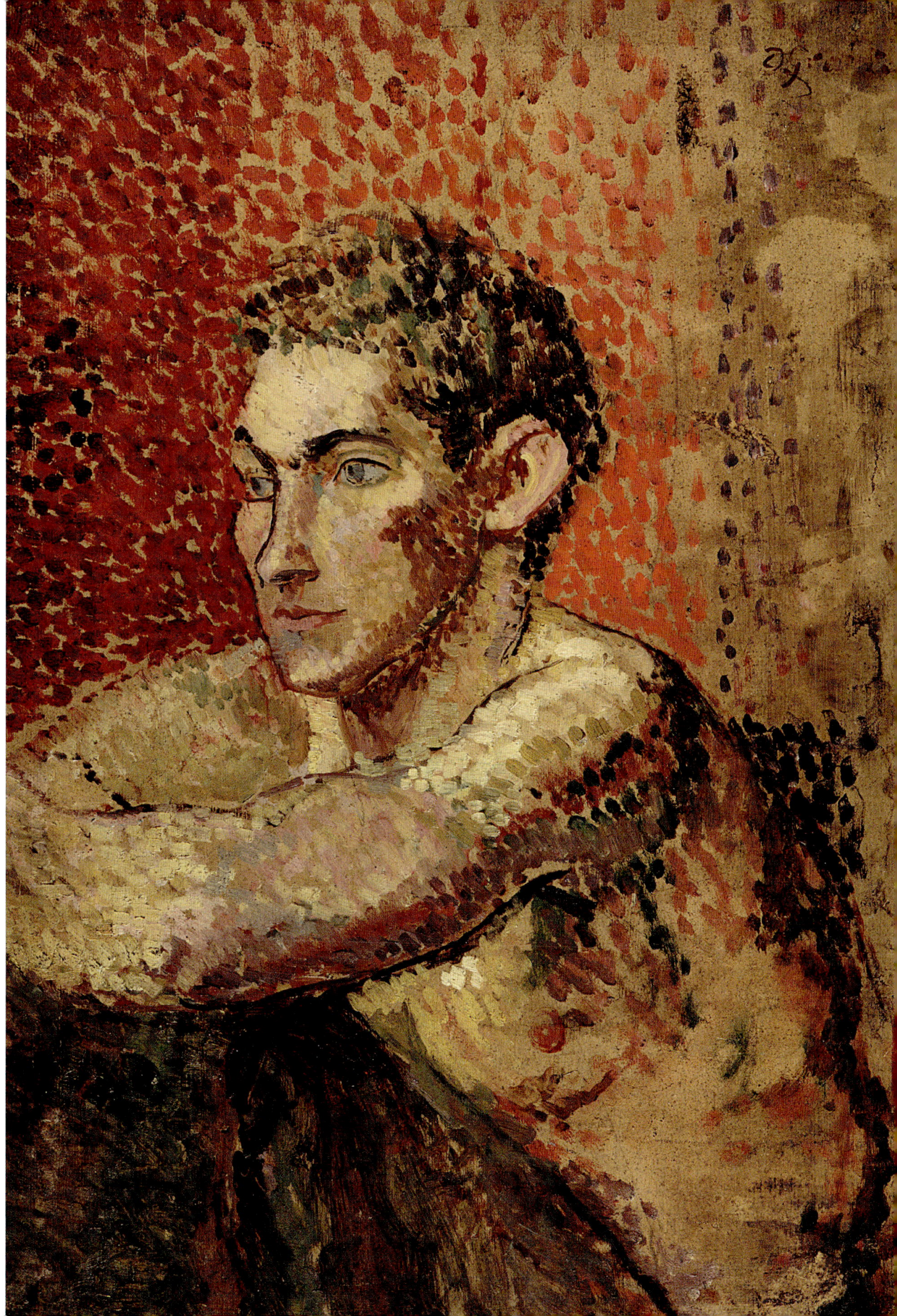

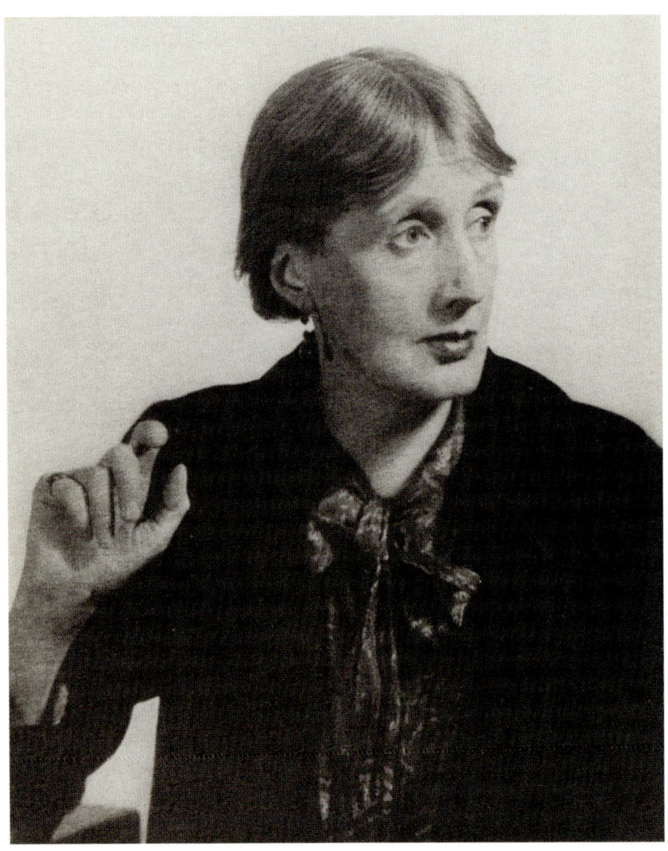

Fig.4 *Virginia Woolf*, 27 November 1934
Man Ray
Gelatin silver print, 246 × 195mm
National Portrait Gallery, London

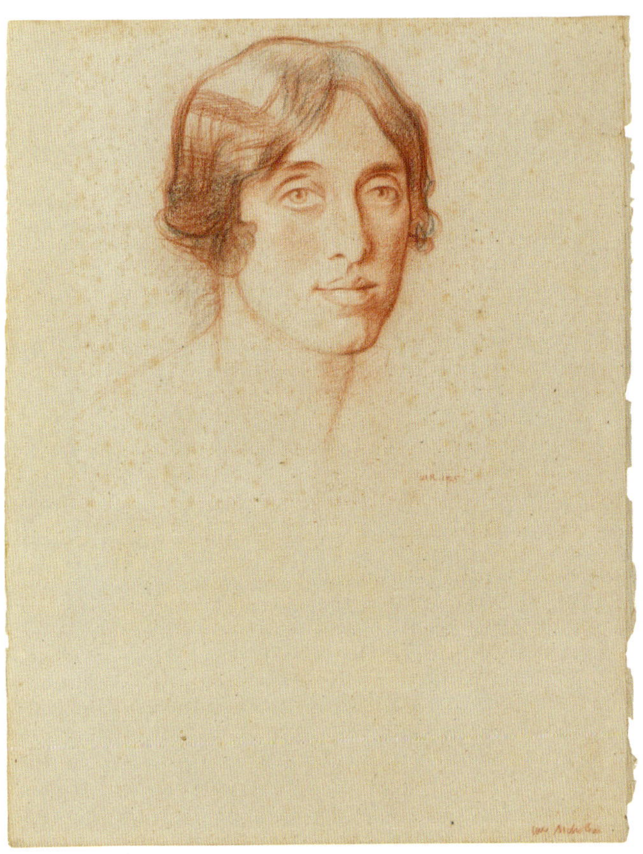

Fig.5 *Vita Sackville-West*, 1925
William Rothenstein
Red and black chalk, 408 × 302mm
National Portrait Gallery, London

developed through her numerous relationships with asexual, homosexual and heterosexual men as well as a lesbian liaison with the writer and gardener Vita Sackville-West, a satellite member of the Bloomsbury Group who, like both Vanessa and Virginia, was in an open marriage. This relationship peaked in 1925, the same year that William Rothenstein made this tender red and black chalk drawing of Vita (fig.5). It shows a thick-set, handsome-faced woman whose heavy-lidded eyes engage us directly. Vita's androgyny inspired Virginia's 1928 novel *Orlando*, a fantasy of sex-changing and gender fluidity which underlined the paradoxes of modern intimacy so central to their relationship and Bloomsbury's queer subculture.

Another associate of the group known for her androgyny was the artist Dora Carrington (fig.8). Her sexuality was also fluid and experimental, conducting relationships with both women and men, most famously with Lytton Strachey, the gay biographer thirteen years her senior. The story of their first encounter is that during a weekend visiting Virginia and Leonard Woolf's Sussex retreat, Dora and Lytton went for a walk during which he tried to kiss her against her will. That night, she

OPPOSITE
Fig.6 *Vanessa Bell*, 1917
Duncan Grant
Oil on canvas, 1270 × 1016mm
National Portrait Gallery, London

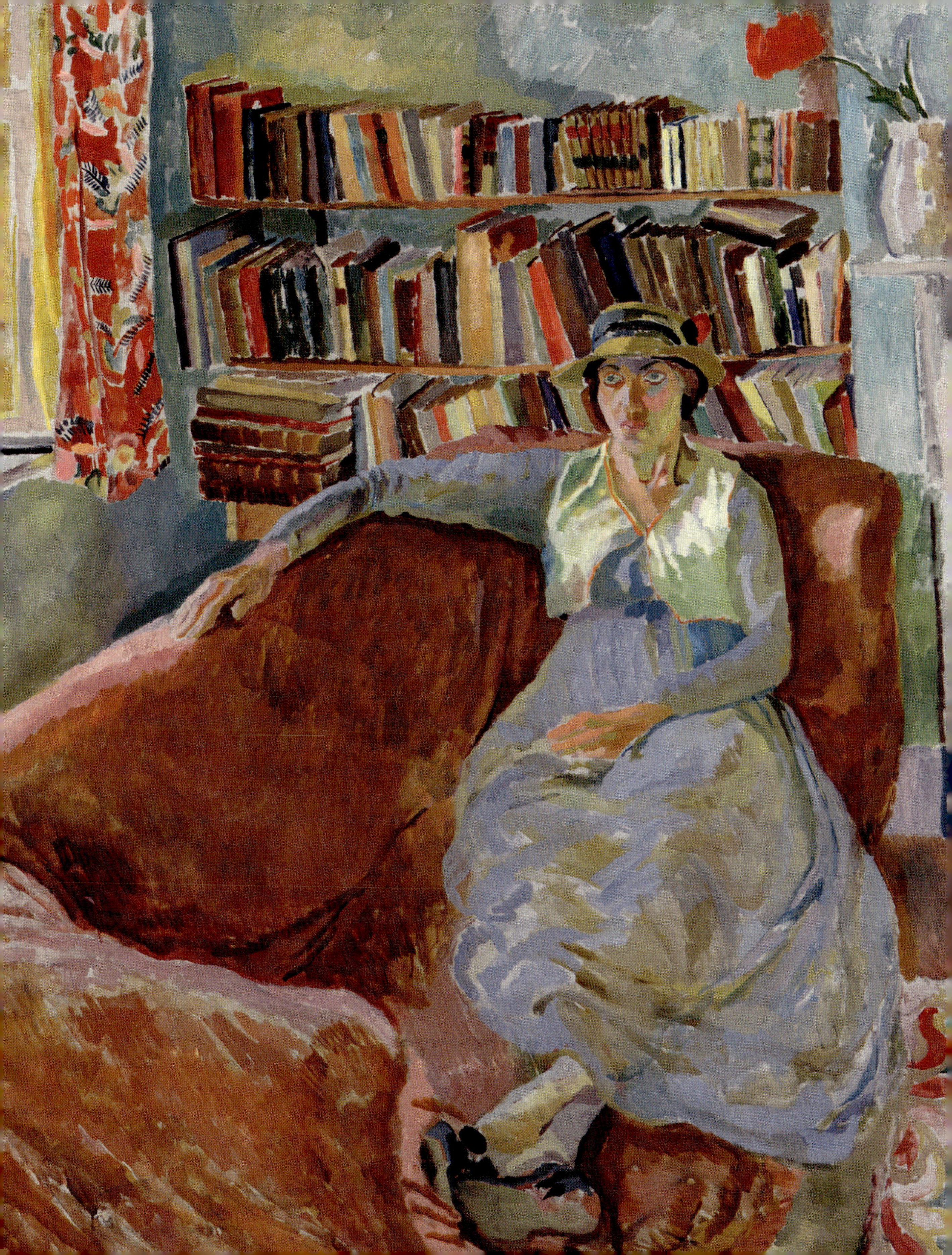

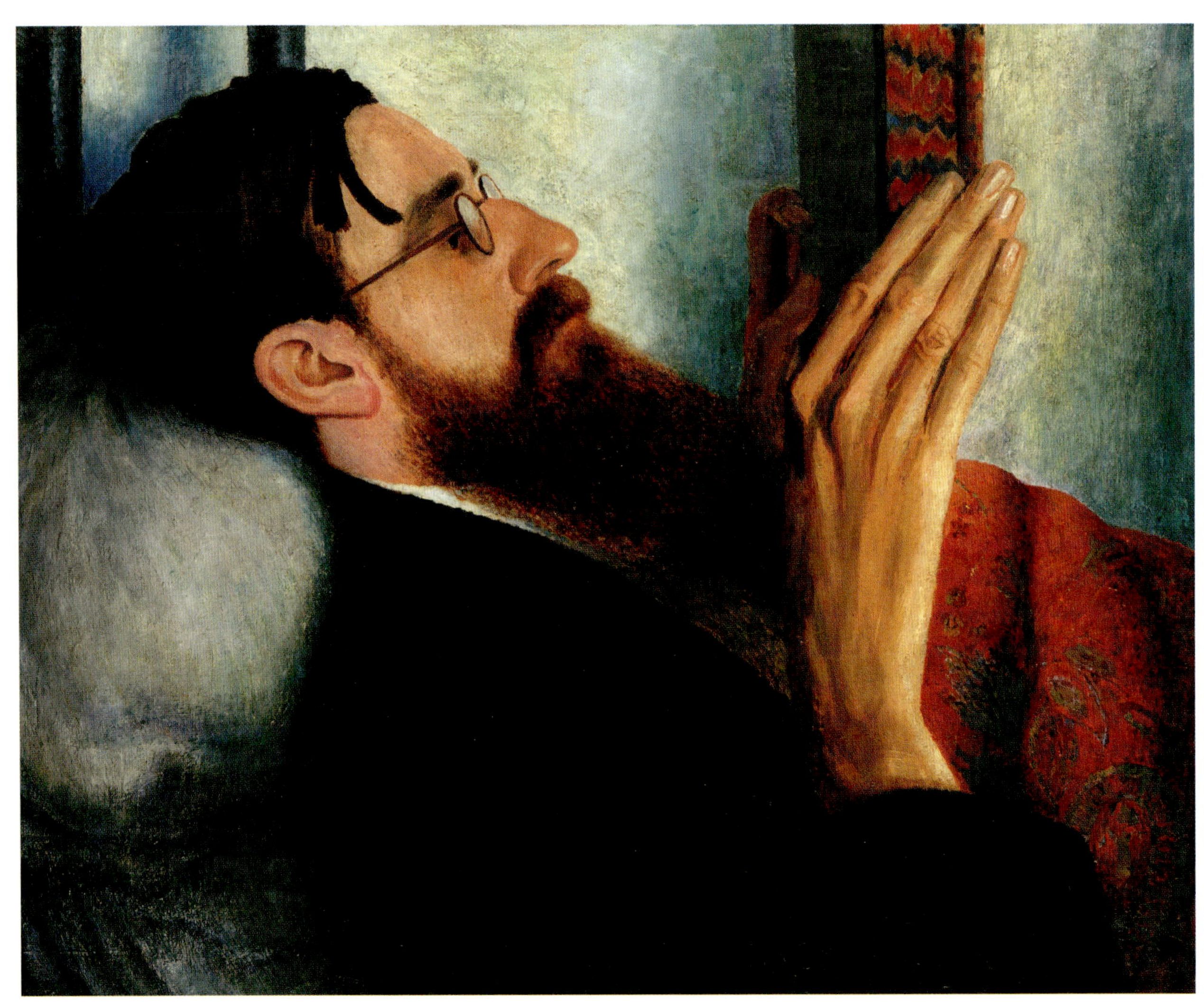

Fig.7 *Lytton Strachey*, 1916
Dora Carrington
Oil on panel, 508 × 609mm
National Portrait Gallery, London

plotted her revenge and slipped into Lytton's room while he was sleeping, intending to cut off his trademark long beard. But before she could do so, he opened his eyes and she fell deeply and obsessively in love. Despite Lytton's homosexuality, the couple entered into a sexual relationship (at first) and set up home together for most of Dora's adult life. They took in another lover, the poet Ralph Partridge, whom Dora married (reluctantly), and they lived temporarily in a *ménage à trois*. There were other lovers too, both male and female, but it was Lytton for whom Dora carried the brightest flame. Stricken by grief when he died of stomach cancer in 1932, she took her own life at the age of thirty-eight.

Carrington's letters reveal that she was utterly absorbed with Strachey.[3] This absorption is at the heart of her portrait of her companion, made shortly after the start of their relationship in 1916 (fig.7). Lying on plumped-up pillows, tucked under a red blanket, Strachey is shown engrossed in a book. Everything is painted with meticulous attention to detail: the creases in the pillow and sheet, the pink of his earlobe, the texture of his beard and the fall of light on his face and fingernails. The book's marbled pages are held gently in his hands, which Carrington dramatically elongated, skewing the perspective to position her – and by extension us – close up to his body, as if she were lying in bed beside him.

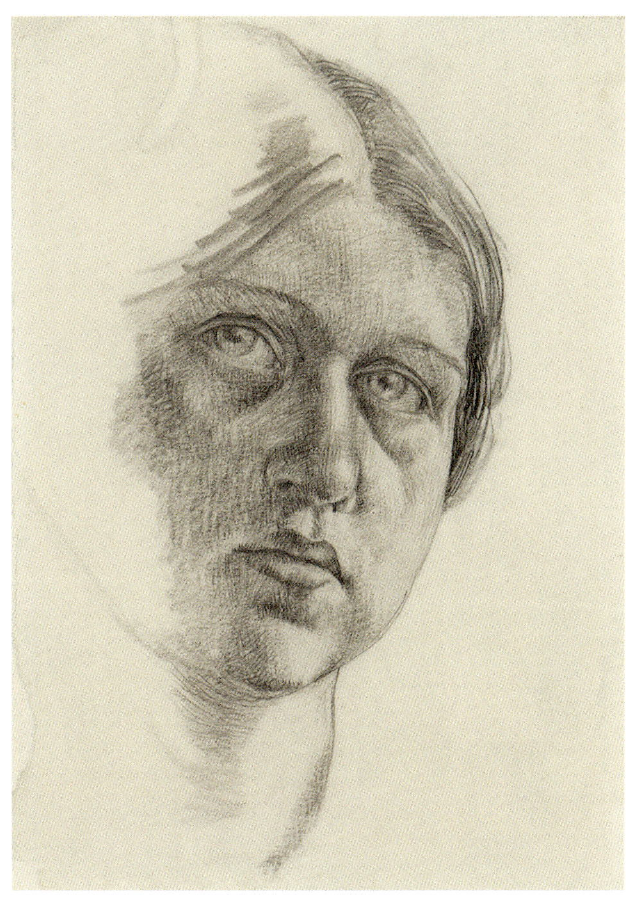

Fig.8 ***Self-Portrait**, c.***1910
Dora Carrington
Pencil, 228 × 152mm
National Portrait Gallery, London

Looked at together, these Bloomsbury portraits speak to the complex entanglements of men and women who, in the first decades of the twentieth century, were radically redefining the structures of intimacy, companionship and sexual identity. Although not without complications, the group usually divided their sexual and emotional energies between multiple partners. This led to the famous quip that 'they lived in squares and loved in triangles'.[4] Fluid and multiple, permissive and adventurous, complex and human: loving in the Bloomsbury Group exploded boundaries and crafted new ways of experiencing and representing love.

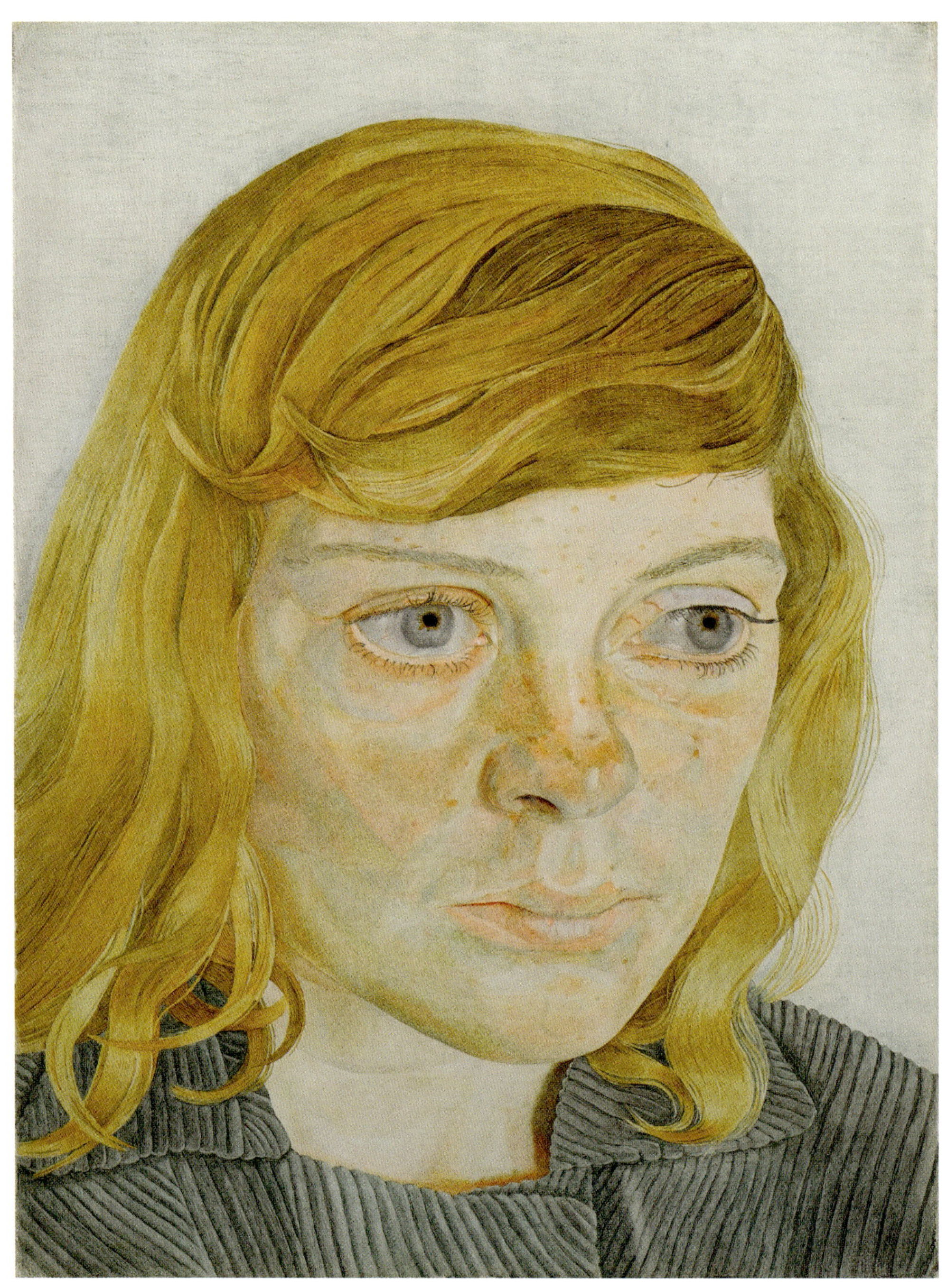

Fig.1 *Girl in a Green Dress*, 1954
Lucian Freud
Oil on board, 325 × 236mm
Arts Council Collection, Southbank Centre, London

GEORGIA HASELDINE

Lucian Freud & Caroline, Lady Blackwood

'A painter's taste', wrote Lucian Freud, 'must grow out of what so obsesses him in life.'[1] It is no surprise then that Freud's many lovers feature prominently in his work. The series of portraits he made during his long courtship and short marriage to the Irish writer Lady Caroline Blackwood between 1950 and 1956 recorded his obsessive desire and forensic attention to her form. His meticulous style recorded every vein and freckle in his early portraits in a style that many of their contemporaries deemed cruel. Blackwood remembered how Freud's portraits of her were 'received with admiration that was tinged with bafflement'. She was 'dismayed' and others 'mystified as to why he needed to paint a girl, who at that point still looked childish, as so distressingly old'.[2] Even though he distanced his subject by titling the portraits 'Girl', and never 'Caroline', these likenesses of her are among his most tender portraits of a woman by whom, for a while, he was utterly possessed.

Blackwood and Freud met at a society ball in 1949 where Princess Margaret took to the stage and sang Cole Porter songs terribly off-key until she was heckled by the artist Francis Bacon.[3] Blackwood, a member of the wealthy Guinness family, was an 18-year-old aristocratic beauty with huge blue eyes. She was just beginning her career as a journalist when she fell for Freud's Byronic good looks. Freud in turn, though still married to his first wife Kitty Garman, became obsessed with the young heiress, following her around debutante balls and having to pawn and sell paintings to keep up with her. Flouting convention Blackwood moved into Freud's Paddington studio in 1952, facing the censure of her family who disapproved of her lover for being a poor, German-Jewish artist who was already married. To escape their critics,

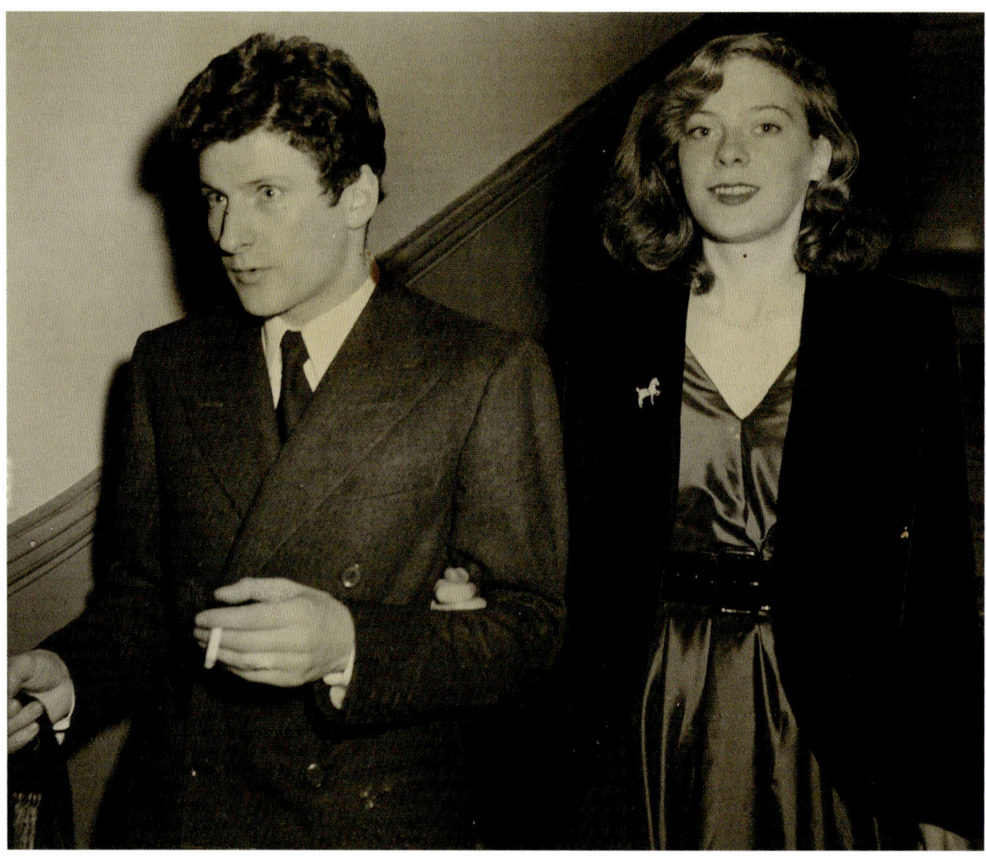

Fig.2 *Lucian Freud and Lady Caroline Blackwood*, 8 December 1953
Unknown photographer
Gelatin silver print, 178 × 211mm
National Portrait Gallery, London

the couple soon fled to Paris, living in a small room in the Hôtel La Louisiane.

Girl in a Green Dress (fig.1) was painted at the French seaside resort, Arcachon. Blackwood read during these sittings and apparently was lost in Henry James' *The Tragic Muse* (1889–90) at the time, a role that she could identify with while sitting endlessly for Freud. She later recalled that modelling for him was not only slow but also 'after six months you can be back where you started. He not only paints "the anguish of our age" but he also paints the "anguish of his sitters"'.[4]

They were married in December 1953 at Chelsea Town Hall. A reporter took a photo of them leaving the registry office in which Freud looks distracted, cigarette in hand, while Blackwood smiles with dazed, soft relief (fig.2). They held a lunch afterwards at Wheeler's in Soho, which was so raucous that the society photographer Cecil Beaton wrote in his diary that 'by four o'clock in the afternoon one had the impression it was four in the morning'.[5]

But once the newlyweds had arrived in Paris for a honeymoon, Freud took up with another woman, the American model Ivy Nicholson who would later go on to be Andy Warhol's muse. Freud told his friend William Feaver that 'my ardour in the long pursuit [of Caroline] was spent; the whole thing exhausted ... instead of happy ever after'.[6] Later in her life Blackwood was often asked about her marriage to Freud. To one enquirer she responded, 'Have you ever driven with him?' The interviewer replied that he had, a terrifying experience where he had thrown himself out of the car when Freud – unusually – stopped at a red light. Blackwood replied, 'Exactly. That's what being married to him was like.'[7]

In 1956 Blackwood left Freud and moved to New York. She married the composer Israel Citkowitz but by 1970 began an affair with the American poet, Robert Lowell. Lowell documented their relationship in his Pulitzer Prize-winning collection *The Dolphin* (1973) where he, like Freud, was obsessed with her 'huge eyes and dawn-gaze'. Lowell's manic depression combined with Blackwood's alcohol-fuelled taunts eventually made the relationship unbearable. Lowell returned to his ex-wife in the autumn of 1977 but died shortly after from a heart attack on the back seat of a New York taxi. In his arms he was clutching a gift from Blackwood: Freud's portrait of her, *Girl in Bed* (1952).

In the same year, Blackwood published her most successful novel, *Great Granny Webster* (1977), which was short-listed for the Booker Prize. Philip Larkin cast the decisive vote against it, claiming that a novel based so closely on her dysfunctional family was too autobiographical to be judged fiction. Having always been described as Freud's muse, Freud can also be considered Blackwood's. Her fiction was a literary version of his ruthless view of humanity. One reviewer commented that she had an 'unblinking, observant eye' and her prose was 'like an etching, sharp, precise and sensitive'.[8]

Reflecting on Freud's career, Blackwood described how 'the amazed interest he once took in the human vulnerability of his sitters', which the portraits of her had been his highest achievements, had been 'replaced by an appalled horror at their condition'.[9] Their divorce sparked this change. After a melancholic period Freud began to stand up whilst painting, freeing his style, and painting human flesh with clinical unsentimentality. He turned this dispassionate gaze on himself in an unfinished self-portrait from 1985 (fig.3). Blackwood and Freud remained close throughout her lifetime. During her final illness in 1996, a living wake was held in her hotel room in New York. A transatlantic phone call from Freud interrupted the event; Blackwood said a private goodbye that lasted half an hour.

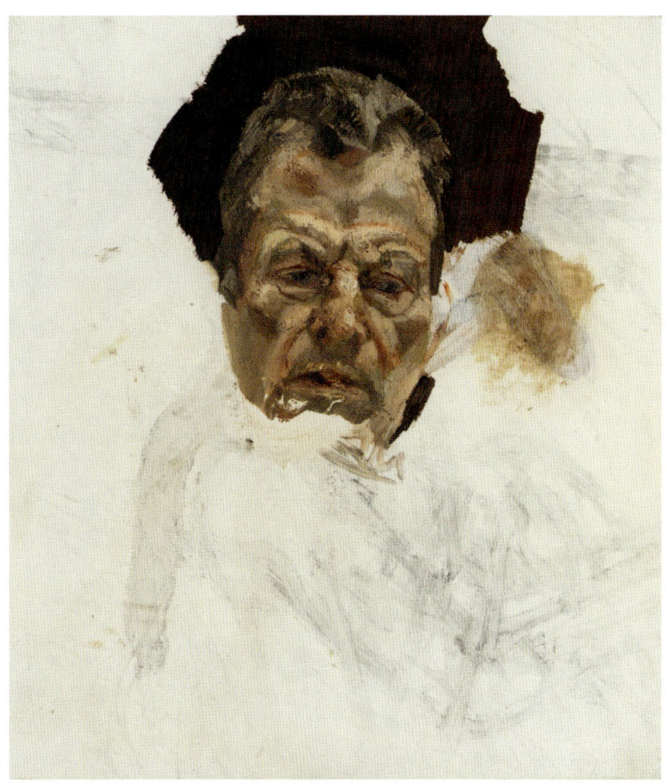

Fig.3 ***Self-Portrait**, c.1985*
Lucian Freud
Oil on canvas, 356 × 306mm
National Portrait Gallery, London

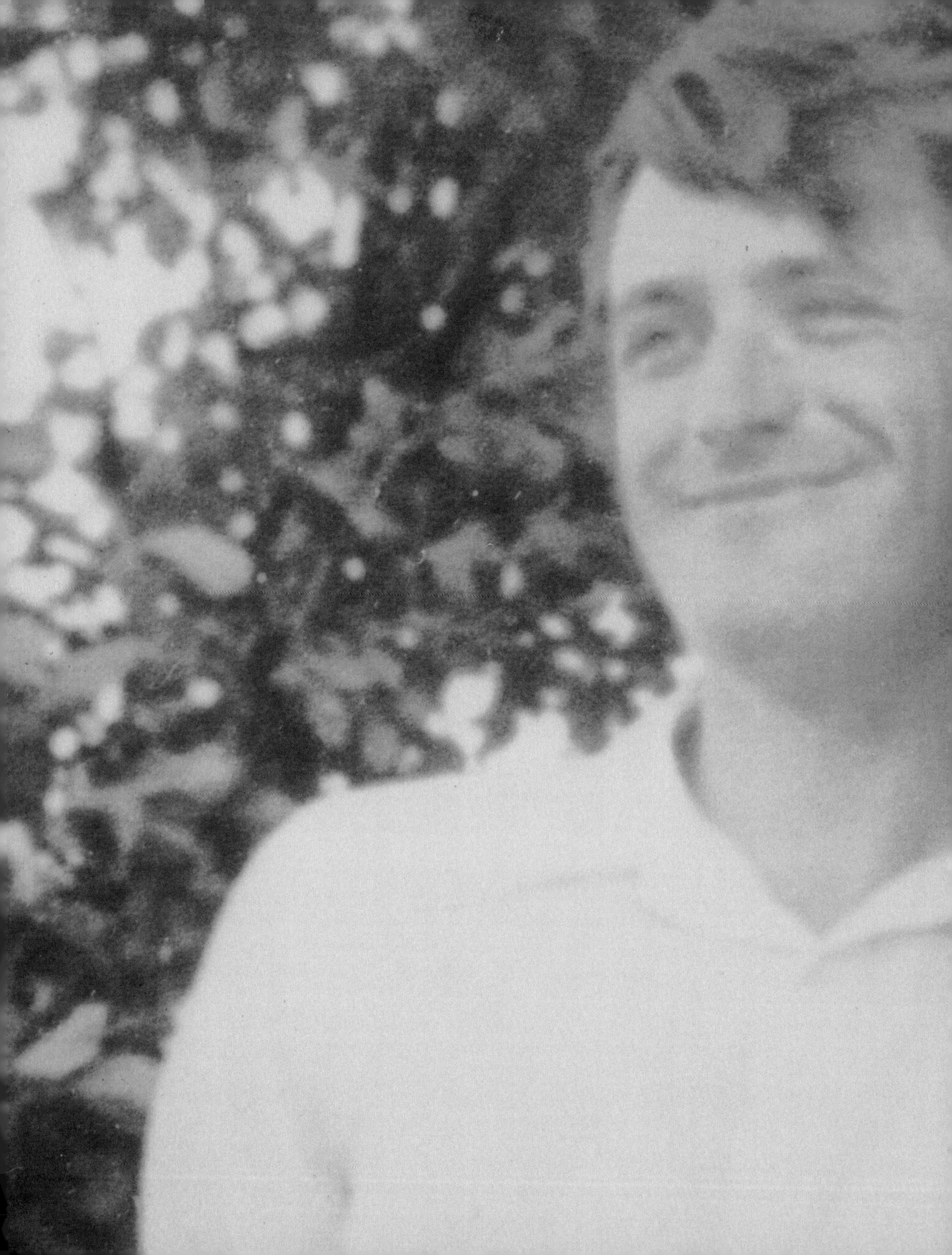

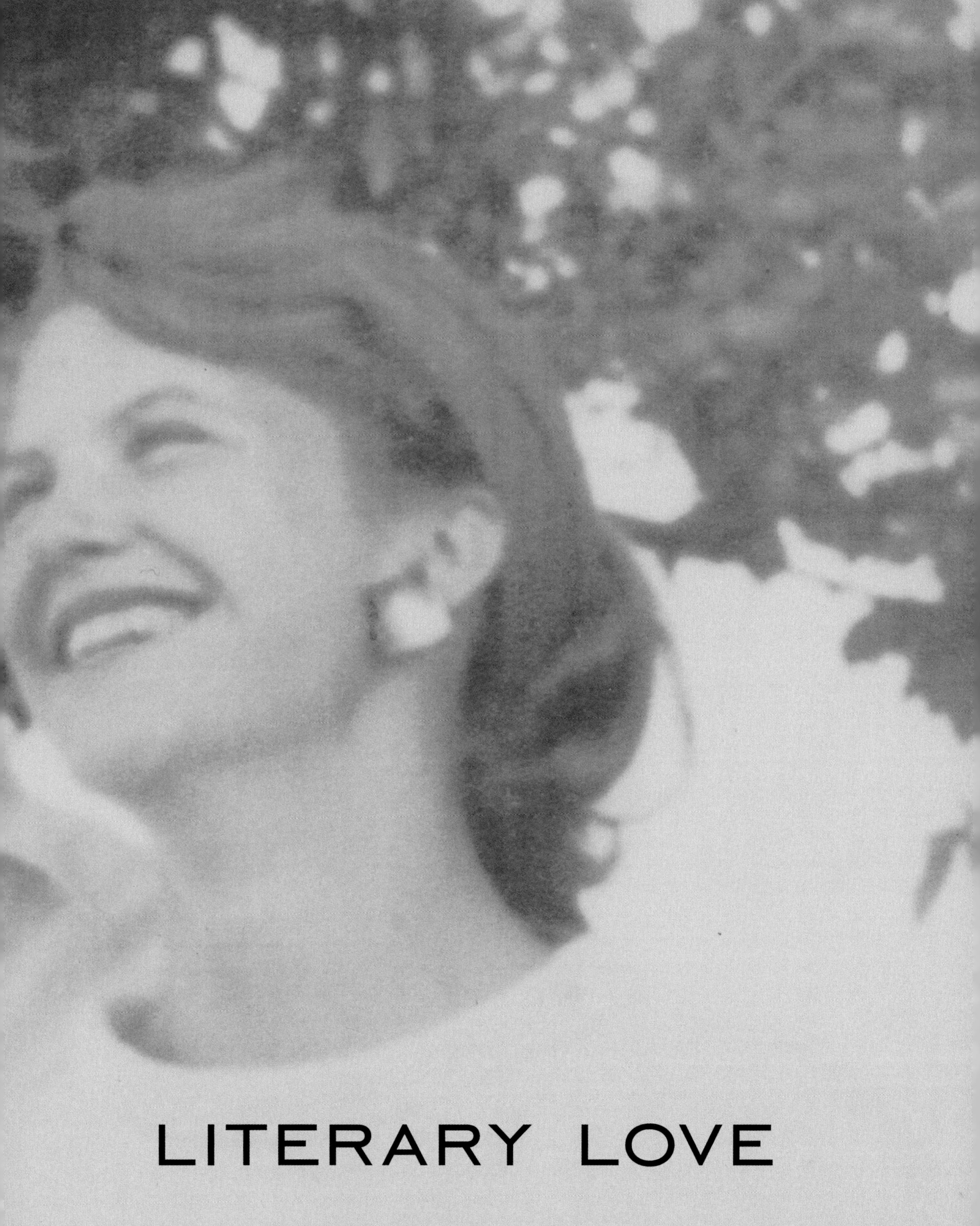

LITERARY LOVE

LOUISE STEWART

LITERARY LOVE

Love is the subject of some of the greatest works in literary history, from Shakespeare's sonnets to Jane Austen's novels and the love poetry of John Keats. 'Bright Star', which is thought to be one of Keats' last poems, was revised for his fiancée Fanny Brawne as he set sail for Italy, seeking a climate that would help cure his consumption. In the poem, he describes his wish to be steadfast as a star, forever listening to his love's 'tender-taken breath'. The pair would never see each other again, as Keats died in Rome in September 1821 at the age of only twenty-five. A posthumous portrait was painted by Keats' close friend Joseph Severn in the two years following his death (fig.1). It represents Keats at home in Hampstead on a morning when Severn was 'struck with the first real symptoms of sadness in Keats' and conveys the yearning, melancholic sensibility, often linked to doomed love, which inspired so much romantic poetry.[1]

Many of the leading figures of English literature have been caught up in romances with other writers, which have inspired some of their greatest works. Lord Byron is one of the most prolific lovers in the literary canon due to his numerous relationships with both men and women. The dashing, romantic hero of Thomas Phillips' portrait (fig.2) rose to prominence following the publication of *Childe Harold's Pilgrimage* (1812–18), and his fame brought him to the attention of Lady Caroline Lamb (fig.3), the wife of the future prime minister William Lamb, Lord Melbourne. Born into the Anglo-Irish peerage, Lamb was a follower of Mary Wollstonecraft and refused to be constrained by social convention. Her tempestuous marriage scandalised polite society and would later be the subject of popular novels including Benjamin Disraeli's *Vivian Grey* (1826–7) and *Venetia* (1837). This is less surprising when we note that she used the material from her own love life as the subject for her first novel, *Glenarvon: A Gothic Novel* (1816), published just as her four-year adulterous relationship with Lord Byron came to an end. This had begun in 1812, when she had been introduced to the glamorous poet but had refused to acknowledge him. She retained this sultry approach in public while embarking on a torrid and passionate affair with Byron, whom she is remembered as

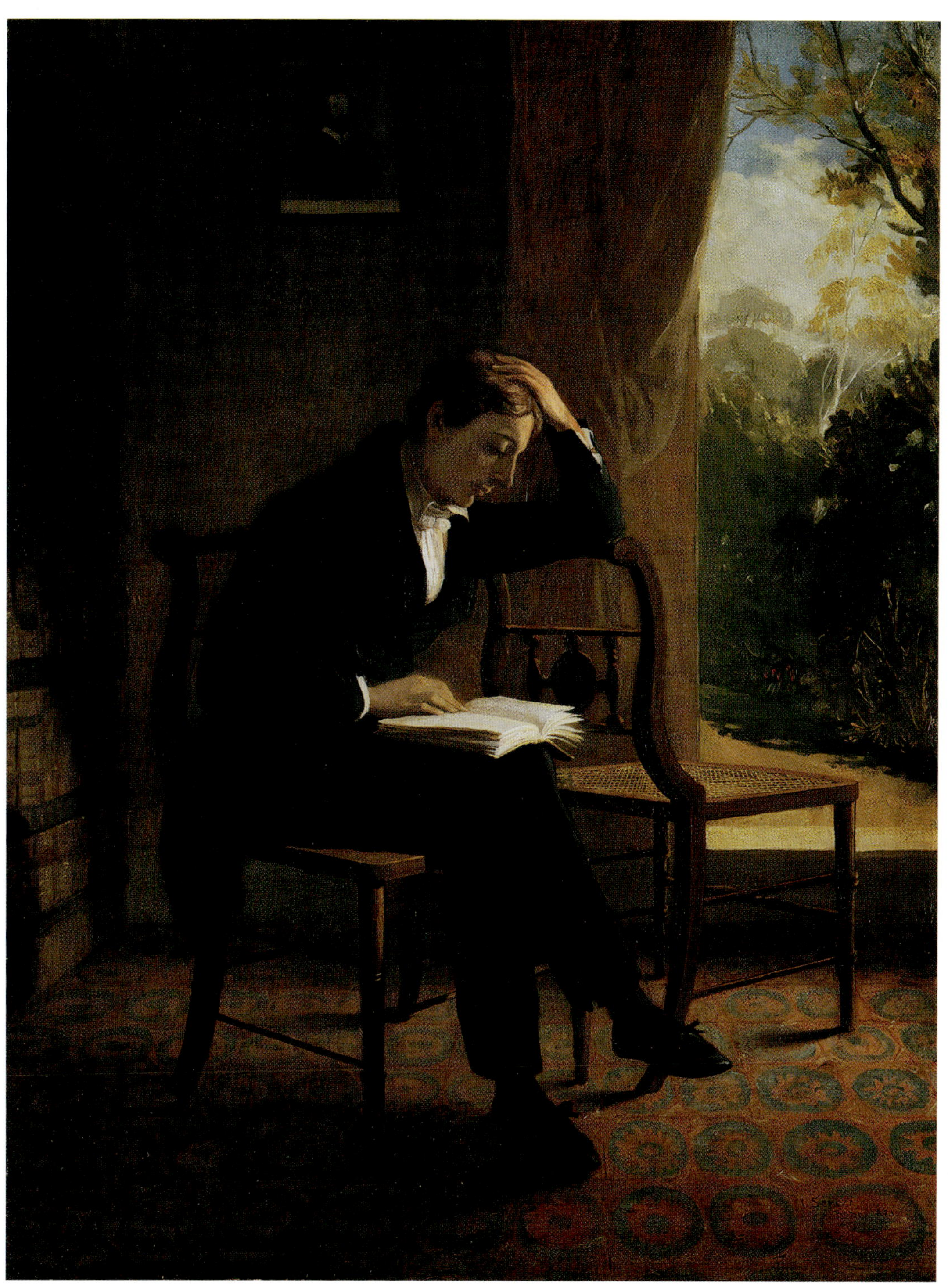

Fig.1 *John Keats*, 1821–3
Joseph Severn
Oil on canvas, 565 × 419mm
National Portrait Gallery, London

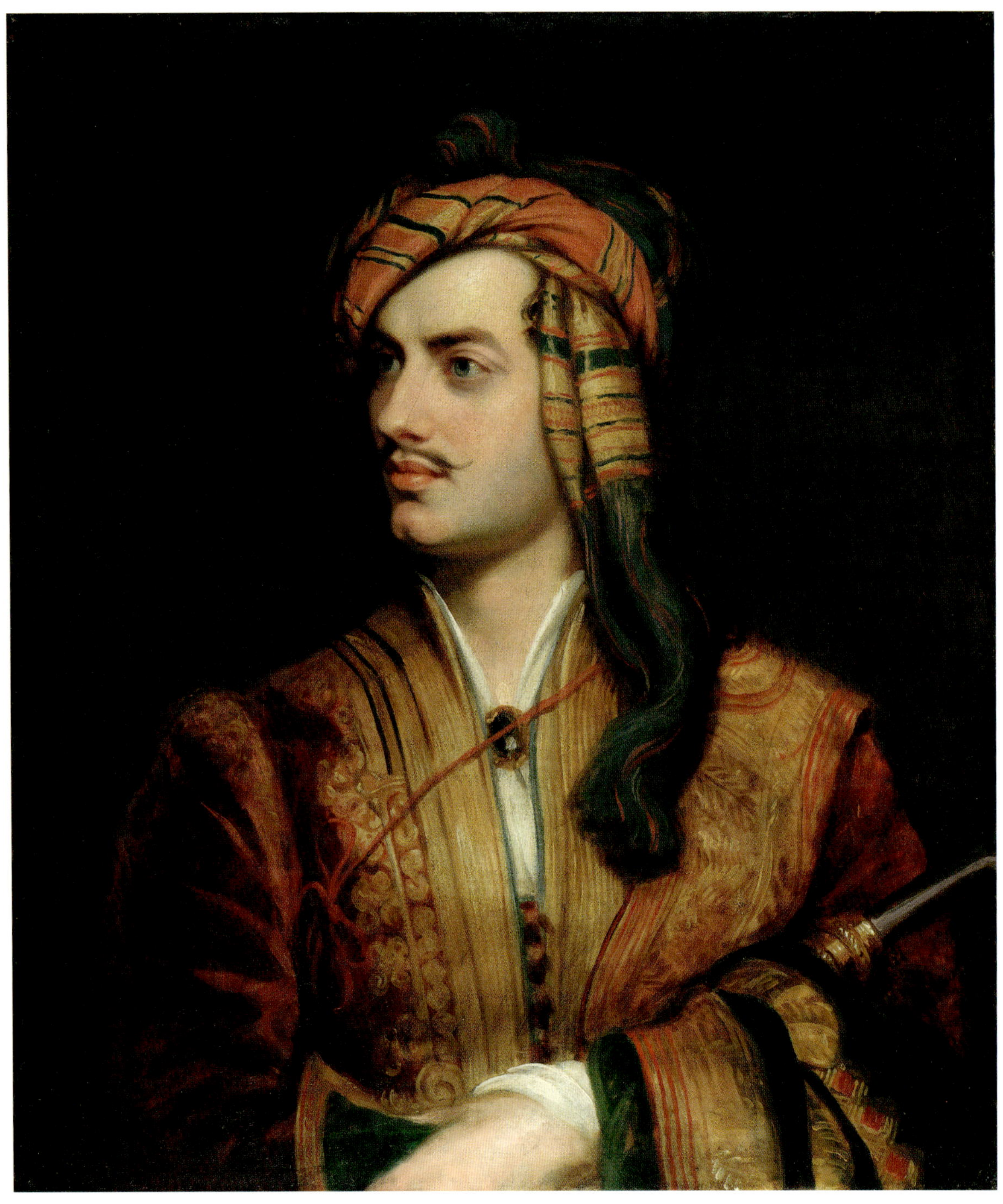

Fig.2 *Lord Byron*, *c.*1835, replica of a work of 1813 by Thomas Phillips
Oil on canvas, 765 × 639mm
National Portrait Gallery, London

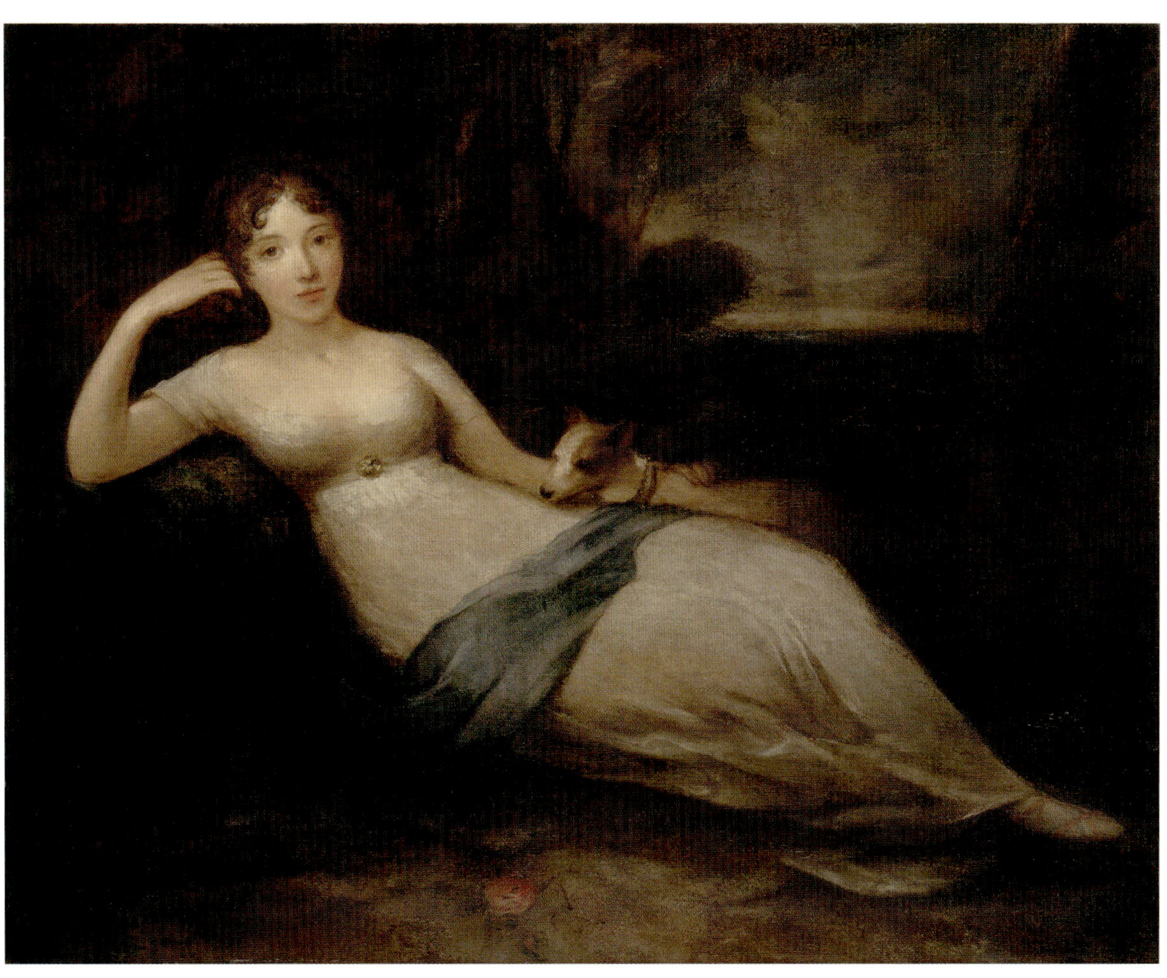

Fig.3 *Lady Caroline Lamb*, *c.*1811
Eliza H. Trotter
Oil on canvas, 1149 × 1403mm
National Portrait Gallery, London

summarising as, 'mad, bad and dangerous to know'.[2] Byron, for his part, summed Lamb up as 'the cleverest most agreeable, absurd, amiable, perplexing, dangerous, fascinating little being that lives'.[3] But Lamb was not just Byron's lover: she went on to forge her own career as a highly successful romantic novelist. There followed an intense literary rivalry which saw Lamb respond to Byron's *Don Juan* (1819) with two anonymous parodies: *A New Canto* (1819) and *Gordon: a Tale* (1821). Like the poets Elizabeth Barrett Browning and Robert Browning (see pp.68–71), the passionate, even obsessive relationship between two writers provided a rich seam of inspiration for their work. The Brownings' creative dialogue and love for one another is fittingly symbolised in a portrait by Harriet Goodhue Hosmer which takes the form of a bronze cast of the couple's clasped hands (see p.69). This work, an unusual addition to the National Portrait Gallery's collection, is a particularly appropriate tribute to their love, a portrait focusing not on their faces but on the hands which wrote some of the most celebrated love poetry in the English language.

Attention to literary love stories sheds light on the achievements of women in more recent times. Mildred Eldridge was a successful artist whose detailed watercolour studies, landscapes and large-scale murals deal with the human relationship with the natural world. In 1940, she married a curate, Ronald Stuart Thomas, who went on to become a distinguished poet. Her influence on his work, which also focuses on spiritual links with the land, is only beginning to be recognised. The nature of the pair's literary collaboration, in which Eldridge often illustrated her husband's poetry, is summed up in this ethereal double portrait made at the start of their life together (fig.4).

Fig.4 *R.S. Thomas and Mildred E. Eldridge*, 1941
Mildred E. Eldridge
Pencil and watercolour, 495 × 381mm
National Portrait Gallery, London

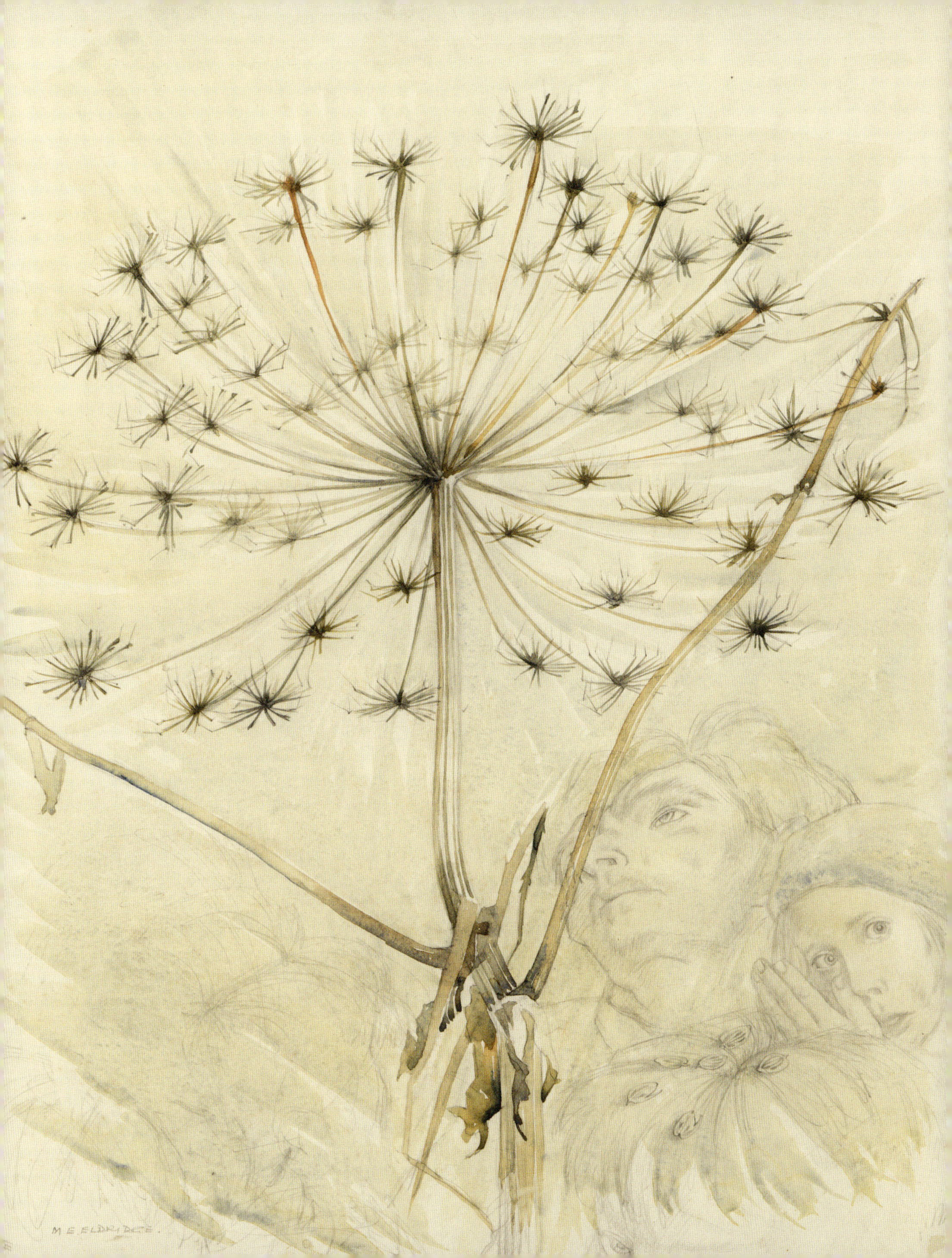
M E ELDRIDGE.

RAB MACGIBBON

Mary Shelley & Percy Bysshe Shelley

The love story of the writer Mary Shelley (fig.1) and the poet Percy Bysshe Shelley (fig.2) was touched by tragedy from the outset. Mary was named after her mother, Mary Wollstonecraft (fig.3), author of *A Vindication of the Rights of Woman* (1792), who died eleven days after her birth. Her father was William Godwin (fig.4), whose *Enquiry Concerning Political Justice* (1793) laid the philosophical foundations for anarchism. Godwin remarried in 1801 and Mary was raised as one of five step-siblings, none of whom shared the same two parents. For the early nineteenth century, it was an unconventional and intellectually stimulating upbringing.

The Godwin home attracted the most radical thinkers of the period, including the young poet Percy Shelley, the son of a prosperous Sussex baronet, who had been educated at Eton and Oxford. Greatly influenced by the revolutionary ideas of Godwin, Shelley had rejected the confines of his privileged upbringing. Aged seventeen, he was cut off by his father after getting expelled from Oxford for atheism and then eloping to Scotland with a friend of his sister, Harriet Westbrook, who gave birth to a daughter in 1813. By the time of his marriage to Harriet the following year, Percy and Mary Godwin had already become infatuated and had declared their love as they stood by her mother's grave in St Pancras Churchyard.

Fig.1 *Mary Shelley*, exhibited 1840
Richard Rothwell
Oil on canvas, 737 × 610mm
National Portrait Gallery, London

Fig.2 *Percy Bysshe Shelley*, 1819
Amelia Curran
Oil on canvas, 597 × 476mm
National Portrait Gallery, London

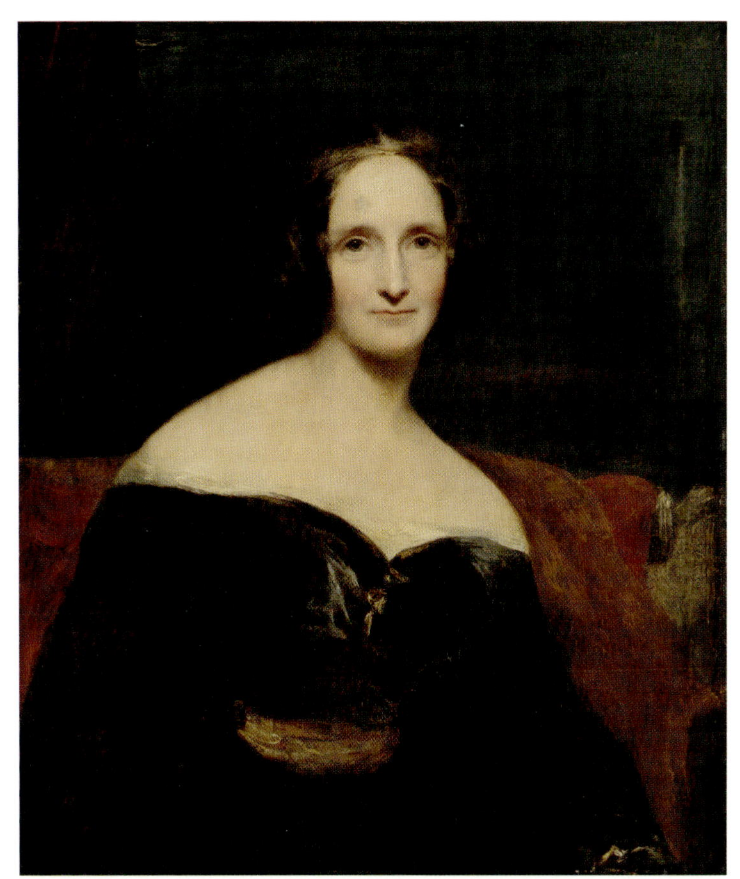

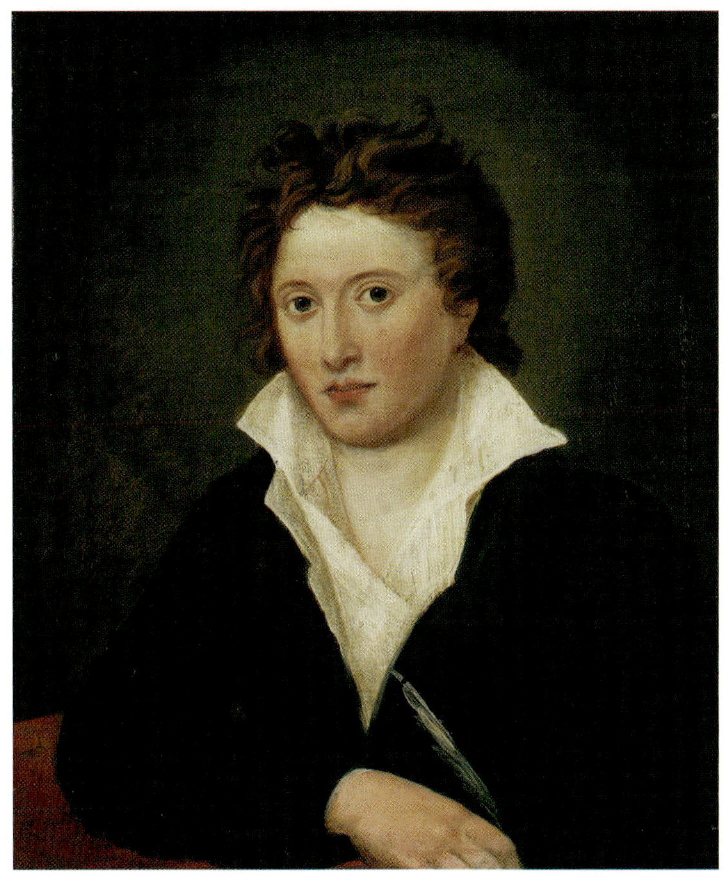

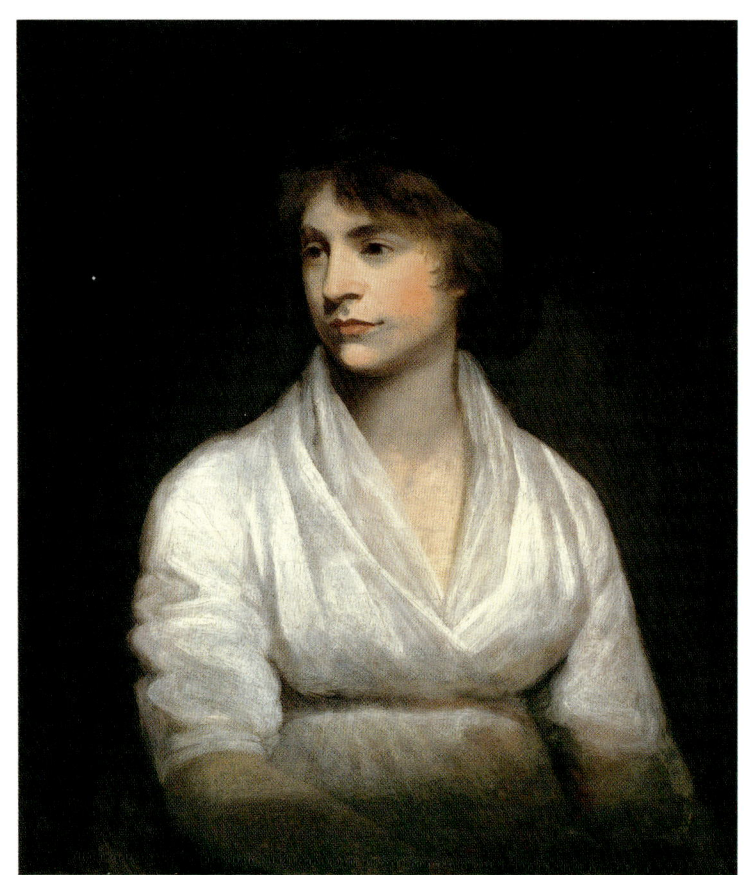

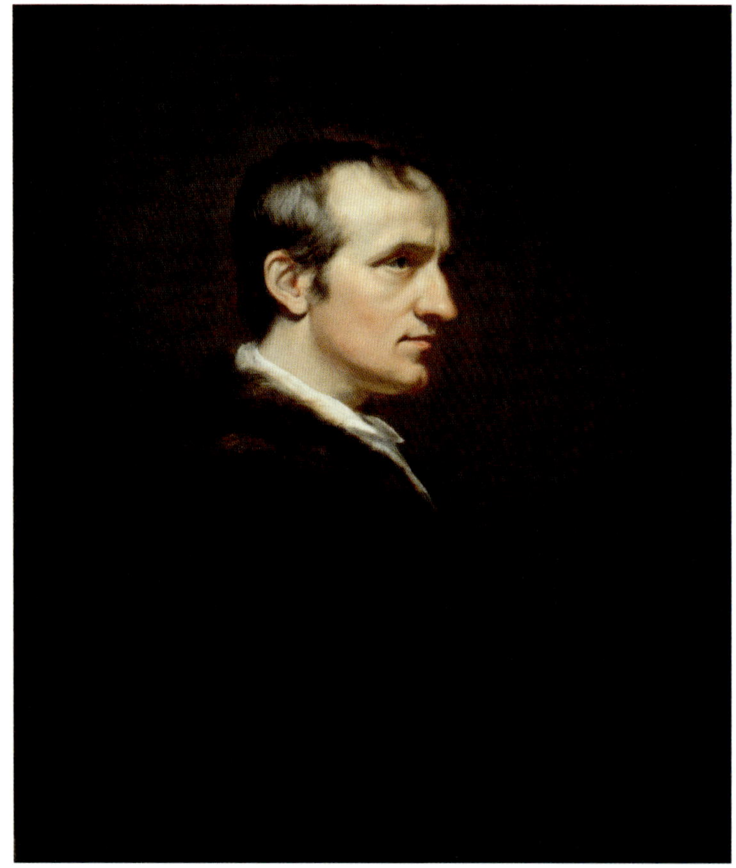

Their life together began at dawn on 28 July 1814, when Mary slipped out of her home to meet Percy in a waiting carriage. Abandoning his pregnant wife Harriet, he and Mary fled to the continent, thus setting in train the peripatetic lifestyle that the couple would lead over the next eight years. From the outset, their relationship involved creative collaboration. In Mary's first published work, *History of a Six Weeks' Tour of France, Switzerland, and Germany* (1817), she recorded their experiences of travelling through a Europe ravaged by the Napoleonic Wars. They returned in September to face the disapproval of both their families and Percy had to go into hiding to escape his creditors. The first surviving letter from Mary to Percy dates from this period of separation. She writes, 'I know how tenderly you love me and how you repine at this absence from me – when shall we be free from the fear of treachery?'[1]

From 1815, an inheritance provided Percy with an annuity but money troubles remained a continual pressure. An experiment in free love, where they lived communally with her step-sister Claire Clairmont and a friend, Thomas Jefferson Hogg, collapsed in recriminations. They moved out of London to Windsor, where Mary give birth to a son, William. They then spent the summer of 1816 with Lord Byron by Lake Geneva in Switzerland. Inspired by a ghost-story contest, Mary returned to England with the idea for her gothic science fiction masterpiece, *Frankenstein* (published anonymously in 1818).

The year ended in tragedy. First Mary's half-sister and Mary Wollstonecraft's first child, Fanny Imlay, killed herself with an opium overdose. Then Harriet Shelley, pregnant again and in despair at being abandoned by both her husband and parents, drowned herself in the Serpentine in Hyde Park. Percy carried his guilt and remorse over her death for the rest of his life. Percy and Mary married on 30 December, twenty days after the discovery of Harriet's body.

The birth of a daughter, Clara, in September 1817 did little to stem the couple's restlessness. Percy suffered from ill health throughout his life and a diagnosis of pulmonary disease motivated a move to the warmer climate of Italy in March 1818. Percy's poetry flourished in response to the landscape and culture, but their constant travelling came at a terrible cost to his family. Clara, aged one, died of dysentery in Venice in September and William, aged four, died from malaria in Rome in June 1819.

While in Rome, Percy sat for his only formal portrait (fig.2). Considering the painting 'so ill done', the artist Amelia Curran almost burned it but later gave it to Mary, who treasured it for the rest of her life. Their fourth child was born in November 1819 and named Percy Florence after the city of his birth. They made their final home together in San Terenzo, Liguria. Mary survived a near-fatal miscarriage on 16 June 1822 but further tragedy was to come. On 8 July, Percy drowned at sea after his boat sank during a storm. His body washed ashore ten days later and he was cremated on the beach near Viareggio on 16 August.

Mary returned to England bereft but determined to secure Percy's poetic legacy. She never remarried. Her portrait in middle age by Richard Rothwell suggests something both of her intelligence and sorrow (fig.1). The intense emotional and intellectual collaboration between Mary and Percy Shelley came at a great personal cost but together they produced some of the most enduring and powerful works in English literature.

Fig.3 *Mary Wollstonecraft*, c.1797
John Opie
Oil on canvas, 768 × 641mm
National Portrait Gallery, London

Fig.4 *William Godwin*, 1802
James Northcote
Oil on canvas, 749 × 622mm
National Portrait Gallery, London

ALISON SMITH

Elizabeth Barrett Browning & Robert Browning

The relationship between Elizabeth Barrett and Robert Browning is widely regarded as one of the great love stories in English literature. The meeting of minds and hearts exemplified by their marriage is sensitively captured by Harriet Hosmer in her cast of their clasped hands and in Michele Gordigiani's pair of portraits in which the couple are shown gently inclining towards one another from their own separate realms (figs 1–3). By the time they first met in 1845 Elizabeth was thirty-nine and a respected poet in her own right. The daughter of a wealthy and over-protective plantation owner (her mother died in 1828), she had led a reclusive existence, virtually imprisoned in the Barrett family home in Wimpole Street in London. Her hermit-like situation was compounded by the pulmonary disorder she had contracted in her teens which was to make her an invalid for life. Robert, junior to Elizabeth by six years, came from a less privileged background and had experienced more of a struggle in establishing himself as a writer, his dramatic monologues having come in for particularly harsh criticism. But Elizabeth was to signal her praise for Browning's work in her *Poems* (1844) and elsewhere she had described him as an 'indubitable genius' and a 'master in clenched passion'.[1] Having discovered an advocate in Elizabeth, Robert wrote to her in January 1845 confessing, 'I do, as I say, love these books with all my heart – and I love you too.'[2]

The declaration sparked a long and impassioned correspondence with nearly 600 letters exchanged over a twenty-month period during which the poets shared their artistic aspirations and ideals. Despite having reservations, Elizabeth eventually agreed to meet Robert in May 1845 although he was to record another ninety-one meetings before she finally agreed to marry him. Her initial resistance may have been due to alarm at the strength of Robert's passion as

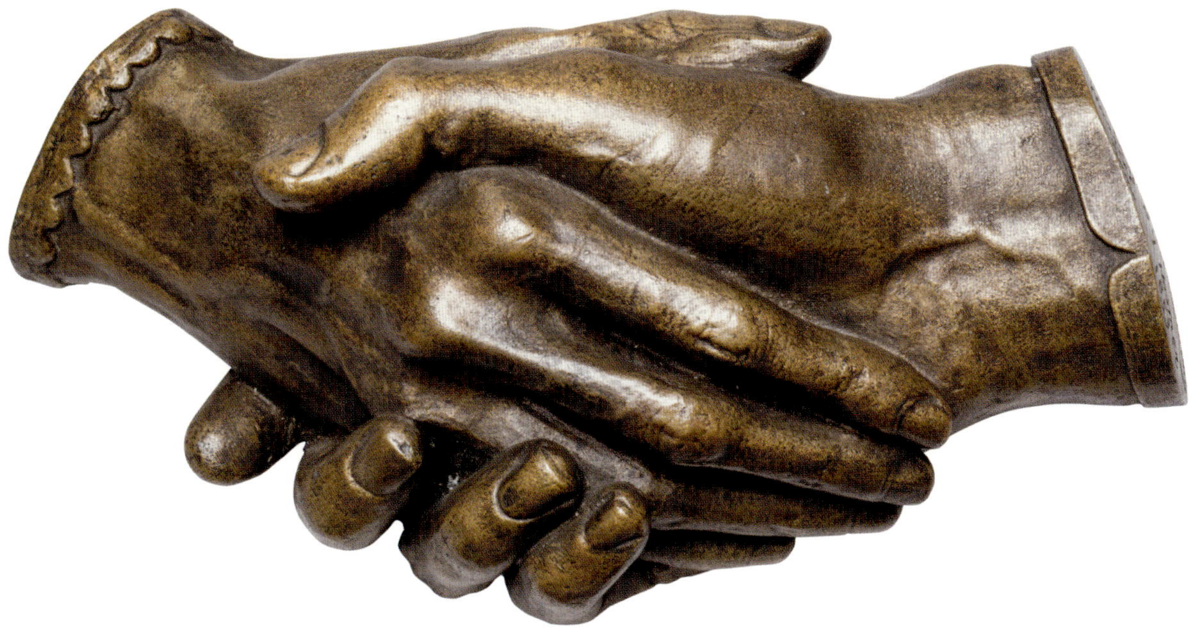

Fig.1 *Elizabeth Barrett Browning and Robert Browning*, 1853
Harriet Goodhue Hosmer
Bronze cast of clasped hands, 210mm long
National Portrait Gallery, London

well as fear at how her father might respond. On 12 September 1846, without her father knowing, she secretly married Robert at nearby Marylebone Church and then returned home for a week before eloping with him to Italy. She was never to see her father again. For a woman who had been largely confined to the family house to suddenly uproot herself in this way was audacious in the extreme. Her friend, the art historian Anna Jameson, described herself as 'out of breath with *wonder* at the marriage', while Elizabeth's father immediately disinherited her, leaving the couple dependent on Elizabeth's independent income for their existence.[3]

There followed a period of enormous creativity and happiness tinged with sadness as Elizabeth suffered three miscarriages before giving birth in 1849 to a healthy son, Robert Wiedeman, whom they called Pen. As writers, the couple encouraged and supported one another in their creative endeavours. Elizabeth's *Sonnets from the Portuguese*, a collection of forty-four poems titled after Robert's pen-name for her ('my little Portuguese'), had been composed during their courtship but she had kept them private, embarrassed by their intimacy. Upon Robert's urging they were published in 1850 and now stand as one of the best-known series of love poems in the English language. The most famous of them, Sonnet 43, opens with the famous lines 'How do I love thee, / let me count the ways'. It acknowledges the struggle she went through to be with Robert and the pure, free quality of her love for him once she had abandoned herself to it.

Robert's compilation *Men and Women*, saturated with allusions to their life together, was published in 1855, his first collection of shorter poems since their marriage. The title is taken from a line in Elizabeth's *Sonnets* and the epilogue

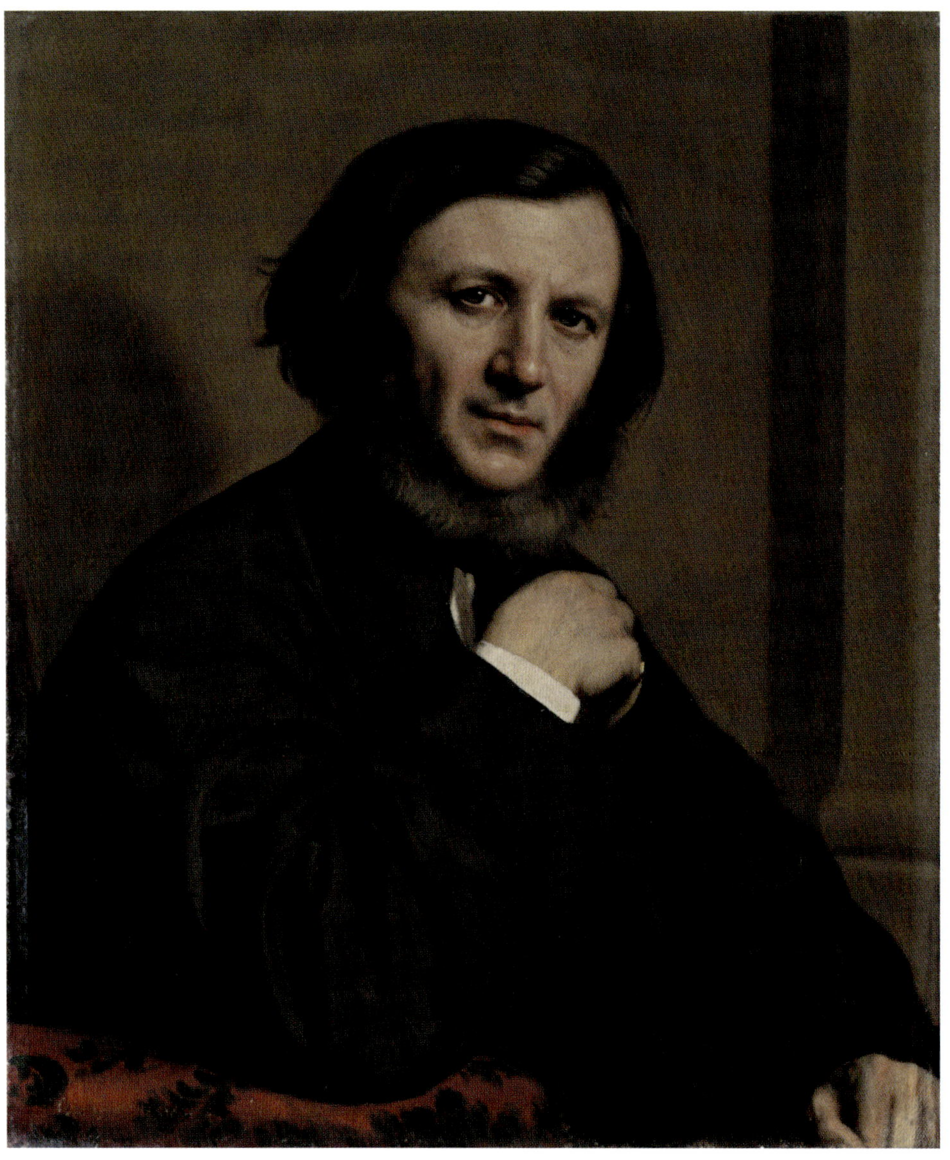

Fig.2 ***Robert Browning***, 1858
Michele Gordigiani
Oil on canvas, 724 × 587mm
National Portrait Gallery, London

('One Word More') acts as a kind of dedication to his wife. The last line of the opening stanza proclaims 'Where my heart lies, let my brain lie also!' testimony to their partnership in love and art. Despite differences of opinion on matters ranging from spiritualism to politics and how to raise their son (Robert favoured sensible trousers while Elizabeth preferred pantaloons), the couple enjoyed an equal relationship at a time when gender inequality was much debated, forming the subtext, for example, of Elizabeth's own controversial 1857 novel-poem *Aurora Leigh*.

The image of two distinct yet closely entwined personalities comes across vividly in Hosmer's cast

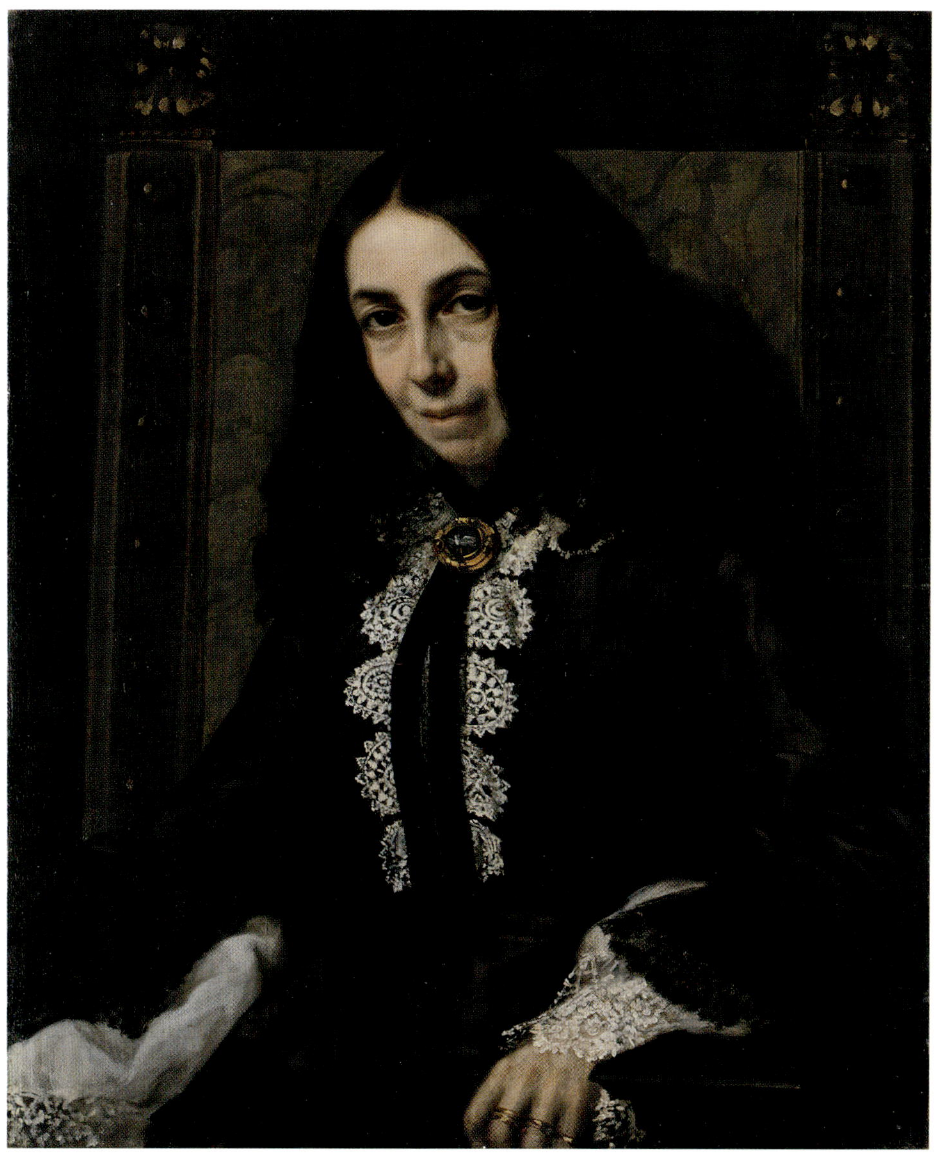

Fig.3 ***Elizabeth Barrett Browning***, 1858
Michele Gordigiani
Oil on canvas, 737 × 584mm
National Portrait Gallery, London

of their interlinked hands (fig.1) and in the twin portraits commissioned by the couple's friend Sophia May Eckley (figs 2 and 3). These paintings had been conceived as likenesses and something of the writers' keen cerebral nature is relayed to the viewer: Robert's warmth and energy contrasting with Elizabeth's frailty and intensity of vision.

Despite the health benefits of living in Italy, Elizabeth remained susceptible to bouts of sickness. In June 1861 she became ill again and never recovered, dying in Robert's arms in Florence. Writing to her brother George, Robert described how she passed away 'smilingly, happily, and with a face like a girl's ... her last word was ..."Beautiful"'.[4]

HELENA CUSS

TED HUGHES & SYLVIA PLATH

The American Sylvia Plath arrived in Cambridge as a Fulbright Scholar in 1955. Her meeting on 26 February 1956 with fellow English Literature student Ted Hughes at the launch party for a student magazine was recounted memorably in her journal: 'he kissed me bang smash on the mouth and ripped my hairband off … and my favourite silver earring: hah, I shall keep [it], he barked. And when he kissed my neck I bit him long and hard on the cheek, and when we came out of the room, blood was running down his face.'[1]

Just four months later they married on James Joyce's 'Bloomsday' – 16 June – in a self-conscious nod to their literary ambitions as a couple. Plath's mother was the only witness. Hughes captured his memories of the day years later in a poem:

In your pink wool knitted dress
Before anything had smudged anything
You stood at the altar. Bloomsday. [...]
You were transfigured.
So slender and new and naked,
A nodding spray of wet lilac.[2]

The fragile happiness and youthful love and hope that Hughes describes is also evident in a photo taken in the same year (fig.1). At this point, Hughes was not aware of Plath's ongoing struggle with her mental health, which had been affected by the sudden death of her father when she was just eight. In 1953 she had suffered a nervous breakdown and had been treated with electro-convulsive therapy after trying to commit suicide by sleeping pills.

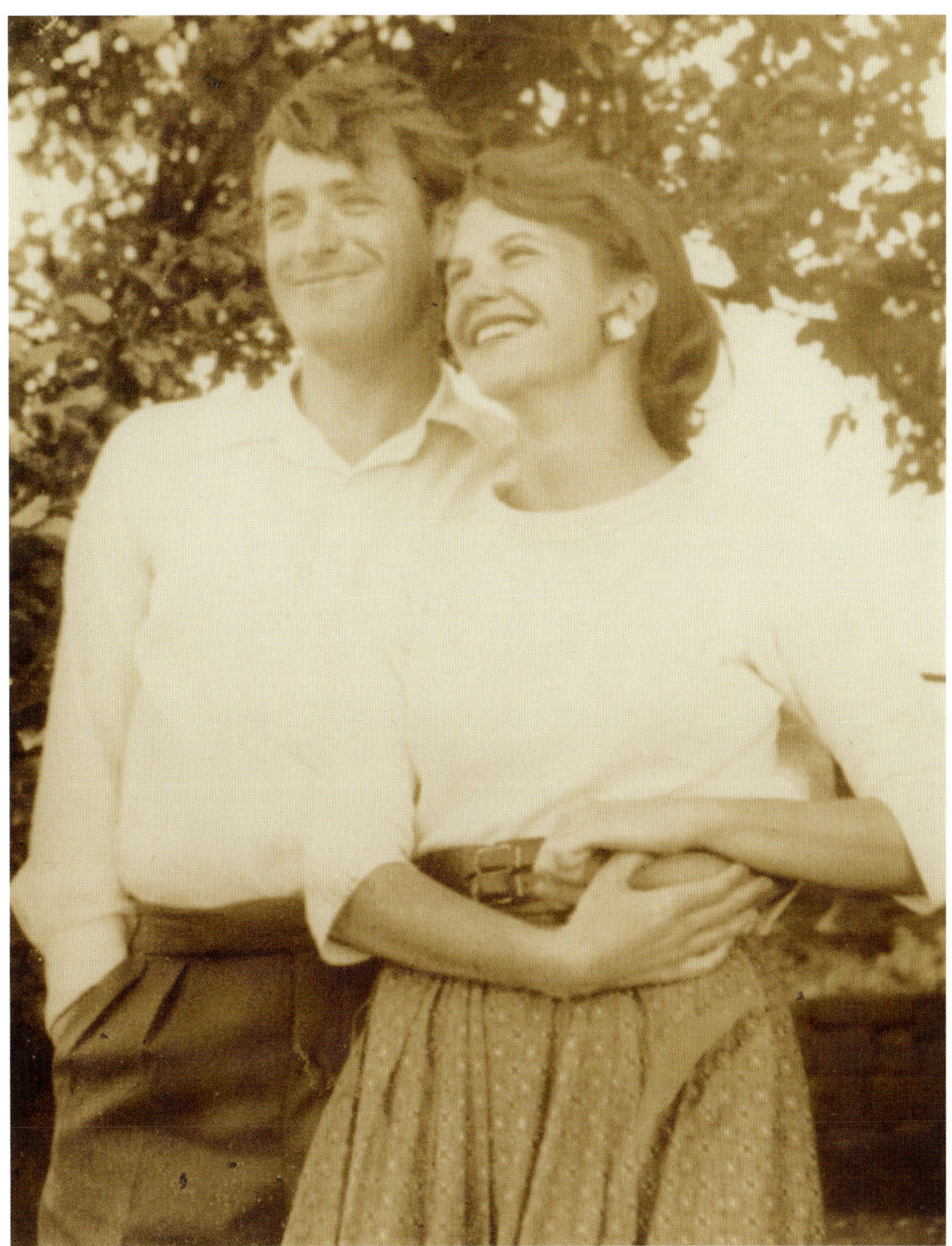

Fig.1 *Ted Hughes and Sylvia Plath ('The Beacon, Yorkshire 1956')*, 1956
Harry Ogden
Gelatin silver print, 250 × 205mm
National Portrait Gallery, London

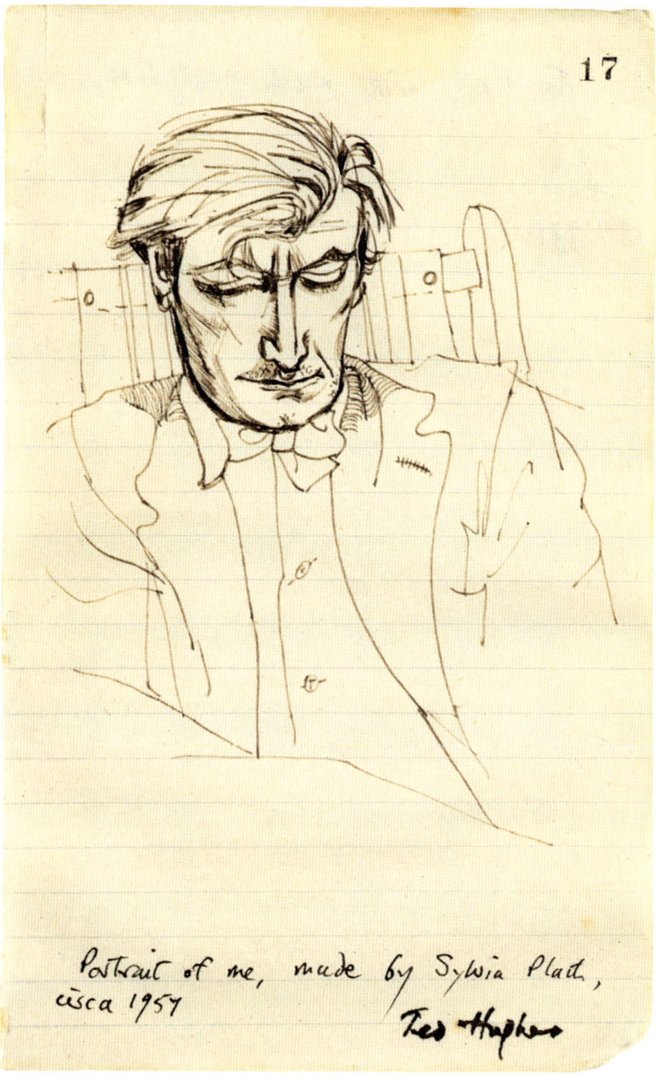

Fig.2 *Ted Hughes*, *c.*1957
Sylvia Plath
Pen and ink, 213 × 130mm
National Portrait Gallery, London

The young couple settled in Cambridge where Hughes had a teaching post. They quickly established a symbiotic working relationship, finding in each other mutual support and inspiration. A poem by Hughes recalling Plath sketching on their honeymoon evokes something of this creative partnership, as he describes 'the contemplative calm / I drank from your concentrated quiet' – which is also illustrated by her only known drawing of him which he inscribed 'Portrait of me, made by Sylvia Plath, circa 1957' (fig.2).[3] The lined paper on which it was drawn was likely a page from her journal. Tellingly, it was one of the few personal papers documenting their relationship that Hughes did not destroy in the years after her death.

In June 1957 they moved to Massachusetts, where Plath took up a teaching position. Three months later, Hughes published his first poetry collection, *The Hawk in the Rain*, to ecstatic reviews, and two of Plath's poems appeared in the *New Yorker* magazine. Despite these achievements, over the following year she began to suffer from writer's block and depression. Plath's memory of her father became intertwined with a fear that Hughes would abandon her so, without mentioning it, she resumed psychiatric treatment. By spring 1959, she was pregnant and feeling significantly better. Hughes had earned enough money that they could both quit teaching to drive across the USA to California, where they stayed in an artists' colony at Saratoga Springs. It was a time of creative rebirth for both, in which Plath wrote the poems that would make up her first poetry collection, *The Colossus*, while Hughes completed his second, *Lupercal*.

In December 1959, they moved back to London, where their daughter Freida was born. In an unusually egalitarian spirit for the period, they split the child-rearing responsibilities in half, with Plath writing in the morning and Hughes in the afternoon. Two years later, while she was pregnant with their second child, the family moved to Devon and it was here that Plath's mental health worsened and the relationship began to break down. Plath found the English countryside depressing and isolating and during 1962 darkness crept into her writing, as she penned the poems that would

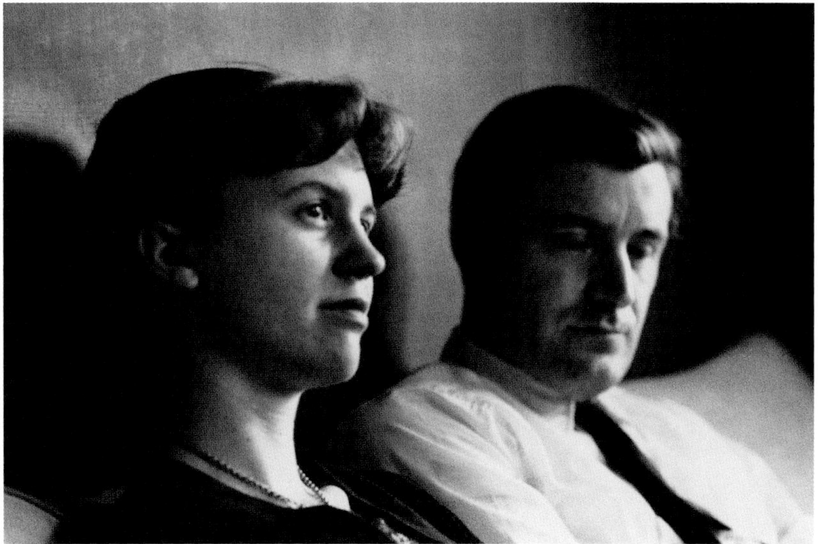

Fig.3 *Sylvia Plath and Ted Hughes*, 1959
Rollie McKenna
Gelatin silver print
National Portrait Gallery, London

make up *Ariel* as well as the semi-autobiographical novel *The Bell Jar.* Although Plath's poetry does more than simply draw on personal experience there is no doubt that her most famous poem, 'Daddy', represents an attempt to exorcise the memory of her father's death. She imagines him as a Nazi and ends, 'If I've killed one man, I've killed two – / The vampire who said he was you / [...] / Daddy, daddy, you bastard, I'm through.'[4]

The presence of 'Daddy' as a ghostly third-player in their marriage appears throughout much of *Birthday Letters*, and Hughes attributed Plath's inability to move past her father's death as a key component of their separation. Both believed that through her writing she could heal the pain of her father's death, but in hindsight Hughes believed it may have actually contributed to her demise. In July 1962 Plath discovered that Hughes was having an affair and by the autumn had left him and taken the children back to London. Although exhausted and depressed she continued to work prolifically and *The Bell Jar* was published to indifferent reviews in January 1963. Many of her poems from this time are sparely written and appear to prefigure her suicide – 'the woman is perfected. / Her dead / Body wears the smile of accomplishment' – but an ecstatic joy also permeates some of the poems in *Ariel*.[5] Nonetheless, on 11 February Plath left milk and biscuits next to the beds of her sleeping children, sealed up their door, and gassed herself in the kitchen.

As Plath died intestate, Hughes was left with the task of converting her drafts and notebooks into publishable collections. He later revealed that he had destroyed her last journal so that their children would never read of her fury towards him in her final months. Upon publishing *Ariel* in 1965 he also eliminated several poems dealing with their relationship. Plath's posthumous critical reception – although partially driven by interest in the events of her death – would not have been possible without Hughes' dedication. In 1971, among other edited works by her, his edition of her *Collected Poems* won the 1981 Pulitzer Prize, establishing Plath as one of the greatest poets of the century. For both Plath and Hughes, their relationship enabled their greatest works and readers will forever pore over the pages of *Ariel* and *Birthday Letters* seeking the truth of one of English literature's most contested love stories.

GEORGIA ATIENZA

Alice B. Toklas & Gertrude Stein

Alice B. Toklas and Gertrude Stein first met in September 1907, in Paris. In her memoir, Toklas evokes their first encounter at the home of Michael and Sarah Stein, Gertrude's brother and sister-in-law:

> She was a golden brown presence, burned by the Tuscan sun and with a golden glint in her warm brown hair. She was dressed in a warm brown corduroy suit. She wore a large round coral brooch and when she talked, very little, or laughed, a good deal, I thought her voice came from this brooch. It was unlike anyone else's voice – deep, full, velvety, like a great contralto's, like two voices. She was large and heavy with delicate and small hands and a beautifully modelled and unique head.[1]

This first meeting was followed by a walk the next day in the Jardins du Luxembourg, and cakes at a patisserie off Boulevard Saint-Michel. From then on, until Stein's death thirty-nine years later, they were never apart.

Born in Pennsylvania, Stein studied psychology and medicine before moving to Paris in 1903 and embarking on her literary career. She lived with her brother Leo at 27, rue de Fleurus on the Left Bank of the city. They collected art and their Saturday evening salon was celebrated as an important artistic and literary hub. Their home became a crossroads for introducing visitors to new and innovative art, particularly the work of Paul Cézanne, Henri Matisse and Pablo Picasso.

Fig.1 *Alice B. Toklas and Gertrude Stein*, 1937
Cecil Beaton
Gelatin silver print, 214 × 170mm
National Portrait Gallery, London

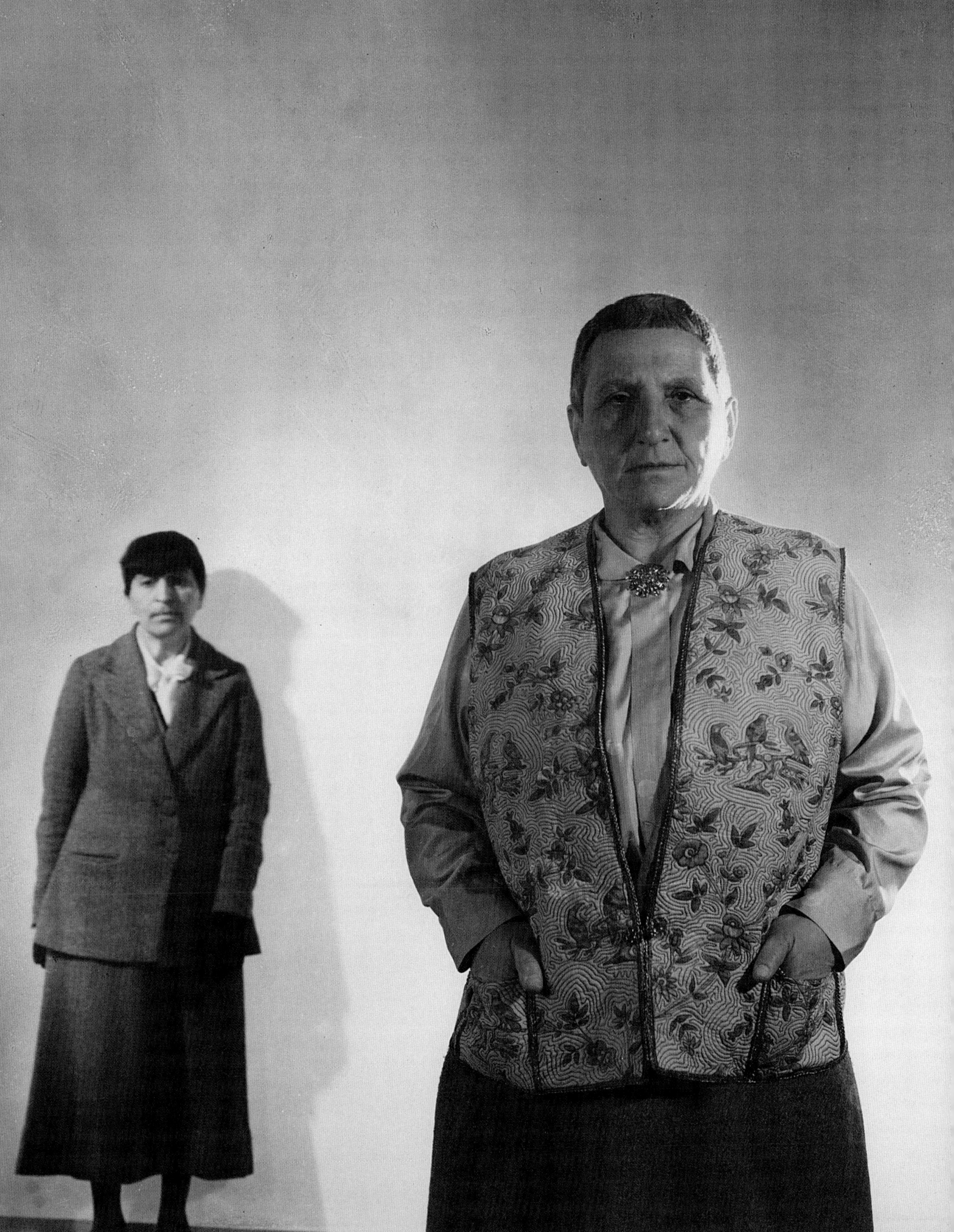

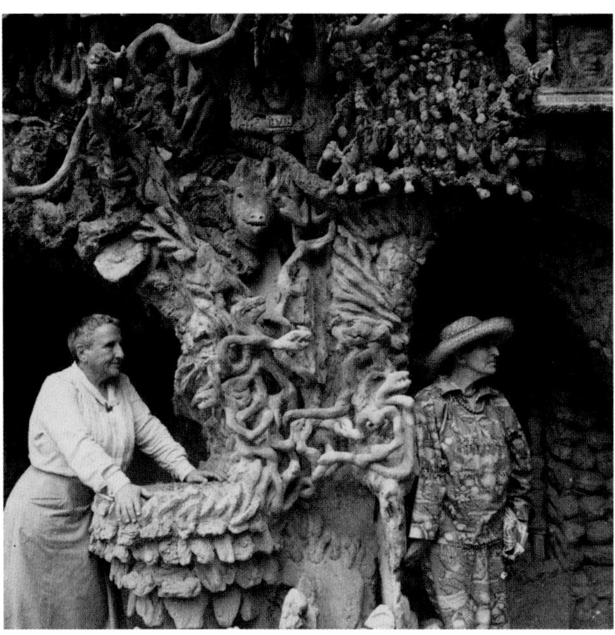

Fig.2 *Gertrude Stein and Alice B. Toklas*, 1939
Cecil Beaton
Gelatin silver print, 196 × 193mm
National Portrait Gallery, London

Originally from San Francisco, Toklas had gravitated to Paris in 1907 attracted by the artistic bustle of the city's Salons.

In 1910 Toklas moved in with Stein at 27, rue de Fleurus, Stein continuing as a tastemaker and collector of modern art, now with her life partner Toklas. Their relationship fulfilled the expectations of conventional romantic love and they regarded themselves as married, living together in domestic harmony. Stein was the writer and conversationalist while Toklas was Stein's typist, editor and archivist, and managed the household. Toklas also shaped and promoted their public image. A prolific writer and speaker, Stein achieved success with *The Autobiography of Alice B. Toklas* (1933), which she wrote in the voice of Toklas. In this work, Stein told the story of their long partnership, identifying Toklas as her close companion and writing from her point of view – the book is evidence of their intense intimacy and fascination for each other. Stein questions the idea of autobiography as a first-person account, an illusion that offered creative licence and hence gave Toklas an important role in Stein's success. The *Autobiography* was also noted for its pioneering account of bohemian Paris. Throughout Stein's career, her writing style challenged literary genres, introducing a cubist idiom to literary forms; she would later be considered the 'mother of modernism'.

Photographs of Stein and Toklas together give us a unique insight into their roles in the relationship and their dedication to each other. Cecil Beaton's portraits capture their intimacy and affection. Beaton worked in London and New York as a prominent fashion and society photographer. He photographed Stein and Toklas as a couple on four separate occasions. The first sitting took place in 1937, when the pair were in London for the opening of a ballet based on one of Stein's plays. Beaton posed the two women standing against a blank white studio background focusing

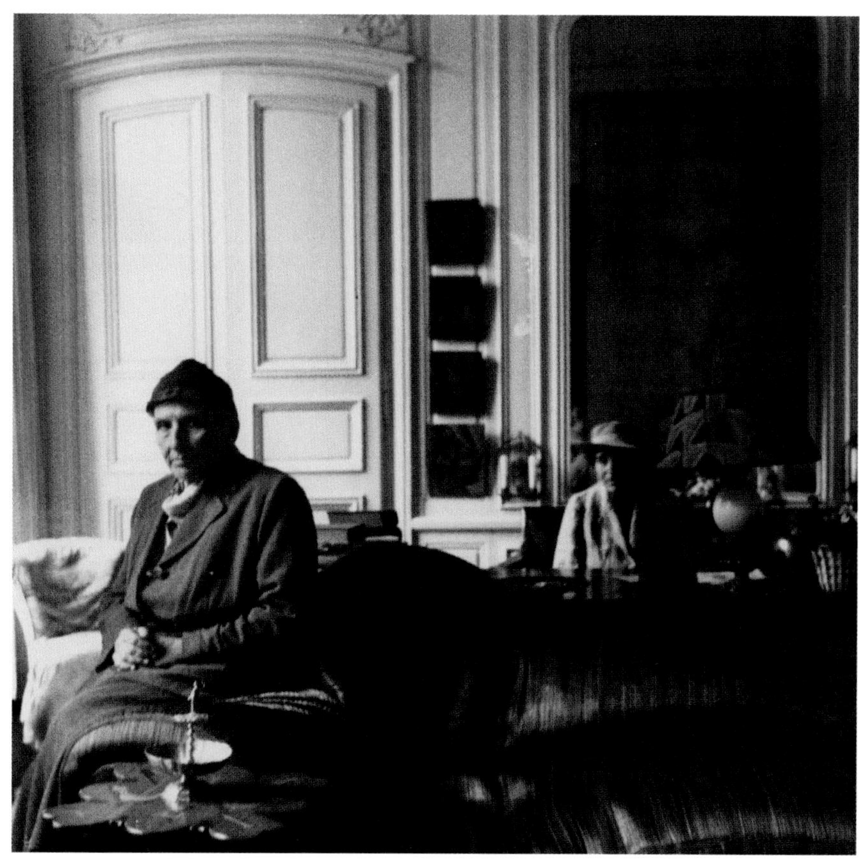

Fig.3 *Gertrude Stein and Alice B. Toklas*, 1945
Cecil Beaton
Gelatin silver print, 196 × 193mm
National Portrait Gallery, London

on the ways Stein and Toklas complemented each other. Stein's outline appears round and tall and Toklas' slight and uneven. In the version here (fig.1) Stein, wearing one of her distinctive waistcoats, possibly made by Toklas, stands confidently in the foreground. Beaton was also the first to portray them in 1938 in the boudoir of their new apartment at 5, rue Christine, Paris. The next sitting with Beaton was in 1939 at Bilignin in the French country house Stein and Toklas rented from the late 1920s. Several portraits were made in the garden and surrounding countryside in which they appear playful and relaxed (fig.2). Beaton's final photographic session with Stein and Toklas took place in 1945 after the Liberation of Paris. These portraits (fig.3) are more sombre than the previous sittings with both women appearing aged. Beaton is still able to depict their union and closeness but Stein looks frail and weak, her face looking drawn as her stomach cancer advanced. She died without regaining consciousness after an operation on 24 July 1946. Toklas lived for twenty-five years after Stein's death, often speaking to friends of her loneliness. During this period of widowhood she published articles, two cookbooks and wrote her memoir. She died on 7 March 1967 at the age of eighty-nine. A poignant indication of her life-long love, she arranged her burial alongside Stein in the Père Lachaise cemetery in Paris, her name being added to the back of Stein's tombstone.

A SHARED STUDIO

LOUISE STEWART

A SHARED STUDIO

Passionate, competitive and sometimes socially transgressive, intimate relationships within the artist's studio have a long history. Focusing on partners in love and art sheds new light on the role of collaboration within artistic production and can shine a light on the role of women in this process. Some relationships have fuelled creativity and spurred artists to their best work, while others have involved one partner subordinating their own talent to support the other and help their career to flourish.

In an unexpectedly early gender-role reversal, the artist Charles Beale supported his successful portraitist wife Mary in the seventeenth century, acting as her studio manager (see pp.88–93). A century later, the marriage of Richard Cosway, the celebrated Regency miniaturist (fig.1), and the history painter and portraitist Maria Cosway (fig.2) enhanced the celebrity and success of them both. Richard was made official miniature painter to the Prince Regent in 1785 and Maria's work was admired by Jacques-Louis David and compared to that of Sir Joshua Reynolds and Angelica Kauffman. Richard portrayed his wife numerous times and after his death Maria enhanced her husband's reputation by producing etchings of his drawings and mounting an exhibition of his work. However creative their marriage appears, it was not an equal union in modern terms but one reflective of contemporary ideas about the different roles that were appropriate for men and women. Despite her successful career before they married, Richard Cosway refused to allow his wife to sell her paintings and Maria wrote that 'Had Mr C. permitted me to paint professionally, I should have made a better painter.'[1] Nevertheless, on his death she set up a tomb monument to her husband's genius, with the epitaph:

> ART WEEPS. TASTE MOURNS, AND GENIUS DROPS HER TEAR O'ER HIM SO LONG THEY LOV'D, WHO SLUMBERS HERE. WHILE COLOURS LAST, AND TIME ALLOWS TO GIVE THE ALL-RESEMBLING GRACE, HIS NAME SHALL LIVE[2]

A creative relationship is visibly played out in a pair of portraits of artist husband and wife, Marian and John Collier. John's portrait of Marian seems,

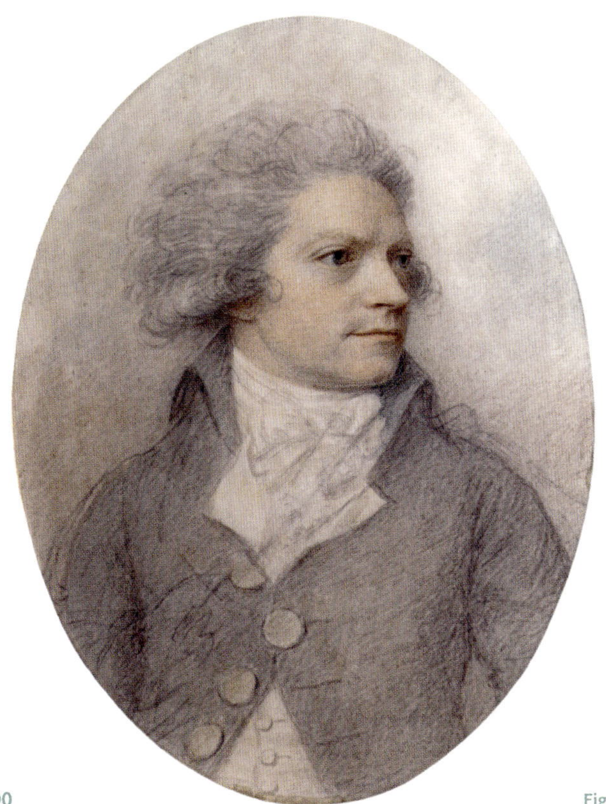

Fig.1 *Self-Portrait*, *c.*1790
Richard Cosway
Pencil and wash, 105 × 79mm
National Portrait Gallery, London

Fig.2 *Maria Cosway*, 1781–5
Richard Cosway
Pencil and watercolour, 286 × 242mm
National Portrait Gallery, London

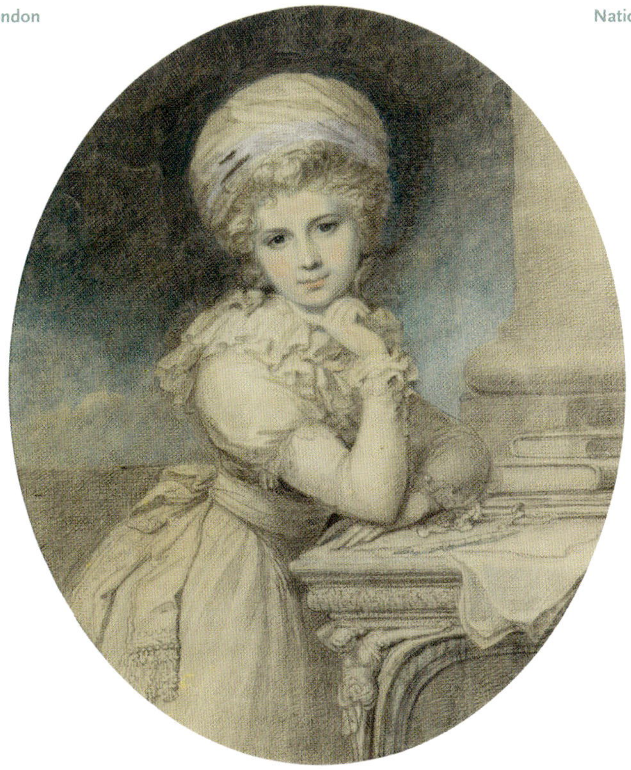

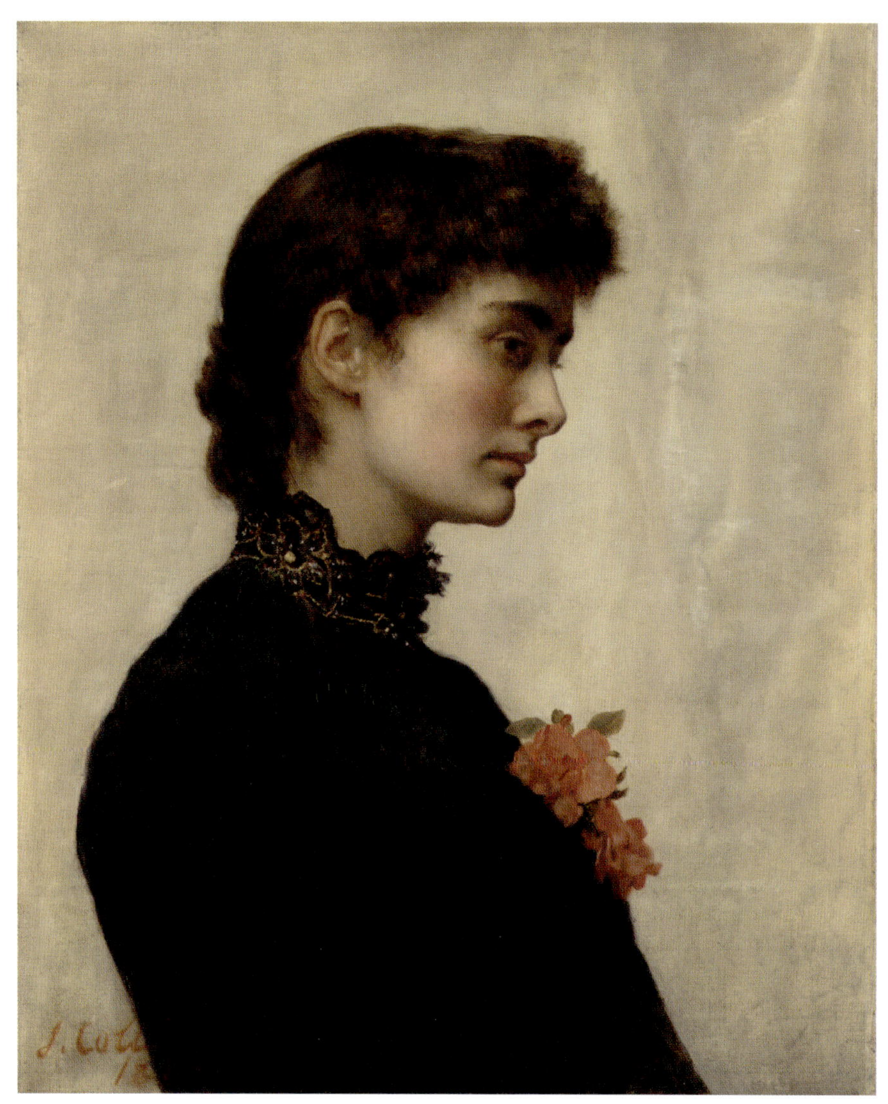

ABOVE
Fig.3 *Marian Collier*, 1882–3
John Collier
Oil on canvas, 619 × 492mm
National Portrait Gallery, London

OPPOSITE
Fig.4 *John Collier*, *c.*1882–3
Marian Collier
Oil on canvas, 1271 × 1080mm
National Portrait Gallery, London

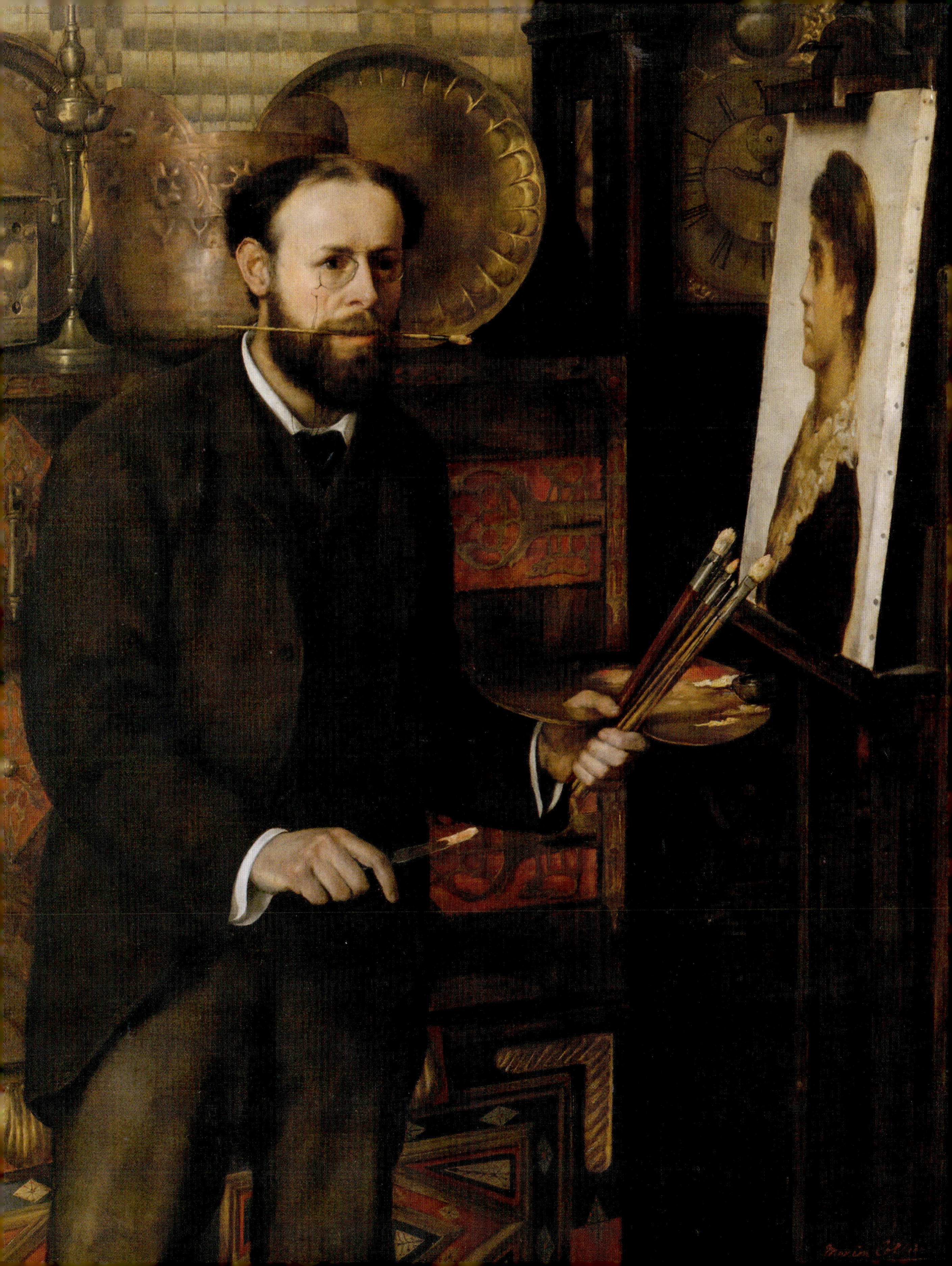

at first glance, to conform to the convention of artists painting their wives as a way of advertising their own talents as fashionable portraitists (fig.3). However, seen alongside her portrait of John (fig.4), in which he appears at work on a portrait of his wife, it is likely that the pair painted each other in tandem, as part of a creative dialogue. This sense of inspiration through linked working practices is also seen in work by great modernist couples Lee Miller and Man Ray, and Barbara Hepworth and Ben Nicholson, who worked together and spurred each other to experiment and innovate (see pp.94–101 and pp.102–5, respectively).

The performance artists and image makers Gilbert and George have taken the tradition of artistic partnership between lovers to the next level, creating all their art works collaboratively and treating their shared life as an artwork in itself. The pair met at St Martin's School of Art in 1967 and George describes their relationship as 'the greatest strength in the world'.[3] Their partnership provides a framework for exploring through their work the fundamentals of human experience: sexuality, faith, identity and death. *In the Piss* (fig.5) is a case in point; the artists are depicted together against a background of enlarged microscopic images of urine. The emphasis on bodily secretions refers to human vulnerability and invokes the link between portraiture, death and memory. The pose, with George's arm looped over Gilbert's shoulder, points to their intimacy, ease and total collaboration, sharing an artistic practice of which their daily life is part. The stories in this section further demonstrate the ways in which relationships between practising artists have allowed them to push the boundaries of art and love as they collaborate, compete, challenge and encourage one another.

Fig.5 *Gilbert & George ('IN THE PISS')*, 1997
Gilbert & George
Photo-piece on nine panels, 2260 × 1900mm
National Portrait Gallery, London

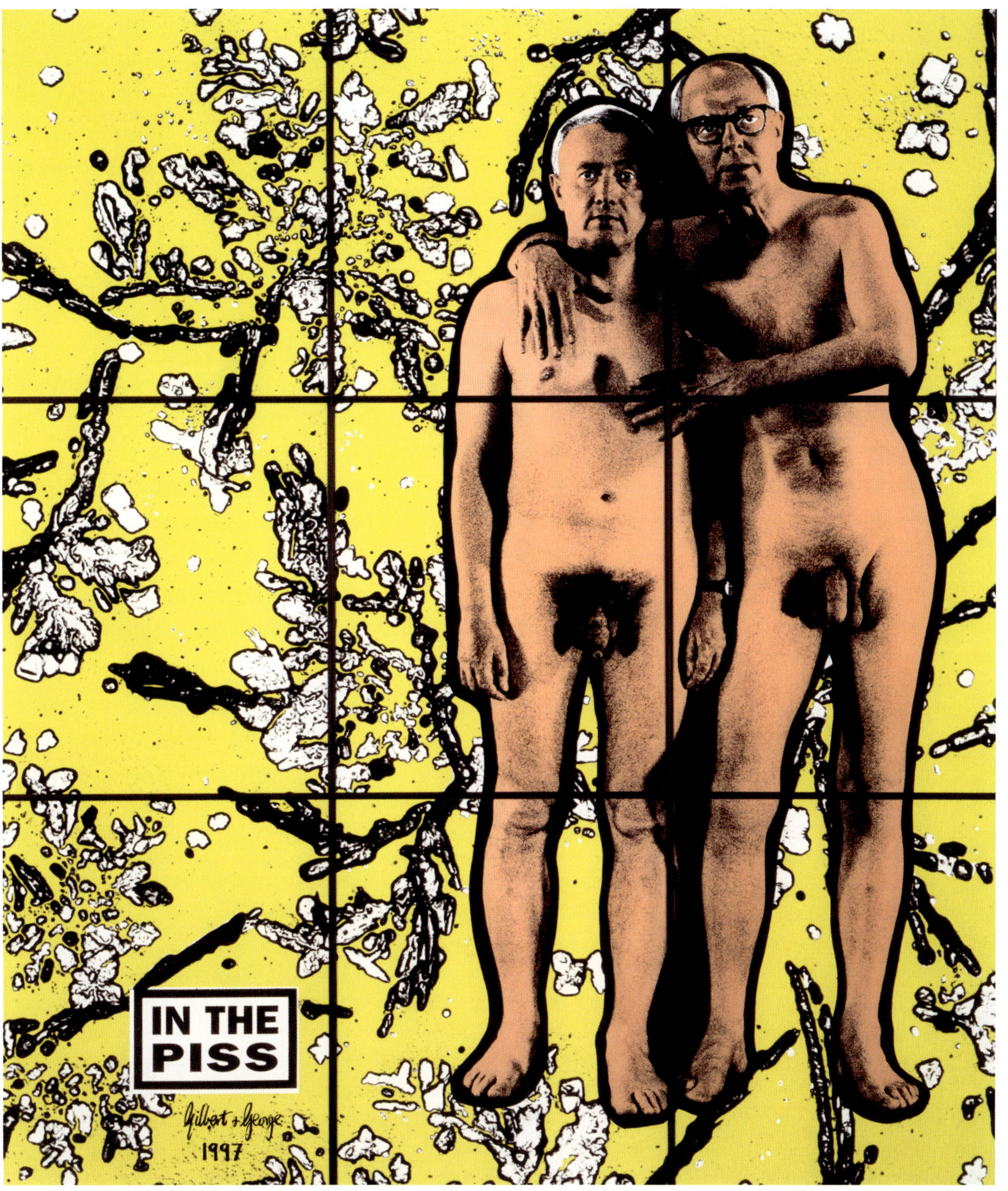
IN THE
PISS
Gilbert + George
1997

RAB MACGIBBON

Mary Beale & Charles Beale

The Restoration period, following the return of the English monarchy in 1660, is regarded as a time of unprecedented licentiousness for a population starved of pleasure during a decade of puritanical oppression. Evidence abounds of moral transgression within the court of Charles II. The king himself fathered at least fourteen illegitimate children with numerous mistresses. An alternative account of love during this period is exemplified by the relationship between the artist Mary Beale and her husband Charles, who enjoyed a remarkably equal and supportive marriage. Mary went so far as to espouse the then radical notion of equality between the sexes. In her *Discourse on Friendship* (1667), she declared that God created Eve, as 'a wife and friend but not a slave'.[1]

Mary was born in 1633 to the Revd John and Dorothy Cradock at her father's rectory in Barrow, Suffolk. For a woman to become an artist in this period was unusual, but not unique. It is likely that she received her first training from her father, an amateur artist, and she may also have received instruction from Robert Walker, favoured portraitist of the parliamentary establishment, who knew her father. Her future husband, Charles Beale was born in 1631 in Walton Manor, Buckinghamshire. The Beales were a prominent Puritan family with close links to the government, Charles' father held the post of Deputy Clerk of the Patents Office, and it is likely that Mary and Charles met through Puritan social circles.

The earliest surviving evidence of their relationship is a love letter written by Charles in 1651. As the final battles of the civil wars shook Wigan and Worcester, his mind could not have been further from the struggle of Parliamentarians and Royalists. He was clearly infatuated with Mary, calling her the 'Quintessence of all Goodnesse' and describing

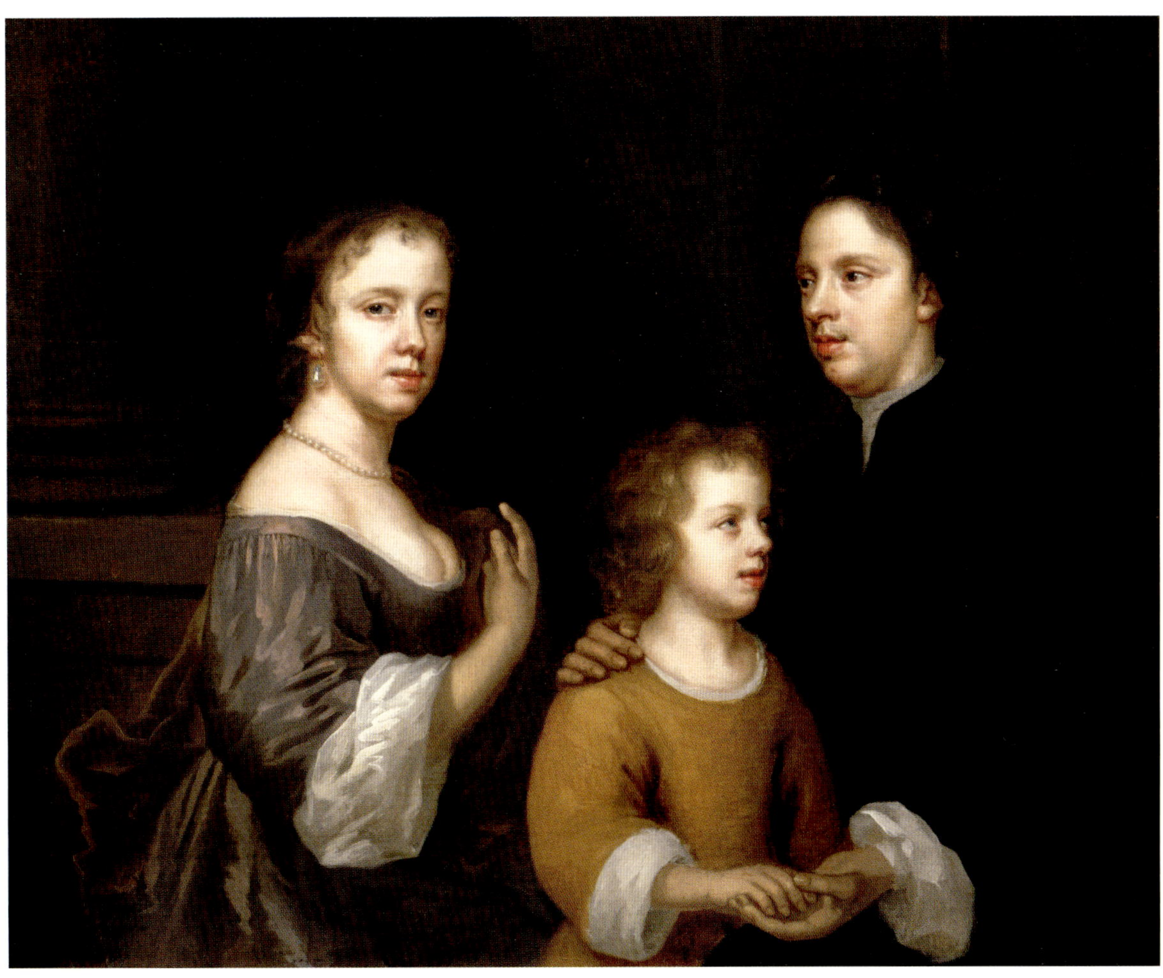

Fig.1 *Self-Portrait with husband, Charles and Son, Bartholomew, c.*1660
Mary Beale
Oil on canvas, 602 × 740mm
The Geffrye Museum of the Home, London

her beauty as Nature's 'best arts Master peece / More worth then Jasons Golden ffleece.'[2] They were married at her father's church the following spring.

By 1656, they had moved to Covent Garden, London, where their son Bartholomew was born. Here they were neighbours with the most fashionable painter of the day, Sir Peter Lely, whose friendship and support was highly valued by the Beales. Mary's arrival as an artist of note was marked by her inclusion in Sir William Sanderson's history of painting up to his own time, *Graphice. The Use of the Pen and Pensil. or, The most Excellent Art of Painting* (1658). Her earliest surviving painting is a self-portrait with her husband and son in a family portrait of exceptional tenderness for this date (fig.1). Mary looks out at the viewer as Charles gazes affectionately at her while embracing their son. It was probably painted while Mary was pregnant with their son Charles, born in 1660.

Charles took over his father's post at the Patents Office and was the main breadwinner of the family until they were driven out of London by the plague and lived for five years in Allbrook, Hampshire. It was here that Mary wrote the *Discourse on Friendship*, an extraordinary insight into her personality and beliefs. Her progressive views were put into practice on the family's return to London in 1670, when they set up studio in the exclusive new development of Pall Mall, with Mary as the principal earner. Charles became her studio manager and assistant and in time both sons joined the enterprise, painting draperies and the architectural surrounds that feature in many of her portraits. The entire family appear in Mary's pendant portraits of husband and wife (figs 3 and 4). Charles is shown as a man of learning, seated before an Italianate landscape, appropriate for a man fluent in Italian and the author of a manuscript treatise on art, *Experimental Secrets found out in the way of Painting* (1647–63). Facing him and unified by the colour scheme of their satin robes, Mary's portrait celebrates her identity as a fashionable woman, an artist and a mother. Her artist's palette hangs in the background and her hand rests on an unfinished painting of her sons. A closely related portrait of her husband also dates from this period (fig.2).

An unusually full picture of their professional and personal lives can be gleaned from their correspondence with friends and the notebooks that Charles studiously kept to record sittings, payments and the preparation of art materials. They reveal the extent to which business and love went hand in hand, with Charles describing Mary as his 'Dearest & Most Indefatigable Heart'.[3] They also reveal a piety conspicuously at odds with the relaxed morals at court. Ten per cent of their earning went into a 'pious and charitable account' for the poor and although they had a taste for the finer things and a wide social circle, they were not decadent. Their friend Samuel Woodforde wrote of a convivial evening with them: 'We were very cheerful, and I hope, without sin.'[4]

By the time of Mary's death in 1699, her son Charles had an independent career as an artist and Bartholomew, having graduated from Cambridge in 1682, had moved to the Midlands to work as a physician. Her husband and business partner retired from London to live with Bartholomew in Coventry, where he died in 1705.

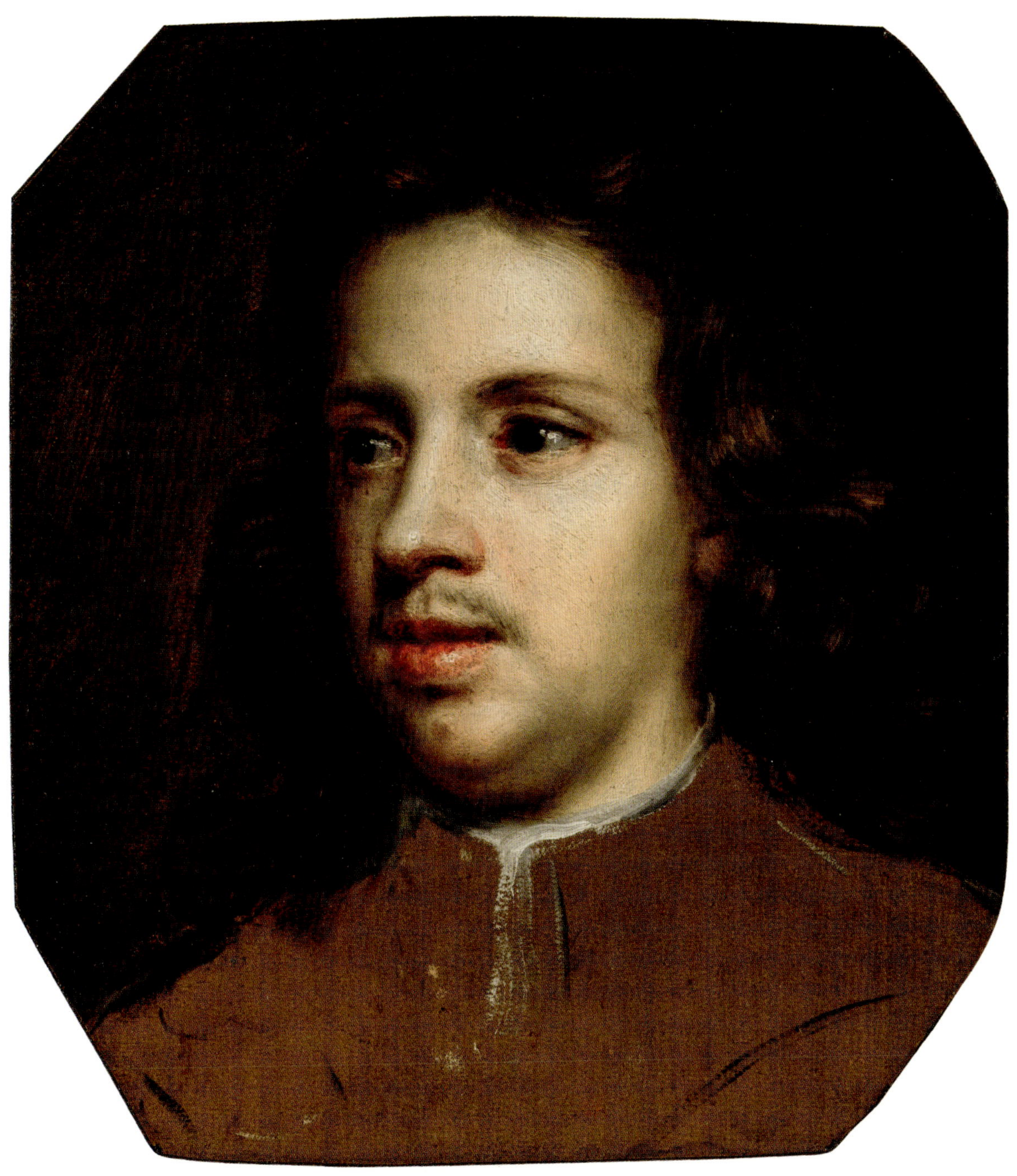

Fig.2 *Charles Beale the Elder*, *c.*1660
Mary Beale
Oil on canvas, 241 × 210mm
National Portrait Gallery, London

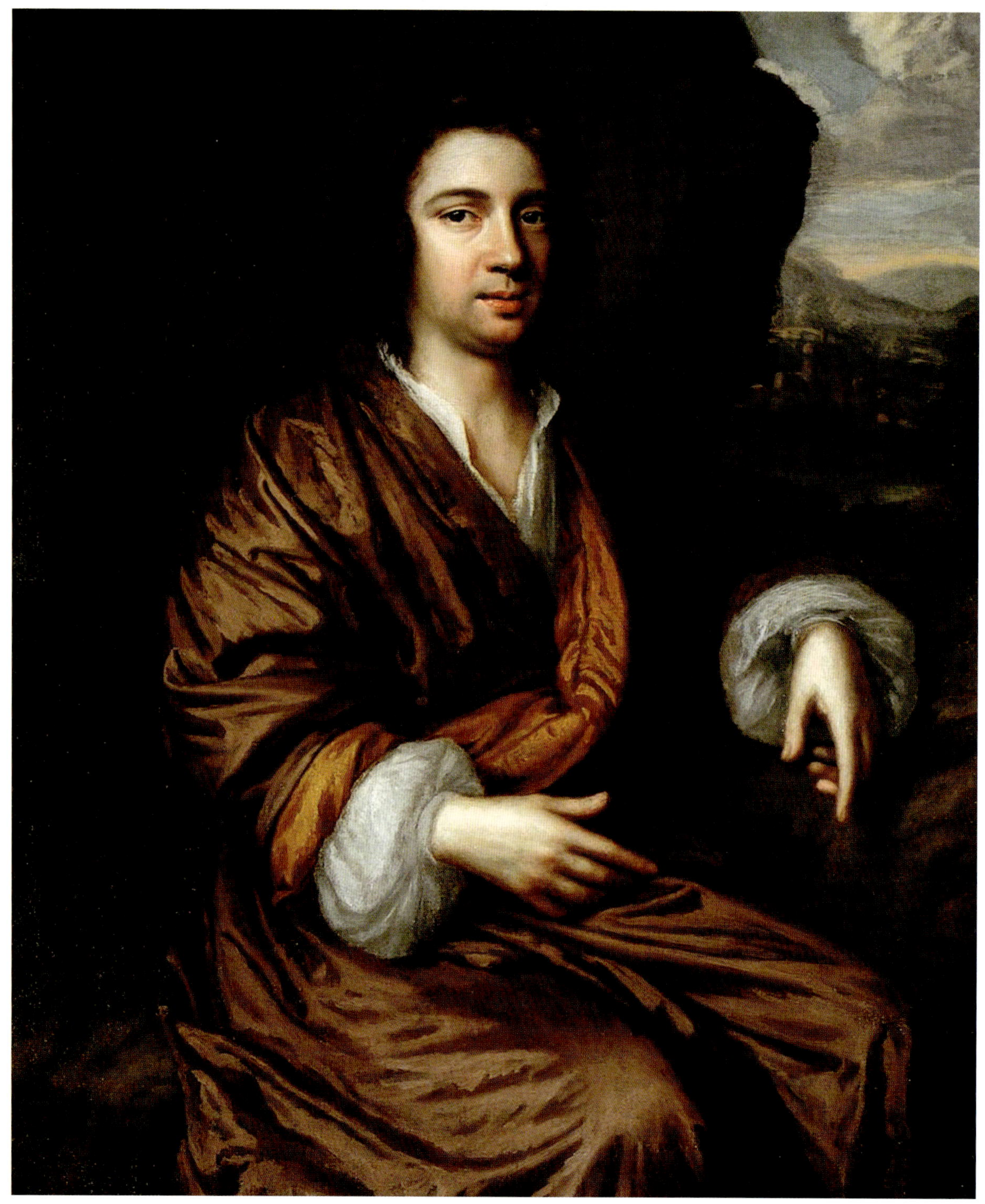

Fig.3 *Charles Beale*, *c.*1666
Mary Beale
Oil on canvas, 1092 × 876mm
St Edmundsbury Museum, West Suffolk Heritage Service

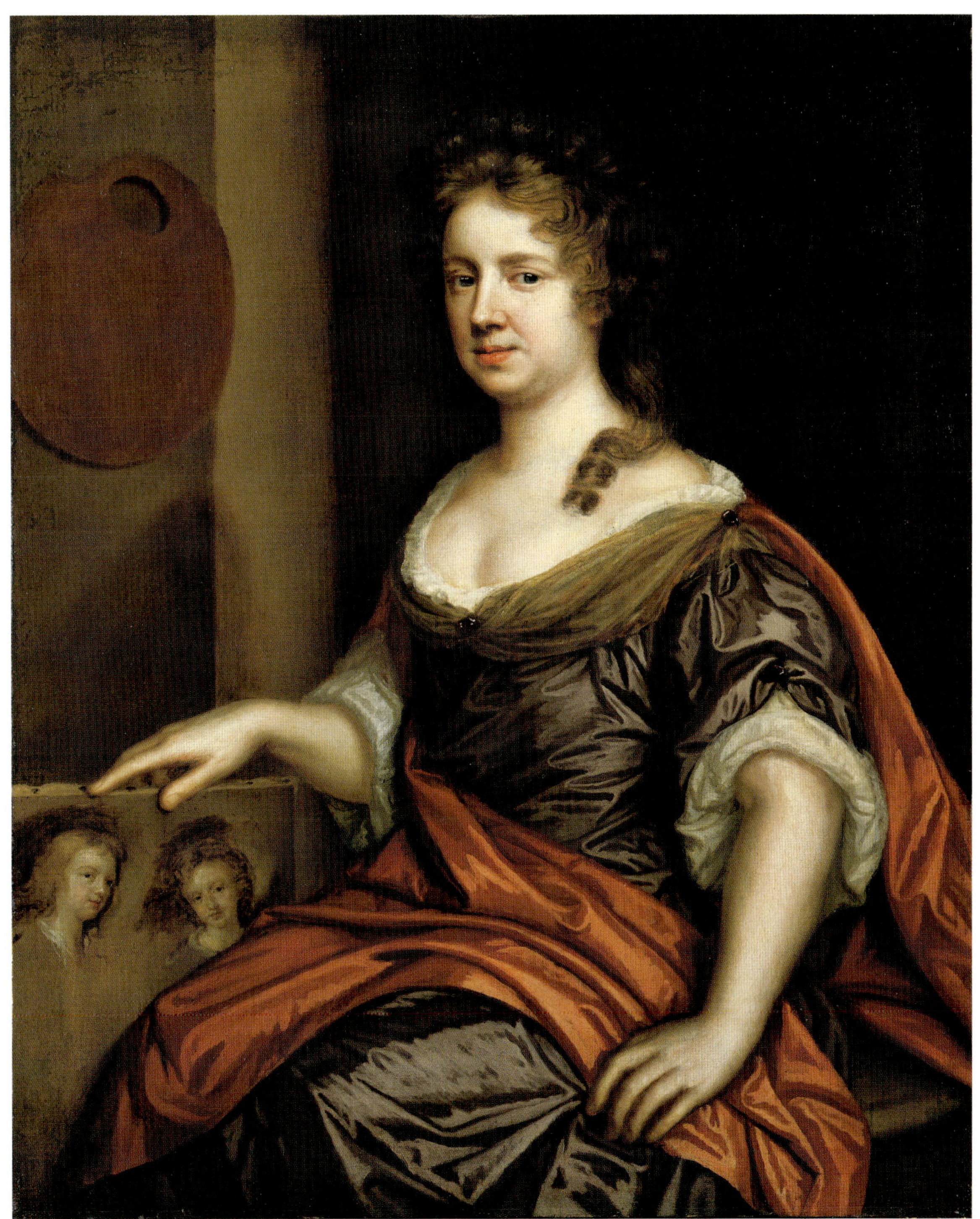

Fig.4 *Self-Portrait*, *c.*1666
Mary Beale
Oil on canvas, 1092 × 876mm
National Portrait Gallery, London

MARINA WARNER

LEE MILLER & MAN RAY

When Lee Miller arrived in Paris in 1929, she radiated light: with her very fair hair and blue eyes, she had the colouring of an ice maiden, but everyone who met her reports instead how, on the contrary, Lee was 'bright', her shining hair 'lustrous'; she looked like 'a sun-kissed goat boy from the Appian way'.[1] Yellow dominates Picasso's palette when he paints Lee's portrait in 1937 (fig.1) – bright yellow and sky blue. The gallerist Julien Levy, seeing her walking down the Boulevard Raspail, exclaimed at her 'bold bright aura'.[2] *Vogue* editor Madge Garland noted that visitors to Man Ray's studio in 1929, were 'greeted by a vision so lovely they forgot why they had come'.[3] Marilyn Monroe had similar incandescence, but by contrast Lee was androgynous, tall, lithe, her eyebrows unplucked, and, in those days, her hair cropped close to her head, revealing her long, slender neck. She exuded natural grace, youth and energy. When she went to a high-society White costume ball (everyone in lace and tulle), she wore tennis shorts by Mme Vionnet. Man Ray, who had been commissioned to take the official photographs, chafed at his lot, stuck in his improvised studio, while Lee 'was continually being taken away to dance' by one partner after another.[4] He remembered the occasion ruefully: 'Lee turned up now and then between dances to tell me what a wonderful time she was having; all the men were so sweet to her.'[5] He added, 'I was in love with her.'[6]

Man Ray was seventeen years older than Lee Miller; she was from wealth in upstate New York, he was brought up in South Philadelphia by his Russian Jewish parents and had arrived in Paris penniless. 'He looked like a bull,' Lee wrote, 'with an extraordinary torso and very dark eyebrows and dark hair.'[7] Her portrait photograph draws attention to slightly bulging eyes and his set mouth

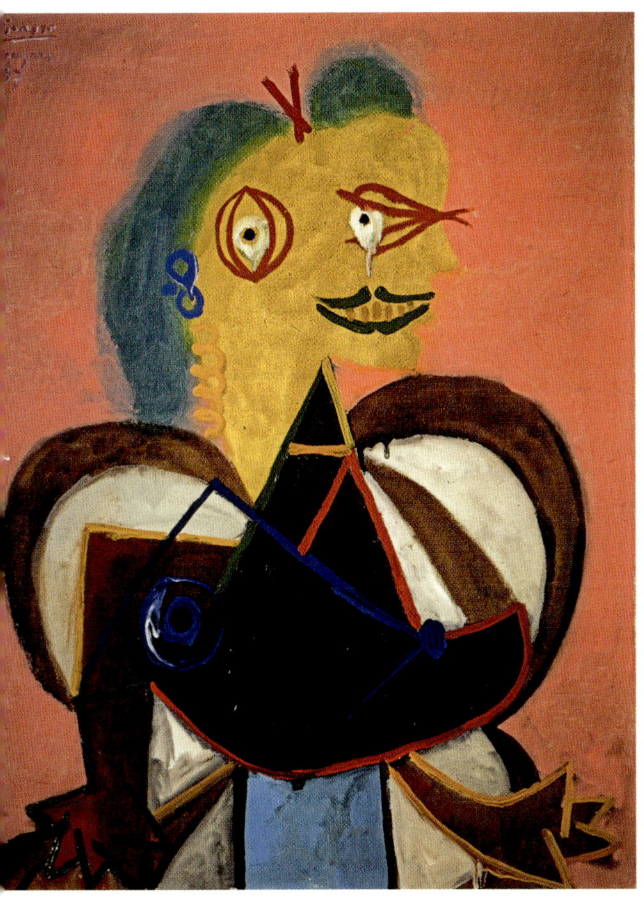

Fig.1 *Lee Miller*, 1937
Pablo Picasso
Oil on canvas, 810 × 600mm
Scottish National Gallery of Modern Art

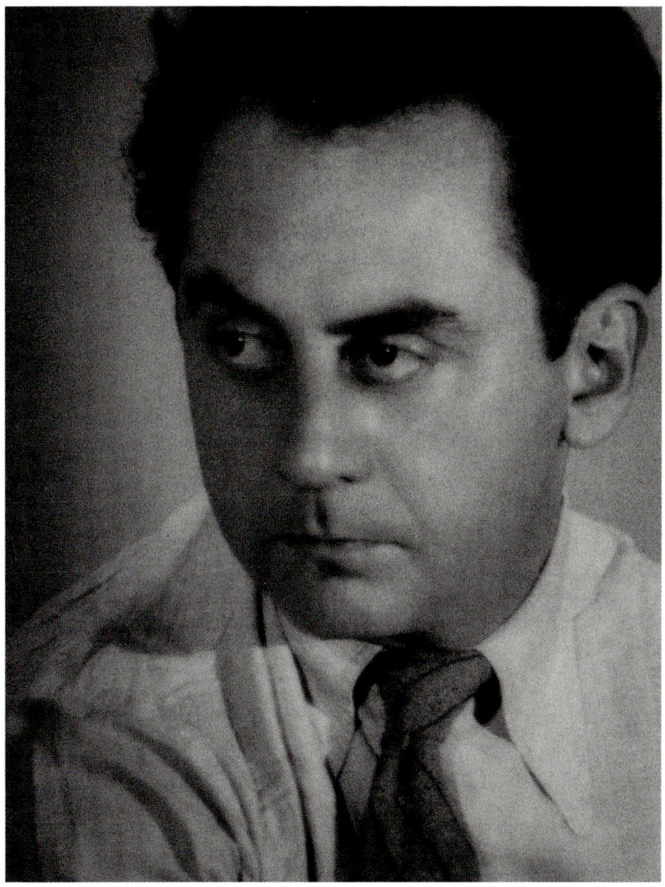

Fig.2 *Man Ray, Paris 1931*, 1931
Lee Miller
Gelatin silver print, 355 × 271mm
Lee Miller Archives, England

and brings out his authority and a certain distance – he is not looking at her (fig.2). At that point in his life Man Ray had abandoned paint and canvas for photography: 'I am working directly from light itself', he said, winning his friend Marcel Duchamp's warm approval.[8] Lee had triumphed as a fashion model in New York – until her appearance in an advertisement for Kotex sanitary towels caused an uproar, blemishing her image (such were the times). In these early fashion images, by some of the finest *Vogue* and *Harper's* photographers, Lee Miller has a classic, poised, uncluttered grace, with an enthralling inward reflectiveness.

But she was now resolved to move behind the camera. The photographer George Hoyningen-Huene told her Man Ray was the leader in the field; accordingly, she sought him out. His studio was a hub of Surrealist and intellectual adventures and Lee presented herself there. The concierge told her Monsieur had left for Biarritz; acting on impulse – Lee would always act on impulse, to the dismay of her family, lovers, husbands and friends – she tracked Man Ray down to a nearby nightclub, Le Bateau ivre. 'I am your new student', she told him.[9] He demurred, he didn't take students. Nevertheless, almost immediately, she was travelling with him to Biarritz and their professional relationship – and intense love affair – was under way.

From that first encounter onwards, Lee, who had a strong streak of daredevilry, set the terms of their artistic partnership (and maybe their love affair – these interactions are, however, hidden from our curiosity today).

His photographs of her have become Surrealist classics (figs 3–6). These images develop the startling aesthetic which Man Ray, in Surrealist mode, began when he transformed Kiki de Montparnasse's back by adding F-scrolls to her torso to produce *Le Violon d'Ingres*, 1924. Man Ray had also played very successfully with extended camera-less exposures, dubbing his dynamic juxtapositions 'Rayographs'. But when Lee Miller started working with him, the images begin to show a greater adventurousness, as model and artist improvise more extreme angles of view on the female body (hers), flouting all tenets of portraiture. Unlike his society sitters, she did not always want a record of what she looked like, nor did she simply seek to be elegant and lovely. She wanted to explore sensual and formal possibilities, often laced with a Sadeian streak (her arms pinned behind her back; her neck stretched vulnerably) (fig.4). She fragmented and masked herself, concealing the individual woman: the images from this period cut out parts of the body, her chin, her lips (fig.3), or show her headless torso barred by shadows from the window blind. In her later solo career, she trained this same courageous, dispassionate eye on startling juxtapositions, during her travels in the Western Desert and her unflinching wartime records of Dachau and other horrors.

Man Ray was evasive about Miller's role in his uses of solarisation, the process which confirmed him as innovatory artist of pure light. Later, Lee described how in l929, she stumbled upon this 'edge reversal' effect by accident when something – a mouse? – ran over her foot in the darkroom and she switched on the light, exposing the photograph in the developing tray.[10] The effect of sudden light at this juncture wasn't wholly unknown, but it hadn't been applied before to aesthetic effect. Numerous iconic studies of Lee, her face and form outlined with a smudged sooty halo, enhance her intrinsic luminosity, giving her the unearthly character of a profane angel (fig.6). Several of the works made during their time together and afterwards cultivate the estranging and unreal effects of the process (fig.7).

The collaboration did not outlast their love, and that love was a short and stormy affair, lasting just three years: Lee tested to the limit May Ray's Surrealist support for free love, and would not commit to him alone. She was filled with passionate curiosity about life and Man Ray's circle of friends was at the heart of the avant garde of that era (fig.8); she loved excitement; the outrageous side of Surrealist events appealed to her restless appetite. Nor was she submissive as a student: 'on one occasion, Man Ray took a low-angle, soft focus photograph of Lee's head, featuring her neck prominently, but the result was not to his liking so he threw away the negative. Lee retrieved the plate and carefully made a print ... working hard to enhance and perfect it until she was satisfied with the image.'[11] Man Ray who now approved the print, became indignant when Lee insisted the work was hers (fig.4). They had a furious row, and Lee walked out. 'A few hours later, when she returned, she found the image pinned to the wall with its throat slashed by a razor and streams of

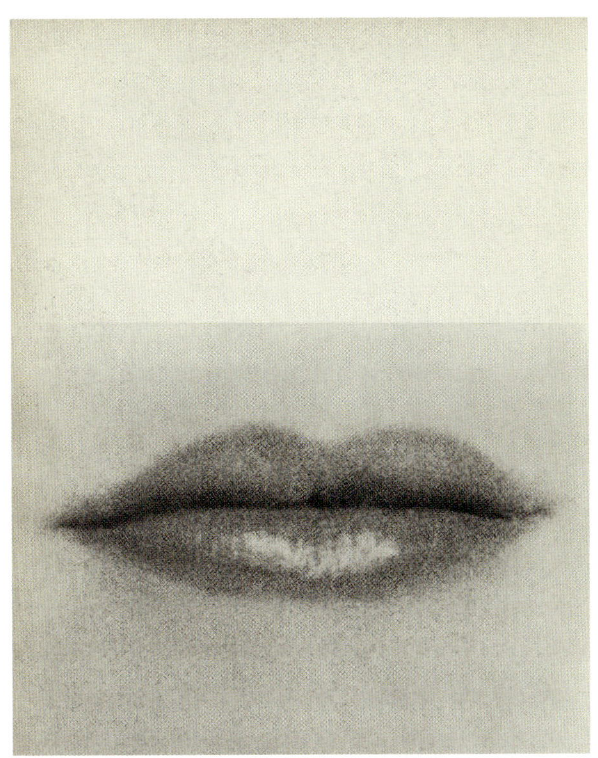

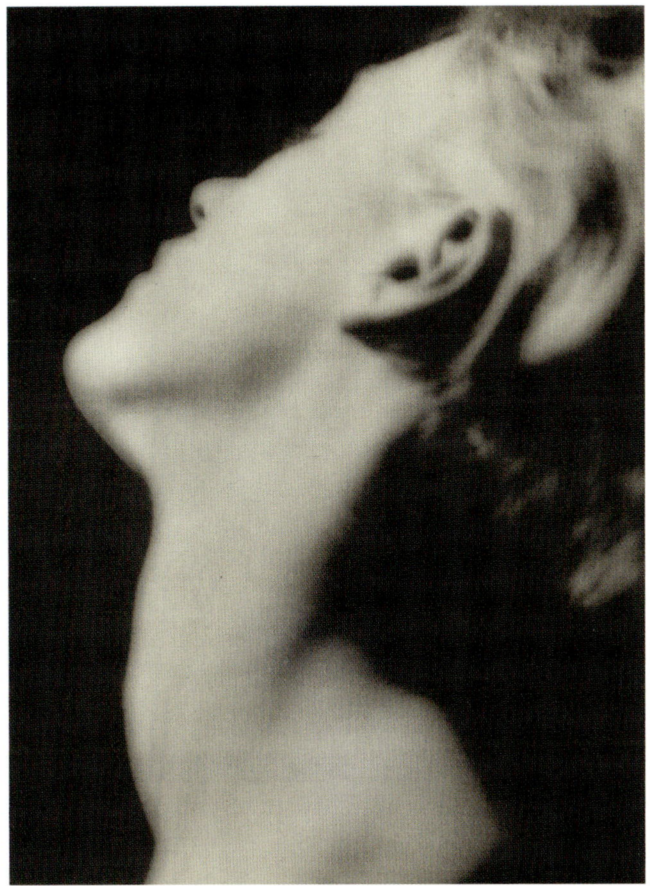

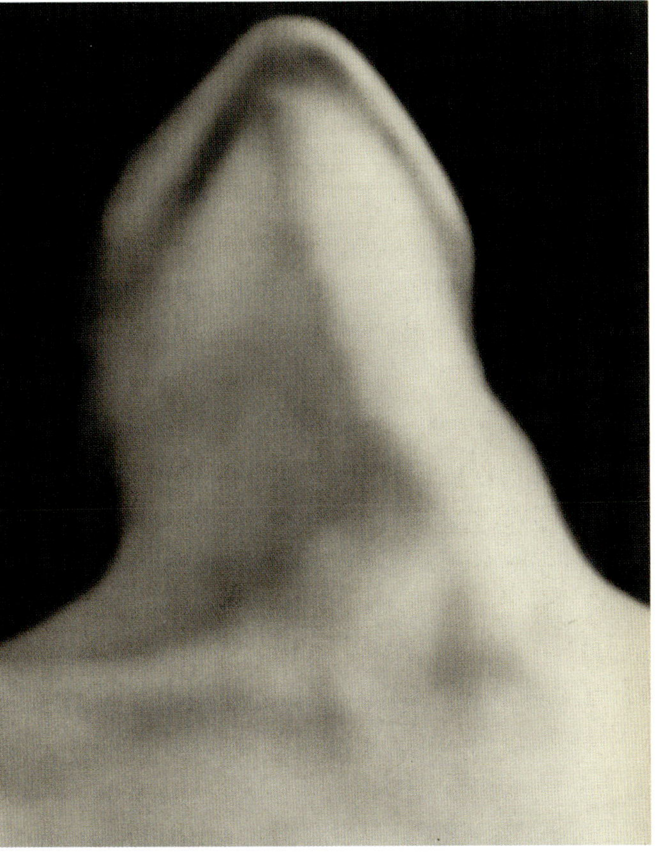

CLOCKWISE FROM TOP LEFT

Fig.3 *Lee Miller*, 1930
Man Ray
Photogravure, 310 × 240mm
National Portrait Gallery, London

Fig.4 *Lee Miller ('Neck')*, 1930
Lee Miller and Man Ray
Photogravure, 295 × 216mm
National Portrait Gallery, London

Fig.5 *Lee Miller ('The Necklace')*, 1929
Man Ray
Photogravure, 310 × 240mm
National Portrait Gallery, London

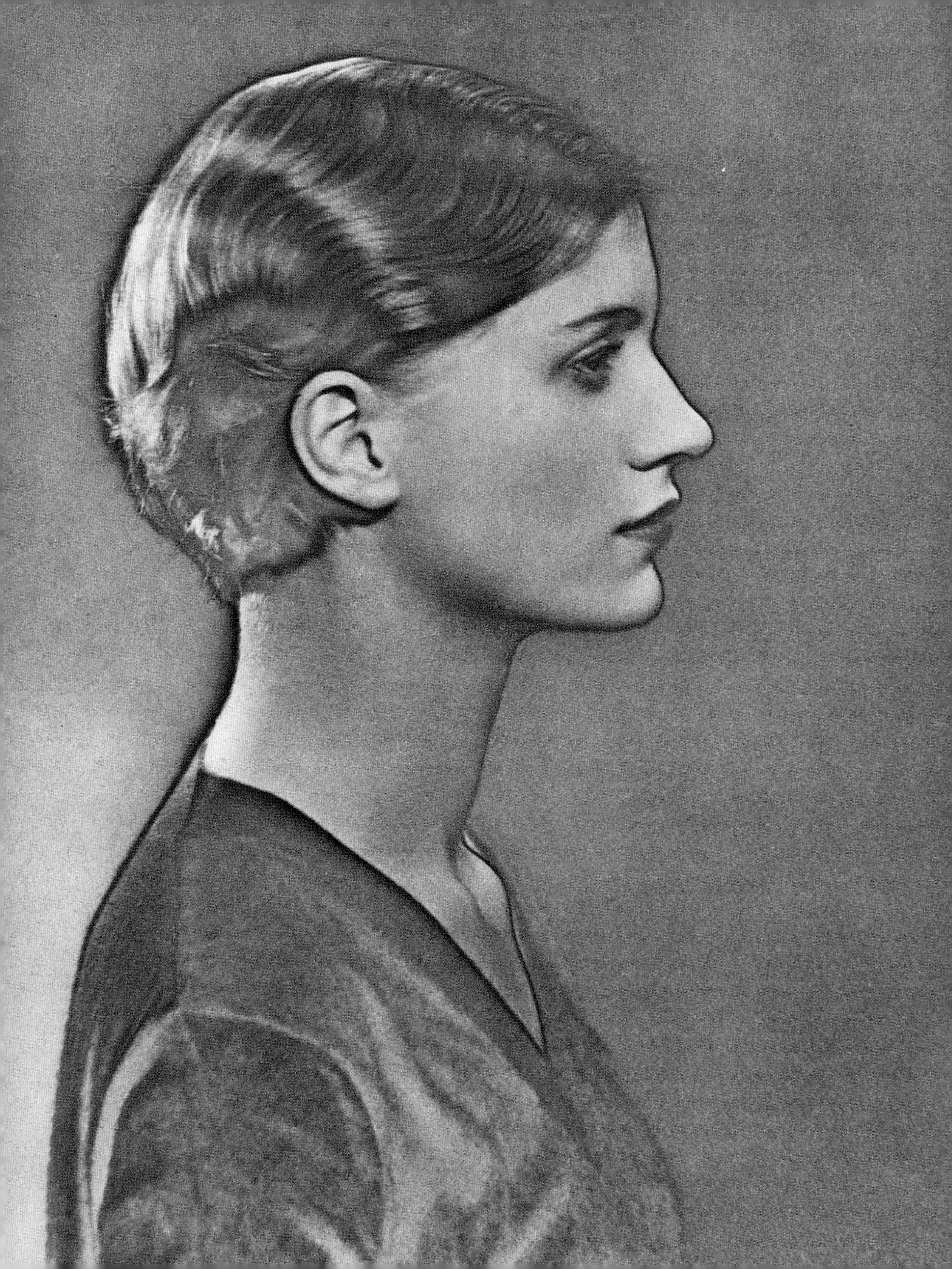

scarlet ink cascading from the wound.' Man Ray then reprised the scene in the painting, *Le Logis de l'artiste* (*c.*1931, fig.9).[12] (One of her photographs of him shows him shaving: the razor isn't in shot, but his neck and cheeks and chin are white with shaving foam, almost like the plaster used to cast a death mask.)

During the time they shared a studio, the balance of power between them shifted and shifted fast, though Lee, as a young woman known for her loveliness, wasn't able to secure recognition for her experiments behind the camera and in the dark room until much later. For his part, Man Ray suffered her loss very deeply; he threatened suicide, but eventually exorcised the pain by customising a metronome, one of his most celebrated Surrealist 'gifts', by sticking to its wand his photograph of Lee's eye (*Object to Be Destroyed*, 1932), and adding instructions how to smash it in order to stop its maddening insistence – an apt correlative for that endless longing of the lovelorn. Her incendiary passage through Man Ray's life had catalysed him to return to painting and sculpture.

Lee Miller was an exceptionally lively, strong-willed, independent character; she moved on, though in the midst of her new amours and marriages she still wrote very tenderly to Man Ray; after a few years they met again and became firm friends. In her old age, she was often depressed; she would never rest on her laurels

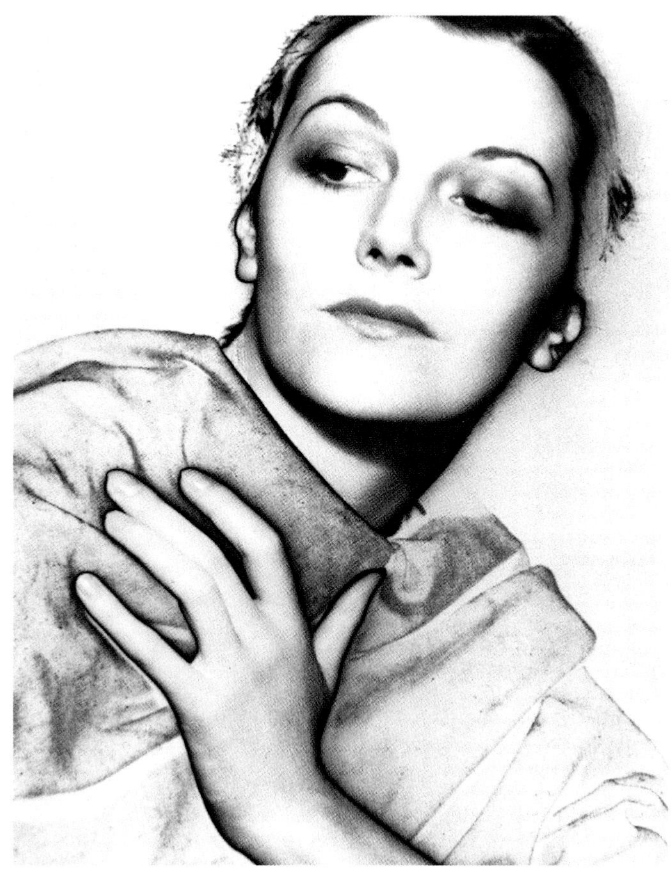

Fig.7 *Solarized Portrait of Unknown Woman*, 1930
Lee Miller
Lee Miller Archives, England

OPPOSITE
Fig.6 *Lee Miller*, 1930
Man Ray
Photogravure, 310 × 240mm
National Portrait Gallery, London

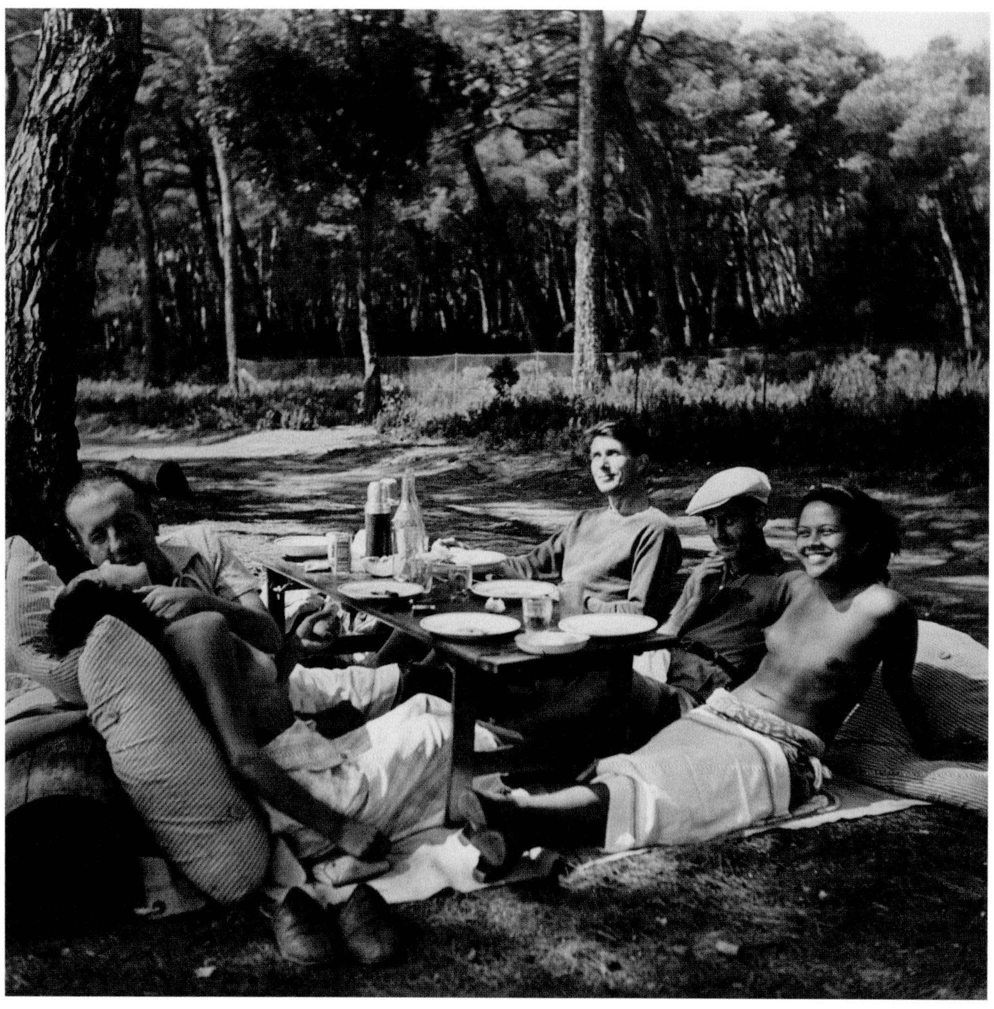

ABOVE
Fig.8 *Nusch Eluard, Paul Eluard, Roland Penrose, Man Ray and Ady Fidelin ('Picnic')*, 1937
Lee Miller
Modern gelatin silver print, 203 × 197mm
National Portrait Gallery, London

OPPOSITE
Fig.9 *Le Logis de L'artiste (The Artist's Home)*, *c.*1931
Man Ray
Oil on canvas, 710 × 520mm
The Roland Penrose Collection, England

or even look backwards – her son Antony Penrose, after her death, unearthed the whole range of her remarkable oeuvre from the family attic; it seemed she had wanted her work to vanish. Man Ray would send her messages and gifts to bring back the brightness which had lit up his and many others' lives. In 1976, the year he was to die, Man Ray was given a retrospective at the Arles Photo Festival, and he asked Lee to take his place at the ceremony in his honour. After half a century, he recognised, in this way, the part she had played.

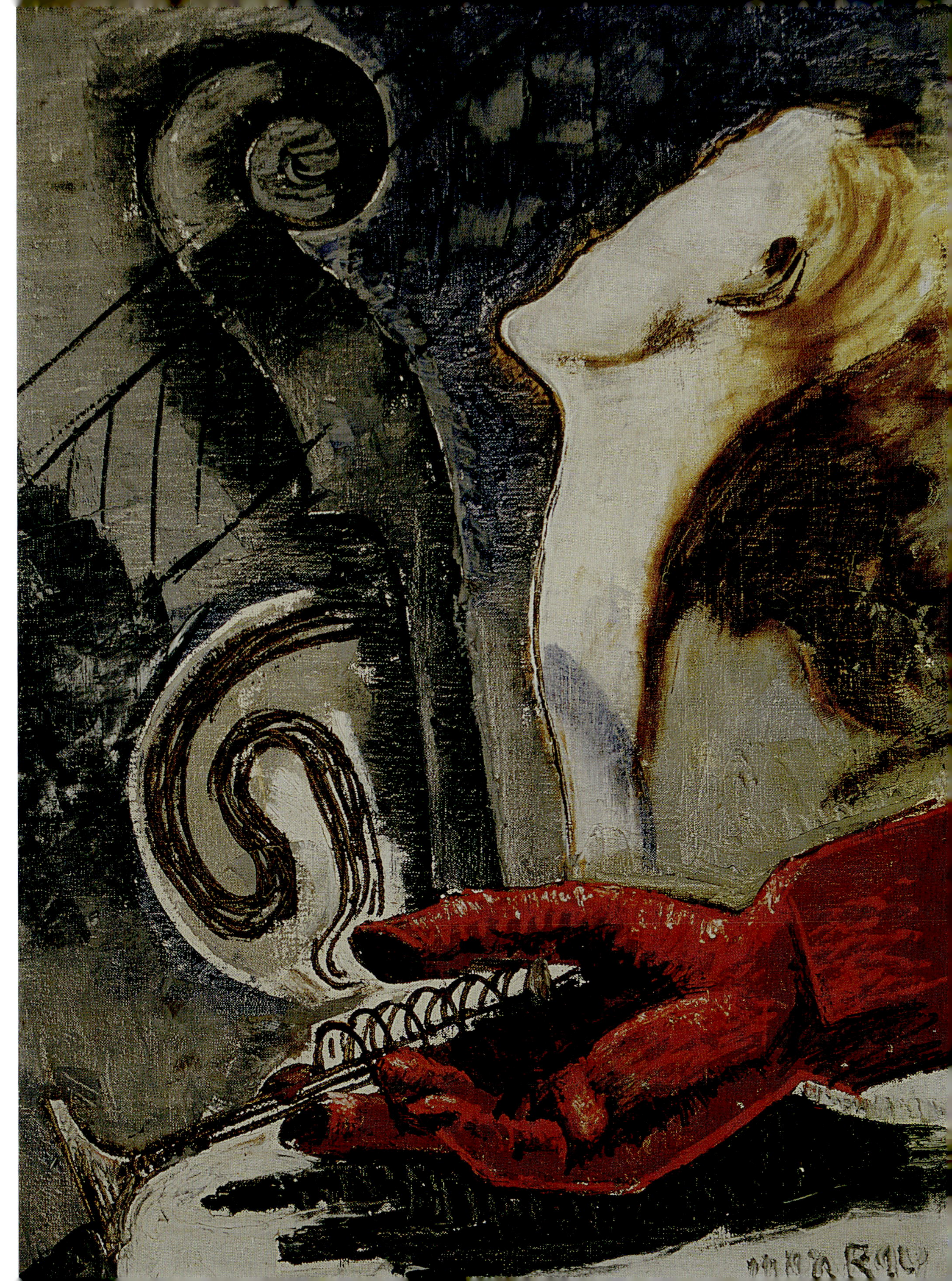

LUCY DAHLSEN

Barbara Hepworth & Ben Nicholson

Barbara Hepworth saw and admired Ben Nicholson's art before she met him. Of her initial encounter with his work, in March 1930, she later wrote, 'The experience helped me to release all my energies for an exploration of free sculptural form.'[1] Hepworth and Nicholson subsequently lived, shared a studio and worked together for over a decade. A meeting of minds and ideas, their relationship facilitated a mutually enabling creative dialogue that had a significant and lasting impact on the art and legacy of both. Together, they played a vital role in bringing continental modernism to Britain as they became leading figures of the international group of abstract artists that formed in the 1930s. This group championed a purely non-representational aesthetic that symbolised a broader ideal of harmonious social interaction and international cooperation in the face of rising fascism. By the end of the decade and the outbreak of war, Hepworth and Nicholson's shared studio, later described by the critic Herbert Read as 'a nest of gentle artists', had become the hub of the avant-garde in Britain.[2]

Hepworth and Nicholson met in person in 1931 while on holiday on the Norfolk coast with artist friends. Both were married to other artists at the time of their meeting, Hepworth to fellow sculptor John Skeaping and Nicholson to the painter Winifred Nicholson (née Roberts), and both had children. Hepworth and Skeaping divorced abruptly but the Nicholsons did not officially separate until later. By the beginning of 1932 Hepworth and Nicholson were working in close proximity and by the end of the year they were sharing a work space at The Mall Studios in Hampstead, which Hepworth had occupied since 1928. In Autumn 1934 Hepworth and Nicholson had triplets and in 1938 they married.

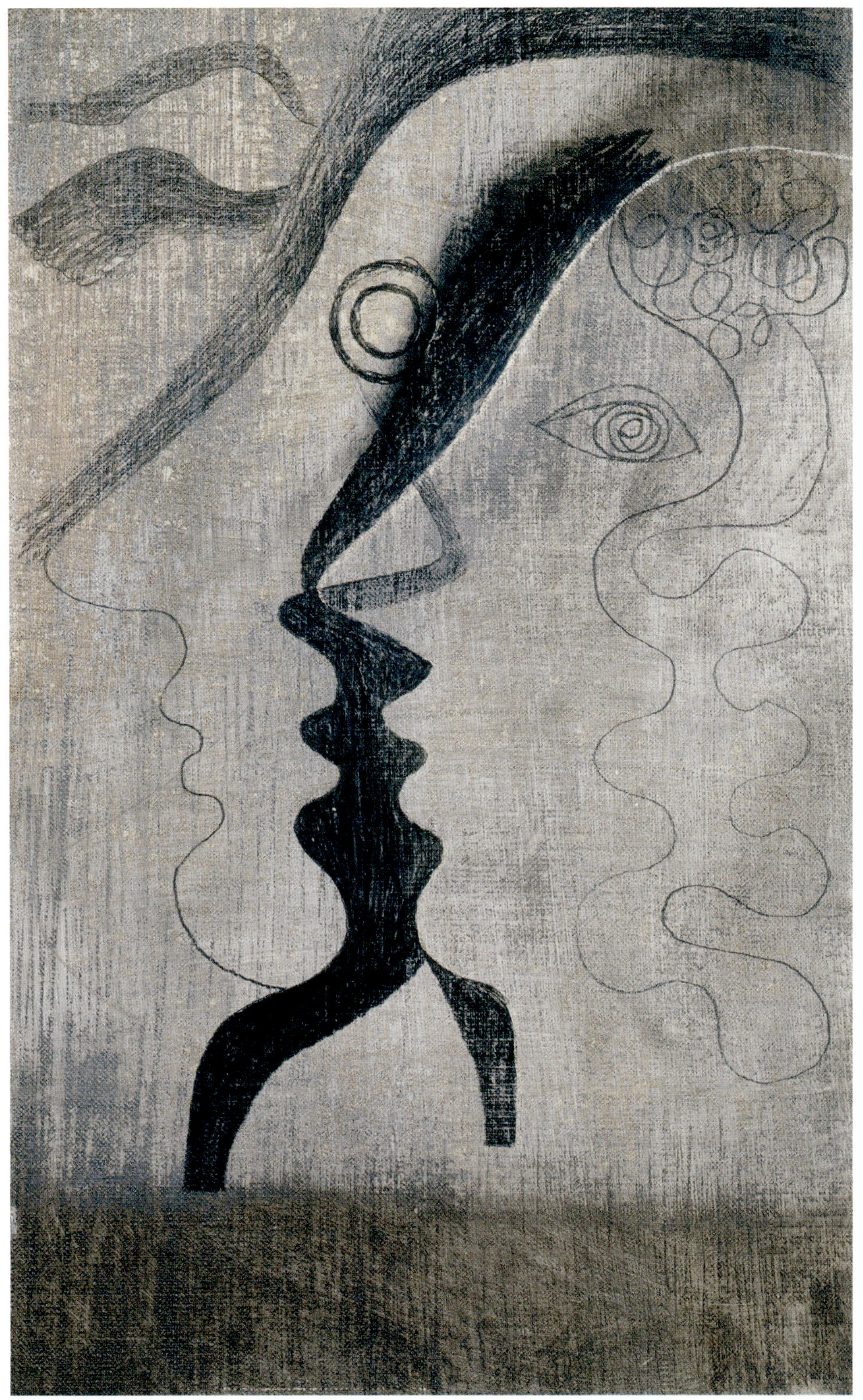

Fig.1 *Self-Portrait with Barbara Hepworth ('1933–St Rémy')*, 1933
Ben Nicholson
Oil on canvas, 273 × 168mm
National Portrait Gallery, London

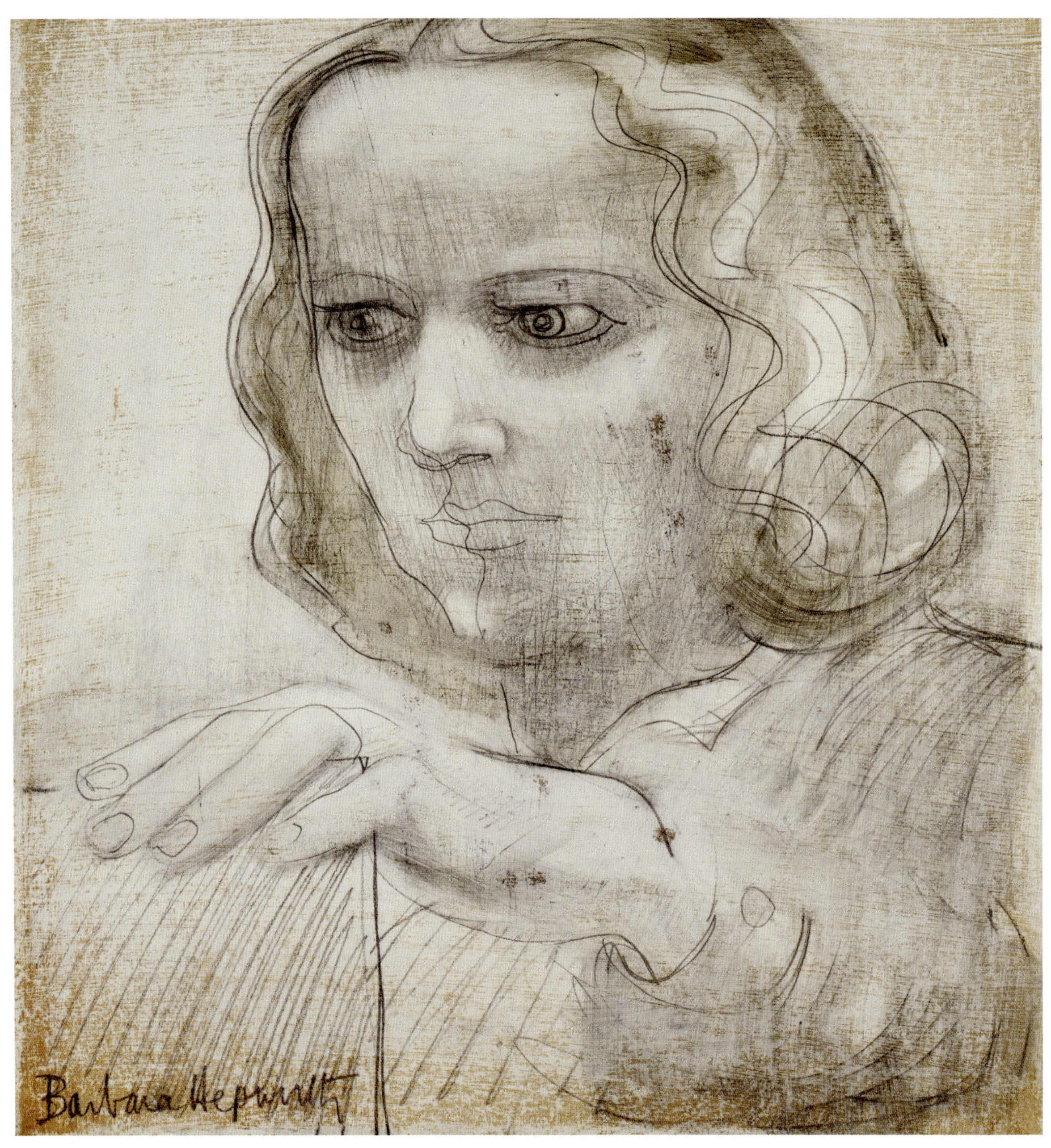

Fig.2 *Self-Portrait*, 1950
Barbara Hepworth
Oil and pencil on board, 305 × 267mm
National Portrait Gallery, London

"Barbara and I are the same ... our ideas & our rhythms, our life is so exactly married that we can live, think and work and move and stay still together as if we were one person."[3]

BEN NICHOLSON, 1932

Although largely based in London during the 1930s, the couple also made a number of trips to France, which they documented in drawings, paintings and photographs. During the summer of 1932, they travelled to Dieppe, where the artist Georges Braque was working, and the following year to Avignon, Saint-Rémy-de-Provence and Paris, meeting and visiting the studios of key international figures such as Hans and Sophie Taeuber-Arp, Pablo Picasso, Alberto Giacometti, Piet Mondrian and Joan Miró. Describing their trip to Provence, Hepworth later recalled,

> It was my first visit to the South of France, and out of three days at Avignon the most important time for me was spent at St Rémy. ... we walked up the hill and encountered at the top a sea of olive trees receding behind the ancient arch on the plateau, and human figures sitting, reclining, walking and embracing at the foot of the arch, grouped in rhythmic relation to the far distant undulating hills and mountain rocks.

Shortly afterwards, Nicholson made this double portrait in which the couple's profiles are superimposed onto one another and the hills of Provence seen in the background. The portrait hung over the mantelpiece in the couple's studio in London, a marker of the early days of their union.

For both Hepworth and Nicholson, the 1930s marked a period of rapid artistic development, influenced both by the work they had seen abroad and by their direct influence on one another. A series of joint exhibitions in London demonstrated the increasing similarity between their styles. As Hepworth's sculptural language became gradually more simplified, Nicholson began to execute his signature carved reliefs, which were no doubt encouraged by the sculptor's presence in his life. As the critic Adrian Stokes emphasised in a review of an exhibition of Nicholson's work in 1933, 'Mr Nicholson's canvases and panels serve him in the role of the carver's block.'[4] The couple's joint progression towards abstraction bought them to the forefront of the avant-garde and they were invited to join leading associations including Abstraction-Création in Paris and the Seven and Five Society and Unit One in England.

In 1939, just before the outbreak of the Second World War, Hepworth and Nicholson left London for Cornwall, a move that was to become an evacuation and a marker of the end of the closest years of their relationship. During the 1940s Nicholson travelled often while Hepworth remained in Cornwall looking after the children and developing her work, which increasingly had less in common with that of Nicholson. Finally, in 1950, the couple took two separate studios, a sign of their diverging paths. Though their marriage was dissolved in 1951, the two remained professionally supportive of one another as they each embarked on prominent and influential post-war careers.

LUCY DAHLSEN

Mervyn Peake & Maeve Gilmore

Mervyn Peake and Maeve Gilmore met in 1936 on Gilmore's first day at the Westminster School of Art, where, at the age of seventeen, she was to study sculpture. Gilmore had grown up in London before attending finishing school in Switzerland and aspired to become an artist. Six years her senior, Peake was already a successful painter and was teaching at the school. Agreeing to go to tea with him, Gilmore was immediately attracted by what she later described as Peake's 'native exuberance', a quality rendered in his charged self-portrait (fig.2).[1] Made a few years earlier, the portrait presents Peake wide-eyed and dishevelled against a background of mountain tops, a playful evocation of his name. The couple were married a year later and stayed together for thirty years until Peake's death from Parkinson's Disease at the age of fifty-seven.

The couple lived for periods in Kent, London and, predominantly, on the Channel Island of Sark. During the 1940s and 1950s, Peake became well known as a painter, illustrator and writer, recognised for his trademark combination of fantasy and the macabre. Gilmore had a number of solo exhibitions in London during the late 1930s before taking the role of wife and mother to their three children as Peake's career burgeoned. Alongside supporting her husband's activity, however, Gilmore continued to paint and her output, ranging from portraits and scenes of pastoral life to abstract and surrealist compositions, was prolific. Despite this, little of her mature work was exhibited or even seen outside of the family home during her lifetime.

Fig.1 *Maeve Gilmore*, 1940s
Mervyn Peake
Oil on canvas, 605 × 458mm
National Portrait Gallery, London

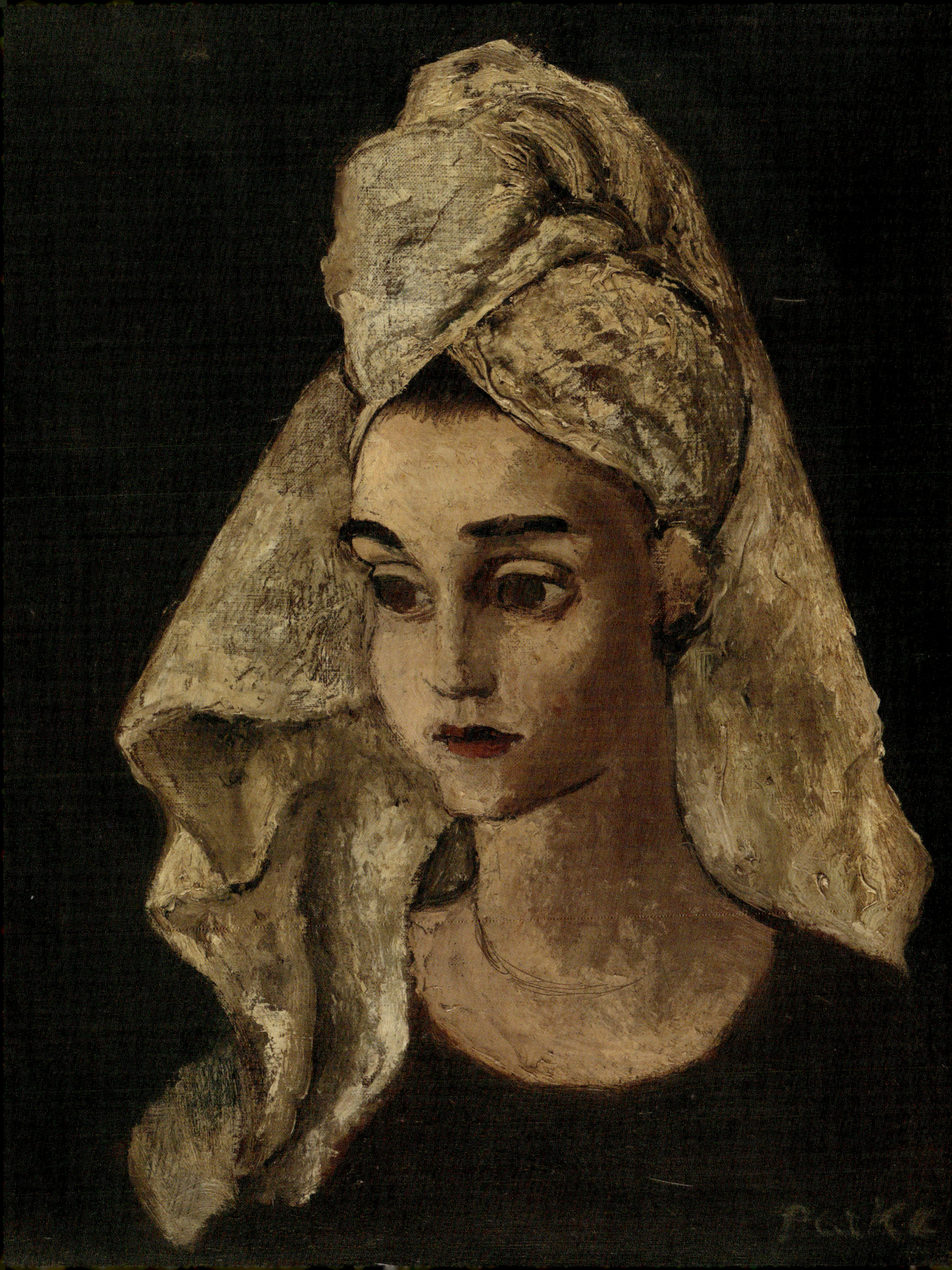

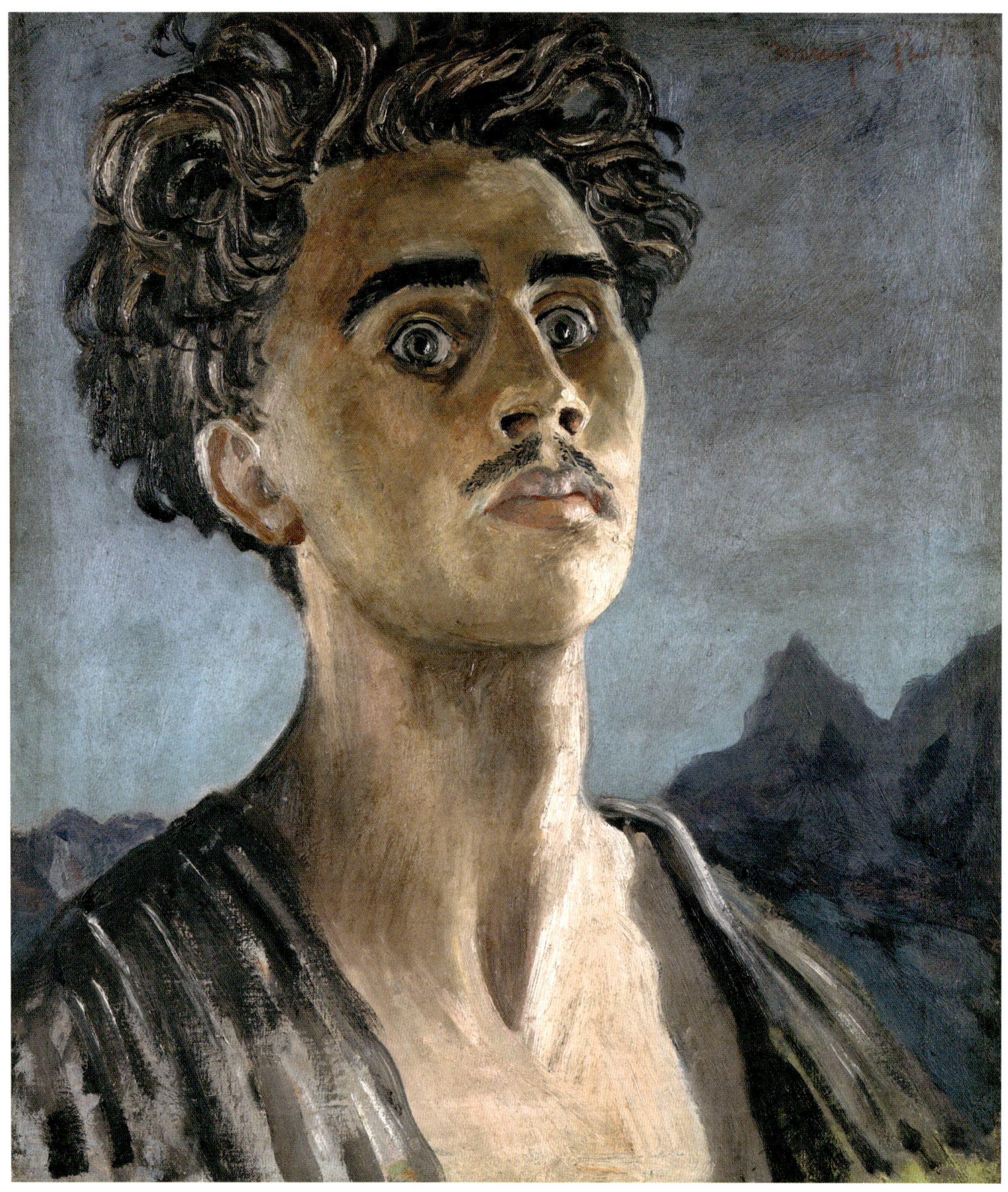

Fig.2 *Self-Portrait*, 1932
Mervyn Peake
Oil on canvas, 600 × 505mm
On loan to the National Portrait Gallery, London, courtesy of Mervyn Peake estate

For Maeve

You are the maeve of me as this my arm
Is the joined arm of me; the heart within
Which I have heard so long yet never seen
Is this – like these, you are my fount, my limb –
Yet more than these: you are the maeve of me.

MERVYN PEAKE[2]

The couple's love and life together is captured in the paintings and drawings they made of one another, poems, illustrated letters and photographs, as well as in Gilmore's memoir, *A World Away: A Memoir of Mervyn Peake* (1970). This portrait of Maeve by Peake is likely to have been made in the 1940s, during the early years of their relationship, when the sitter was in her twenties. An intimate work, the bust-length portrait shows Gilmore with a towel wrapping her damp hair, seated in private contemplation yet at ease in Peake's presence. In capturing an everyday domestic moment, the portrait attests to the central role that art played in the couple's home as they lived and worked side by side.

During the late 1950s, Peake's health began to decline as he was finishing *Titus Alone* (1959), the third novel in his series of *Titus* books, following *Titus Groan* (1946) and *Gormenghast* (1950). In 1960, Peake and Gilmore worked together to illustrate his poem, *The Rhyme of the Flying Bomb*, which was broadcast on BBC Radio and widely celebrated. Despite initiating a spark of interest in his art, Peake's condition had worsened and he was unable to continue working. Following his death in 1968, Gilmore began to work on a fourth book in the *Titus* series using detailed notes left by Peake. She finished the book before her death in 1983 but it was only published in 2010 after being discovered in the attic of the family home by their granddaughter. Titled *Titus Awakes*, the novel recounts the protagonist Titus travelling through a series of sites recalling those that Peake had visited in real life. Eventually Titus reaches an unnamed island that is reminiscent of Sark, returning to a place of love and happiness with the concluding sentence, 'There's not a road, not a track, but it will lead him home.'[3] Gilmore's confident sense of permission in continuing Peake's series is testament to the deep connection and intimacy that existed between the couple.

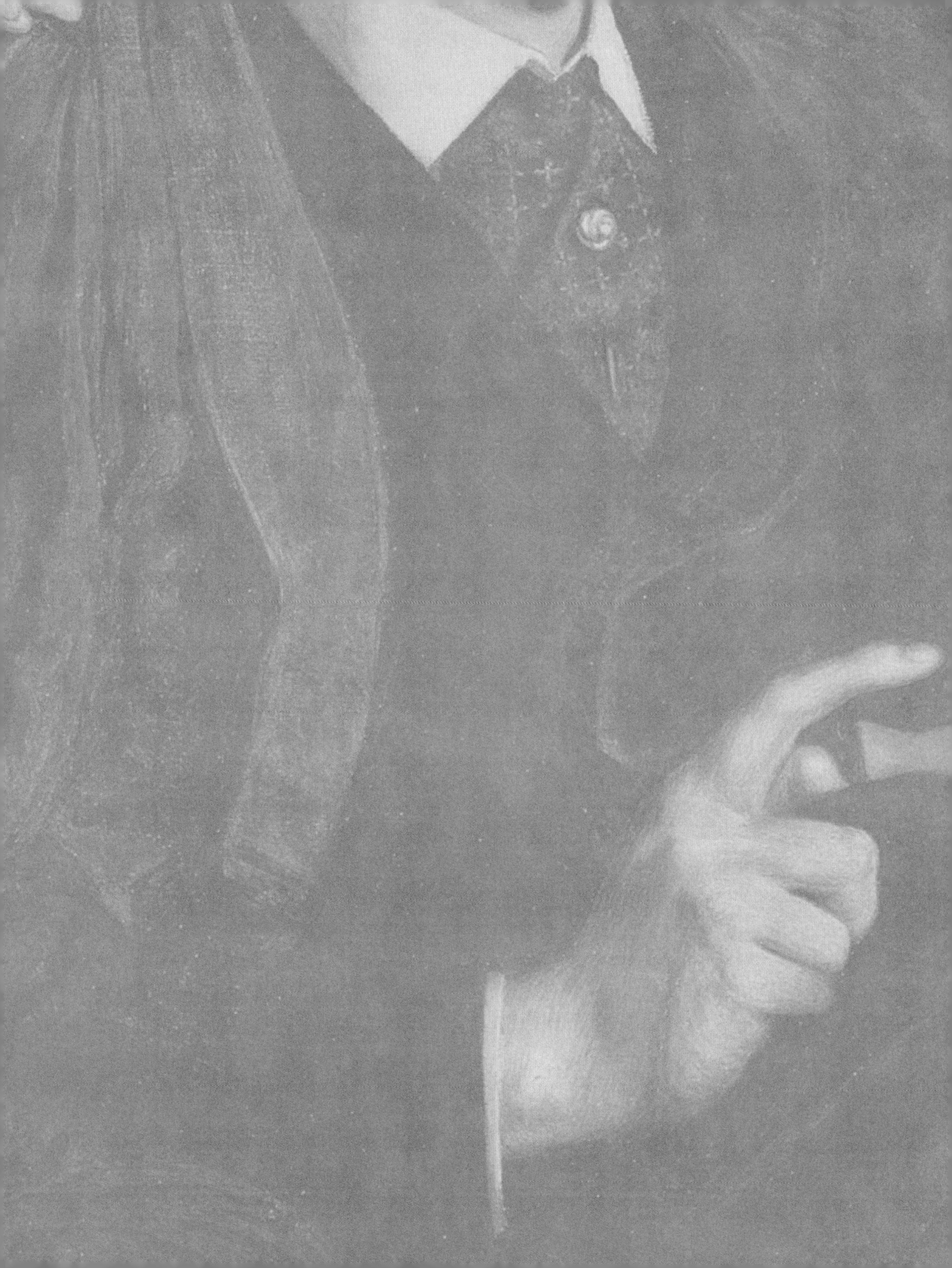

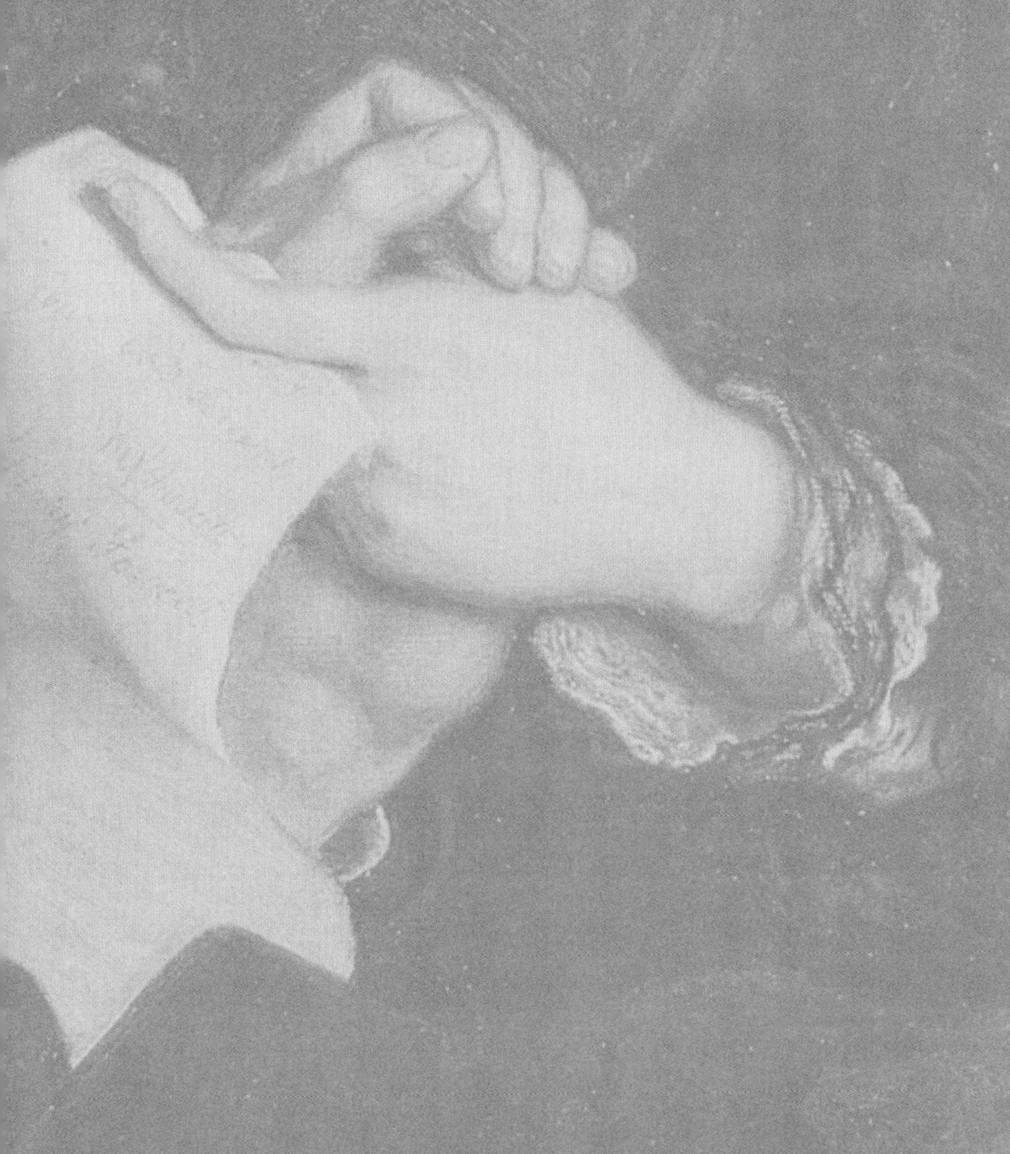

PORTRAYING PARTNERSHIP

LOUISE STEWART

PORTRAYING PARTNERSHIP

From sixteenth-century marriage portraits to contemporary wedding photography, portraits of couples have formed a distinct category of image-making in Britain for at least 500 years. Paired images, whether pendant (twin) or in a single composition, have usually been made to mark key life events, such as marriage, the birth of a child or a professional achievement. They celebrate a couple's relationship whilst simultaneously providing a setting for the expression of shared interests and evidence of lives lived together.

Daniel Mytens' depictions of the Earl and Countess of Arundel (figs 1 and 2) are an important early example of a portrait pair in British art. This is unsurprising as the Arundels were leading patrons and collectors of art in early seventeenth-century England. Funded by Aletheia's fortune, the couple fostered the careers of Inigo Jones, Daniel Mytens, Anthony van Dyck and Peter Paul Rubens and are widely credited with introducing the collecting of European renaissance art to England. Fittingly, they are depicted against backgrounds that signal their joint interest and showcase their status as art collectors; Thomas gestures towards their sculpture gallery while Aletheia is pictured in front of a portrait gallery. A recent painting of collectors and patrons of the arts Sir Harry and Lady Carol Djanogly, commissioned for the National Portrait Gallery, provides a contemporary counterpoint to these images (see pp.136–9).

Similarly, a portrait of the Shudi family (fig.3) situates their success and social status as a joint endeavour between Burkat, a celebrated harpsichord maker, and his wife Catherine. In the portrait we find evidence of Burkat's professional achievements as he sits at a harpsichord he had made for his patron Frederick, Prince of Wales, who can be identified as the subject of a print hanging on the wall behind him. Catherine's excellent taste is demonstrated through her fashionable silk dress and the furniture and china which indicate their consumption of exotic and expensive drinks like tea and chocolate. The inclusion of the children denotes Burkat and Catherine's success in founding a dynasty and their eldest son's gesture suggests that he has already developed an interest in the family business. Importantly, Catherine holds a document

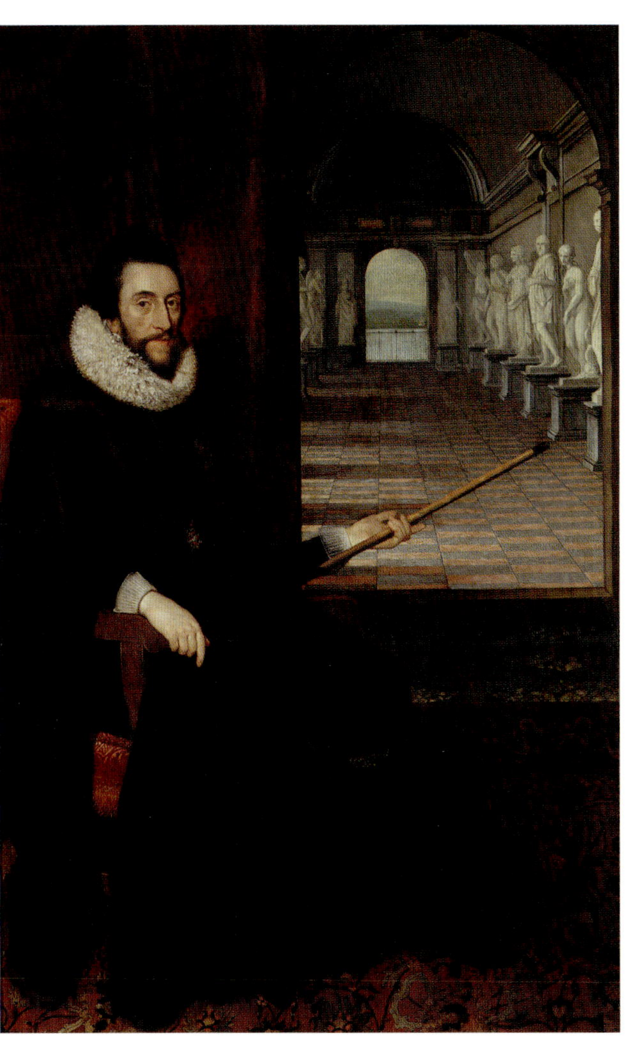

Fig.1 *Thomas Howard, 14th Earl of Arundel*, *c.*1618
Daniel Mytens
Oil on canvas, 2070 × 1270mm
National Portrait Gallery, London

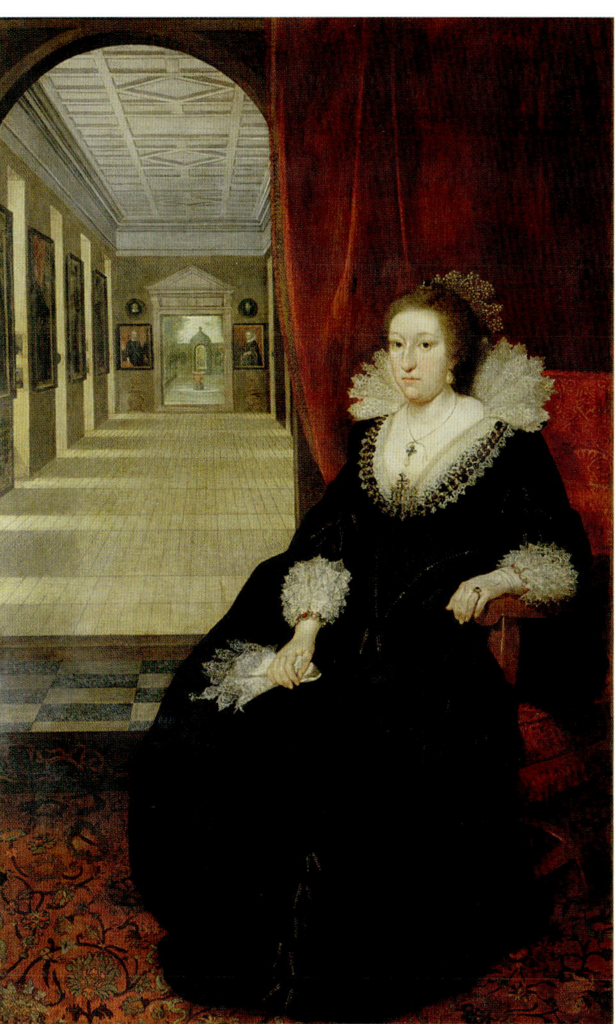

Fig.2 *Aletheia Howard, Countess of Arundel*, *c.*1619
Daniel Mytens
Oil on canvas, 2070 × 1270mm
National Portrait Gallery, London

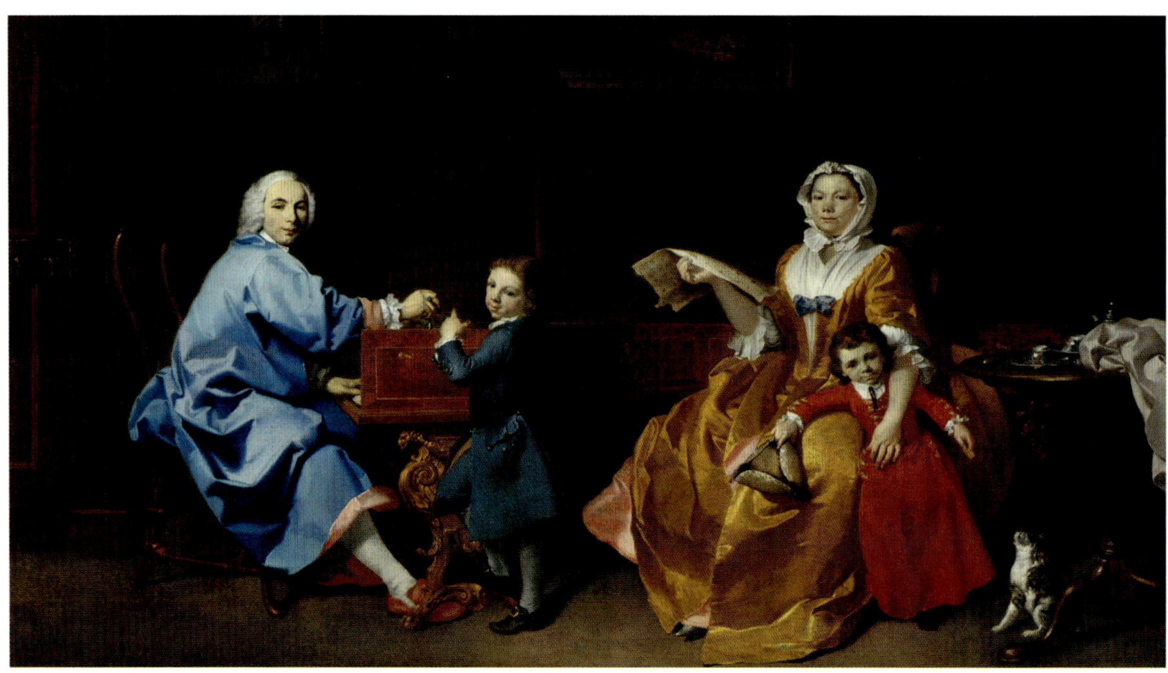

Fig.3 *The Shudi Family, c.*1742
Marcus Tuscher
Oil on canvas, 834 × 1415mm
National Portrait Gallery, London

which is thought to be her father's will, a reference to the recent inheritance which secured the family's prosperous, middling status. This sense of success and shared identity is a typical feature of portraits of married couples.

Framed very differently, Lucy Willis' portrait of the historian and biographer Elizabeth, Countess of Longford and her husband the politician Francis, Earl of Longford, does not refer at all to their considerable professional achievements (fig.4). Instead, it shows the couple together in a thoroughly domestic space, the bedroom of their flat in Chelsea, with photographs of their eight children in the background. It is significant that in a work commissioned for the National Portrait Gallery in response to both sitters' contributions to public life in Britain, the result focuses on their relationship and family life rather than their public achievements. This emphasis on the personal links that underpin public and professional success is a theme which recurs frequently in the portraits discussed here.

Historically, the painted portrait as a means of celebrating a life lived together has been available only to the wealthy. However, the development of photography, in the nineteenth century, made portraiture more widely available. From its first decades, photography has not only been an adjunct to the marriage ceremony it has been an ever-increasing component of the ritual. In the 1860s, couples began to be photographed in their wedding clothes

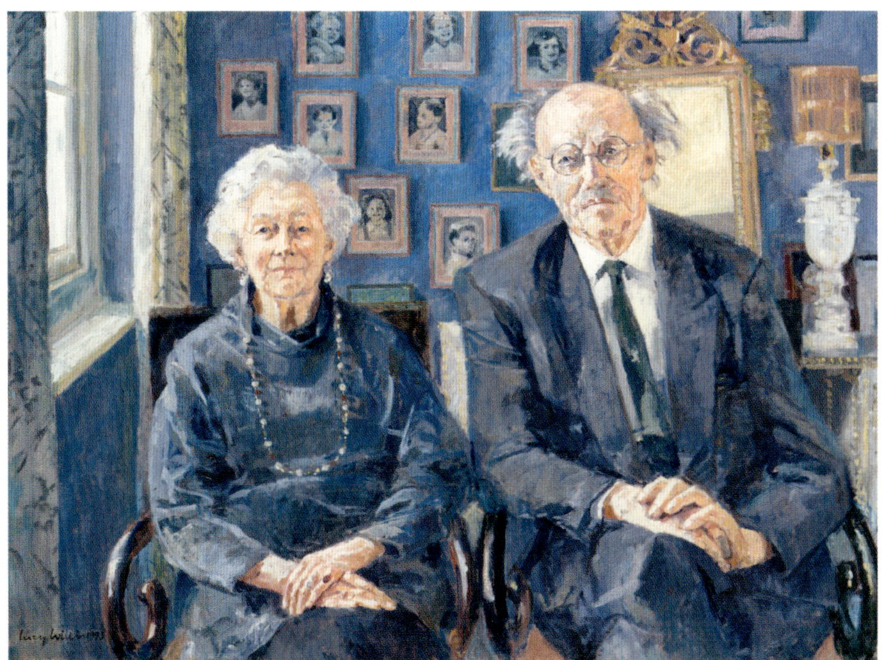

Fig.4 *Elizabeth, Countess and Francis, 7th Earl of Longford*, 1993
Lucy Willis
Oil on canvas, 762 × 1011mm
National Portrait Gallery, London

and formal studio photography was an important means by which a couple would celebrate their marriage. As photography became more mobile in the early twentieth century, it was used to showcase the key moments of the wedding day. These include formal family groups, beauty-shots of the bride, the couple arriving at and leaving the place of marriage and the cutting of the cake. Later displayed or viewed within the marital home, these photographs highlight the role of ritual in marriage portraiture and the ritual role of the photographic record in married life.

Wedding photos have not always been a private or personal matter. Throughout the twentieth century, readers of newspapers and society magazines have been able to indulge in illustrated accounts of high-profile weddings (fig.5). These included the lavish nuptials of film stars and aristocrats as well as more modest celebrity weddings. In 1931 the wedding of Peter Carl MacKay, known as Ras Prince Monolulu, and Nellie Adkins was widely featured in the press (fig.6). MacKay, who claimed to have been born in Addis Ababa, was a celebrity horse-racing tipster and performer who went on to appear in films and on BBC radio and television in the late 1930s. This image, taken for the *Daily Herald* newspaper shows MacKay and Adkins leaving St Pancras Register Office after marrying, with MacKay dressed in his trademark 'Abyssinian' costume and feathered headdress.

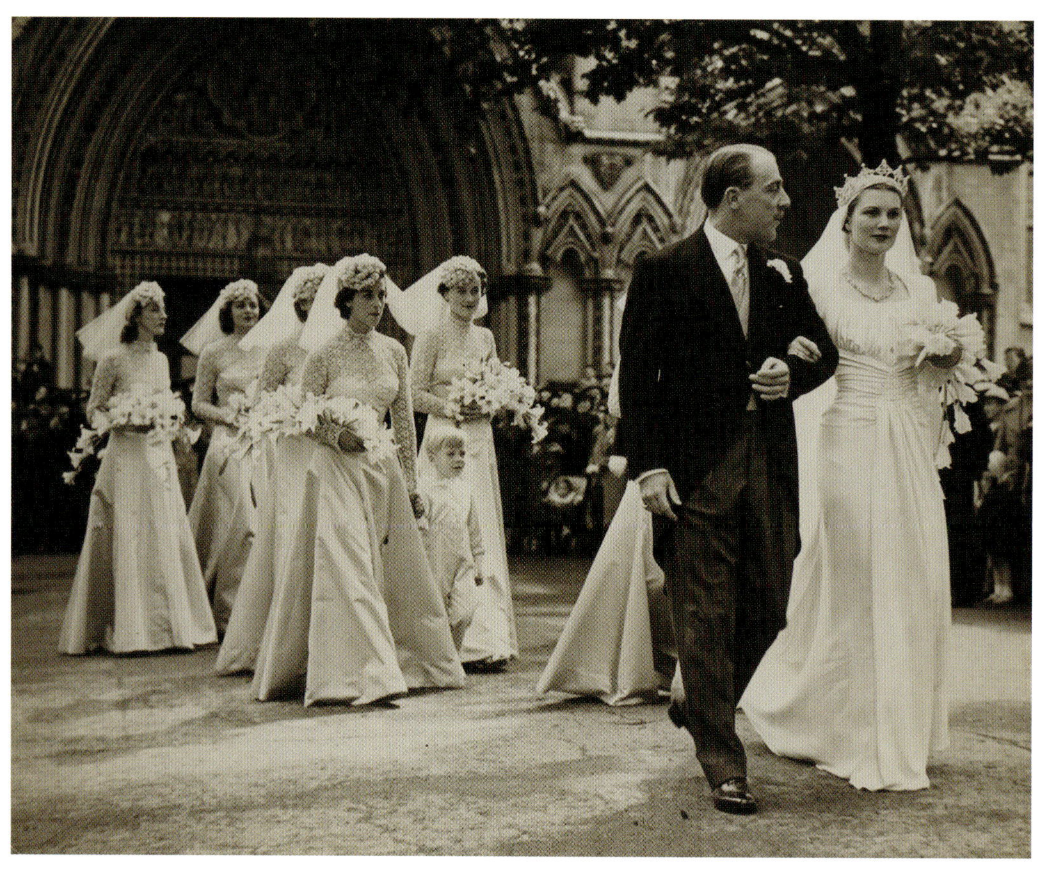

Fig. 5 *Viscount and Viscountess Cowdray with their Bridesmaids and Page Boy*, 19 July 1939
Unknown photographer
Gelatin silver print, 241 × 292mm
National Portrait Gallery, London

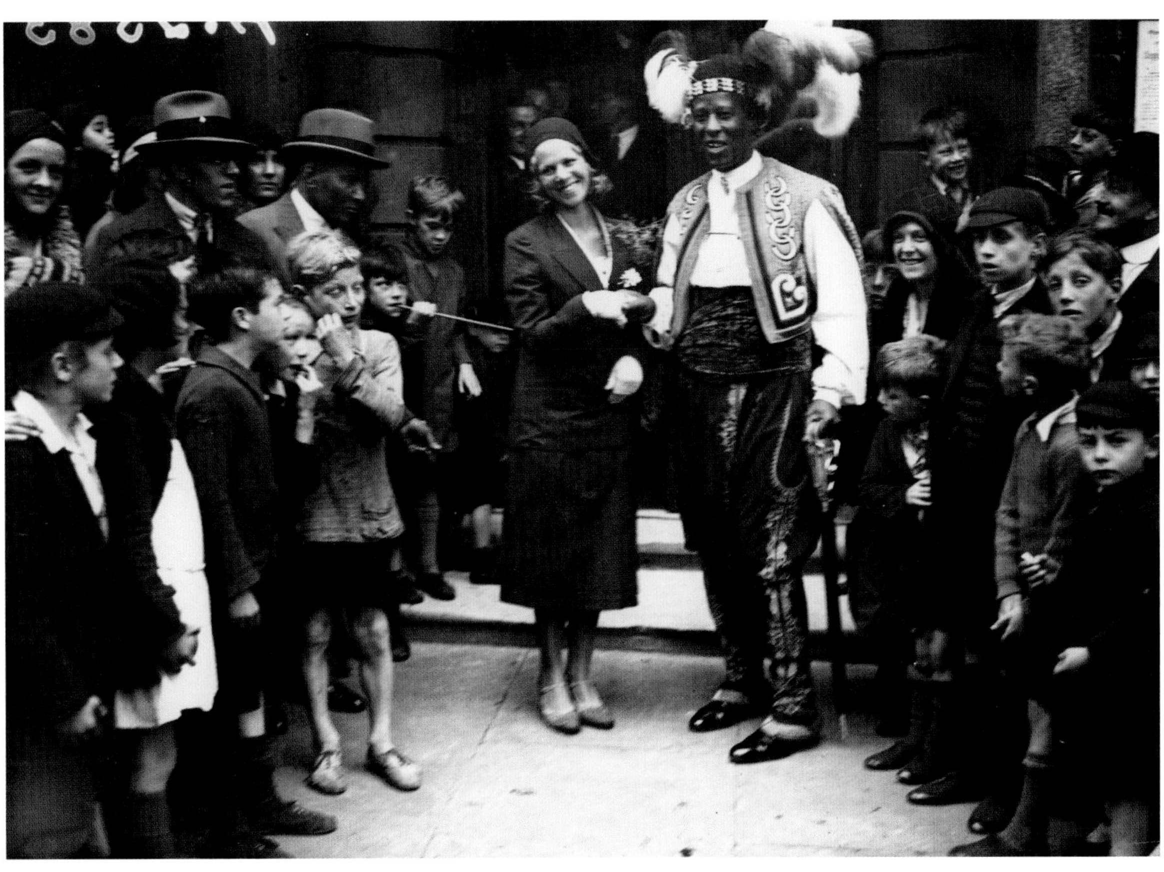

Fig.6 *The Wedding of Nellie Adkins and Ras Prince Monolulu (Peter Carl MacKay)*, George Woodbine, for *The Daily Herald*, 21 August 1931
Modern gelatin silver print, 140 × 192mm
National Portrait Gallery, London

RAB MACGIBBON

David Garrick & Eva Maria Garrick

When David and Eva Maria Garrick sat for a double portrait by their friend Sir Joshua Reynolds, they had been married for twenty-four years and the warmth and ease of their partnership is evident in the picture (fig.1). David Garrick was the actor-manager who transformed the British theatre, introducing a more natural and intuitive style of acting. Eva Maria Veigel, from Vienna, had been an internationally celebrated dancer. At first glance, this quiet, intimate, portrait appears to represent a wealthy gentleman and his wife, rather than two acclaimed performers. Indeed, as his success grew, David Garrick sought to elevate the status of the actor at a time when the profession was widely considered disreputable. In this respect, Garrick was not unimpeachable, having previously lived 'out of wedlock' with the actress Peg Woffington.

With Eva Maria, Garrick was able to use his substantial income as manager of the Drury Lane Theatre to cultivate an elegant lifestyle to match that of the gentry and aristocracy whose friendship they enjoyed. While marriage meant that Eva Maria was expected to retire from her professional life, and the desire for children remained unfulfilled, she appears to have found satisfaction in maintaining their elegant homes and hosting their wide circle of friends, including the artists Johan Zoffany and William Hogarth, both of whom painted portraits of the celebrity couple. Hogarth's portrait (fig.2) is especially telling, capturing the couple's delight and affection as Eva Maria pretends to snatch the quill out of her husband's hand as he is absorbed in thought, writing a prologue to Samuel Foote's comedy *Taste*.

They met in 1746 when they were both enjoying exceptional professional success. David Garrick had performed to packed houses at Covent Garden

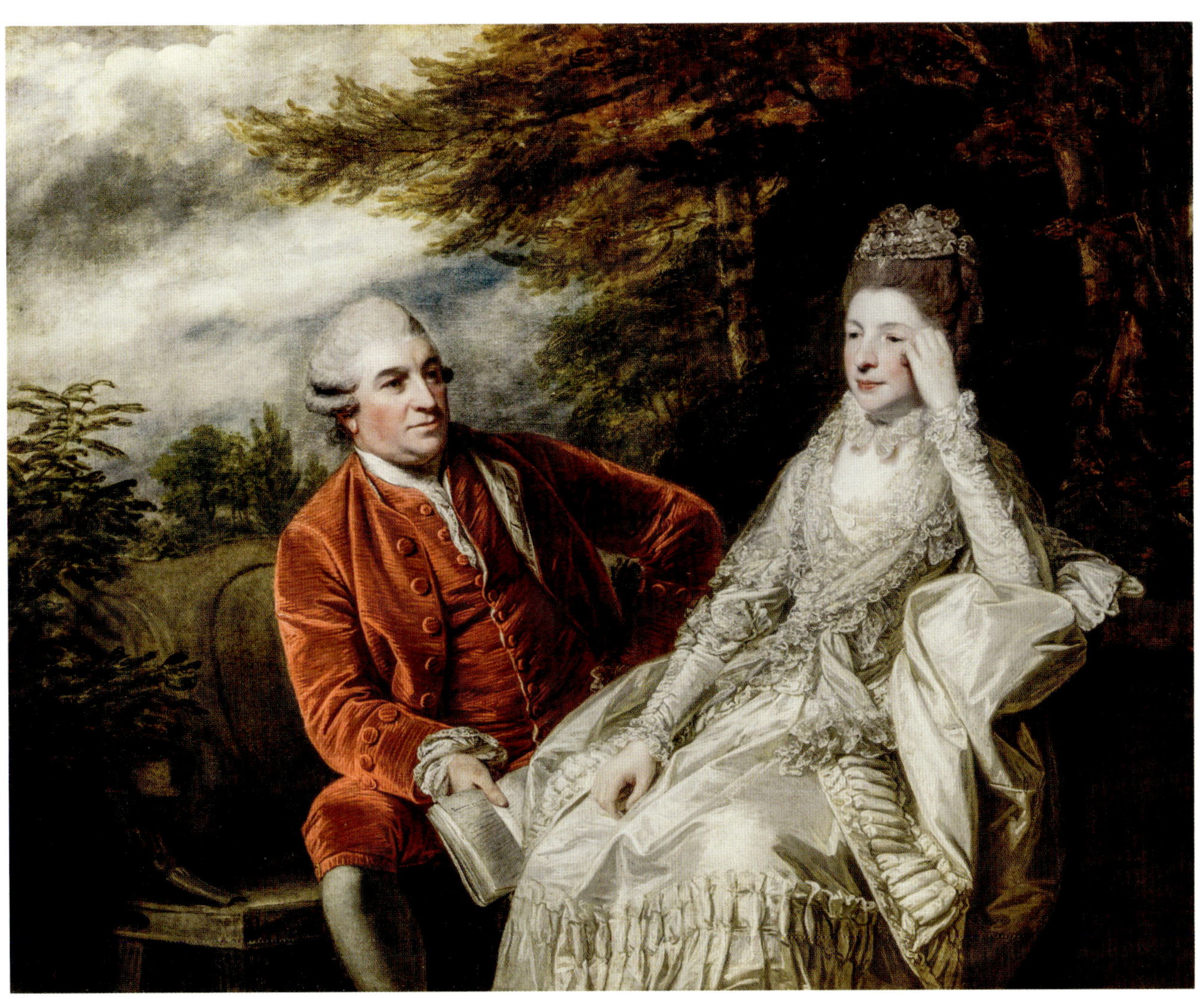

Fig.1 *David Garrick and Eva Maria Garrick*, 1772–3
Sir Joshua Reynolds
Oil on canvas, 1403 × 1699mm
National Portrait Gallery, London

and had just signed up to co-manage the Drury Lane Theatre. Eva Maria, professionally known as 'Violette', had made her debut at the King's Theatre, where the Prince of Wales had apparently changed seats for a better view of her performance. Socially, Eva Maria was considered to be more elevated than most other dancers, having enjoyed the patronage of Viennese nobility and spent time at court. As with Garrick, her charm and good taste earned her invitations to the finest homes in London and it was in this society that they first met.

Their fame ensured that details of the burgeoning romance were gleefully picked over by contemporary observers, including the diarist Horace Walpole who described a love-struck Garrick 'ogling and sighing' in Eva Maria's direction at the Duke of Richmond's fireworks party.[1] The Earl and Countess of Burlington acted as the dancer's chaperones in London and planned a more prestigious match for her with the Earl of Coventry, but Eva Maria was in love with David so the Burlingtons eventually gave their blessing to the marriage along with a substantial annuity.

Following their wedding in June 1749, they spent part of their honeymoon at the Burlingtons' villa, Chiswick House. Garrick described his wife's exceptional qualities in verse:

A gaiety with innocence
A soft address, with manly sense,
Ravishing manners, void of art
A cheerful, firm, yet feeling heart,
Beauty, that charms all public gaze,
And humble amid pomp and praise.[2]

When David died in 1779, Eva Maria justified her quiet form of grief: 'Groans and complaints are very well for those who are to mourn but a little while, but a sorrow which is to last for life will not be violent and romantic.'[3]

Fig.2 *David Garrick with his Wife Eva Maria*, c.1757–64
William Hogarth
Oil on canvas, 1327 × 1042mm
The Royal Collection / HM Queen Elizabeth II

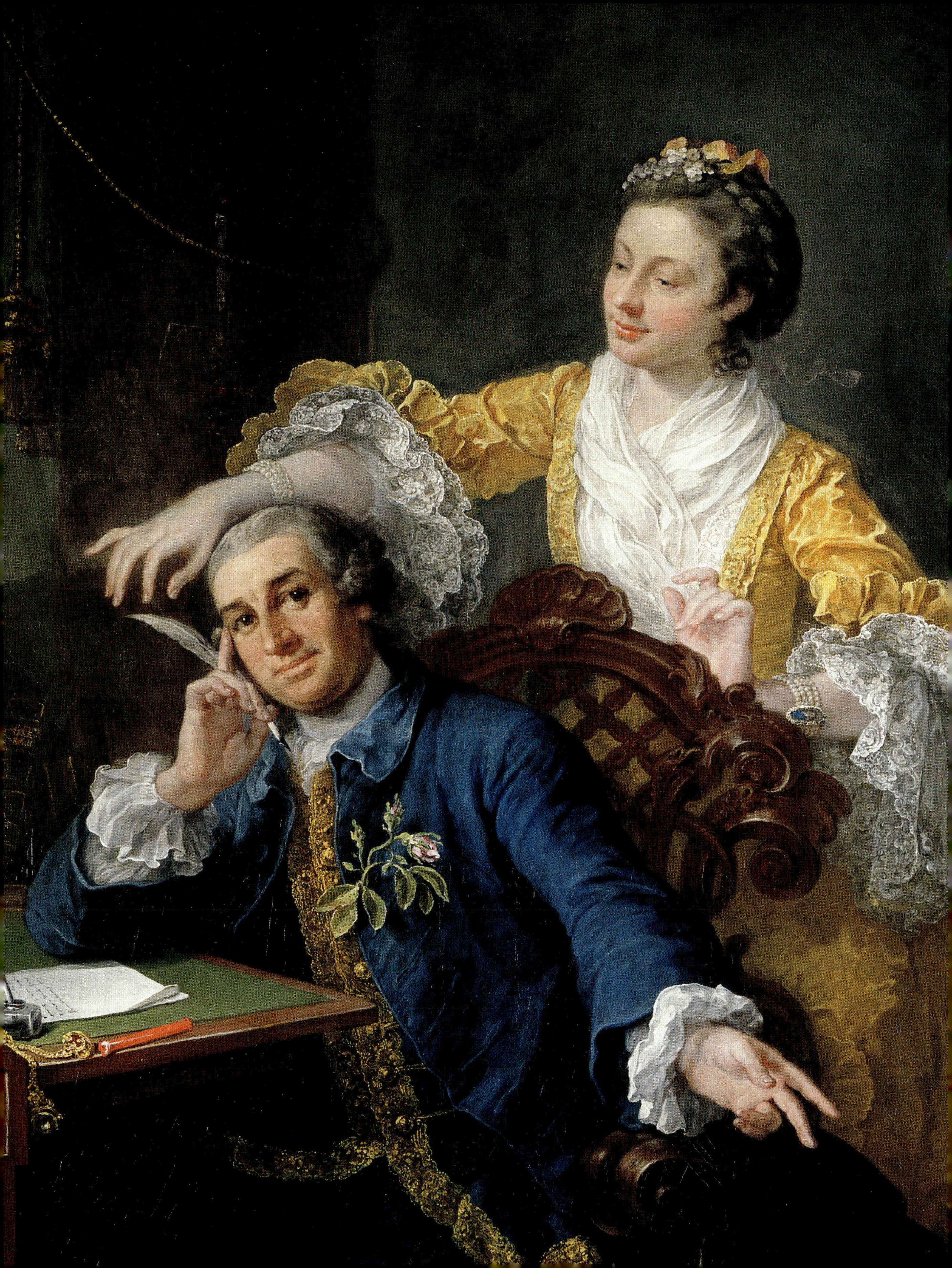

PETER FUNNELL

DAME MILLICENT GARRETT FAWCETT & HENRY FAWCETT

The relationship of the radical Victorian politician, Henry Fawcett, and the campaigner for women's suffrage, Millicent Garrett Fawcett, has been described as 'one of the most celebrated marital partnerships of the era'.[1] Fawcett had been blinded in a shooting accident in 1858 leading him to give up his ambitions for a legal career and turn to academia and politics: he published his *Manual of Political Economy* in 1863 and became Professor of Political Economy at Cambridge University in the same year. Millicent Garrett was born in Aldeburgh, Suffolk in 1847 and, from her teenage years, became involved in women's emancipation and was to be a leading pioneer of the women's suffrage movement in the nineteenth and early twentieth centuries. She and Henry married in 1867. She assisted Fawcett to overcome his blindness in the conduct of his public affairs, acting as his guide and secretary (his 'eyes and hands'), and this is how she is portrayed in Ford Madox Brown's painting (fig.1). The artist, a close associate of the Pre-Raphaelite Brotherhood, wrote of the way the portrait 'might be made of them full of character and pathos'.[2] Shared beliefs and a marriage in which they contributed equally to each other's work shine through in contemporary accounts. As Fawcett's great friend and Cambridge contemporary Leslie Stephen wrote, 'their alliance implied the agreement of independent minds, not the relation of teacher and disciple'.[3]

The Fawcetts represent a particular intellectual and political strand in Victorian Britain. They were radical Liberals, followers of the leading political thinker of the previous generation, John Stuart Mill, and advocates of progressive ideas across politics and society, who were emphatically advocating greater political emancipation and flirting with republicanism. Henry developed a

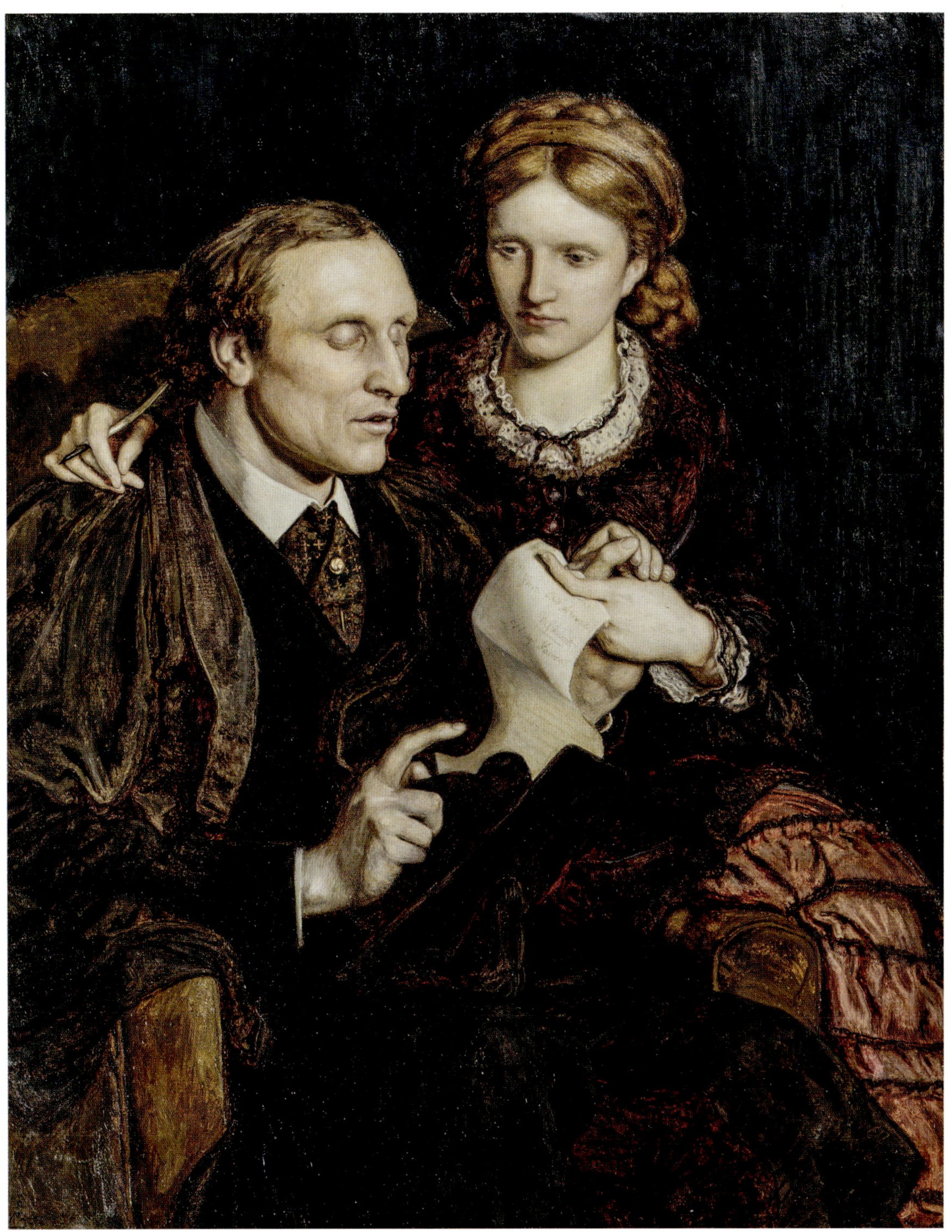

Fig.1 *Henry and Dame Millicent Garrett Fawcett*, 1872
Ford Madox Brown
Oil on canvas, 1086 × 838mm
National Portrait Gallery, London

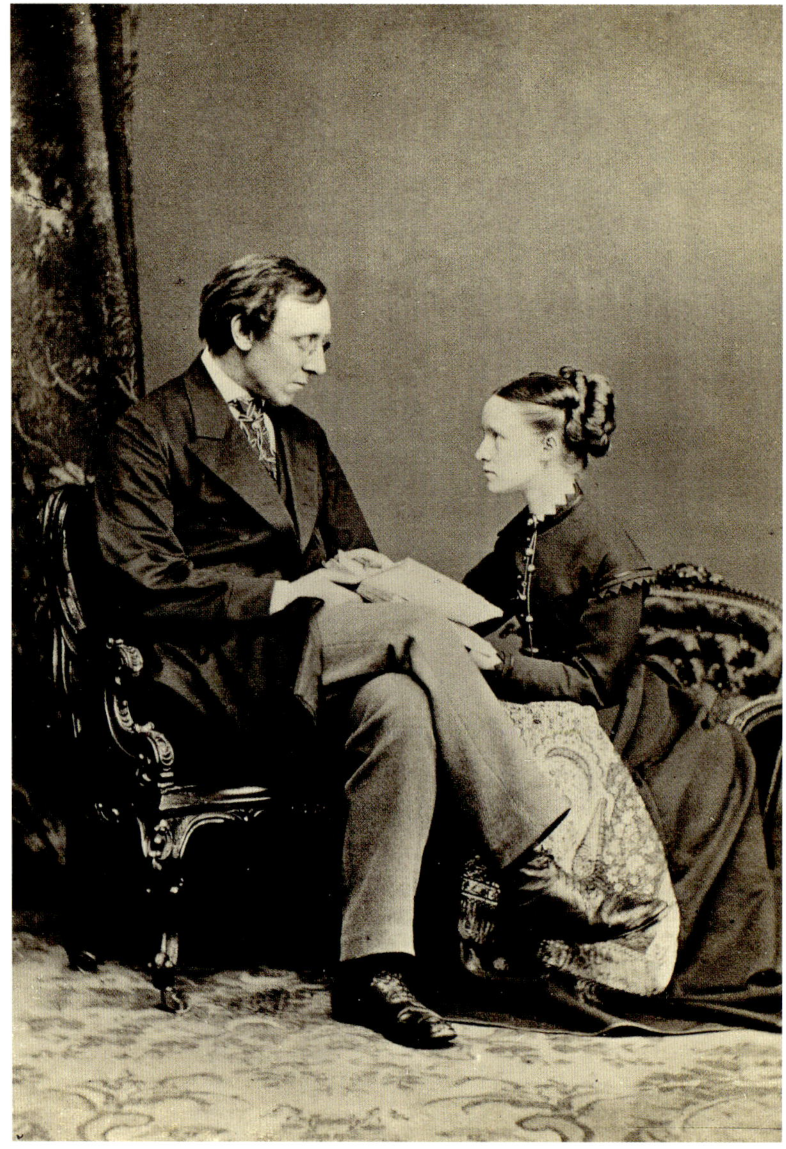

Fig.2 *Millicent Garrett Fawcett with Henry Fawcett, c.*1880
Unknown photographer
Photograph, 102 × 153mm
The Women's Library, LSE, London

special interest in issues of poverty and labour in Victorian society and became an important champion of workers' rights and ally of the developing trades union movement. He was also influenced by Mill's promotion of the rights of women and this drew him into the circle of feminist thinkers with whom Millicent and her sisters were also associated in the 1850s. Millicent had always protested her beliefs in this regard: 'I cannot say I *became* a suffragist. I always was one, from the time I was old enough to think about all the principles of Representative Government.'[4]

Henry and Millicent met at a party in London in May 1865 and it is said that Fawcett was impressed by hearing her expressing her dismay at the assassination of President Lincoln. Henry became a Member of Parliament in July 1865, firstly for Brighton and then for Hackney, East London, and the couple had homes in both Cambridge and London. Women's emancipation became a key tenet of their shared beliefs leading to a rift for Henry with his trades union associates who were wary of support for women's role in the workplace. A further concern was the acceptance of women in higher education and the Fawcetts were largely instrumental in the establishment of Newnham College, Cambridge in 1871. Their close intellectual and political association found expression in a book of 1872 entitled *Essays and Lectures on Social and Political Subjects*. Eight of the fourteen articles were by Millicent who also edited the volume. Henry's parliamentary career led to his becoming postmaster-general in William Ewart Gladstone's second administration in May 1880, but his strongly held independent views put him at odds with Gladstone and the Liberal political establishment. He died on 6 November 1884. Millicent lived on until 1929, continuing her campaign for women's suffrage and eventually witnessing the winning of limited voting rights for women in 1918. Although she, like Henry, has in the past been associated with what seemed to be outdated Victorian values in terms of social and sexual politics, her important role in the feminist movement is now acknowledged. She was honoured by a statue by the artist Gillian Wearing unveiled opposite Parliament in 2018 (fig.3).

Ford Madox Brown's portrait was commissioned by the Fawcetts' friend and fellow political radical, Sir Charles Dilke, probably on the initiative of one of the original founders of the Pre-Raphaelite Brotherhood and later art critic, Frederic George Stephens. Brown suggested the three-quarter-length format and, by February 1872, had made a highly finished chalk study. In July he discussed framing the picture with Dilke but requested the portrait be returned by Dilke in September since 'Mr Fawcett has not yet sent me his signature, to put on the paper along with *her's* as I intended in the picture.'[5] It shows Millicent seated on the arm of Henry's chair while he talks to her about a letter which he has apparently dictated and which she, a pen held in her right hand, has written. The letter is inscribed, as Brown had intended, with his sitters' signatures: *Your Ob[edien]t. Servants / MG Fawcett / Henry Fawcett.*

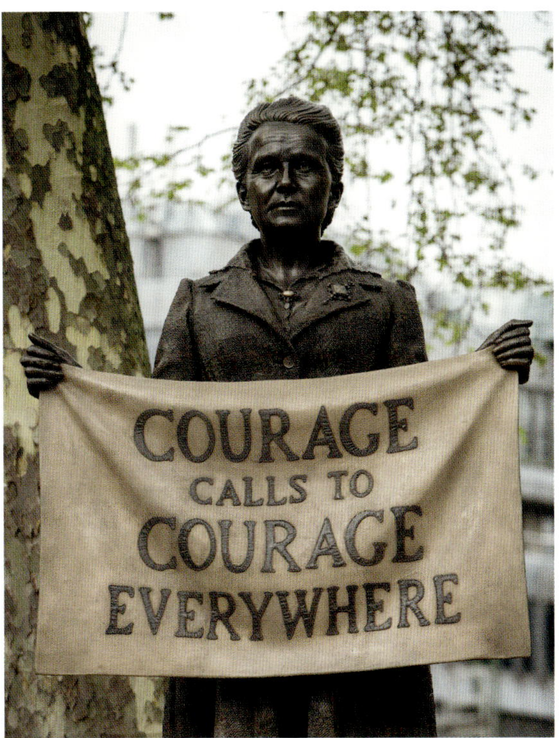

Fig.3 *Millicent Garrett Fawcett*, 2018
Gillian Wearing
Bronze sculpture, Parliament Square

SARAH MOULDEN

Charles Shannon & Charles Ricketts

These companion paintings (figs 2 and 3) were made in 1897 and 1898 respectively by the artist Charles Shannon. One, a self-portrait, shows a clean-shaven Shannon tilting his head to meet our gaze. The other presents a profile view of his lifelong partner, the artist Charles Ricketts, bearded and enveloped in a black cape. Each man is shown in the same stark golden-beige interior and on canvases of a similar size surrounded by matching frames, calling to mind the Victorian painter Jacques-Emile Blanche's description of the sitters as 'two inseparables'.[1]

Shannon and Ricketts steadfastly refused to define their relationship. At a time when same-sex love was strictly prohibited by law, 'coming out' was practically impossible. Yet we can detect a notable queerness to their shared life which signals a particularly close male bond, if not a homosexual relationship. The love story of Shannon and Ricketts is thus one of an affectionate, mutually-supportive, inseparable partnership. For almost fifty years, that inseparability was played out through their home life, their circle of friends, shared cultural pursuits, personal writings and, as suggested here, this pair of portraits.

The two artists met on Ricketts' sixteenth birthday in 1882 when they were beginning their artistic training at the City and Guilds Art School in Kennington, south London. Within four years, they were living together in rented rooms near the school and had soon planned for Ricketts to be the sole breadwinner while Shannon devoted himself to painting. Mutual financial support was a feature of their partnership with Shannon later doing the same for Ricketts. Both went on to become professional artists, with Shannon specialising in lithography and painting and Ricketts in illustration, book design and printmaking.

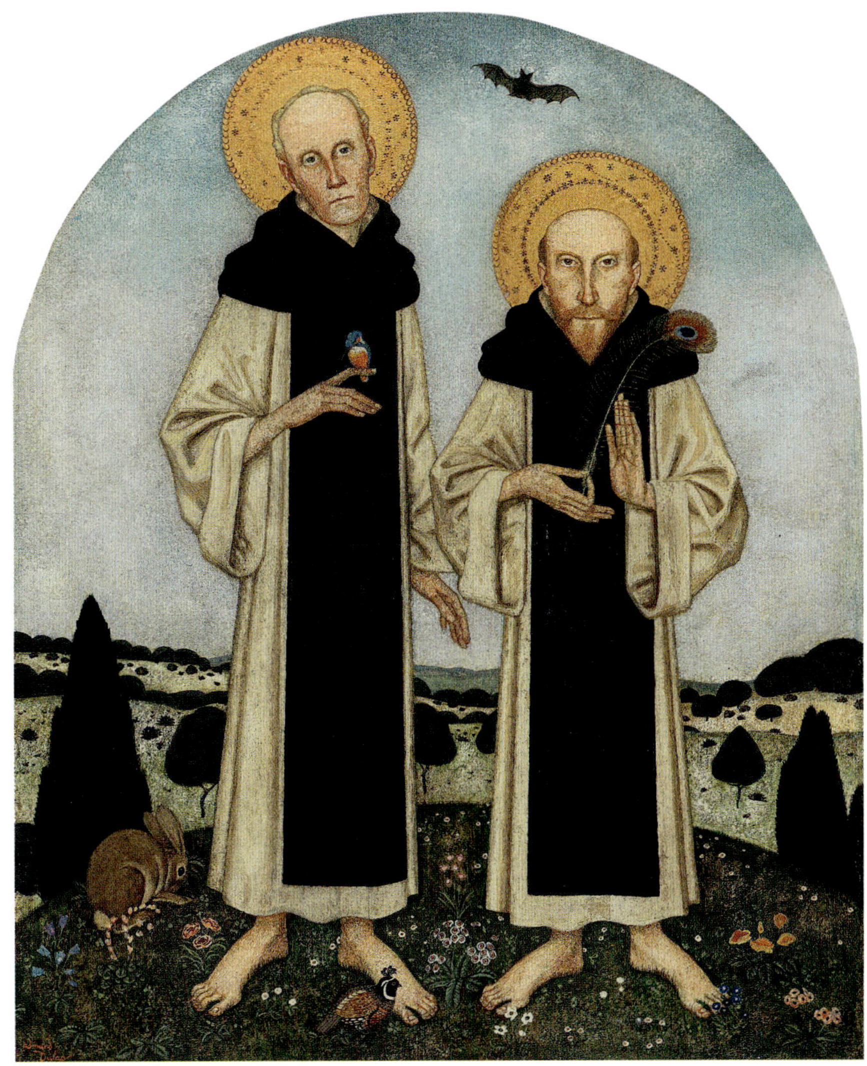

Fig.1 ***Charles Shannon and Charles Ricketts as Medieval Saints*, 1920**
Edmund Dulac
Tempera on linen, 387 × 305mm
The Fitzwilliam Museum, Cambridge

Over the course of their lives, Shannon and Ricketts co-habited in various homes in London and Kent, often sharing a bedroom. There they entertained a bohemian network of liberal friends and acquaintances, including the homosexual playwright Oscar Wilde, the poet John Addington Symonds, who was an advocate of male love, and the queer aunt-and-niece couple Katherine Bradley and Edith Cooper who, as authors, went by the joint pseudonym 'Michael Field'. These artistic and literary types gathered for conversation in Shannon and Ricketts' carefully composed domestic spaces, their magnificent art collection claiming pride of place. Indeed, the pair's shared passion for interior design and collecting fine and decorative arts was one of the foundations of the relationship. At home, they arranged their collection in ways that spoke to a particular *fin de siècle*

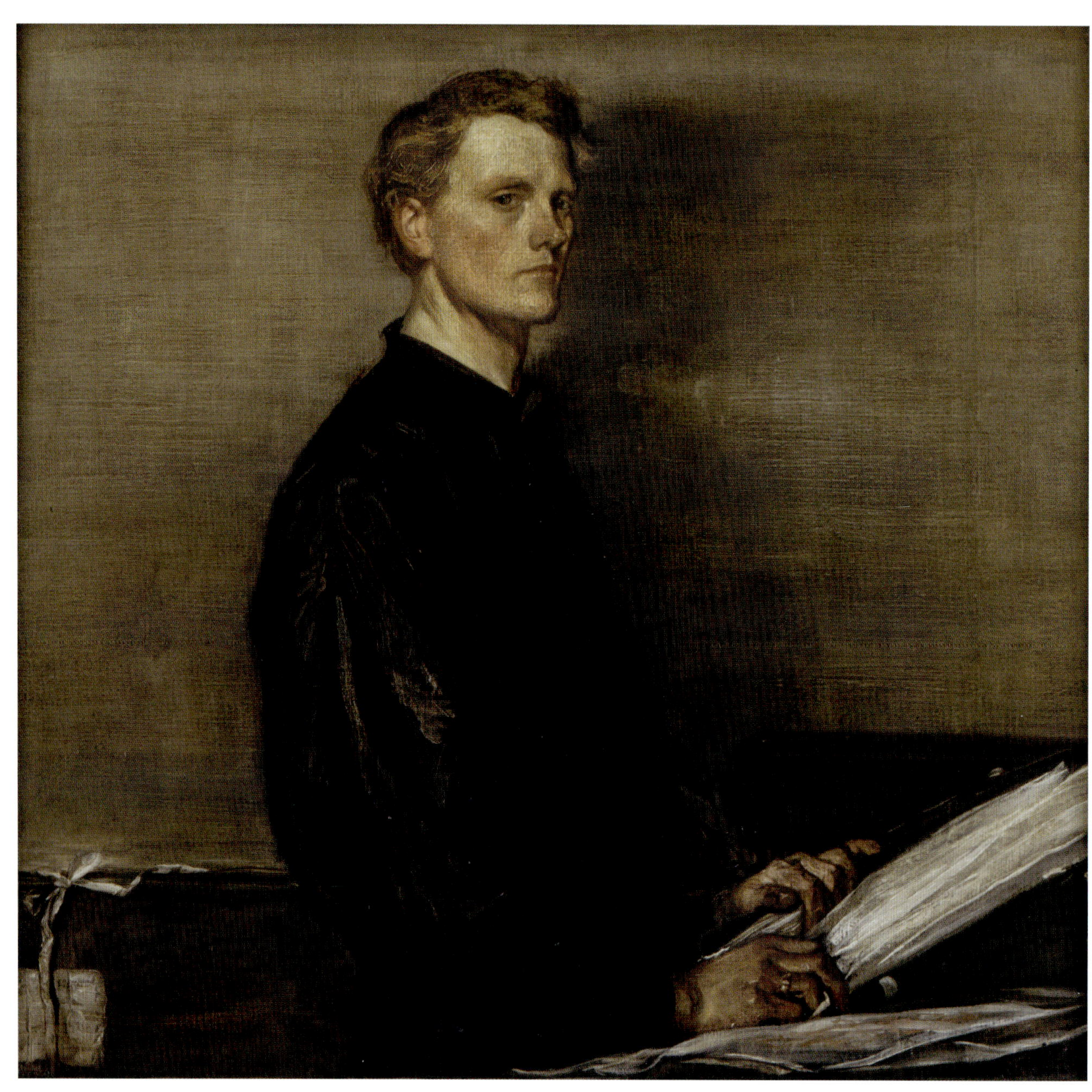

Fig.2 *Self-Portrait*, 1897
Charles Shannon
Oil on canvas, 942 × 989mm
National Portrait Gallery, London

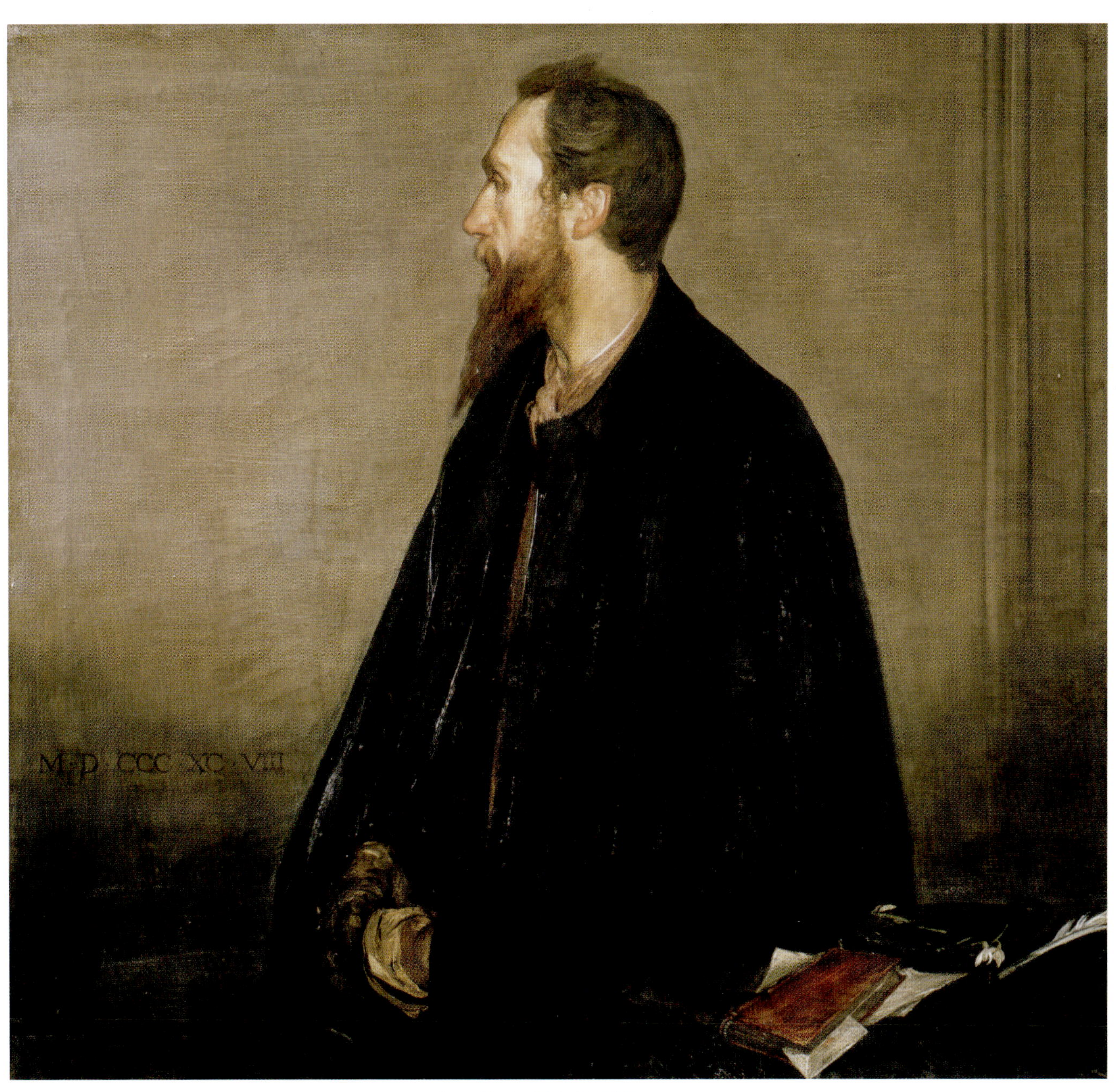

Fig.3 *Charles Ricketts*, 1898
Charles Shannon
Oil on canvas, 972 × 1006mm
National Portrait Gallery, London

aestheticism, characterised by the primacy of beauty, an interest in the art of the past and, as was recognised at the time, a queer sensibility.

The artwork Shannon and Ricketts made also spoke to these aesthetic concerns and is seen in these companion portraits. The sober colours and square format evoke the paintings of Whistler who championed the aesthetic mantra 'Art for Art's Sake'. Yet Shannon's main reference is the Renaissance. The poses, particularly Ricketts' profile stance, and the inclusion of dark, heavy garments recall Titian's portraiture which the two artists admired. Ricketts was pleased for Shannon to exhibit his portrait at the New English Art Club in 1898 and, in a letter to 'Michael Field', confirmed its tacit associations with the past: 'I am turning away from the 20th century to think only of the 15th.'[2] This love of the early Renaissance was captured, even parodied, in Edmund Dulac's portrait of the two men (fig.1). Renaissance references are also found in Shannon's inclusion of a black-glossed Castulo cup from the couple's collection. Beyond nodding to the antique, the cup stands in for their collection, the pursuit that was so integral to Shannon and Ricketts' shared life.

So when Shannon announced that he was thinking about marrying one of his female models, Ricketts' dismay was expressed (at least outwardly in writing) through reference to their joint passion, bemoaning to 'Michael Field' 'what would become of the collection?'[3] Yet Shannon never did marry and the two men grew old together, with the last years largely consumed by Ricketts nursing Shannon following a fall in 1929.

These paintings show Shannon and Ricketts over thirty years earlier in the prime of their lives. Ricketts appears to look longingly towards Shannon and, while not returning his gaze, Shannon's body is turned towards the left picture edge and thus towards his partner. These compositional decisions create a strong visual connection between the sitters, only intensified by their separation from each other by dint of their format and frames.

Imagine these divisions removed and we arrive at an arrangement similar to that taken by the photographer George Charles Beresford five years later (fig.4) on the day after Ricketts' thirty-seventh birthday. It speaks to the two men's easy affection for one another with Shannon staring blankly outwards and a heavy-lidded Ricketts turned dotingly towards him. Beresford draws attention to their heads and the slight overlap of their shoulders with an almost heart-shaped smudge on the glass-plate negative, indicating the area on which he would wish to focus when it came to retouching. Applied with a brush, the smudge serves to unify the sitters, quite literally highlighting their inseparability. For Shannon and Ricketts, love at the turn of the twentieth century could be formulated less through conspicuous and binary sexual identifications than through nuanced and fluid bonds of belonging.

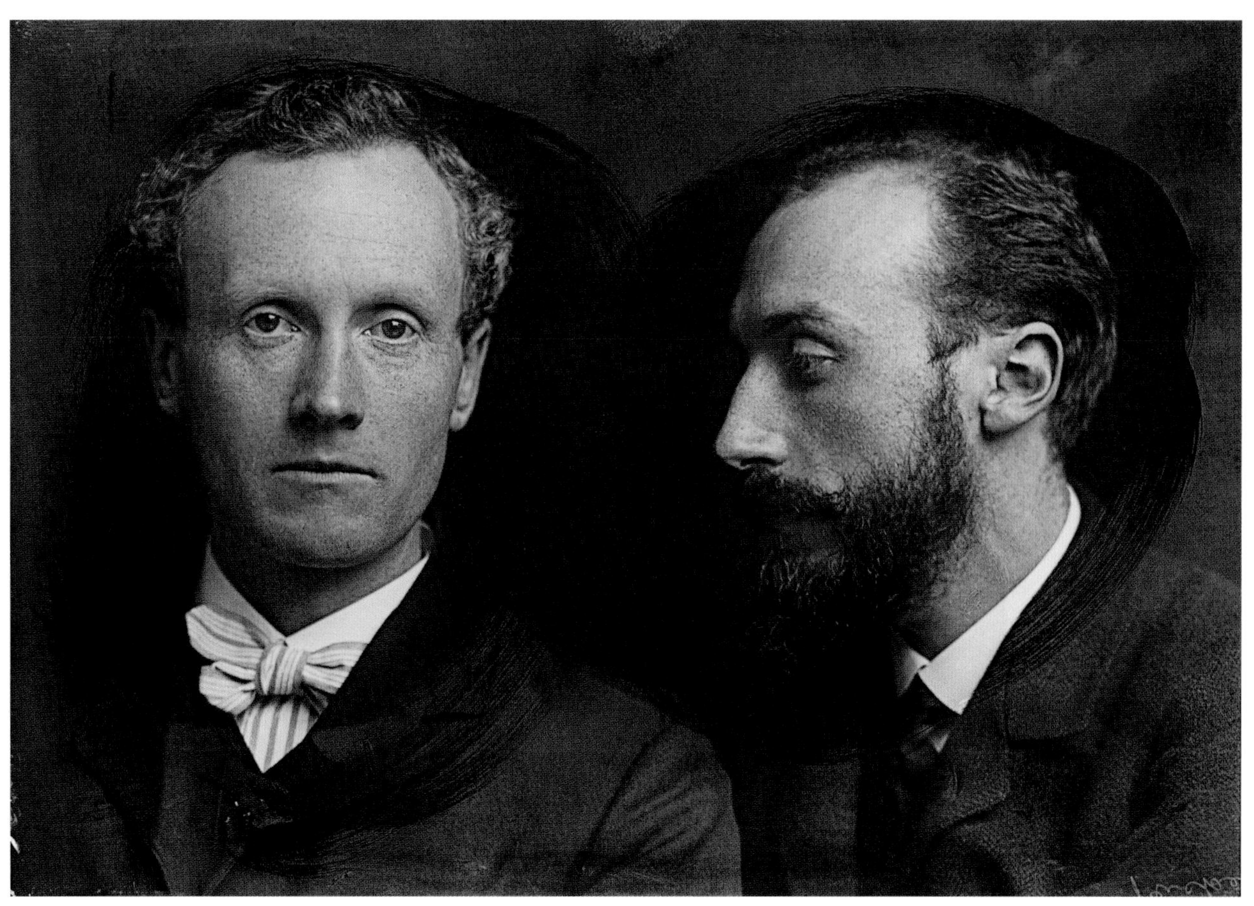

Fig.4 *Charles Shannon and Charles Ricketts*, 13 October 1903
George Charles Beresford
Half-plate glass negative, 113 × 157mm
National Portrait Gallery, London

HELENA CUSS

John Maynard Keynes & Lydia Lopokova

The perceived unlikeliness of a great love story between the most brilliant economist and the greatest comic ballerina of the twentieth-century gave rise to a popular anonymous ditty upon their marriage in 1925:

> What a marriage of beauty and brains
> The fair Lopokova and John Maynard Keynes.

This incongruity was furthered by the fact that Maynard Keynes, until he fell in love with Lydia Lopokova, appeared to be a confirmed homosexual as well as a lover of the bachelor lifestyle. His friends in the infamously snobbish Bloomsbury Group were both confused and horrified by his devotion to a woman whom they considered beneath his intellectual standing. Indeed, the first time Keynes saw Lopokova on the stage in 1918 as part of Serge Diaghilev's Ballet Russes he declared her a 'poor' dancer, an unpromising start for what would become a relationship of enduring affection, loyalty and great happiness.[1]

Maynard and Lydia met for the second time in 1921. The intervening years between their first and second meetings in London were as turbulent for the ballerina as they had been comfortable for the economist. In 1916 Lydia had married Rudolf Barocchi, Diaghilev's business manager. In July 1919, as the Ballet Russes was nearing the end of another run in London she disappeared abruptly, not resurfacing in public until February 1921, when she appeared on the stage in New York. Although unexplained at the time, it's now known that Lydia had discovered that Barocchi was already married.

In May 1921, Keynes wrote to his friend Vanessa Bell, 'Loppy came to lunch last Sunday, and I again fell very much in love with her. She seems to me

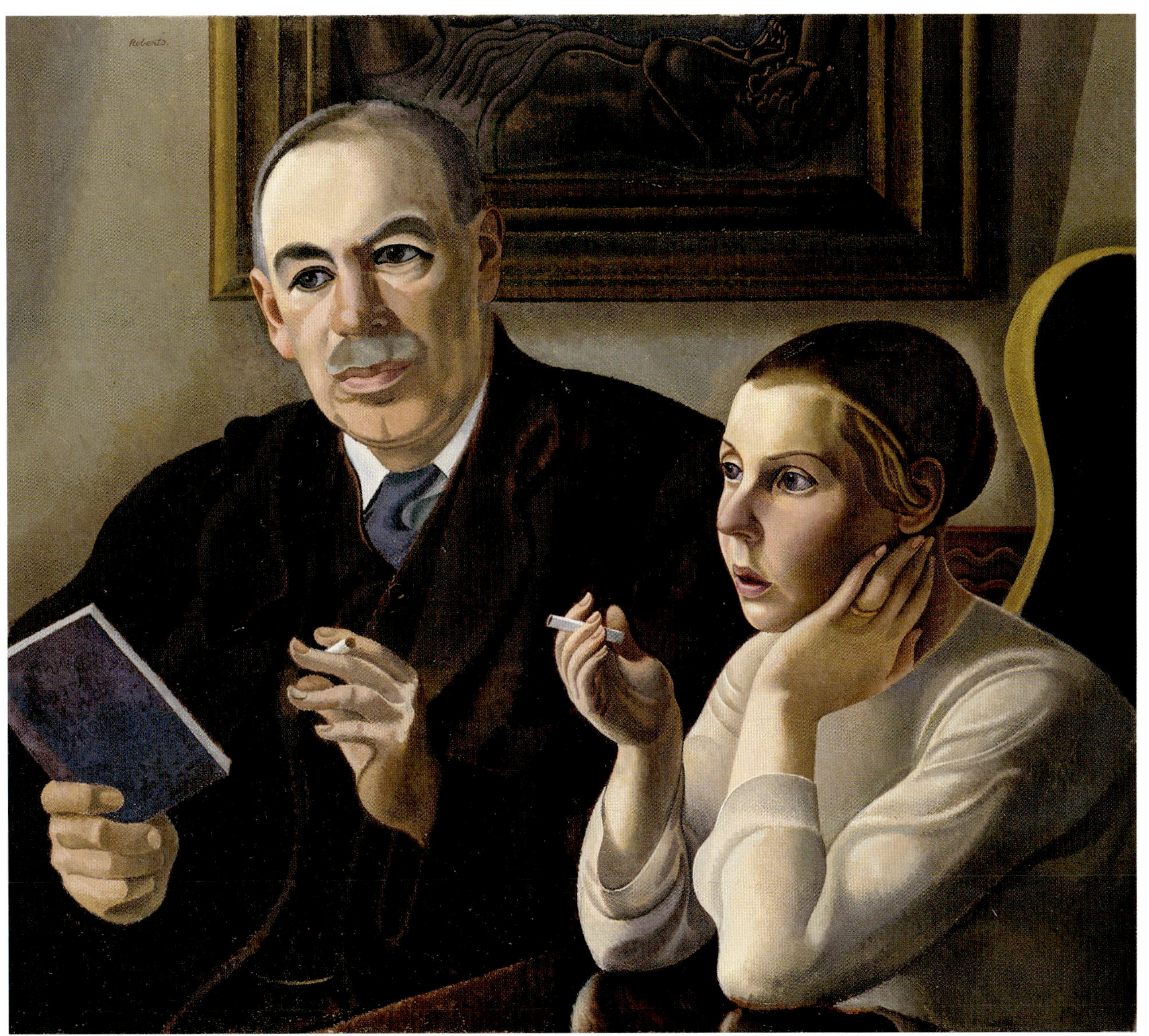

Fig.1 *John Maynard Keynes, Baron Keynes and Lydia Lopokova*, 1932
William Roberts
Oil on canvas, 740 × 810mm
National Portrait Gallery, London

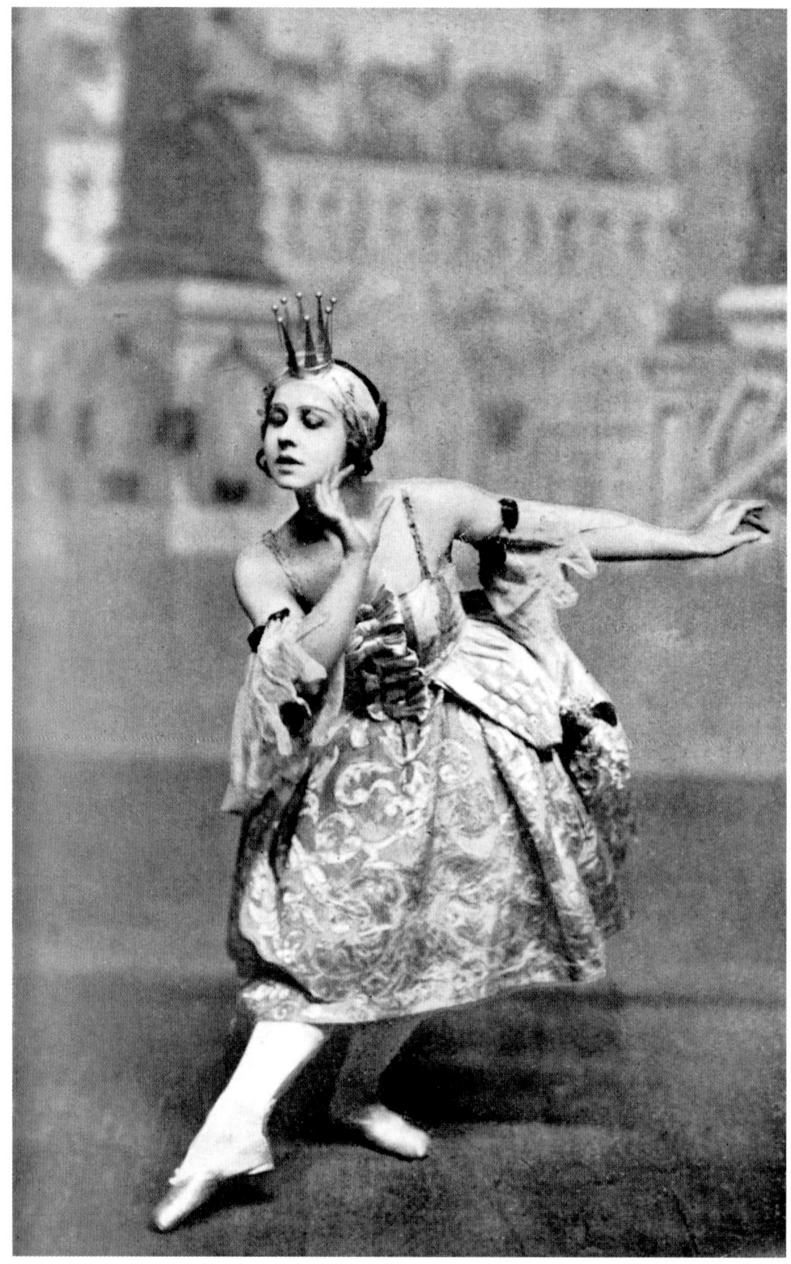

Fig.2 *Lydia Lopokova in the Sleeping Princess by Tchaikovsky*, 1921
Unknown photographer

perfect in every way. One of her new charms is the most knowing and judicious use of English words.'[2] From here their affair progressed rapidly, alarming Keynes himself with the force of his passion for Lydia. His Bloomsbury friends, meanwhile, advised that the dancer was not his intellectual match, and worthy only of being a mistress. Keynes could not be deterred. Throughout the 1921 autumn season he sat in the stalls night after night watching Diaghilev's production of *The Sleeping Princess*, drawn principally to Lydia's Lilac Fairy (fig.2).

The early letters between the couple reveal their burgeoning romance from 1922 to 1925. They exhibit her idiosyncratic 'Lydian English' – a term coined by Maynard and reflective of the affection she inspired. She often signed off her letters with phrases such as 'I gobble you', sending him 'primitive love kisses' or 'boundless caresses'.[3] Maynard, for his part, demonstrated his feeling for her by adopting her own brand of English, on one occasion writing, 'I kiss you very hard (that is not English – I have translated it from the Russian).' Nicknames proliferated the pages, also usually from Russian, such as 'Pupsik', 'Lydochka' and 'Lady Talky'.[4] As well as infusing her letters with love, Lydia was careful to flatter Maynard's immense intellect and self-importance – in which she believed totally – and made great efforts to immerse herself in his work. Her lively intelligence, much commented upon outside Maynard's Bloomsbury set, was intuitive rather than trained; in fact, it aligned with Keynes' own creative approach to economics and sustained their relationship for many years to come.

The couple married in August 1925. With Lydia at his side, Keynes produced much of his best work. Chief among these was *A Treatise on Money* (1930), and his magnum opus *The General Theory of Employment, Interest and Money* (1936) which would shape the economic policies of Western democracies for the next several decades. He also made significant contributions to the arts. Among many other endowments and contributions, in 1925 he co-founded the London Artists' Association to provide financial assistance to artists, which from 1927 included William Roberts, an artist whom Maynard greatly admired. The double portrait of Maynard and Lydia (fig.1) was commissioned from Roberts in the early 1930s, and shows them smoking companionably – then an indication of an emancipated lifestyle. The sculptural solidity of the figures and their compactness within the composition conveys the deep intimacy and comfort of the relationship between these two forceful personalities.

The domestic bliss which the couple created for themselves, walking their dogs across the Sussex Downs, playing tennis or sunbathing naked in the courtyard, was marred only by their inability to have children, which they had both longed for. They devoted their lives to one another, and when Maynard suffered an acute coronary artery thrombosis in 1937, Lydia gave up her own career to nurse him in order that he might continue with his. When Maynard died in 1946, the words of ballet choreographer Frederick Ashton were perhaps the most fitting tribute to Lydia:

> You will go down in history as the most devoted wife a great man could have had. I always thought that it was through your will, devotion and care that Maynard was spared to do the great work that he did, for your vigil was incessant both on his pleasure and his work.[5]

Lydia never remarried, and lived out the rest of her days in quiet seclusion until her own death in 1981.

LUCY DAHLSEN

Carol, Lady Djanogly & Sir Harry Djanogly

The British industrialist Sir Harry Djanogly and his late wife, Lady Carol Djanogly, who married in March 1964, have been active philanthropists since the 1970s. Most noted for their invaluable support of the arts, the British national institutions they have supported together include Tate, the Victoria and Albert Museum, the Royal Academy of Arts, the British Museum, the National Gallery and the National Portrait Gallery. They have also given important support to the education and health sectors. In Nottingham, they founded the Djanogly Learning Trust, which has been responsible for the education of some 6,000 students in Nottingham, as well as funding the Sir Harry and Lady Djanogly Learning Resource Centre and Nottingham Lakeside Arts at the University of Nottingham.

In 2014 the couple were jointly awarded the Prince of Wales Medal for Arts Philanthropy. Alongside their philanthropic activity, the Djanoglys have been prolific art collectors, and have created one of the most extensive collections of British decorative art and works by L.S. Lowry in the United Kingdom.

The Djanoglys' joint love of the visual arts, collecting and their commitment to one another is documented in this double portrait made by the Dutch artist Wim Heldens in 2017 (fig.1). Painted from photographs taken by the artist, the portrait depicts the couple together in the living room of their London home. They are looking at a Lucian Freud drawing from their collection, titled *Pet Mouse*, which is being held up by their daughter, Simone and seen by us in a reflection in the mirror on the wall (fig.2). The artist explained:

> They have been amazing benefactors to the arts and I wanted to express that in a very

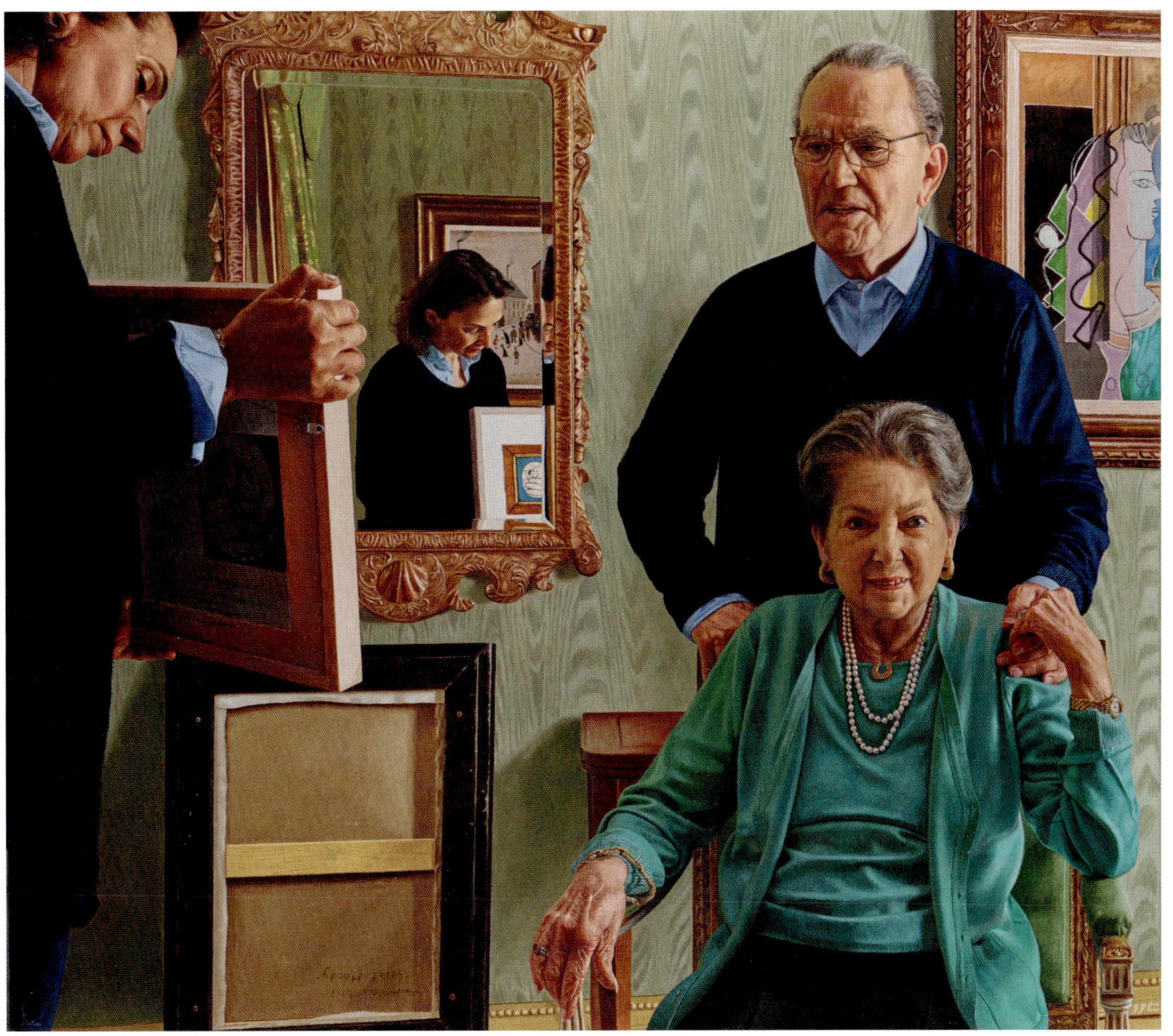

Fig.1 *Sir Harry Djanogly and Carol, Lady Djanogly (with their Daughter, Simone)*, 2017
Wim Heldens
Oil on canvas, 1250 × 1400mm
National Portrait Gallery, London

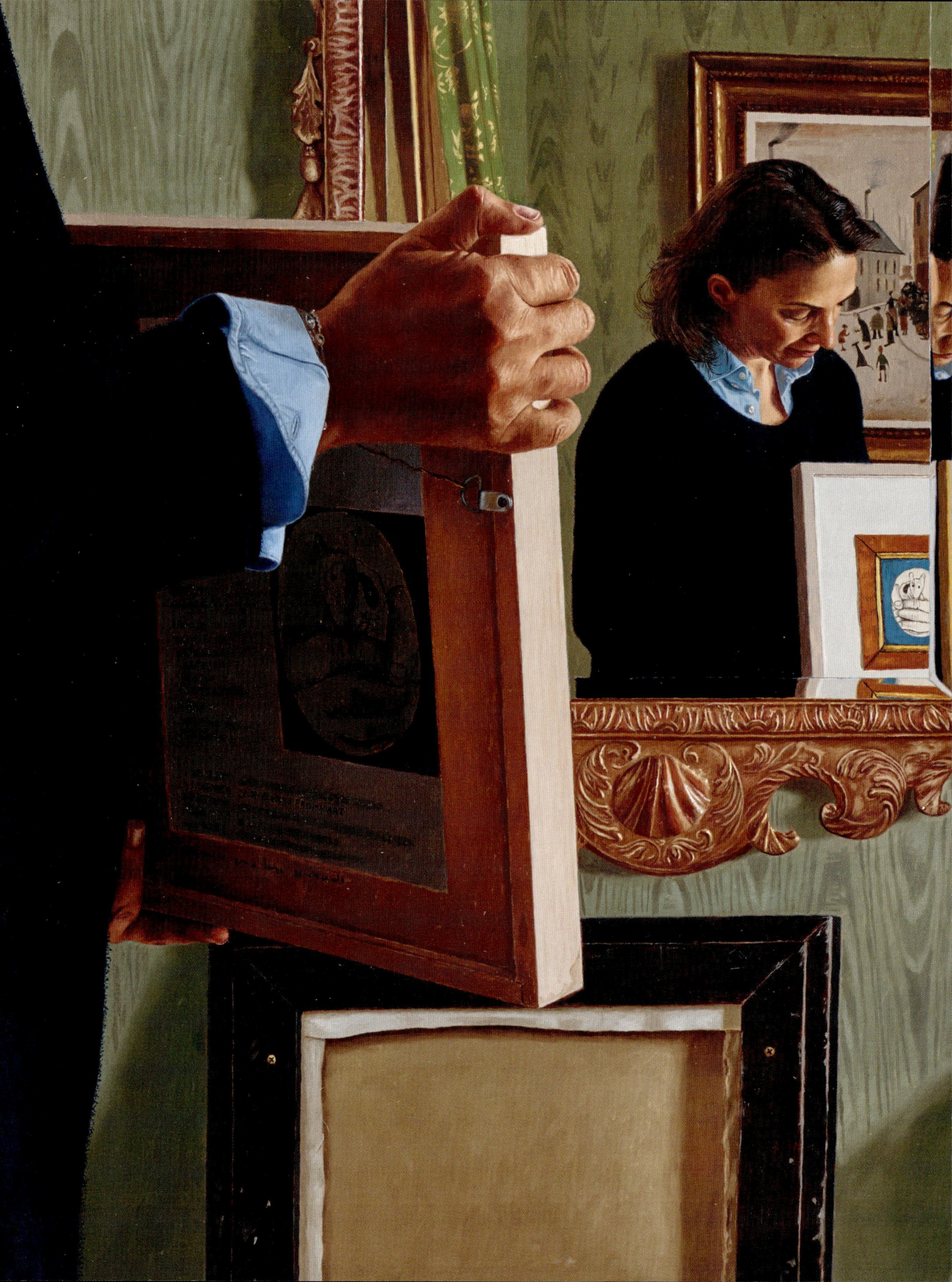

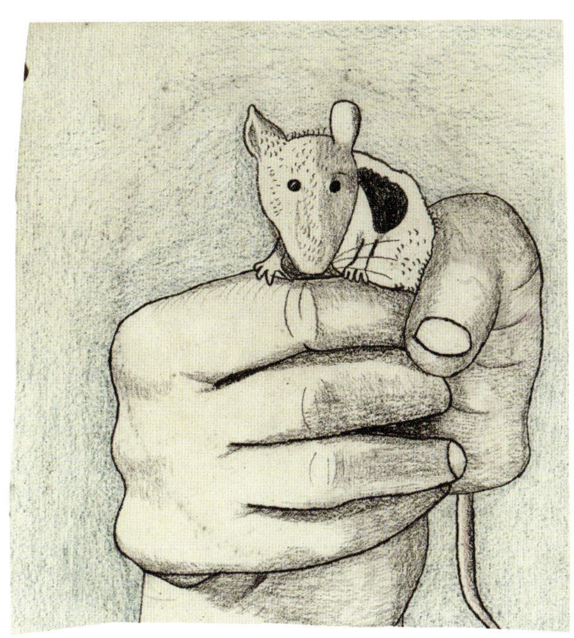

OPPOSITE
Sir Harry Djanogly and Carol, Lady Djanogly (detail), 2017
Wim Heldens
Oil on canvas, 1250 × 1400mm
National Portrait Gallery, London

ABOVE
Fig.2 *Pet Mouse, c.*1944
Lucian Freud
Pencil and crayon on paper, 89 × 70mm
Private Collection

simple way by depicting them as collectors who are looking at one of their works ... I thought that the person holding the art work should be someone who is close to them and [Sir Harry] immediately said, it should be my daughter. Their daughter then helped me to rearrange the room for the photo shoot.'

Of the Freud drawing that the couple are looking at in the painting, the artist explained:

'[Sir Harry] once gave the work to [Lady Carol] because her nickname was mouse. When I met them what I picked up was that they are very dedicated to each other, very devoted to each other and it was very sweet to see.'

The other artworks depicted in the painting include a painting by Picasso on the right of the composition and a painting by Lowry, also reflected in the mirror, both of which are in the Djanoglys' collection. Shortly after the painting was completed Lady Carol Djanogly's health declined and this is the final portrait that was made of the couple before she died in 2018. The painting, which was shown to Lady Carol in her final days, serves as a memorial to their lives together and their shared love of the arts.

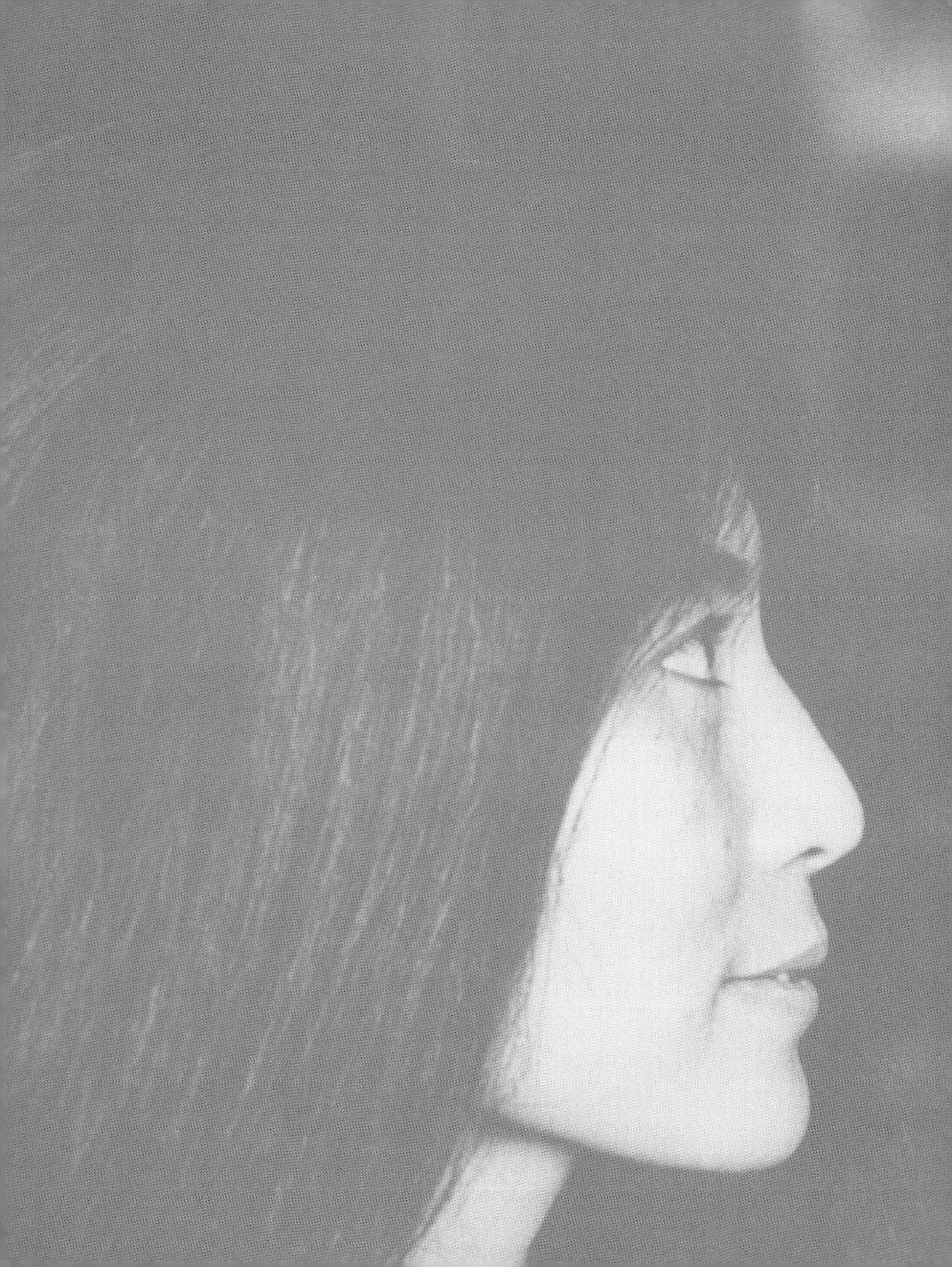

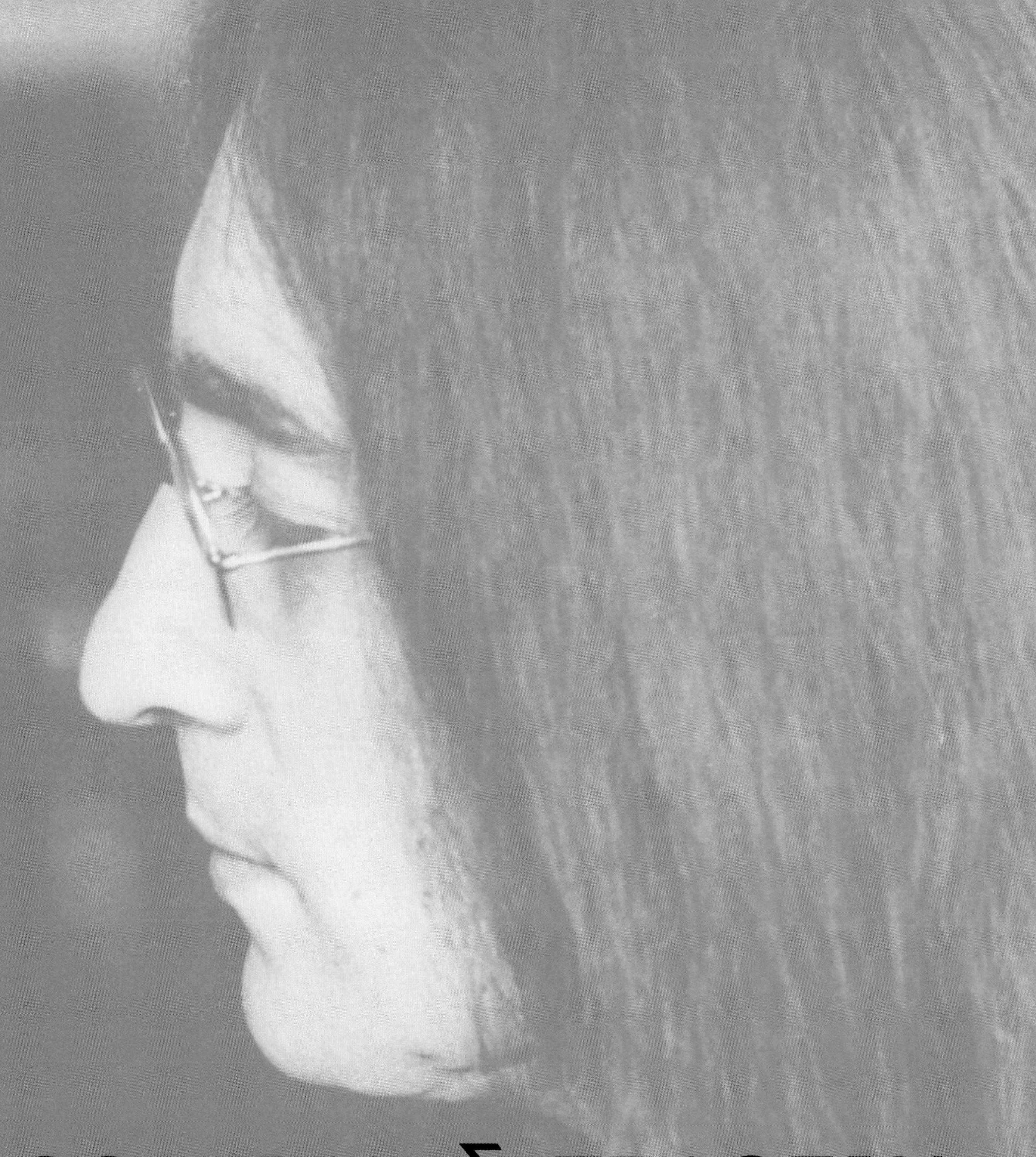

SCANDAL & TRAGEDY

LOUISE STEWART

SCANDAL & TRAGEDY

From Paris and Helen of Troy to Romeo and Juliet, tales of forbidden and tragic love have long captured the imagination. The consequences for the star-crossed lovers of these tales are often catastrophic and, in literature, these stories tend to end in the death of one or both of the protagonists. The power of love to convince people to transgress social expectations or take extreme risks is not confined to myth and fiction, and British history is strewn with real life love stories that scandalised society or ended in tragedy.

Because of the high stakes involved in royal marriage, there are many instances of scandal and tragedy in the true love stories that involve kings, queens and their heirs. In 1558, Elizabeth I came to the throne aged only twenty-five. She immediately appointed her childhood companion, Robert Dudley, as her Master of the Horse. This assured his intimate access to the queen and she insisted on his constant presence at court. Elizabeth was expected to marry a foreign prince, but in the early years of her reign her close relationship with Dudley was widely thought to be preventing a foreign match from taking place. Their intimacy provoked scandalous rumours throughout Europe in the 1560s: that Elizabeth had secretly borne Dudley's child, and he had murdered his wife in order to free himself for marriage to the queen. Ultimately, her understanding that marriage meant sacrificing at least some of her power and risking her life in childbirth seems to have convinced Elizabeth to remain unmarried. Nevertheless, Dudley endured as her only love. The queen treasured his portrait in the form of a miniature, a type of small painting often given as a love token. According to the Scottish diplomat James Melville, who visited her in 1564, Elizabeth kept the miniature of Dudley in her private rooms wrapped in a paper labelled 'my Lord's Picture'.[1] Although this portrait is now lost, many other images of Elizabeth and Dudley survive, including two by the celebrated miniaturist Nicholas Hilliard, now in the collections of the National Portrait Gallery (figs 1 and 2).

In the 1930s, Edward VIII was faced with a similar dilemma to that of Elizabeth I. He was forced to choose between the British crown and marriage to Wallis Simpson who, as an American divorcée, was then thought

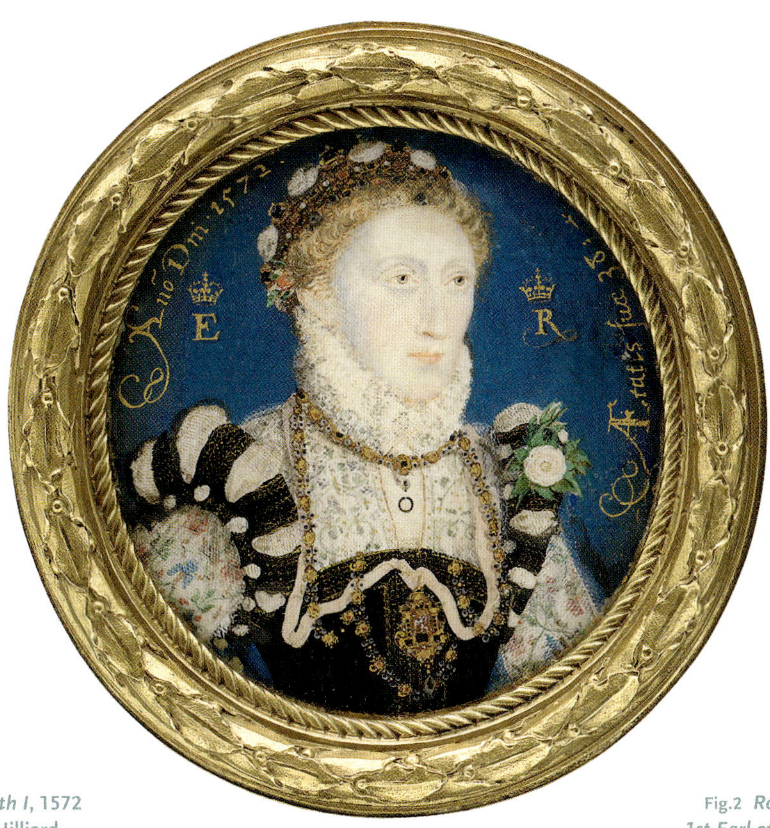

Fig.1 *Elizabeth I*, 1572
Nicholas Hilliard
Watercolour on vellum, 51 × 48mm
National Portrait Gallery, London

Fig.2 *Robert Dudley, 1st Earl of Leicester*, 1576
Nicholas Hilliard
Watercolour on vellum, 44mm diameter
National Portrait Gallery, London

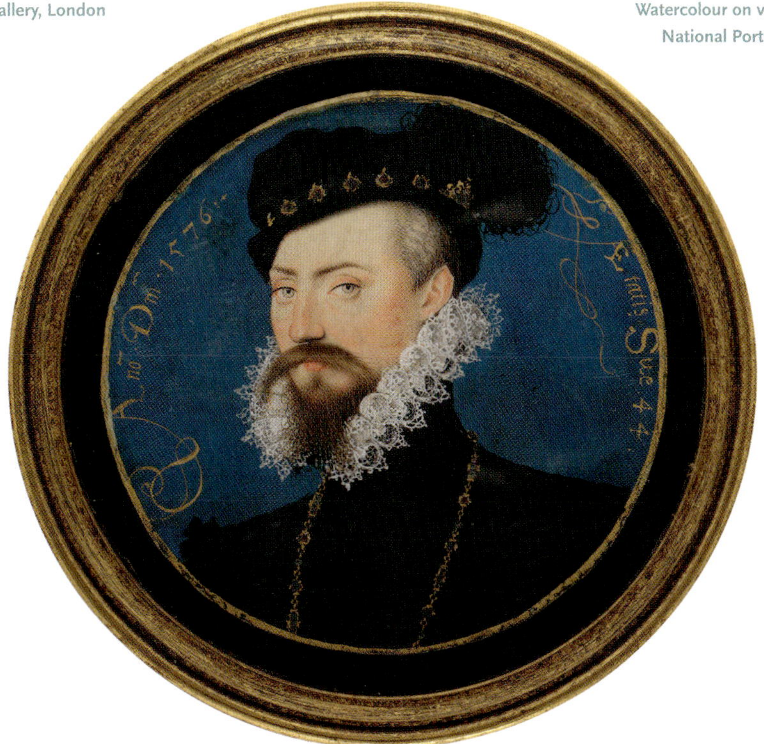

unacceptable as a potential queen. In contrast to Elizabeth, Edward famously chose to abdicate in favour of the woman he loved (see pp.161–5).

Changing ideas regarding what is acceptable, or morally right, in relation to love have meant that stories which would be unremarkable, or even celebrated today, caused scandal in the past. By the mid-1790s Mary Wollstonecraft was the most widely read female political writer in Europe. After her death in childbirth, her broken-hearted widower William Godwin published a frank memoir of her life. In trying to underpin Wollstonecraft's philosophy by presenting her as a role model, Godwin was forthright about female sexual appetites. He described Wollstonecraft's life in revolutionary Paris living with another man and bearing his child out of wedlock, her anguished suicide attempts after that relationship failed, and her subsequent resistance to marriage to Godwin. The book left the middle-class reading public in horror. Mary Wollstonecraft was damned as the archetype 'unsex'd female' who 'O'er humbled man assert the sovereign claim / And Slight the timid blush of virgin fame'.[2] Godwin may have been blinded by his grief, but Wollstonecraft's disregard for conventional female morality left her personal reputation in tatters and her writing largely disregarded, only to be resurrected in the late nineteenth century by early campaigners for votes for women.

In Britain, sex between men was first targeted for prosecution by an act passed by parliament in 1533. From then until 1861, the death penalty could be used to punish men convicted of a sexual liaison. This meant that gay couples faced intolerable risk, as was the case for Oscar Wilde and his lover 'Bosie' whose relationship led to Wilde's ruin (see pp.157–9). Unlike some couples, Wilde and Bosie escaped with their lives; the last execution for sex between men took place in 1835 when James Pratt and John Smith were hanged (fig.3). They were pardoned in 2017 under 'Turing's law', named in commemoration of the computer scientist and now-celebrated World War Two codebreaker Alan Turing. Turing committed suicide after being convicted for gross indecency when his relationship with another man came to police attention in 1952. This section explores a sequence of tragic and scandalous love stories, in which partners contravened the expectations of society or family to realise their love – however briefly.

Fig.3 *Particulars of the Execution of James Pratt and John Smith*, 1835
Printed by T. Birt, Bloomsbury
Print on paper, 370 × 202mm
Harvard Law School Library, Harvard University

PARTICULARS OF THE EXECUTION OF

JAMES PRATT & JOHN SMITH,

Who were Executed at the Old Bailey this Morning. Friday, Nov. 27, 1835

With the Copy of a Letter written by Smith on Wednesday last;

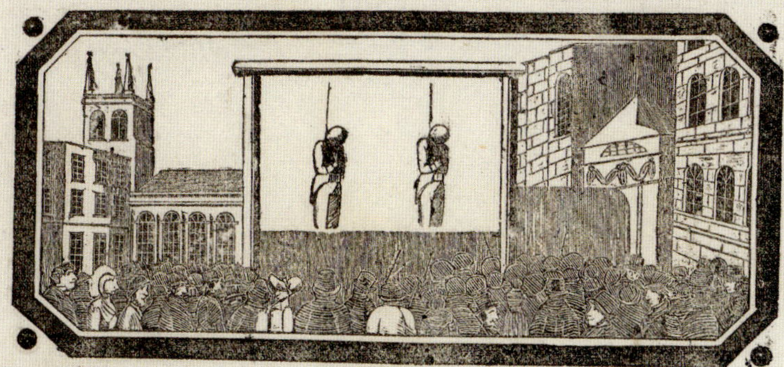

JAMES PRATT, aged 30, and JOHN SMITH, aged 40, were convicted at the last September Sessions, at the Old Bailey, of an unnatural crime, committed in the Borough of Southwark.— Wm. Bonnell, aged 68, was also convicted of aiding in and procuring the commission of the said crime and sentenced to fourteen years' transportation.—The evidence against these wretched men was so conclusive, that not the least shadow of doubt remained of their guilt. On their receiving sentence of Death, the Recorder directed that they should be brought up to receive judgment by themselves, as he felt it to be his duty to separate & distinguish them from the rest of the prisoners who had been called upon to receive the dreadful sentence of the law, because he felt that, however great their crimes might have been, they would have been contaminated by the prisoners' presence. Feeling so satisfied respecting the verdict of the Jury, he could not hold out the least hope of his being of any use to them in the subsequent investigation which their cases would undergo before his Majesty, assisted by his Privy Councillors. He entreated them, therefore, to reflect upon their positions as men on the brink of a period when their lives would, perhaps, close, and when they would be called upon to render an accouut at a far more awful tribunal than that before which they were called to account by the law. He would not now aggravate their sufferings, but would at once proceed to pass upon them the awful sentence of the law which was, that they should be taken to the prison from whence they came, and from thence to a place of execution where they should be hanged by the neck until they sould be severally dead

The prisoners appeared considerat bly affected during this address, & left the dock in tears.

After condemnation, every exertion was made by the Rev. Clergyman to bring them to a just sense of their awful situation & to acknowledge the justice of their sentence, which they did, devoting most of their time in prayer. On Wednesday Smith sent the following letter to a friend of his living in the neighbourhood where he resided, and through great interest we have procured a copy, which is as follows :—

"Newgate, November 25, 18 5.

"Dear William,—The awful period is nearly arrived when the offended laws of my country demand the forfeit of my life for the crime I have committed—a crime the most heinous & disgraceful What possessed me. I am at a loss to conceive, nor can I attribute it to any thing but the baneful effects of liquor and bad company, which must have rendered me void of every feeling of decency. The grave will soon close over me, and my name entirely forgotten. But remember from the knowledge we had of each other, that I die a sincere penitent for my sins & feel confident that you will drop a tear for one who has disgraced himself as a Christain & a friend. Let your prayers be offered up to the Throne of Mercy for that forgiveness which I have anxiously prayed to receive, & when you think of my fate, may it check any growing evil on your part and be the means of rendering you a fit companion for that society I have so much degraded. That the Almighty may bless you is the sincer prayer of "Your lost Friend

"JOHN SMITH.

The prisoners having been conveyed from their cells early in the morning, were at the usual hour conducted to the fatal spot, and soon after launched into eternity, amidst the yells & groans of the spectators.

Printed by T. BIRT, 39, Great St, Andrew Street, Bloomsbury.

CATHARINE MACLEOD

Sir Kenelm Digby & Venetia, Lady Digby

The passionate and tortured romance between Venetia Stanley and Kenelm Digby first began, according to Kenelm, when they were children living near one another in rural Buckinghamshire. Venetia, two and half years older, moved away, but the couple met again in their teens, and love rekindled. At this time, Kenelm gave Venetia a diamond ring in exchange for a lock of her hair. His mother, who was his only surviving parent, disapproved of the relationship, hoping for a more politically and financially advantageous marriage. In 1620 she sent Kenelm away on a tour of continental Europe to complete his education and to get him away from Venetia.

Kenelm's time away from England was eventful. While in France, he attracted the attention of the Queen Mother, Marie de Médicis, who, according to Kenelm's memoir, tried to seduce him. At this time a rebellion, centred on the Queen Mother, rose up against King Louis XIII and, in order to escape being caught up in the fighting, Kenelm decided to fake his own death. He travelled to Italy, where he indulged his intellectual interests, collecting books and manuscripts and presenting learned papers. He also narrowly escaped death from smallpox. After a period at the Spanish court, Kenelm finally returned to England in the autumn of that year.

Meanwhile, Venetia had heard of Kenelm's 'death', but had failed to receive the letter he sent reassuring her that he was still alive. Subsequent letters to her were confiscated by his mother, and so Venetia continued to believe that she had lost her love.
A beautiful but not wealthy young woman, romantically linked with a man who seemed to have either died or deserted her, was in a precarious position in early seventeenth-century England. Venetia acquired a reputation – whether deserved or not – for having affairs with several prominent courtiers.

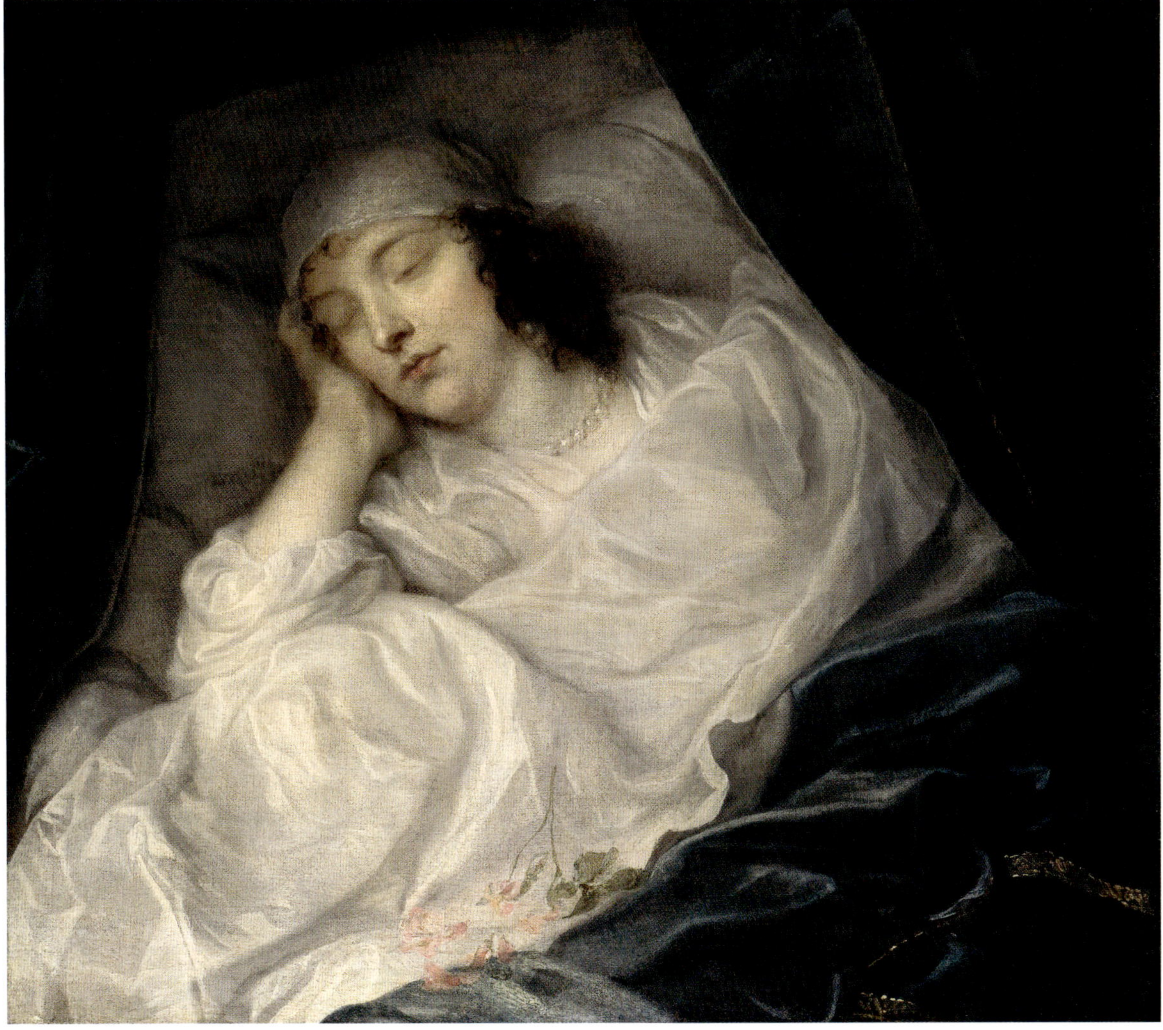

Fig.1 *Venetia Digby on her Deathbed*, 1633
Sir Anthony van Dyck
Oil on canvas, 743 × 818mm
Dulwich Picture Gallery, London

When Kenelm returned to England, he and Venetia were not immediately reunited. He had some concerns about her reputation; it seems likely that she would also have had views on his long absence and apparent silence. However, they eventually met in 1624, when a riding expedition together reignited their love. Venetia subsequently demonstrated her devotion by selling most of her jewellery to finance Kenelm's expenses on a diplomatic trip to France. Kenelm was finally convinced to act against parental wishes and marry Venetia, although the marriage remained secret for three years. The birth of their second son, and Kenelm's departure on a dangerous maritime expedition, led him to instruct her to make the marriage public at last.

The marriage was apparently a happy one, although there is evidence that Kenelm was not faithful to Venetia, despite expecting her to be so to him. Venetia was notably devout and generously

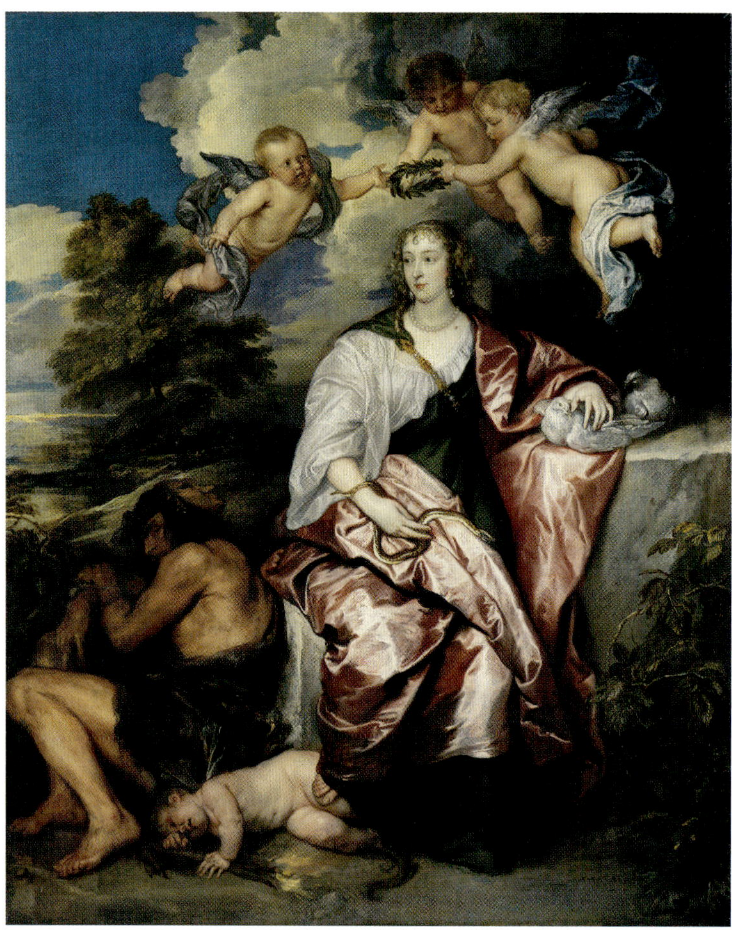

Fig.2 *Venetia, Lady Digby*, *c.*1633–4
Sir Anthony van Dyck
Oil on canvas, 1011 × 802mm
National Portrait Gallery, London

funded various charities, rather surprisingly through a very successful gambling habit. However, on the night of 1 May 1633, apparently with no prior warning, Venetia died in her sleep, probably of a brain haemorrhage. Kenelm was distraught. One of his first thoughts was to summon his close friend the artist Sir Anthony van Dyck to paint her on her deathbed (fig.1). Van Dyck depicted Venetia as though asleep, exactly as she was 'the second day after she was dead', according to Kenelm, the only addition being 'a rose lying upon the hemme of the sheete, whose leaves being pulled from the stalke in the full beauty of it ... is a fitt Embleme to expresse the state her bodie then was in'.[1] The impulse to know, to record and to create that made Kenelm both an enthusiastic scientist and a patron of the arts also found expression in this time of grief in his commissioning an autopsy of his wife, and writing long letters to his family and friends examining his own feelings and detailing her virtues.

As part of his on-going campaign to re-establish Venetia's reputation, Kenelm also had Van Dyck depict her in an elaborate allegorical composition, which symbolises Venetia's virtue in the face of vice (fig.2). Dressed in a timeless, vaguely classical manner, she sits in a landscape holding a dove and

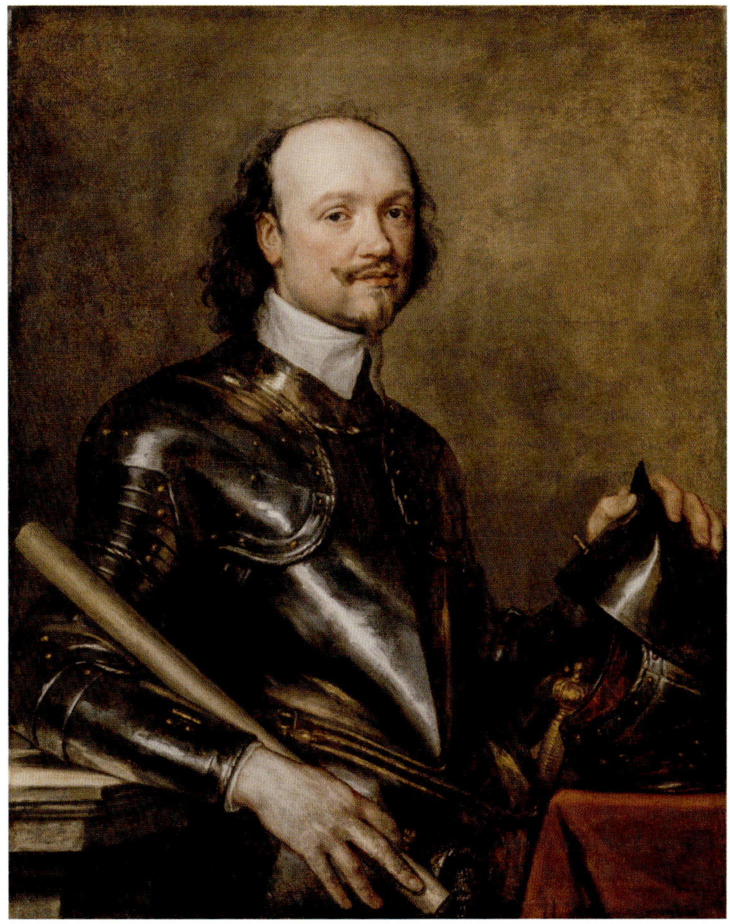

Fig.3 *Sir Kenelm Digby*, *c.*1640
Sir Anthony van Dyck
Oil on canvas, 1172 × 917mm
National Portrait Gallery, London

snake, symbols, respectively, of innocence and wisdom. Her foot rests on Cupid, representing carnal love, and two-faced Deceit lies bound alongside. Over her head, three cherubs hold a wreath. Van Dyck also recorded Kenelm's feelings of desolation and devotion in portraits of him with a long, unkempt beard, wearing a mourning cloak. One version has a sunflower, symbolising constancy; another has a broken armillary sphere, symbolising the destruction of his harmonious domestic life, what Digby himself described as his 'shippe-wracked affection'.[2]

Kenelm retreated initially into a life of scientific investigation and intellectual enquiry. However, Van Dyck's last portrait of him shows him in armour, as a man of action (fig.3). The outbreak of civil war led to periods of arrest for the Royalist, Catholic Kenelm, as well as travels in Europe, which combined efforts at fundraising for the Royalist cause with more opportunities for scientific research. Exiled on the continent during the Interregnum, he returned to England with the Restoration of King Charles II to the throne. Although he was not as faithful to Venetia's memory as he set out to be, Kenelm never remarried and specified in his will that his 'dust [should] lie by hers who was my greatest worldly blessing.'[3]

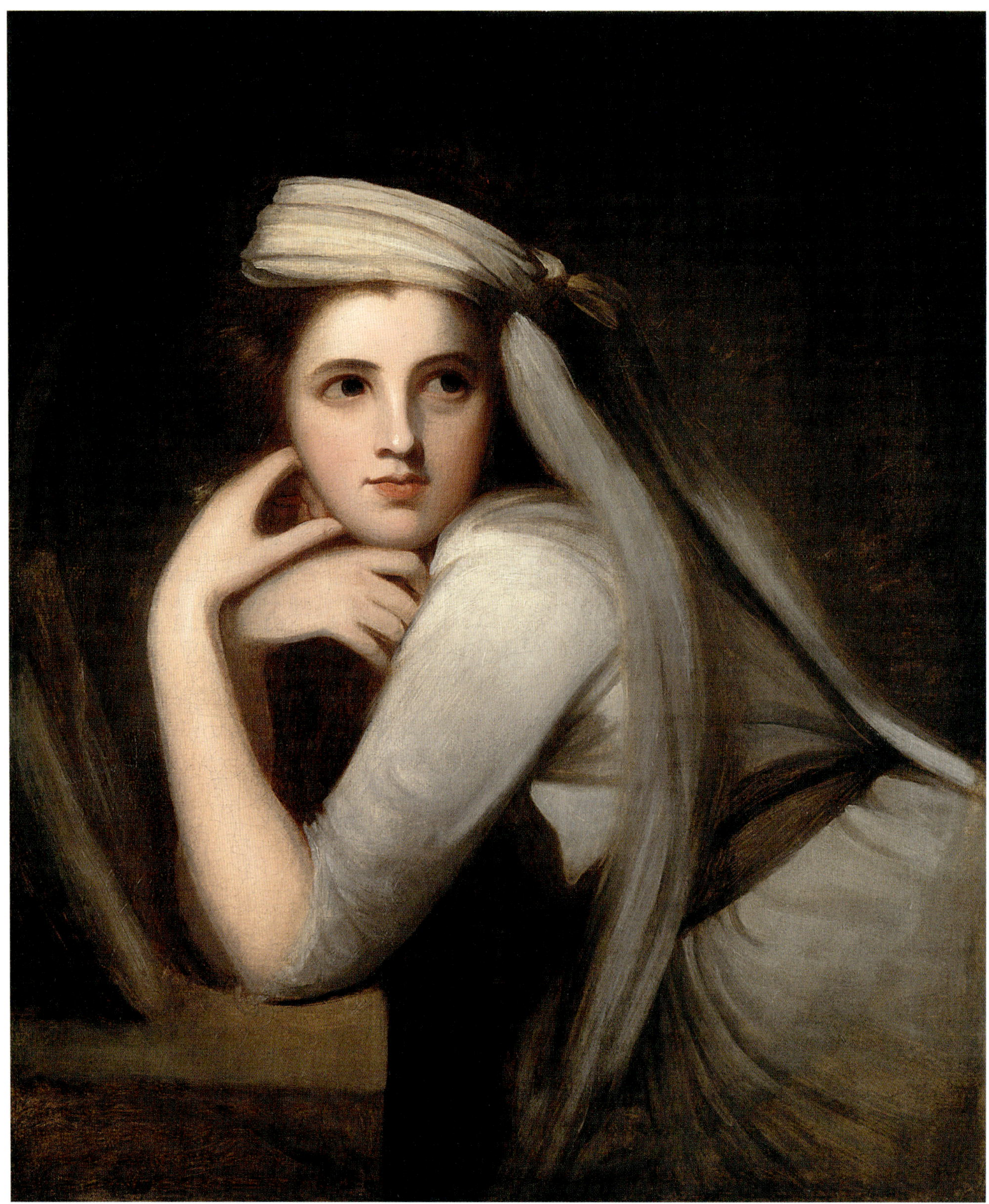

PROFESSOR KATE WILLIAMS

Emma Hamilton & Admiral Lord Nelson

In 1798, Emma, Lady Hamilton, former maid, mistress, muse and all out survivor, was already an accomplished political operator at the Court of Naples (fig.1). When she heard that the brilliant Rear-Admiral Sir Horatio Nelson (fig.2) had won the Battle of the Nile against the French, she created a plan to seize him to protect her beloved Naples – and ensure her own fame.

Emma wrote Nelson an astonishing letter, telling him she was 'swelling' with pride and she had a 'fervour caused by agitation and pleasure', and promising him that Maria Carolina, the Queen of Naples, was in 'transports'. She said she and her husband – Sir William Hamilton, British Ambassador at Naples (fig.3) – longed to embrace him. She continued my 'dress head to foot is alla Nelson' and pleaded with him to come to Naples.[1]

Fig.1 *Emma Hamilton*, *c.*1785
George Romney
Oil on canvas, 737 × 597mm
National Portrait Gallery, London

Emma was à la mode; the victory in Egypt had inspired an outpouring of Nelson-mania – anchor jewellery, Nile outfits, a Wedgwood jelly mould with a sphinx on top. All Britain was dressing to celebrate Nelson. But Emma, who had only briefly met Nelson once before when he passed through Naples five years previously, was doing it most flamboyantly of all.

Nelson received the letter and set off to Naples, although it ran against his orders. When he arrived, Emma, with her superb instinct for drama, put on an unforgettable show of loyalty and patriotism. He had expected to arrive and see the King and Queen of Naples, Ferdinand and Maria Carolina. Instead, Emma took her own boat, sailed up beside his and clambered up on deck. All glamour and flowing hair, much taller than

Nelson, she declared 'O God, is it possible,' and fainted into his arms.

Emma's political, dramatic and romantic brilliance captivated Nelson. She and the Queen of Naples had hoped his presence would scare off Napoleon, who was in the process of invading Italy. But it was not enough. Napoleon's troops were coming and within two months of Nelson's arrival, on 21 December 1798, Nelson evacuated the Royal Family and the Hamiltons to Sicily in HMS *Vanguard*. It was a dreadful journey. Maria Carolina's son, 6-year-old Prince Albert, died in Emma's arms on Christmas Day.

In Palermo, the second capital of the kingdom of King Ferdinand, Nelson, Emma and Sir William lived together, and with Nelson's money supporting the three of them, the great love affair between Nelson and Emma began. Soon, caricatures of the lovers were all over London, with Sir William cuckolded (usually shown studying broken pots, a nod to his interest in antiquity, see fig.4) while Vesuvius exploded in the background. On return to Naples, Nelson punished the rebels who had allied with the French too brutally and his naval commanders decided they had let him remain too long 'at a foreign court'.[2] In 1800, the British government called back both Nelson and Sir William.

Just before the return journey, Emma fell pregnant with Nelson's child and secured his heart forever. He had longed for a child. Emma, Nelson and Sir William paraded back over mainland Europe, greeted by thrilled crowds everywhere they went. By the time they arrived in England, Emma was visibly pregnant, a great shock to Nelson's wife, Frances, who had been

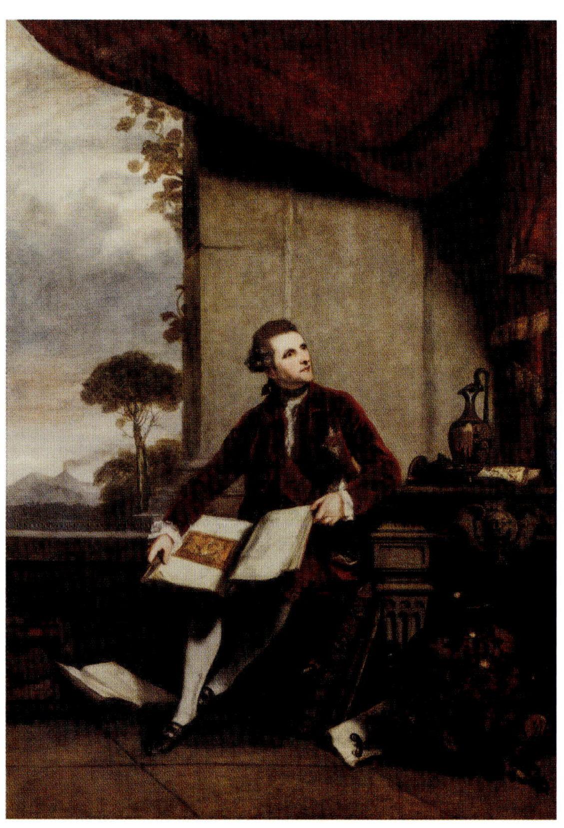

Fig.3 *Sir William Hamilton*, 1777
Sir Joshua Reynolds
Oil on canvas, 2553 × 1752mm
National Portrait Gallery, London

OPPOSITE
Fig.2 *Horatio, Lord Nelson*, 1797
Lemuel Francis Abbott
Oil on canvas, 749 × 622mm
National Portrait Gallery, London

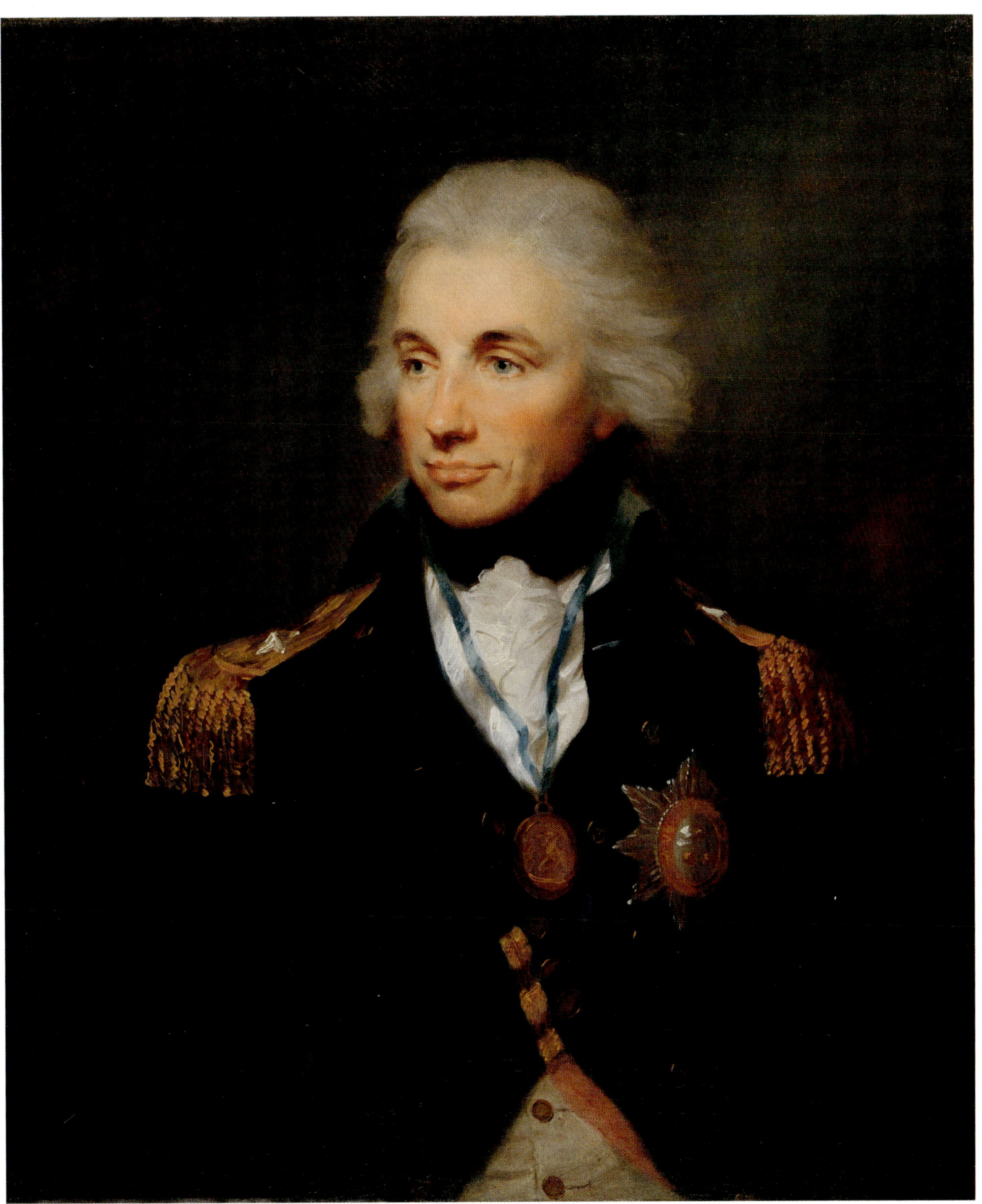

waiting patiently for her husband. He treated her dismissively but gave her half his income (a rare act of fairness from a man at this point) and she had no choice but to retire to live quietly.

Emma, Nelson and Sir William went everywhere together – the *tria iuncta in uno* – and became the most sought after guests in town. Nelson bought a house in Merton, near Wimbledon, to be their home together – 'Paradise Merton' (even though, for propriety's sake, it was Nelson's house and Sir William and Emma's official address was at Clarges Street, near Green Park). Paradise Merton was bedecked with Nelsonia, as, in the words of one visitor, a 'looking glass' to admire himself in. Emma gave birth to their daughter, Horatia, in early 1801 and Nelson was delighted. Nelson's genius and Sir William's willingness to provide a socially acceptable shroud, meant that Emma and Nelson could live together openly and continued to do so after Sir William died in 1803.

Before she met Nelson, Emma had lived multiple lives. Born Amy (or Emy) Lyon in 1765 and raised in Wales in relative poverty, she arrived in London before she was a teenager to work as a maid and after she was fired, moved through the fringes of London's theatre and shows. By fifteen, she had been mistress to Sir Harry Featherstonehaugh, who abandoned her when she fell pregnant. Desperate, she begged his friend, Charles Greville, to help her. Greville took her as a mistress, called her 'Mrs Emma Hart' and, after her baby had been born and boarded with a family, sent her to model for George Romney. Artist and model created the beautiful, expressive portraits that made her celebrated. When Greville tired of her, he dispatched her off to his uncle, Sir William

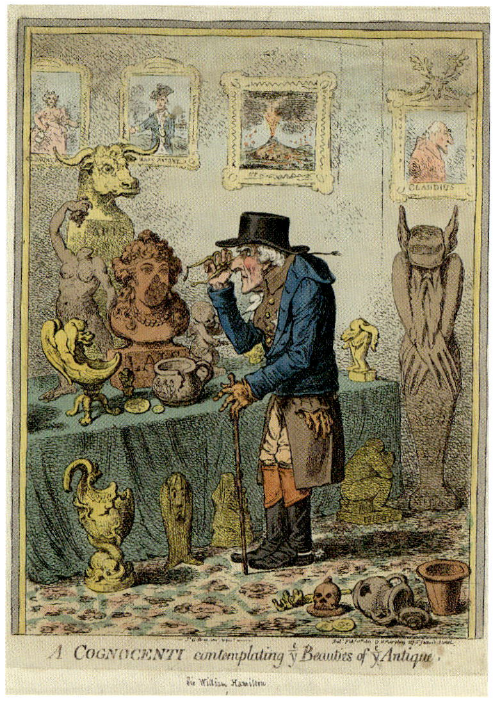

Fig.4 ***Sir William Hamilton ('A Cognocenti contemplating ye Beauties of ye Antique'),*** 1801
James Gillray
Hand-coloured etching, 357 × 258mm
National Portrait Gallery, London

Hamilton, diplomat, celebrated antiquarian and volcanologist. Emma arrived in Naples on her twenty-first birthday, believing she was coming for a short holiday. When Sir William told her the truth, she was heartbroken at what she felt was Greville's rejection.

Sir William had intended to host Emma as his mistress, following the death of his wife of more than twenty years, but he found himself bowled over by his young guest. Her 'attitudes', performances of classical postures, electrified visitors. Emma acted as his wife until 1791, when they came back to England and were quickly married. Romney's books on the day of her marriage tell a story: in the morning Emma is entered as 'Mrs Hart'. In the afternoon, she returns to complete her marriage portrait and she is 'Lady Hamilton'.

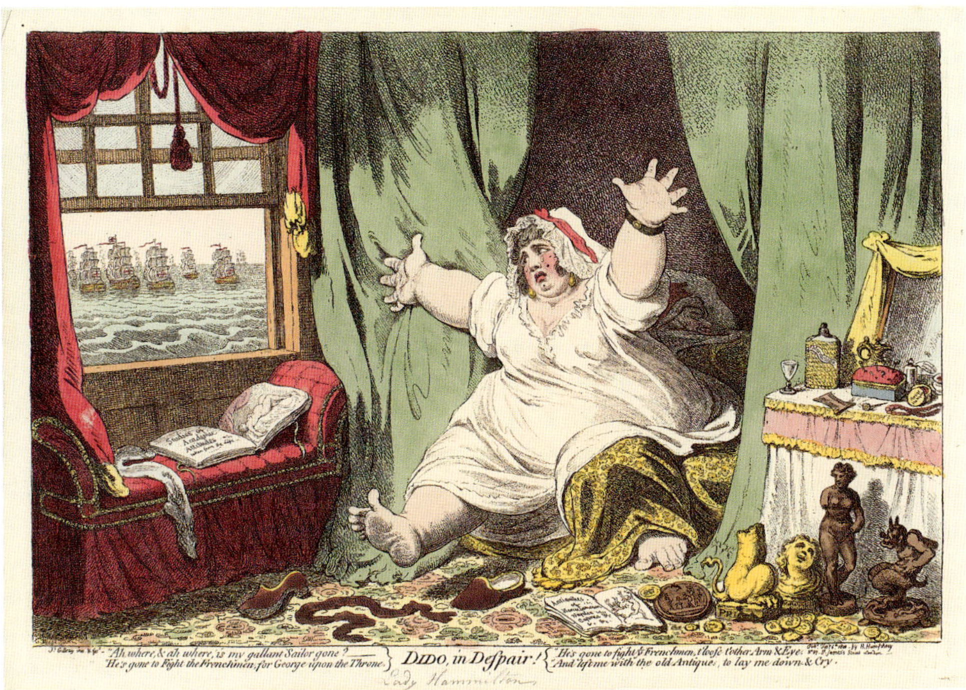

Fig.5 *Emma Hamilton ('Dido, in Despair!')*, 1801
James Gillray
Hand-coloured etching and stipple engraving, 267 × 376mm
National Portrait Gallery, London

As Lady Hamilton, Emma quickly became the first confidante of the Queen of Naples, gaining more power and influence than Sir William, although she always worked for his benefit. But everything was to change when Nelson arrived in 1798. She fell in love with Europe's genius – and a man who finally appreciated her for herself, rather than objectifying her as a muse. Nelson was entranced by Emma's quick wit, enthusiasm for celebrating him dramatically and her ability to charm monarchs – he had always felt rather excluded by the aristocracy. It was a passionate romance. As he once described a dream of her: 'I kissed you fervently and we enjoy'd the height of love. Ah Emma I pour out my soul to you.'[3] He burned all her letters – but she kept his.

At Trafalgar, Nelson's dying words have always been interpreted as 'Kiss me, Hardy', but they could well have been 'Kiss Emma for me, Hardy'. Nelson died a great hero, having done his duty, and near the end he begged his country to 'Look after Lady Hamilton.' Caricatures showed Emma weeping over Nelson, a sobbing Britannia (fig.5). But the nation wanted a hero and so Nelson was painted as a saint. Emma was put aside and the government gave her nothing.

Emma died in poverty in Calais in early 1815, just short of fifty, after fleeing debtors' prison, her terrified 14-year-old daughter, Horatia, by her side. It had been a story of rags to riches – and then back to poverty once more. She had flamed high but society turned on her, her star collapsed and died. Yet still the great love story and the great, luminous portraits remain. Emma fought to be recognised, and it was a brave fight. If Nelson had lived a little longer, she might have won.

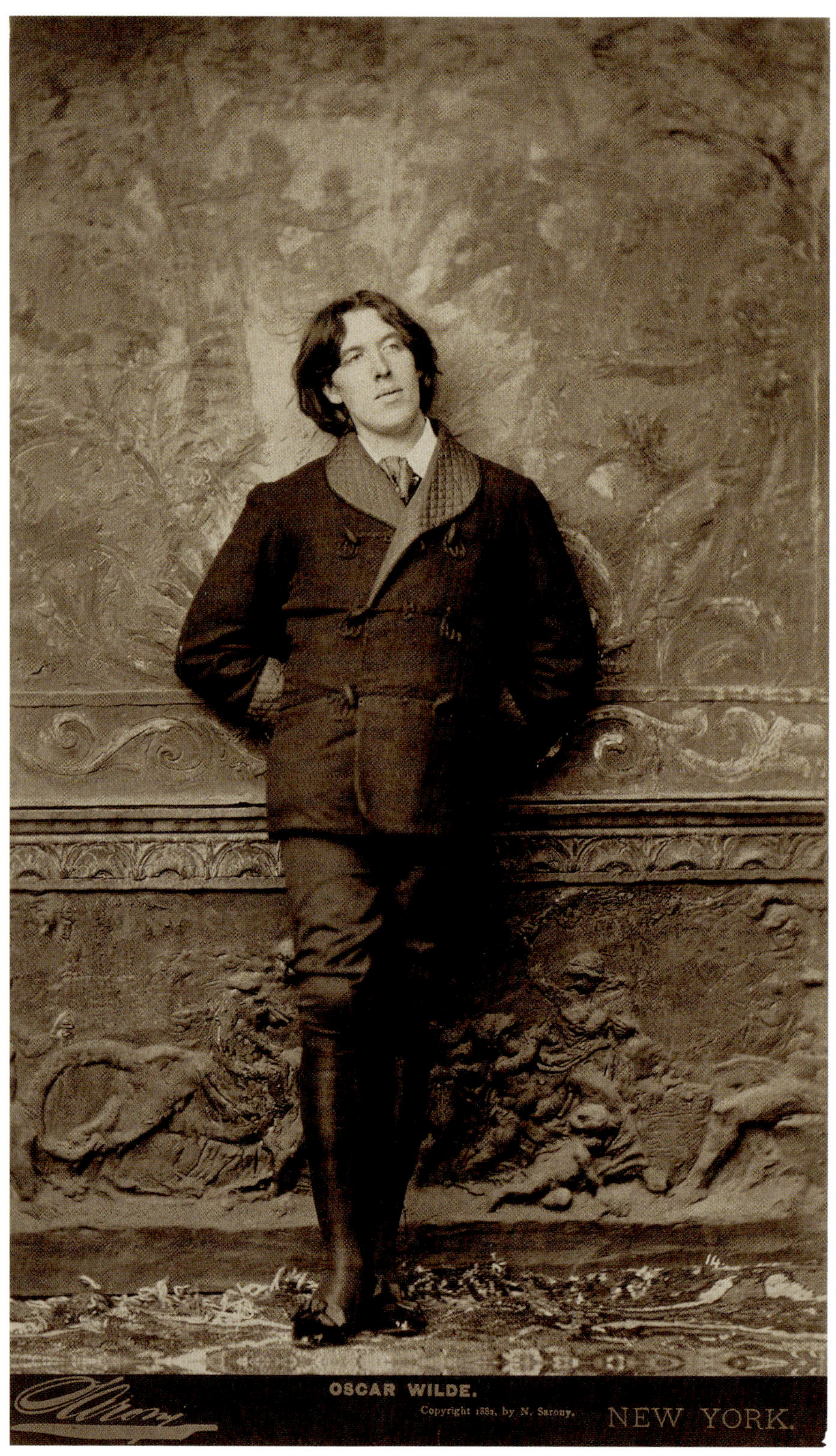

Fig.1 *Oscar Wilde*, 1882
Napoleon Sarony
Albumen panel card, 305 × 184mm
National Portrait Gallery, London

PETER FUNNELL

Oscar Wilde & Lord Alfred Douglas

The celebrated playwright and wit Oscar Wilde met Lord Alfred Douglas in the summer of 1891 and their friendship began the following year. Douglas was then a student at Oxford and an aspiring poet, dubbed by his mother 'Bosie', a name of affection that was taken up by Wilde. Letters between the two over the following years reflect the depth of their attachment to each other. The novelist Colm Tóibín has written insightfully about their relationship, tracing Wilde's expressions of intense love for Douglas to later moments when he chides him for making 'scenes' – 'they kill me – they wreck the loveliness of life'.[1] 'Thus', Tóibín observes, 'the tone was set for the most famous gay relationship in history.'[2] It also led to one of the most celebrated of downfalls when in 1895, following Wilde's unsuccessful suit of libel on Douglas' father the Marquess of Queensberry, he was found guilty of gross indecency for homosexual offences and sentenced to two year's hard labour in prison.

Wilde's public career was cut short by his early death but was remarkable, until his fall, for its success. He was born in Dublin to Protestant parents who espoused Irish nationalism: the eye doctor Sir William Wilde and his wife, who wrote poetry under the name 'Speranza'. She held literary salons in Dublin and London, and was a flamboyant and fiery dissident to convention who much influenced Oscar's view of life. Wilde studied at Trinity College Dublin and Oxford University, taking a double first in Greats (classics). He moved to London in 1879 where he formed friendships with leading actresses of the day – Lillie Langtry, Sarah Bernhardt and Ellen Terry – and cultivated his image as an aesthete, famously satirised by Gilbert and Sullivan in their opera *Patience* (1881). A highly successful lecture tour to the United

States in 1882–3, when he was photographed in New York in aesthetic garb by Napoleon Sarony (fig.1), was followed in the 1880s by a career back in London in literary journalism and his marriage to Constance Mary Lloyd with whom he had two sons. In 1890 he published his controversial novel, *The Picture of Dorian Gray*, and in the following years wrote a series of highly successful comedies culminating in *The Importance of Being Earnest* that opened to popular acclaim on 14 February 1895.

The Marquess of Queensberry had developed a reputation for his bullying and belligerent public behaviour. Relations between him and his son were marked by mutual hostility, intensified by Queensberry's revulsion at Douglas' affair with Wilde. At an especially fraught moment, Douglas called him 'a violent and dangerous rough'.[3] Inflamed by his hatred of Wilde, Queensberry attempted to make a demonstration against him at the first night of *The Importance of Being Earnest* but was barred from the theatre. On 28 February Wilde received a card from him accusing him of 'posing as a Somdomite (*sic*)'. Against the advice of friends, but encouraged by Douglas, Wilde launched his unsuccessful libel suit against Queensberry who turned over the evidence he had gathered concerning Wilde's gay activities to the authorities. After two further trials, Wilde was found guilty. His public reputation was shattered and the two years in prison – mostly under a very harsh regime in Reading Gaol – were to prove disastrous both psychologically and to his physical health. His remaining years were spent abroad: impecunious, in ill-health and an outcast to all but his closest friends. As his biographer Richard Ellmann has written, 'Wilde was as infamous as he had been famous in the early Nineties.'[4]

The photograph featured here (fig.2) records an early moment in the relationship between Wilde and Douglas before the trials and Wilde's imprisonment. Showing the two men together, it was taken in Oxford in the studio of photographers Gillman & Co. in May 1893 when Wilde visited Douglas for an extended stay. Wilde was much fêted there and was the focus of almost nightly dinner parties surrounded by Douglas' like-minded friends. This rare portrait records their early relationship during an often joyous, but not untroubled phase. Already tensions between the two had begun to emerge and it was in 1893 that Queensberry was tipped off about Wilde and Douglas' relationship.

Douglas' blame for the disaster that overtook Wilde has been the subject of much discussion. Wilde himself criticised Douglas' failings in his *De Profundis* (1897), a prose letter that he wrote in Reading Gaol and sent privately to his friend and supporter, Robert Ross. Douglas could certainly be self-centred, quarrelsome, demanding and, on occasion, cruel and later lived a life blotted by dispute and disappointment, until his death in 1945. But when the two men reunited after Wilde's release from gaol, spending time in France and Italy, Wilde was candid about both his undying love for him but also the danger it entailed. 'Of course I shall often be unhappy', he wrote to Ross, 'but I still love him: the mere fact that he wrecked my life makes me love him.'[5]

Fig.2 *Oscar Wilde and Lord Alfred Douglas*, May 1893
Gillman & Co
Gelatin silver print, 136 × 97mm
National Portrait Gallery, London

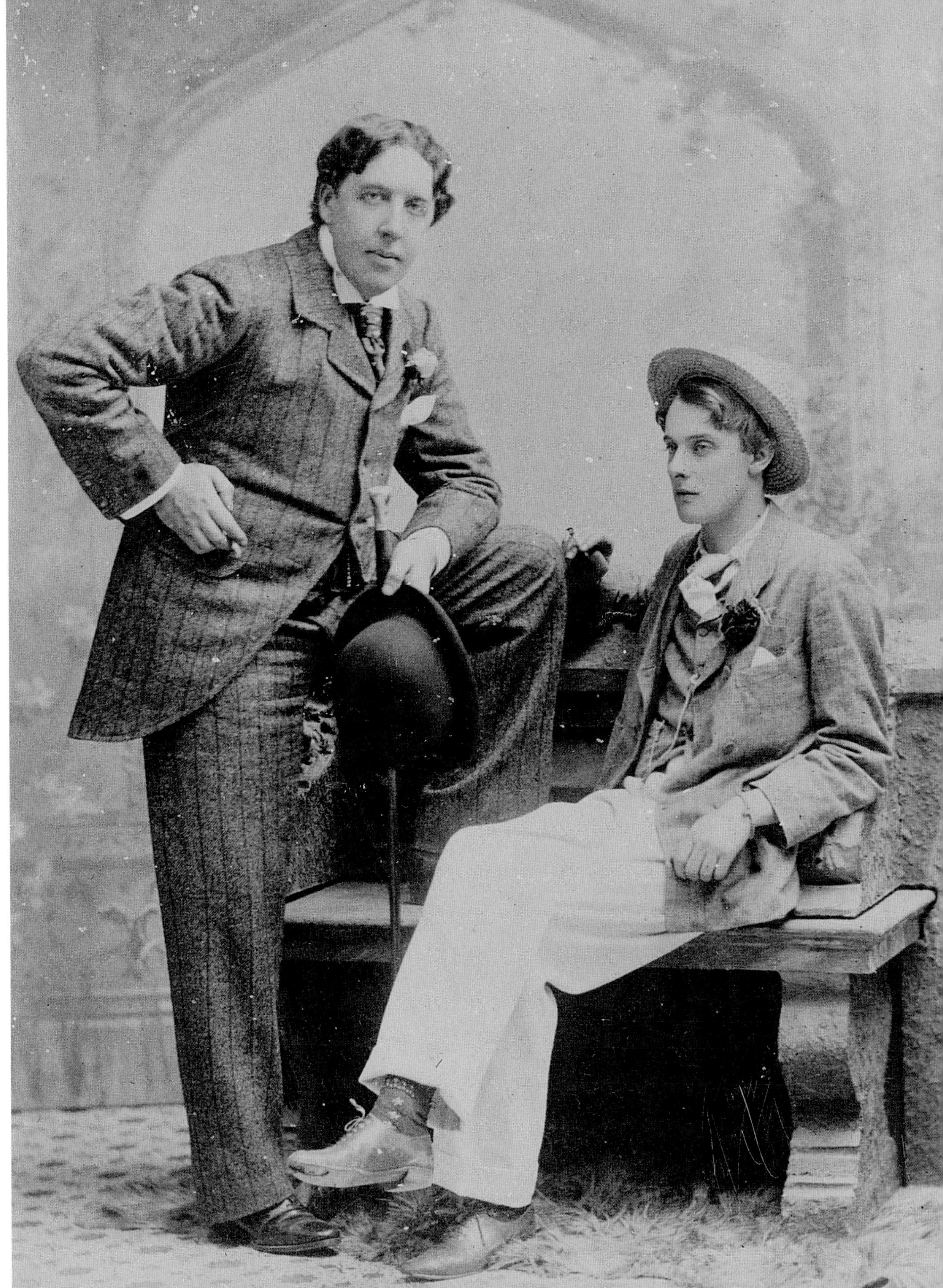

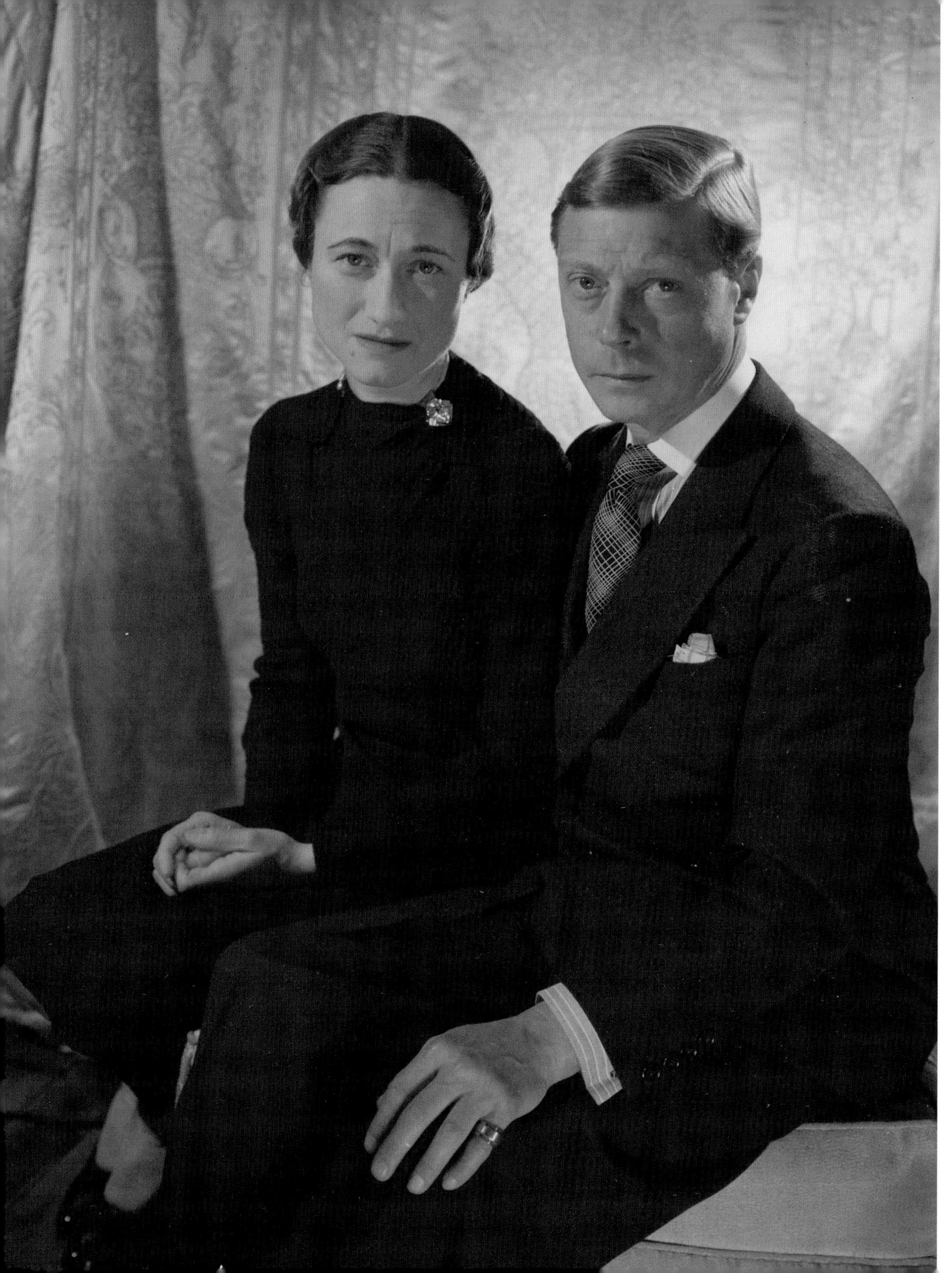

CONSTANTIA NICOLAIDES

EDWARD VIII & WALLIS SIMPSON

In early December 1936, after months of rumours circulating and despite widespread reporting in the foreign papers, the British press finally broke the silence it had maintained in deference to the king. The news of the constitutional crisis facing the country was revealed: King Edward VIII, who had ascended the throne just months earlier, was in love with an American divorcée, Mrs Wallis Simpson, and was on the brink of abandoning his royal duty in favour of life with his beloved.

The eldest child of King George V and Queen Mary, Edward had been groomed since birth to be king and was created Prince of Wales following his father's accession in 1910. Throughout the 1920s, his good looks and easy manner had gained him public popularity, and likewise attracted admirers and affairs. As a bachelor who enjoyed nightclubs and parties, Edward became a leader of fashionable London society and, as heir to the throne, his reckless, womanising ways outraged and distressed his parents. It was at the home of one mistress – Thelma, Viscountess Furness – that Edward first met Wallis in 1931. Wallis had divorced her first husband in 1927, and her subsequent marriage to businessman Ernest Simpson brought her to Britain. By January 1934, Edward and Wallis were allegedly lovers, and he soon became completely besotted with the elegant and charismatic socialite.

King George V died on 20 January 1936, and the prince became King Edward VIII, but his accession failed to curb his socialising or his affair. That summer, the couple cruised the Mediterranean, and it was becoming increasingly apparent within court and government circles that they intended to marry. Their fears were confirmed when Wallis was granted

Fig.1 *Wallis, Duchess of Windsor and Prince Edward, Duke of Windsor*, 2 June 1937
Cecil Beaton
Gelatin silver print, 230 × 168mm
National Portrait Gallery, London

a decree nisi on 27 October and Edward expressed his marriage intentions to the Prime Minister. As monarch, Edward was Supreme Governor of the Church of England and his desire to marry Wallis conflicted with the Church's disapproval of the remarriage of divorced persons (this remained unchanged until 2002). With Wallis deemed wholly unsuitable as a prospective queen consort, government opposition to the marriage was also strong. Faced with Edward's determination not to give up Wallis and no acceptable resolution, it was decided that the king should abdicate. As the scandal spread in the media, Wallis left for Cannes.

Edward signed the abdication papers on 10 December and, the following day, parliamentary laws were passed that officially ended his reign, which had lasted only 327 days. His younger brother, the Duke of York, reluctantly ascended to the throne as King George VI. In a radio speech broadcast worldwide that evening, Edward publicly declared:

> You must believe me when I tell you that I have found it impossible to carry the heavy burden of responsibility and to discharge my duties as King as I would wish to do without the help and support of the woman I love.[1]

On 12 December, the new king announced he was to make his brother HRH the Duke of Windsor. Edward departed for Austria that same day, remaining apart from Wallis to avoid compromising the completion of her divorce proceedings.

The couple were reunited at the Château de Candé, near Tours in France, on 4 May 1937, where they married one month later in a private ceremony. None of Edward's family attended. The prominent fashion and society photographer, Cecil Beaton, was invited to photograph Edward and Wallis on the day before the wedding. Photographs were taken on the steps and terrace of the medieval porch to the castle, but those taken indoors, with a bedspread as an impromptu backdrop that captured the muted, improvised nature of the occasion, are the most revealing. During the sitting – firstly showing Wallis in a black dress adorned with two diamond clips (fig.1), and then depicting the couple in their wedding clothes (fig.2) – Edward received a message, probably the news that the title 'Royal Highness' would be denied to his new wife. Their faces clearly show the effect of this discovery, as Beaton noted: 'Through the lens I saw the Duke become worried, frowning and contorting his face ... Wallis, too, seemed troubled.'[2] The financial settlement issued to the Duke added to the ongoing conflict and resentment, and King George VI, embarrassed by the whole episode, made it clear the couple must not return to Britain without invitation, effectively leaving them in exile.

Edward and Wallis continued to live in France for the remainder of their lives, leaving only at the onset of the Second World War when Edward was awarded the governorship of the Bahamas. The studio photographer Dorothy Wilding photographed the couple during this time at her New York premises. Their body language in her portrait – one of many taken that day – clearly expresses the intimacy and informality of this fashionable couple who moved on the periphery of royal circles (fig.3). After the war, no other official roles were offered, and the couple spent their days as society figures, travelling frequently between Europe and the United States.

Edward died on 28 May 1972 and was buried in the Royal Burial Ground at Frogmore. Wallis spent her last years as a recluse and died on 24 April 1986. She was buried beside her husband. Accused of being manipulative and ambitious, she remains a controversial figure in British history. While they remained loyal to one another until their deaths, questions abound about Edward's real motivations for abdicating, and whether Wallis truly loved Edward or intended for their relationship to progress so far. Indeed, she reportedly remarked: 'You have no idea how hard it is to live out a great romance.'[3]

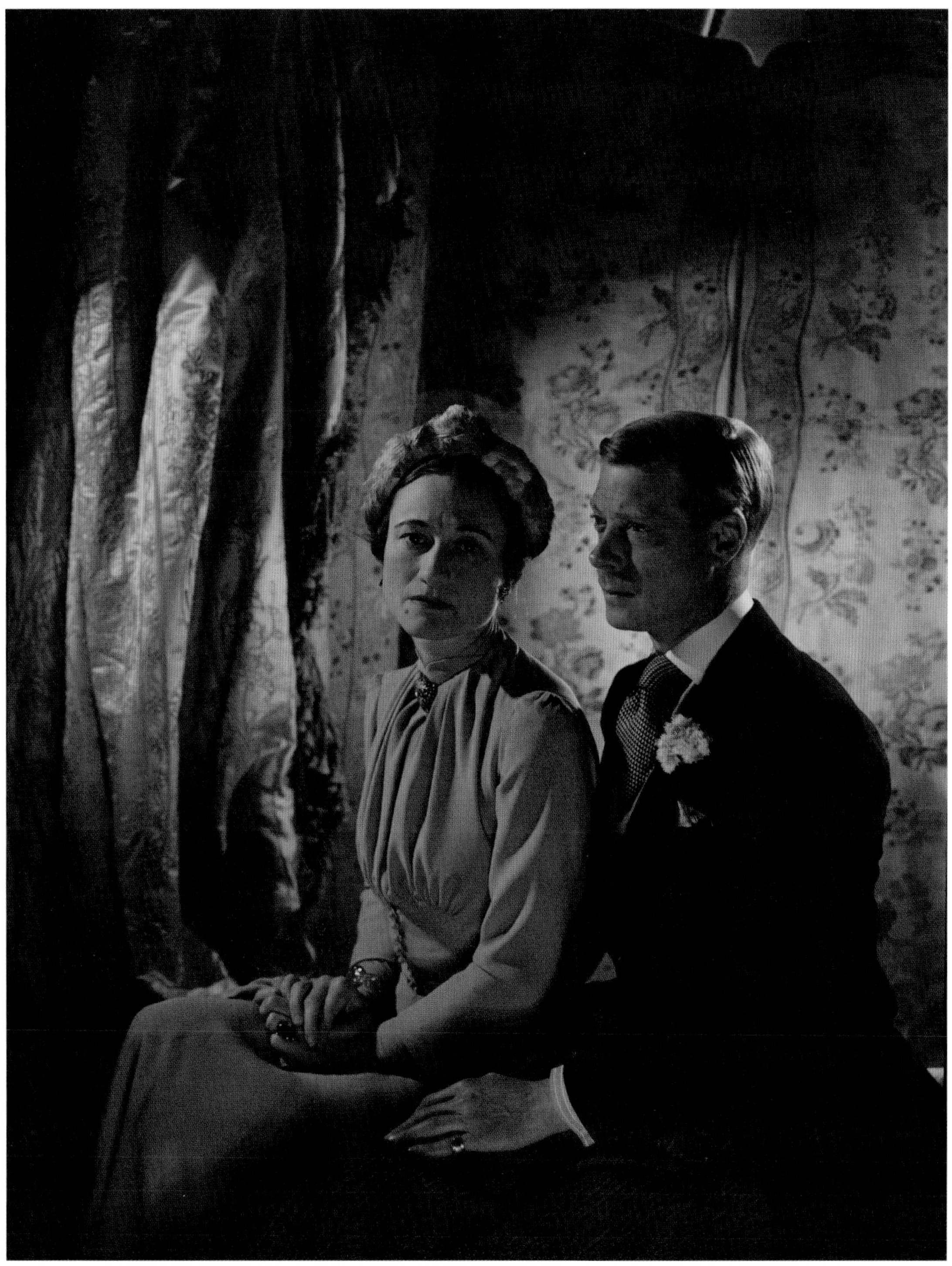

Fig.2 *Wallis, Duchess of Windsor and Prince Edward, Duke of Windsor*, 2 June 1937
Cecil Beaton
Gelatin silver print, 230 × 168mm
National Portrait Gallery, London

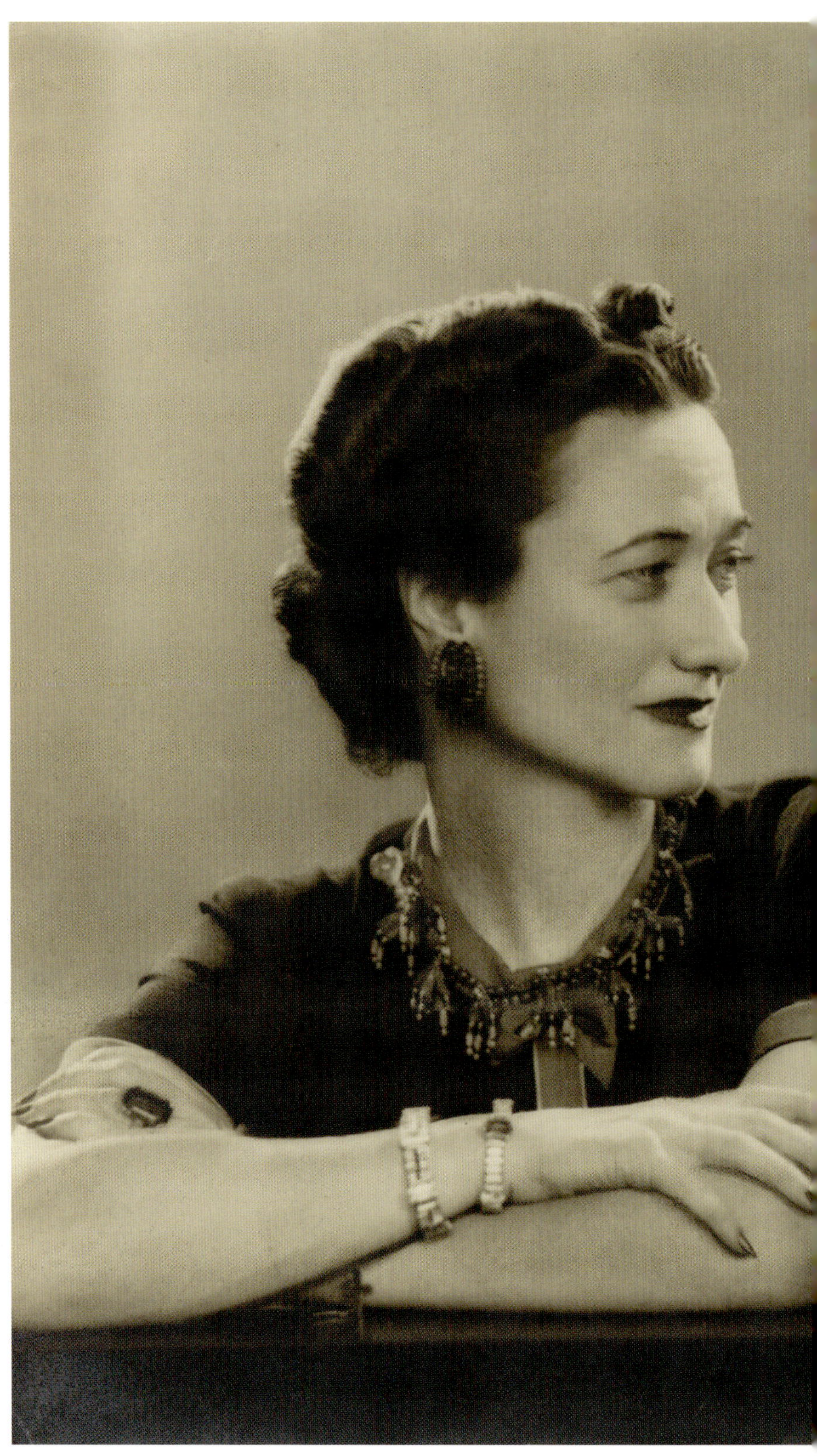

Fig.3 *Wallis, Duchess of Windsor and Prince Edward, Duke of Windsor*, 2 June 1943
Dorothy Wilding
Gelatin silver print, 221 × 282mm
National Portrait Gallery, London

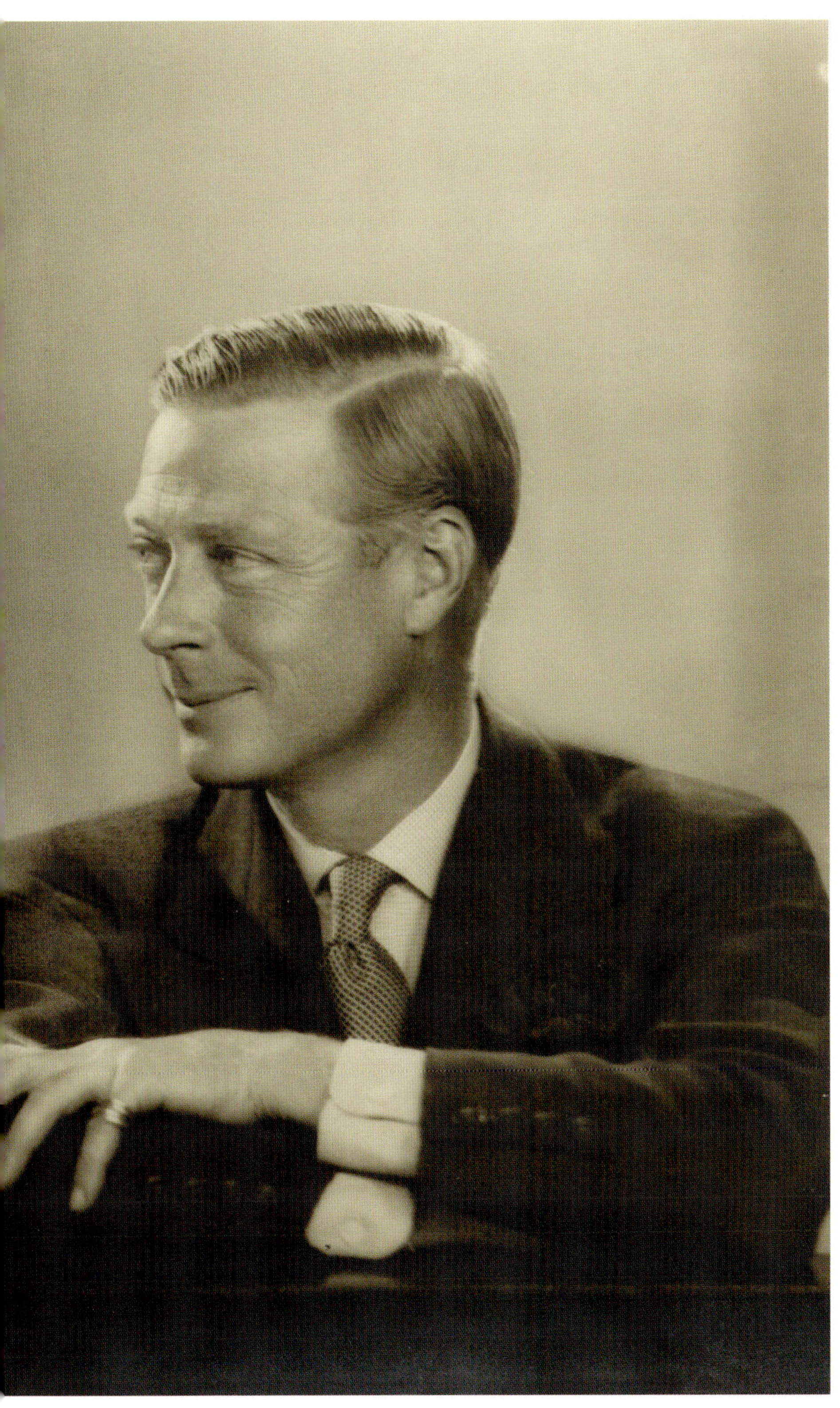

SABINA JASKOT-GILL

JOHN LENNON & YOKO ONO

'Beatlemania' swept the globe in the Sixties, with scenes of adulation and hysteria greeting appearances by the pop band known as 'the Fab Four', and founding member John Lennon proclaiming the Beatles 'more popular than Jesus'.[1] One of the most controversial relationships in music history remains that of John and performance artist Yoko Ono, who is often cited as the decisive factor in the breakup of pop's biggest band.

Born in Tokyo, Yoko grew up between Japan and America, settling in New York in 1962 where she became active in the avant-garde art scene. In the same year, the Beatles released their debut single, 'Love Me Do', and John married his childhood sweetheart, Cynthia Powell. The course of both lives changed after they met in London in November 1966 at an exhibition of Yoko's work. John remembered being surprised: 'I was a working-class macho guy who was used to being served and Yoko didn't buy that. From the day I met her, she demanded equal time, equal space, equal rights.'[2] Afterwards, Yoko sent John a copy of her book, *Grapefruit* (1964), which he reportedly kept by his bedside.

Their platonic friendship evolved as the two collaborated artistically. They recorded *Unfinished Music No. 1: Two Virgins* (1968) at John's Surrey home while Cynthia was away. The album's title refers to the consummation of their relationship, once recording was complete: 'Yoko came to visit me. ... instead of making love, we went upstairs and made tapes. ... And then as the sun rose we made love.'[3] The experimental music proved less controversial that the accompanying album artwork, which featured two full-length photographs of the pair naked (fig. 2). The photographs were taken in Ringo Starr's London flat, using a time-delay camera, and developed in secret for

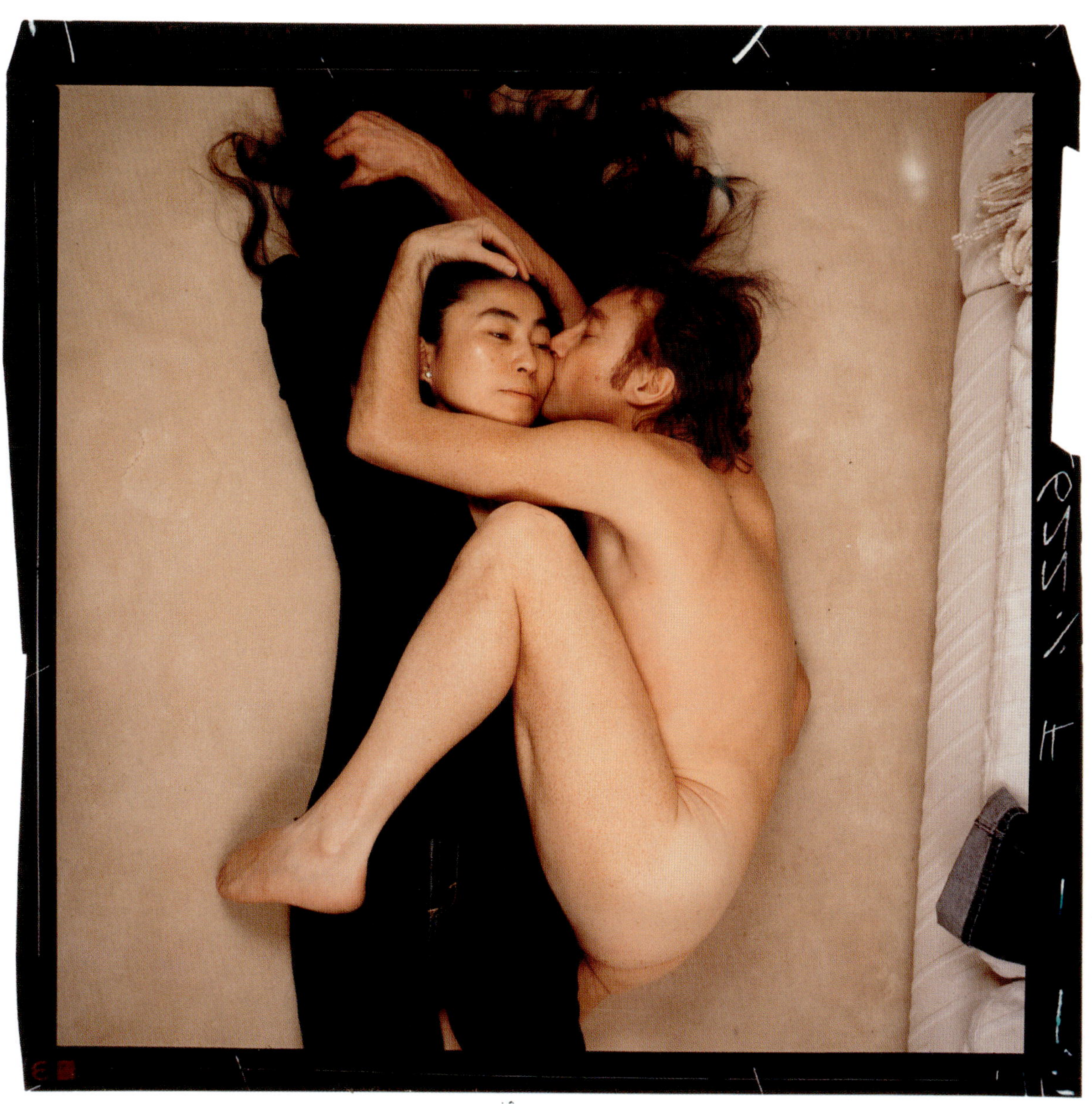

Fig.1 *Yoko Ono and John Lennon*, 1980
Annie Leibovitz
Chromogenic colour print, 327 × 327mn
National Portrait Gallery, London

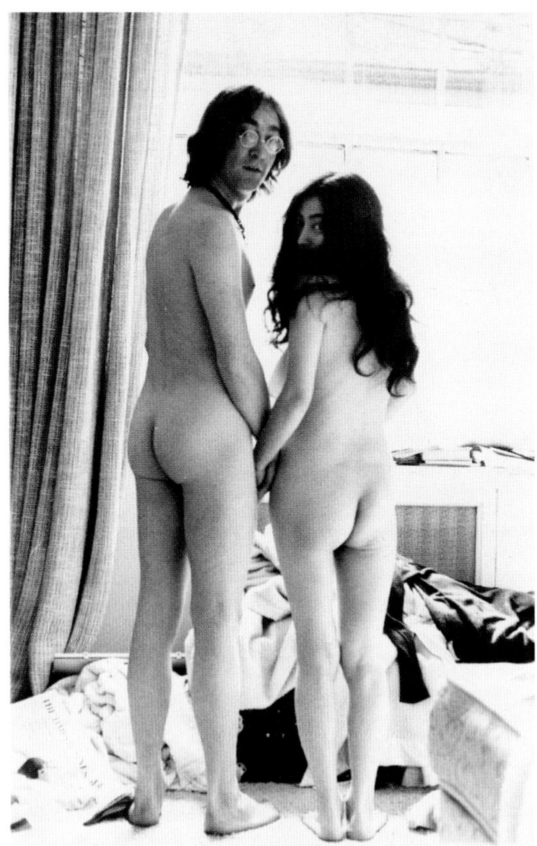

Fig.2 *John Lennon and Yoko Ono*, 1968
John Lennon
Gelatin silver print, 367 × 230mm
National Portrait Gallery, London

the record cover. Their nudity provoked outrage, with American authorities banning the album as obscene and distributors covering the sleeve in plain brown wrapping.

By May 1968, the two were living together and Yoko was present throughout the recording of the Beatles' *The White Album*, contributing to several tracks. For John, Yoko's presence was vital: 'Being with Yoko makes me whole. I don't want to sing if she's not there. We're like spiritual advisers.'[4] For his bandmates, Yoko's continual presence generated resentment, leading Lennon to announce he was breaking up the group in 1969.

Once both were divorced, John and Yoko married in Gibraltar in November 1968, with John changing his middle name from Winston to Ono. Knowing their honeymoon in Amsterdam would generate media interest, the newlyweds sent invitations for journalists to join them. The press were surprised to find the couple sitting in bed, wearing pyjamas, surrounded by flowers and hand-written peace signs (fig.3). Their 'bed-in for peace' lasted seven days, with the couple giving

OPPOSITE
Fig.3 *John Lennon and Yoko Ono*, 27 March 1969
Unknown photographer for *Central Press*
Gelatin silver press print, 253 × 203mm
National Portrait Gallery, London

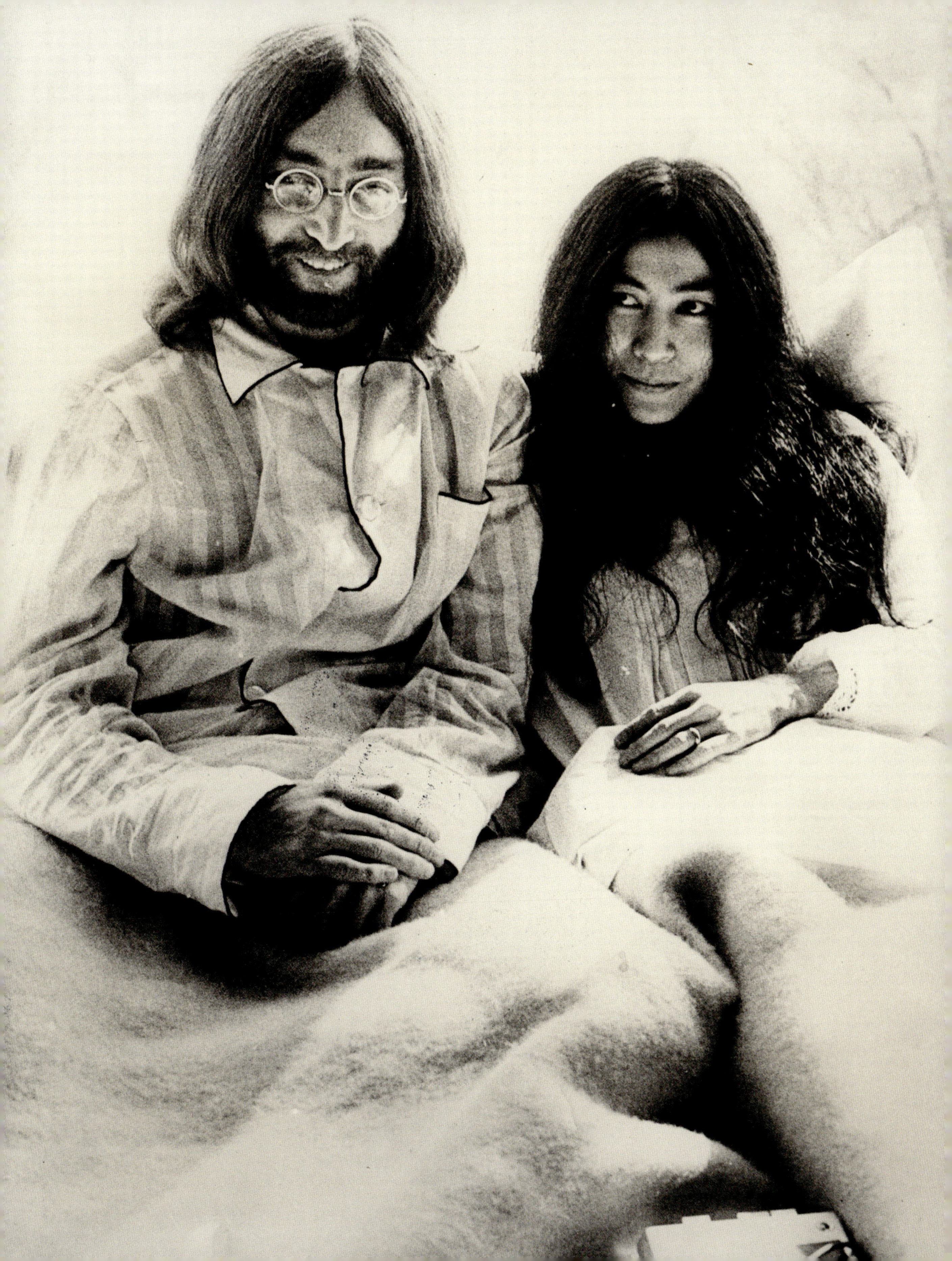

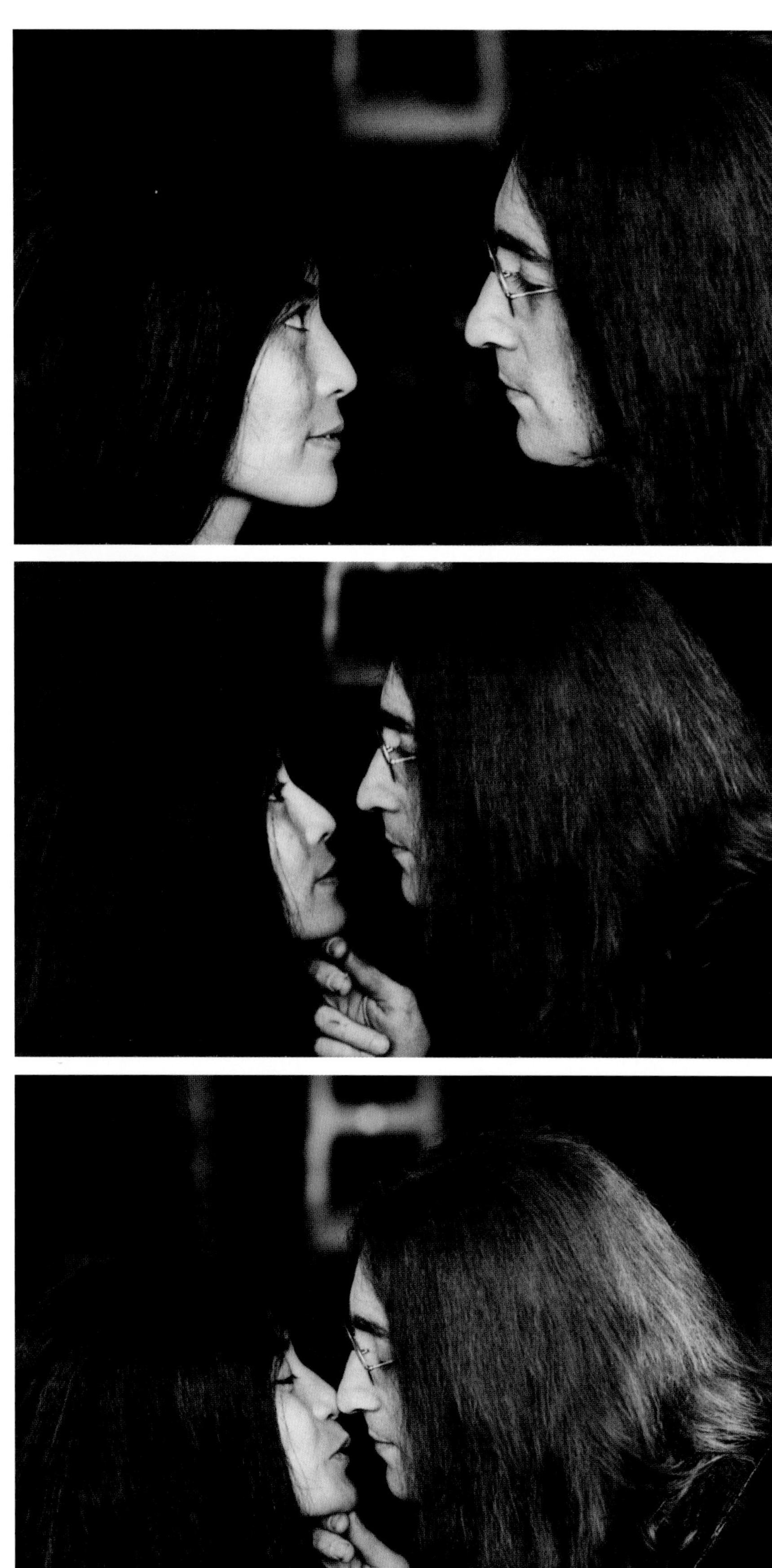

OPPOSITE
Fig.4 *Yoko Ono* and *John Lennon*, November 1969
Tom Blau
Modern gelatin silver prints,
171 × 265mm, 181 × 265mm, 182 × 265mm
National Portrait Gallery, London

RIGHT
Fig.5 *Yoko Ono and John Lennon*, early 1970s
Herb Schmitz
Gelatin silver print, 143 × 131mm
National Portrait Gallery, London

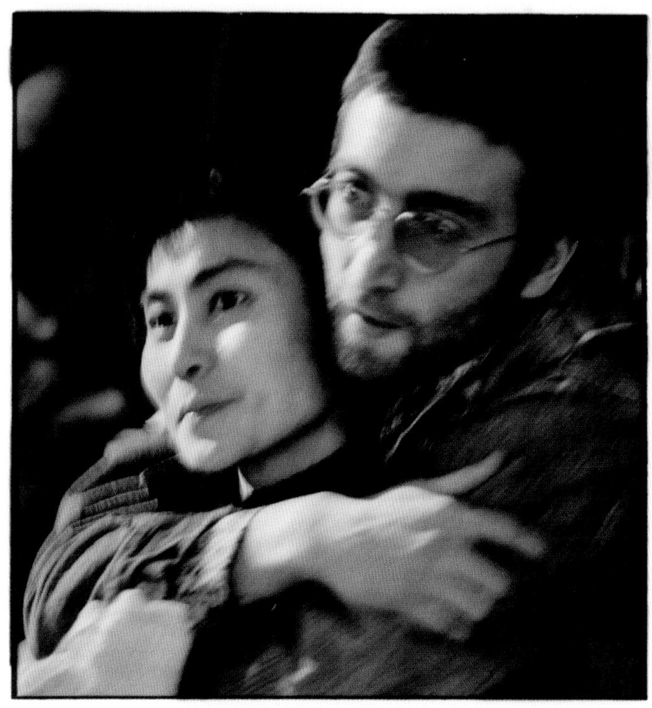

hundreds of interviews, 'to register our protest against all the suffering and violence in the world'.[5] Against the backdrop of the Vietnam War, further non-violent protests followed, and John's first solo album, *Imagine* (1971), featured lyrics that called for a world without division. The album, co-produced by Yoko, became the most successful and critically acclaimed of his career.

The two formed the Plastic Ono Band, collaborating with musicians on experimental releases, and John adopted a more confessional approach in his songwriting. 'God' (1970) featured the lyrics: 'I don't believe in Beatles / I just believe in me / Yoko and me / And that's reality.' Yoko helped John realise happiness outside of the Beatles, and the couple's closeness is recorded in photographs taken by Camera Press photographer Tom Blau, at their Berkshire home (fig.4). Yoko spoke of a telepathy between the two that inspired their creativity and collaboration, and John was influenced by Yoko's artistic sensibility; in a 1980 interview he stated, 'there's only two artists I've ever worked with for more than one night's stand, as it were. That's Paul McCartney and Yoko Ono. I think that's a pretty damned good choice.'[6]

By 1973, the marriage had entered a difficult period and the couple separated. Yoko later reflected, 'I was very aware that we were ruining each other's careers and I was hated and John was hated because of me.'[7] Following an affair with his wife's assistant, May Pang, a liaison that received Yoko's blessing, the couple reconciled in 1975, with John reflecting, 'our separation was a failure'.[8] When Yoko gave birth to their son, Sean, in October that year, John took a five-year hiatus from music to focus on his family.

Returning in 1980 with the album *Double Fantasy*, John was interviewed by *Rolling Stone* magazine, and celebrity photographer Annie Leibovitz was commissioned to take his portrait. Leibovitz was instructed to photograph John alone, due to the animosity still felt towards Yoko, but John insisted upon her inclusion. Taken in the couple's New York apartment, on 8 December 1980, Lennon is depicted naked and vulnerable, as he wraps himself around his clothed wife, tenderly kissing her cheek (fig.1). John's devotion is laid bare in this intimate image, and upon seeing a Polaroid, he admitted to Leibovitz, 'you've captured our relationship exactly'.[9] Within hours, Lennon was shot dead outside his apartment. Leibovitz's portrait has come to symbolise the couple's poignant 'last kiss', immortalising their love.[10]

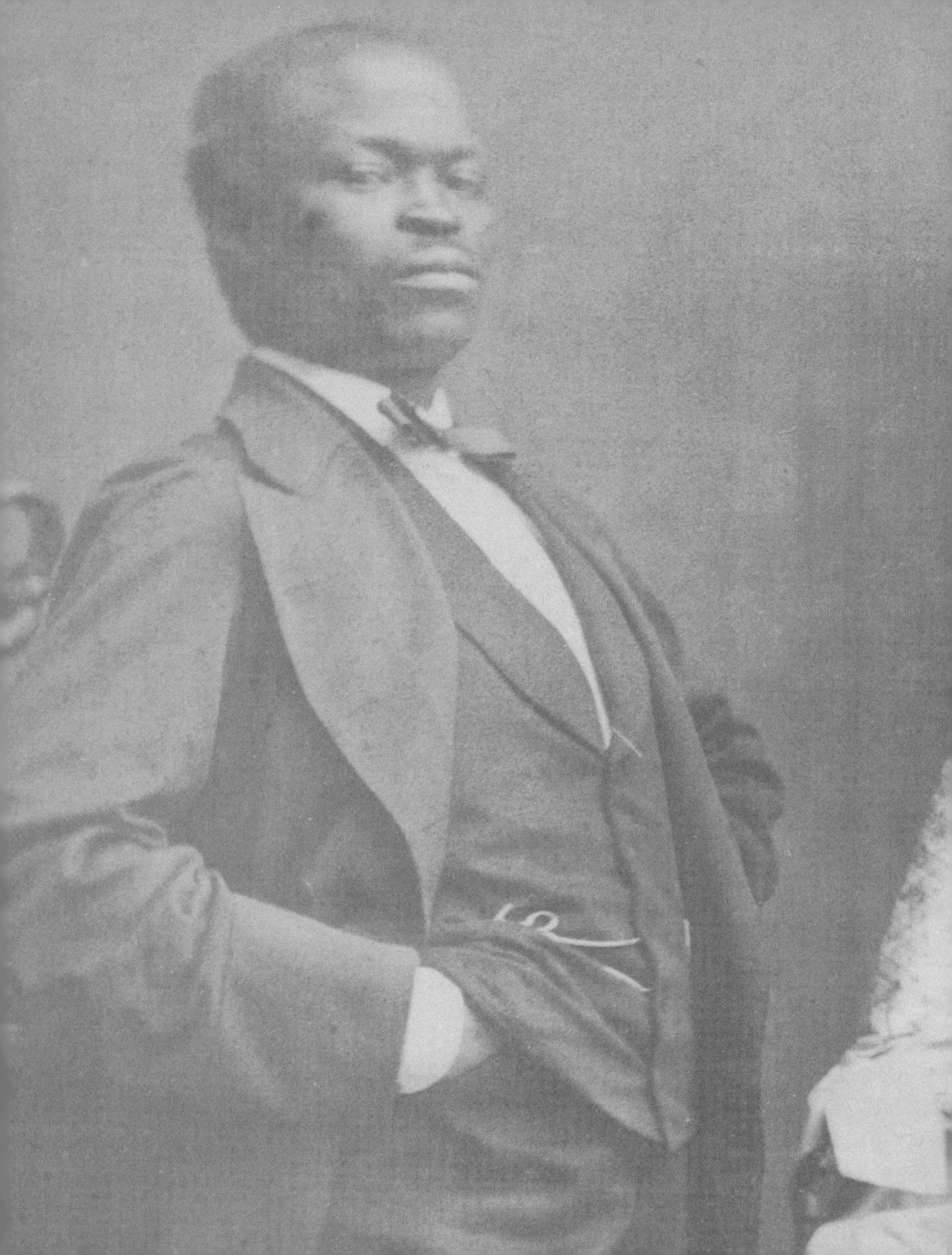

LOVE AGAINST THE ODDS

LOVE AGAINST THE ODDS

Forbidden or contentious relationships, crossing the lines of class, politics or race, have often ended unhappily and couples have been torn apart, ostracised by society or forced into arranged marriages against their will. However, some couples have defied expectations, pursuing lives and loves which have, against the odds, resulted in happy endings. People like Sir William Temple and his eventual wife Dorothy, whose families were on opposing sides during the English civil wars opted to play an extended waiting game. Eventually, years of mutual devotion convinced their families to allow them to marry (see pp.178–81).

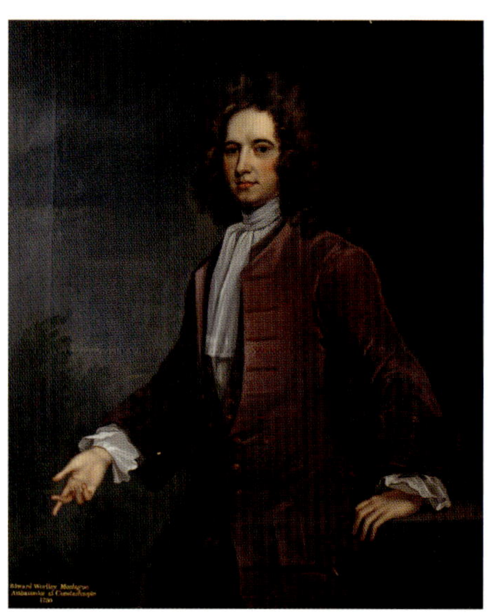

Fig.1 ***Edward Wortley Montagu*, 1730**
John Vanderbank
Oil on canvas, 1240 × 990mm
Government Art Collection, London

Others chose to elope. In 1710, Evelyn, Earl of Kingston, rejected the lawyer and politician Edward Wortley Montagu's request for his daughter Mary's hand in marriage (figs 1 and 2). The couple continued to send each other love letters, but in 1712 Mary's father tried to force her to marry another man. In response, she and Edward eloped, and were married secretly at Salisbury. This was to be the first of many adventures for Lady Mary. She accompanied Edward to Constantinople where he served as British Ambassador, recording local customs and adopting Turkish dress. On her return, she introduced smallpox inoculation to Western medicine and became an important figure in the 'bluestocking' circle of intellectual women. The pair had two children and, although their relationship was tumultuous and they often lived apart, they corresponded constantly. Lady

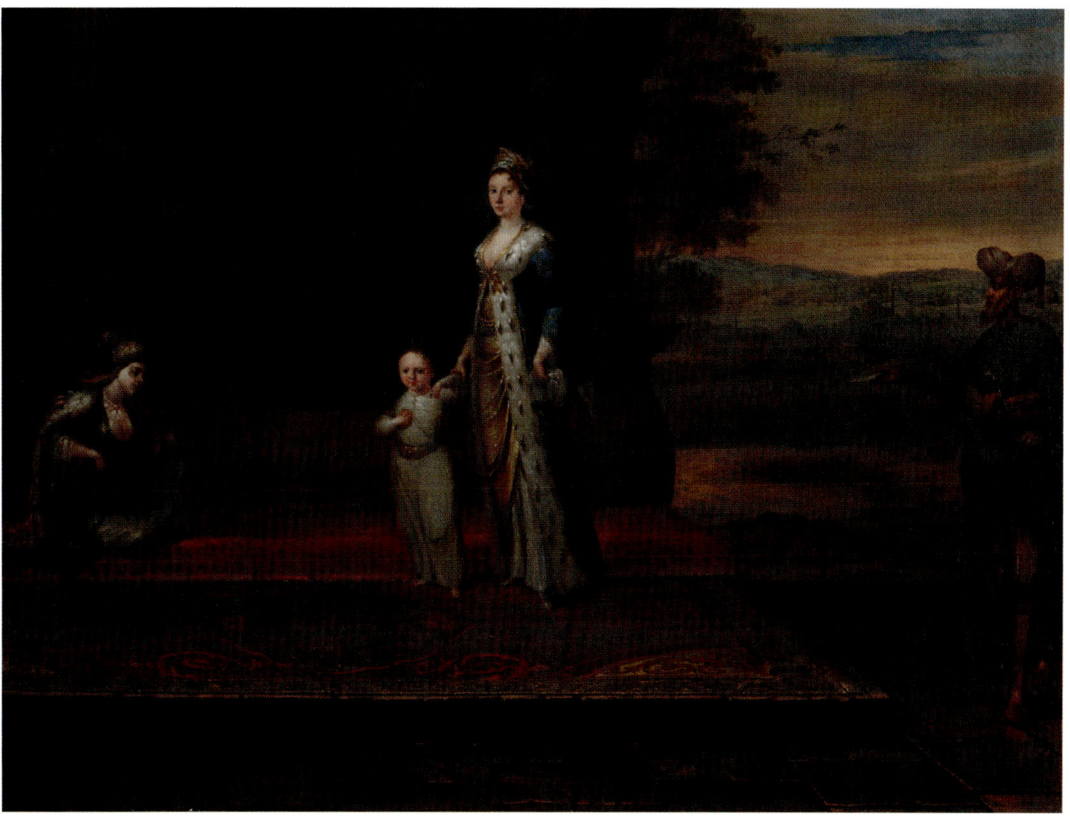

Fig.2 *Lady Mary Wortley Montagu with her Son, Edward Wortley Montagu, and Attendants*, c.1717
Attributed to Jean Baptiste Vanmour
Oil on canvas, 693 × 909mm
National Portrait Gallery, London

Mary's thoughts on marriage were published in a series of extracts from her letters in the *London Magazine* in the 1760s. She reflected that 'If [a couple] can but live together, what does it signify at what price, or by what means, their union is accomplished. Where love is real, and, well founded, it is impossible to be happy but in the quiet enjoyment of the beloved object.'[1]

Some lovers have overcome the prejudices of wider society with regard to race, class or same-sex love in order to forge a life together. The Irish aristocrats, and childhood friends, Lady Eleanor Butler and Lady Sarah Ponsonby first attempted to elope and live together in 1778. They ran away from their home in Castle Kilkenny – dressed as men and carrying pistols – but were apprehended at Waterford. Later that year their families relented and allowed them to move to Plas Newydd in Llangollen, Wales, where they remained for nearly fifty years, engaging in 'improving' pastimes including gardening, reading and turning their home into a gothic haven (fig.3). They dressed in riding habits and wore their hair cropped, giving them a distinctive masculine appearance. Dubbed simply the 'Ladies of Llangollen' their

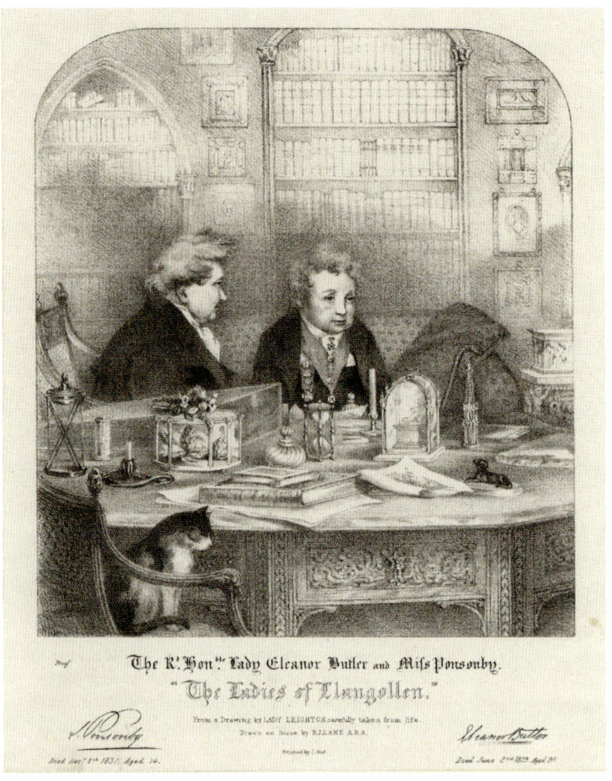

Fig.3 ***Sarah Ponsonby and Lady (Charlotte) Eleanor Butler* (*'The Ladies of Llangollen'*), 1836**
Richard James Lane
Lithograph, 434 × 331mm
National Portrait Gallery, London

relationship was a subject of ongoing popular fascination and speculation, nevertheless their life-long devotion was idealised as perfect friendship. Poems were written about them and their motives in choosing their unusual way of life were discussed in fashionable correspondence. They became something of a tourist attraction, being visited by many national and literary celebrities including the Duke of Wellington, William Wordsworth, Sir Walter Scott and Josiah Wedgwood. Although the exact nature of their relationship is unclear, today Butler and Ponsonby are celebrated as early lesbian icons and 'queer romantics'. Like the other couples featured here, they undoubtedly showed courage in choosing a life which did not confirm to society's expectations.

Similarly, the composer Samuel Coleridge-Taylor and his wife Jessie defied the expectations of middle-class Victorian Britain, and Jessie's family, in order to marry. The pair met through the Royal College of Music where both were studying in the early 1890s. Their romantic relationship began in 1896 and in 1898 Coleridge-Taylor visited Jessie's father to ask for her hand in marriage. The next day, he told Jessie that he had been 'kicked out of the house' and

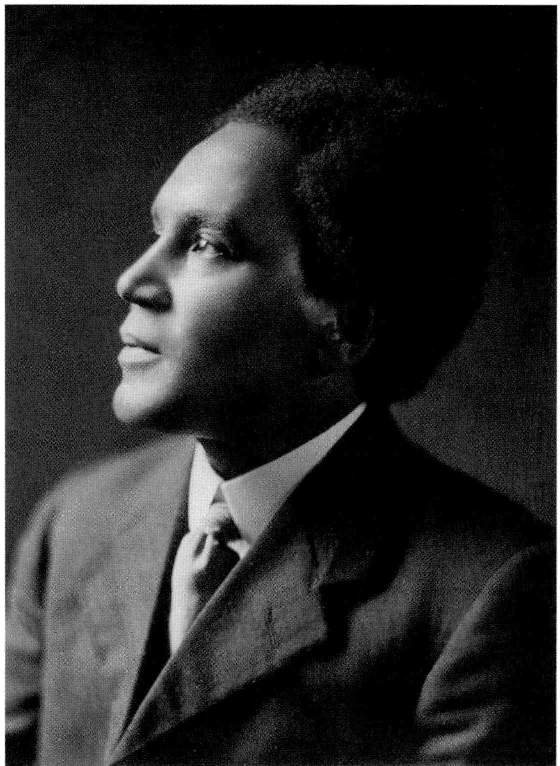

Fig.4 *Samuel Coleridge-Taylor*, 1912
E.O. Hoppé
Gelatin silver print, 204 × 146mm
National Portrait Gallery, London

subsequently the couple were forced to meet in secret as her family vehemently disapproved of the match.[2] Samuel Coleridge-Taylor was the child of an unmarried English mother and a black doctor from Sierra Leone. Both his lack of social status and his mixed-race heritage can, according to values of the day, be assumed to be the reasons that Jessie's middle-class family were set against him as a match for their daughter. Nevertheless, they persevered. Coleridge-Taylor began to enjoy professional success and the pair were formally engaged in 1899, marrying at the end of the year. The day before the wedding Jessie's family finally acquiesced. Her father was a witness to the marriage although Jessie recorded in her memoirs that her sisters continued to try to dissuade her until the very last moment. The pair went on to have two children and she used her musical knowledge to support his career until his death, in 1912, at the age of just thirty-seven. Just before their wedding, Samuel and Jessie had sealed up their years of love letters in a casket. At her husband's funeral, Jessie arranged for the casket to be opened and the letters scattered into his coffin, testament to the couple's enduring love and their courage in the face of adversity.

CATHARINE MACLEOD

Sir William Temple & Dorothy, Lady Temple

The political and social turmoil of civil war in England during the 1640s, the execution of King Charles I in 1649 and the tensions of the eleven years of interregnum that followed provided the problematic backdrop to many romances. However, unlike most such relationships, that between Dorothy Osborne and William Temple is recorded in a collection of surviving letters, written by Dorothy to William during the years in which they longed to marry. These are a testament to the couple's mutual devotion and to Dorothy's engaging, lively personality. Most of William's replies, unfortunately, do not survive.

Dorothy Osborne was the daughter of Sir Peter Osborne, lieutenant-governor of Guernsey and a supporter of King Charles I. As was the case with many wealthy families in this period, the political allegiances of her wider family network were complex and often encompassed support for both sides of the conflict. Accordingly, for some of the civil war period Dorothy lived with her maternal uncle, an influential supporter of the Parliamentarian side. Then, in 1646 her Royalist father was forced into exile in Saint Malo in France, and in 1648 Dorothy set out to visit him, a journey that was to change the course of her life.

William Temple was the son of Sir John Temple, a judge in Ireland and a supporter of the Parliamentarian side during the civil war years. In spite of his father's politics, William lived for much of his youth with a Royalist uncle. In 1648 William embarked on a continental tour in order to further his education. He broke his journey on the Isle of Wight, where Dorothy Osborne and her brother had also stopped on their way to France. It was here that the two met.

Dorothy and William, aged twenty-one and twenty respectively, were evidently strongly

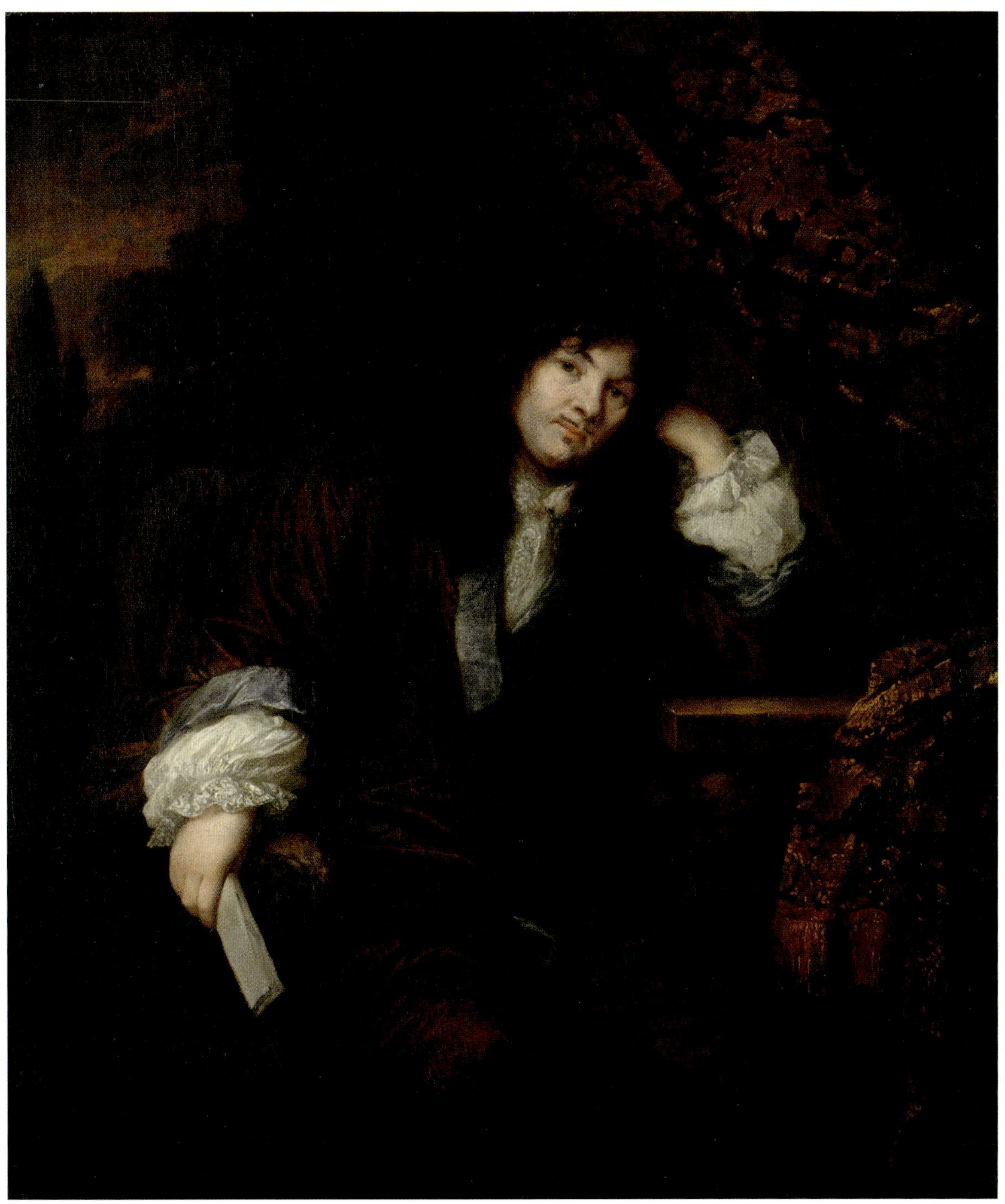

Fig.1 *Sir William Temple*, 1675
Caspar Netscher
Oil on canvas, 521 × 432mm
National Portrait Gallery, London

attracted to one another but had to go on their separate journeys. Another meeting two years later in London rekindled the spark between them, but circumstances forced them apart again for another two years while William was travelling. On his return, in December 1652, he wrote to Dorothy asking if she was engaged to anyone else. Her negative and witty response evidently delighted him and led to a devoted, lively and regular correspondence that, however, they had to keep a secret. Both families objected to a relationship, partly based on political affiliations but probably more importantly on financial considerations; both fathers wanted their children to marry into more money. Dorothy's family presented her with numerous alternative suitors, including Henry Cromwell, son of the Protector Oliver Cromwell, but she wrote amusingly to William about each one's shortcomings and dismissed them all. She commented, 'Tis much easier sure to get a good fortune than a good husband, but whosoever marries without any consideration of fortune shall never be allowed to do it out of so reasonable an apprehension.'[1]

Finally in 1654, after her father's death, Dorothy and William managed to overcome their families' objections and began to plan their marriage. Just before it was due to take place, however, Dorothy suffered a life-threatening attack of smallpox. William came to her side during her illness, Dorothy recovered, and they married a month later, on Christmas Day, 1654. They went on to have eight or possibly nine children, all of whom died in infancy except one daughter, Diana, who died of smallpox as a teenager, and one son, John, who drowned himself in adulthood. Their portraits, painted during periods of diplomatic work in The Hague, show them in poses that were understood at the time to indicate melancholy, perhaps referring to their bereavements (figs 1 and 2). Although William and Dorothy's marriage seems to have been strong, their great love for one another sadly became the backdrop to a family life repeatedly punctuated by tragedy.

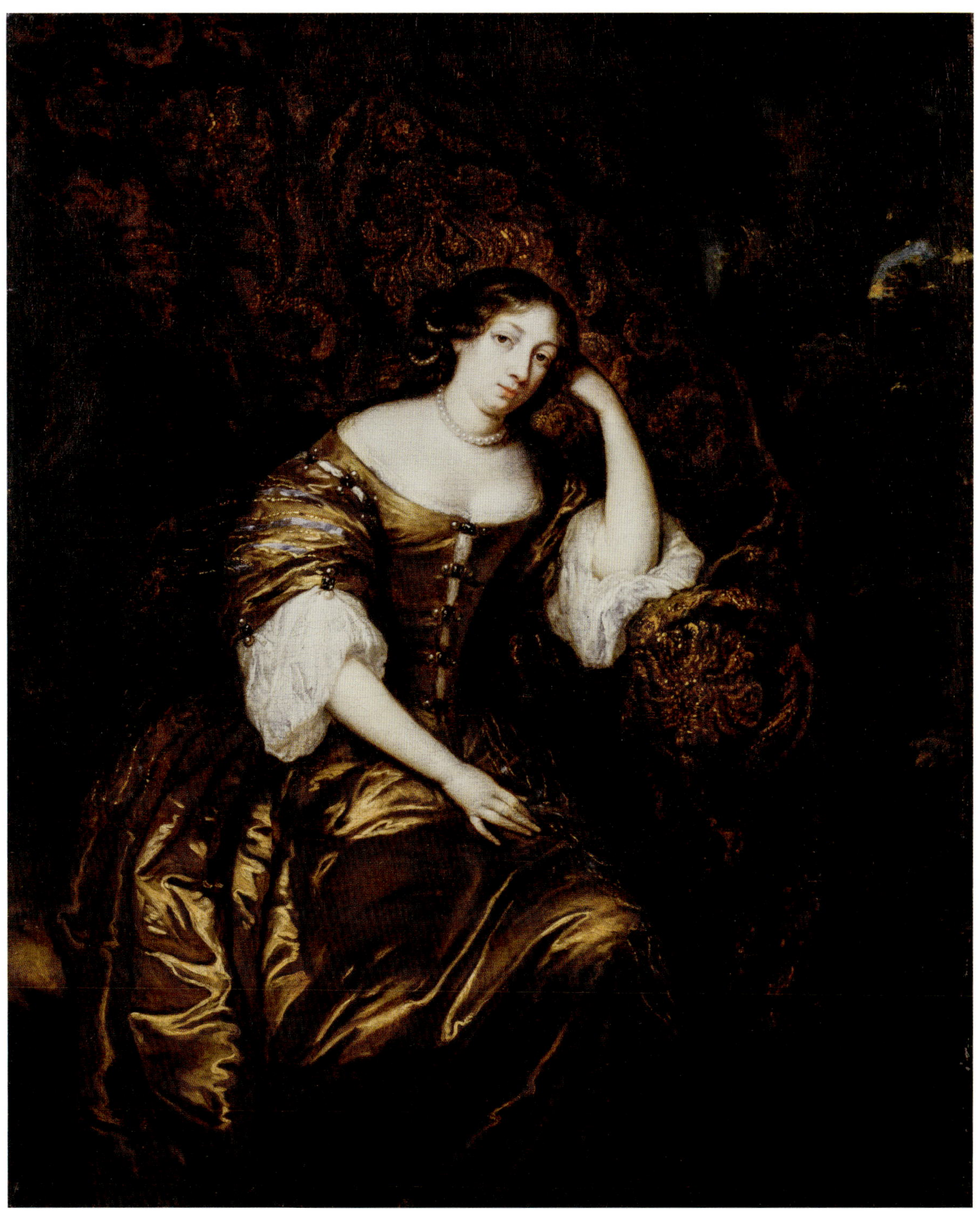

Fig.2 *Dorothy, Lady Temple*, 1676
Caspar Netscher
Oil on canvas, 476 × 387mm
National Portrait Gallery, London

CLARE FREESTONE

SARAH FORBES BONETTA
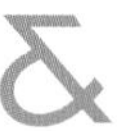
JAMES PINSON LABULO DAVIES

In 1860, 17-year-old Sarah Forbes Bonetta received a proposal of marriage from James Pinson Labulo Davies. Her suitor was fourteen years her senior – and although Sarah was not initially enthusiastic, it was the will of her protector Queen Victoria that the marriage should take place. Their story is one of a union that grew in spite of an inauspicious beginning, and only because of the extraordinary events which led an orphan from West Africa to become a ward of the Queen of England.

Naval officer turned merchant and missionary, Captain James Davies had met Sarah Forbes Bonetta only once before his proposal, when she was being schooled in Sierra Leone. Sarah had been sent there by Queen Victoria as the climate was thought better for the health of an African girl. Her given name Sarah Forbes Bonetta recorded how, in 1850, she had been brought to England by Captain Frederick Edwyn Forbes upon the Royal Navy vessel HMS *Bonetta*. Forbes had been given the 'captive girl' by King Gezo of Dahomey (now Benin), during negotiations intended to persuade him to give up his part in the slave trade. The Yoruba girl's fate would otherwise have been sacrificial death or a future in slavery, following the death of her parents in the slave-hunts that took place as part of the Okeadon War. As Britain was actively engaged in spreading the lessons of the abolition of slavery around the world, Forbes decided to accept the child, whose original name was Ina or Aina.

On his return, Sarah was presented to Queen Victoria in November 1850. The Queen wrote in her diary; 'Capt. Forbes saved her life, by asking for her as a present ... She is 7 years old, sharp & intelligent, & speaks English.'[1] From that date, Sarah became attached to the royal household. Margaret Phipps and Sir Charles Beaumont

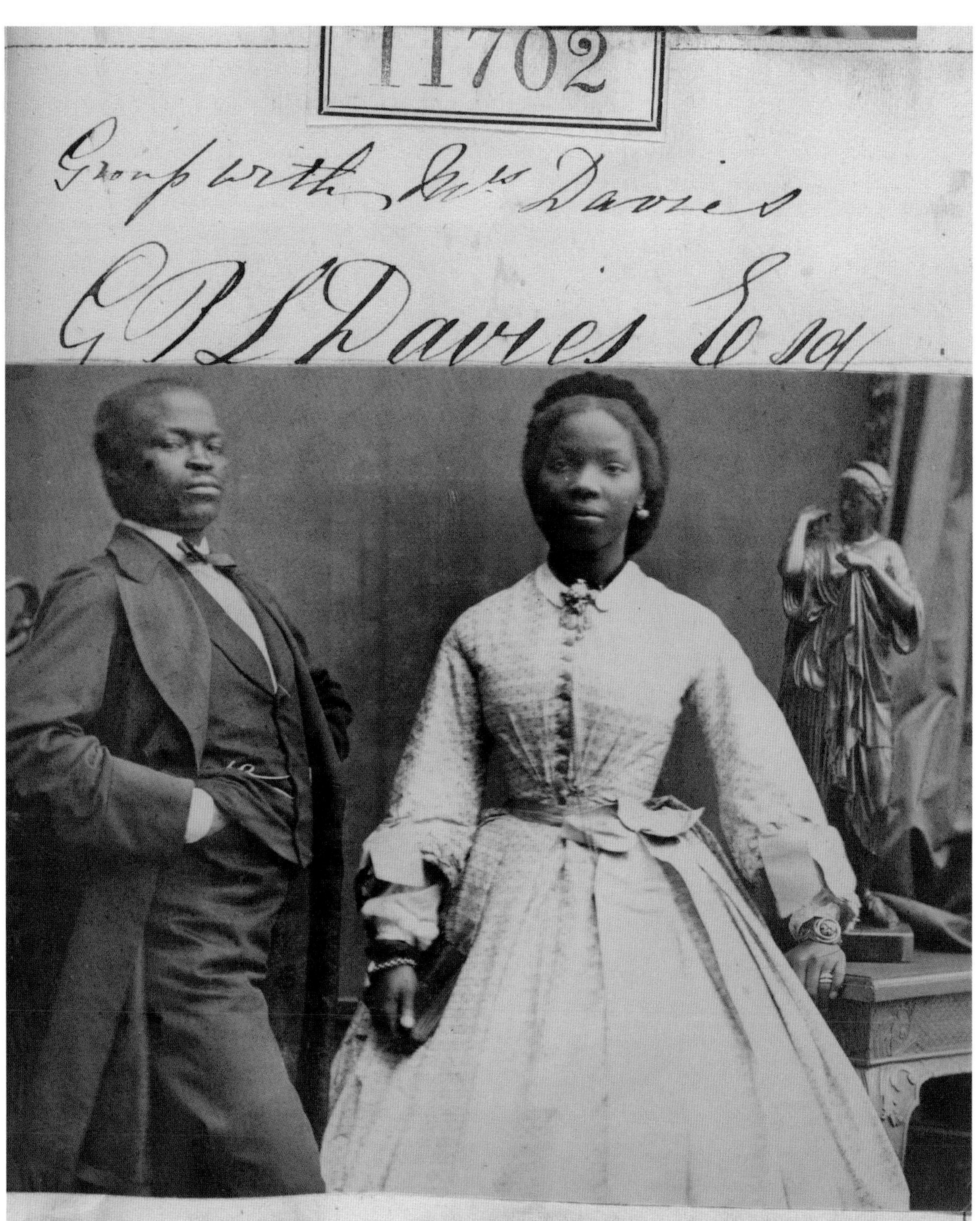

Fig.1 *James Pinson Labulo Davies and Sarah Forbes Bonetta (Sarah Davies)*, 15 September 1862
Camille Silvy
Albumen print, 108 × 129mm
National Portrait Gallery, London

Phipps, Equerry to Queen Victoria, oversaw her care with money designated for her upkeep. The story of Sarah's 'rescue' was brought to public attention in Captain Forbes' book *Dahomey and the Dahomans* (1851) where he stated that 'her mind has received a moral and religious impression, and she was baptized, according to the rites of the Protestant church Sarah Forbes Bonetta'.[2]

Following her education through which Sarah became an accomplished linguist and pianist, the final duty for Sarah's royal protector was the arrangement of a suitable marriage. When James Davies declared his interest in marrying her, the match was well thought of but Sarah was reluctant to accept his offer. This is likely to have encouraged the decision to relocate her to Brighton, where Sarah felt isolated and unhappy. She questioned marrying Davies against choice; 'I don't feel a particle of love for him and have never done so, though now it is a year since he last asked me. What am I to do?'[3]

Sarah eventually acquiesced and married James Davies on 14 August 1862. The pressure of royal approval had no doubt steered her decision. The lavish ceremony took place at St Nicholas Church in Brighton, led by the Bishop of Sierra Leone with sixteen bridesmaids in attendance and ten carriages in the procession. Just before the couple sailed for Africa, where Davies' work was based, they were photographed by the fashionable photographer Camille Silvy who made a series of portraits to mark their marriage in his thriving Bayswater studio (figs 1 and 2).

Once settled in colonial Lagos, Sarah's letters indicate her growing affection and respect for her husband and soon after the marriage she was pregnant. Their firstborn Victoria (b.1863) became a goddaughter of the queen. Sarah and James had two more children; Arthur (b.1871) and Stella (b.1873). By the time the family travelled back to England thirteen years later, Davies' failing businesses and a fraud claim against him were causing the marriage strain and Sarah's health had begun to deteriorate. Diagnosed with consumption (tuberculosis) she reluctantly agreed to go to Madeira for treatment. 'My husband who has had enough trouble to kill two ordinary men, made up his mind at the instigation of the doctor to send me here for some months change and here I am with Stella and her nurse for an indefinite period.'[4] Sarah died on 15 August 1880 – the news reached her daughter, Victoria, in England over a week later.

Davies, despite his shortcomings, was credited for pioneering cocoa farming in West Africa and contributed funds to establish a grammar school in Lagos, where he died and was buried in 1906. Sarah had been buried in Madeira regardless of her wish to be laid to rest at sea. The sea over which she was carried and over which her fortune was changed more than once.

Fig.2 *James Pinson Labulo Davies and Sarah Forbes Bonetta (Sarah Davies)*, 15 September 1862
Camille Silvy
Albumen print, 108 × 129mm
National Portrait Gallery, London

11699

G P L Davies Esq
Group with Mrs Davies

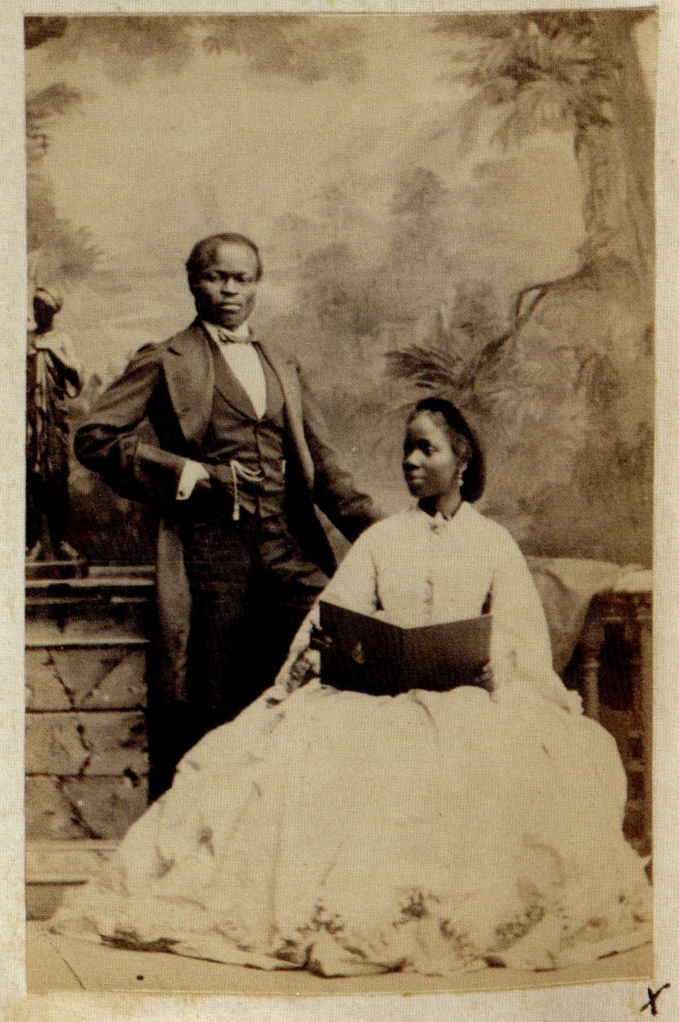

x

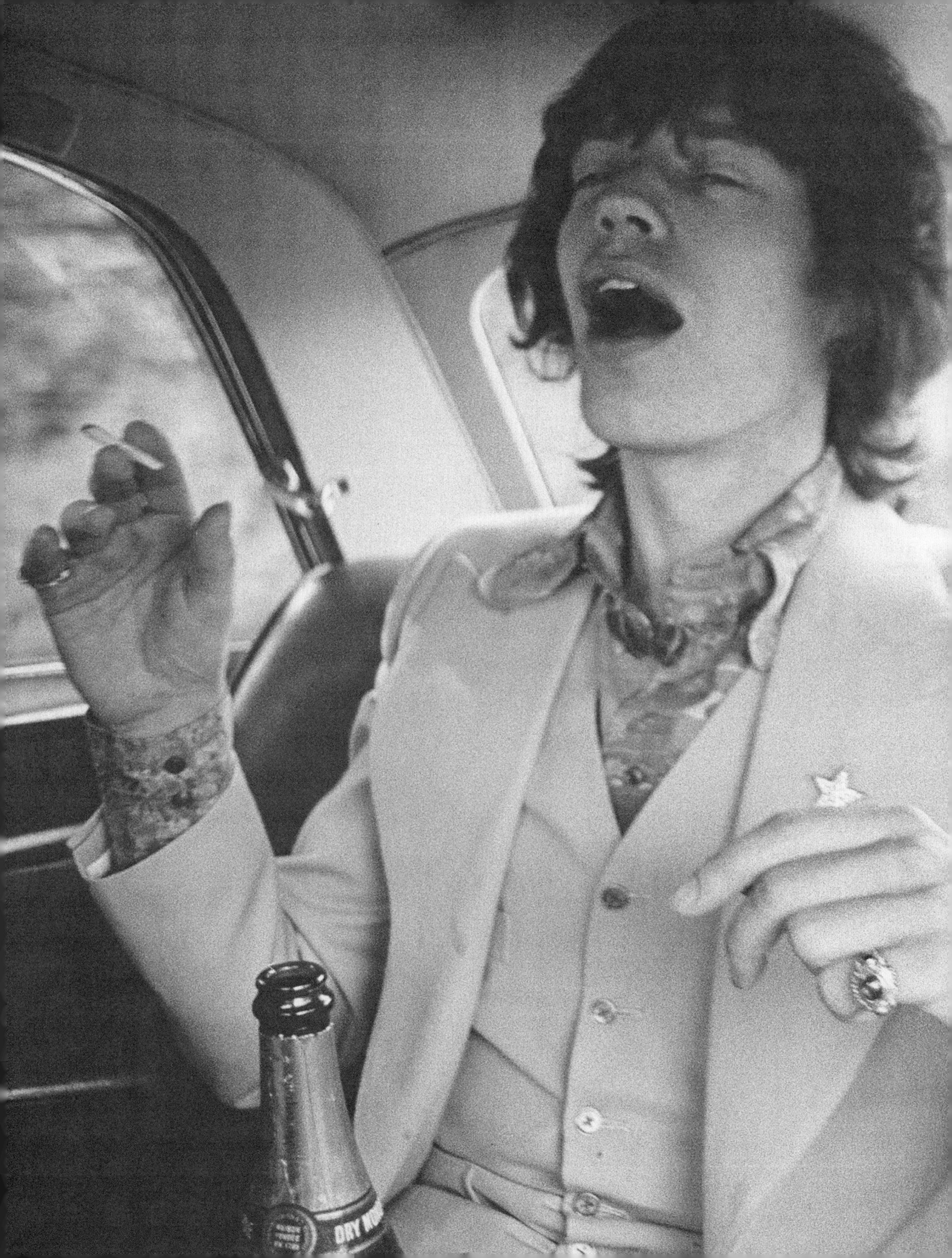

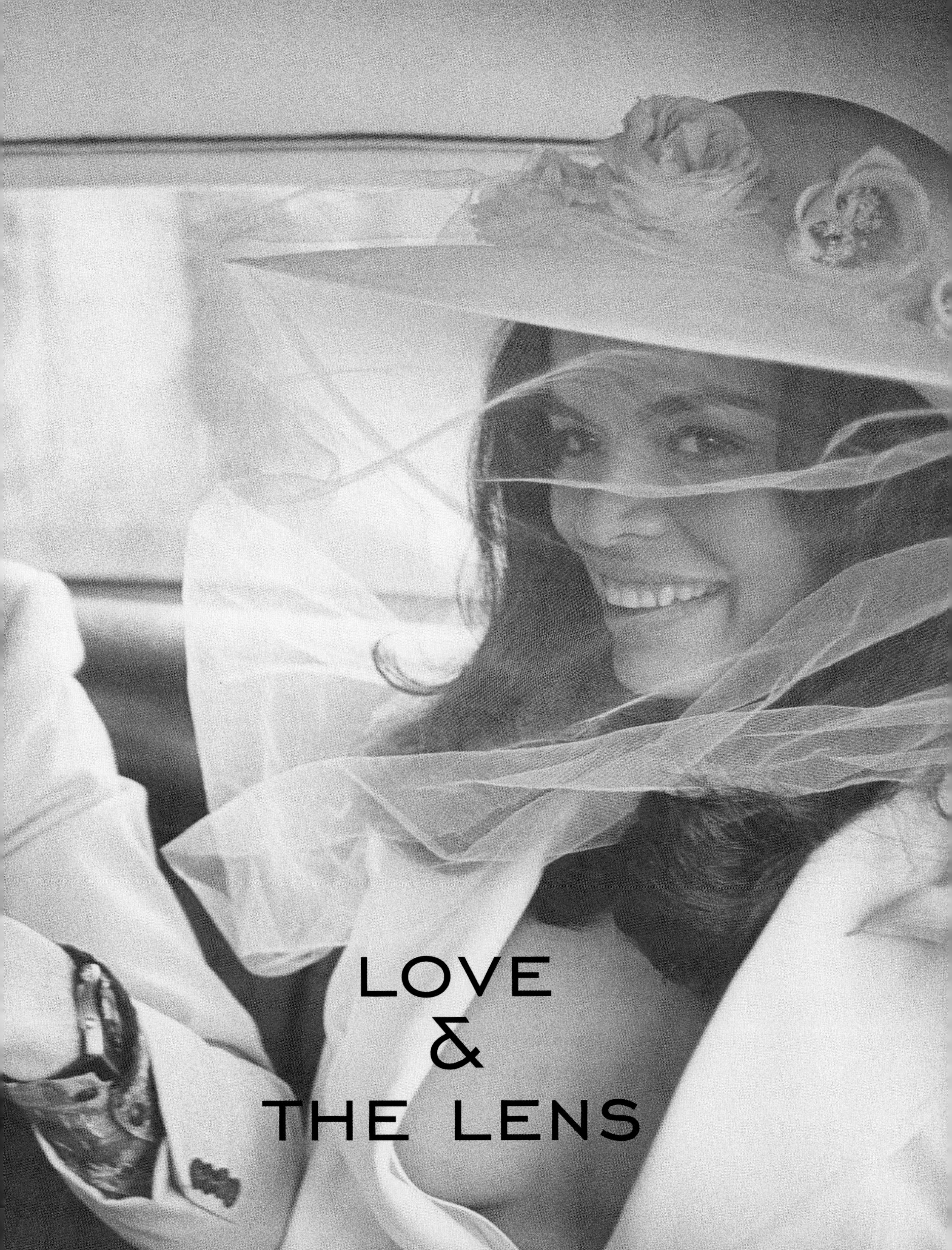

LOVE & THE LENS

LOUISE STEWART

LOVE AGAINST THE ODDS

We are a star-struck society that has an obsession for celebrity romance, from its first glimmers to its 'kiss and tell' break-ups. Indeed, throughout the twentieth and twenty-first centuries, the link between celebrity, love and photography has had a huge and ever-increasing impact on visual culture. The 'Golden Age' of film, in the early and mid-twentieth century, saw the avid consumption of photographs of glamorous couples and a fascination for the love affairs and personal lives of film stars and other media celebrities. Press photographs of the likes of Laurence Olivier and Vivien Leigh and Marilyn Monroe and the playwright Arthur Miller, pictured here at the opening of one

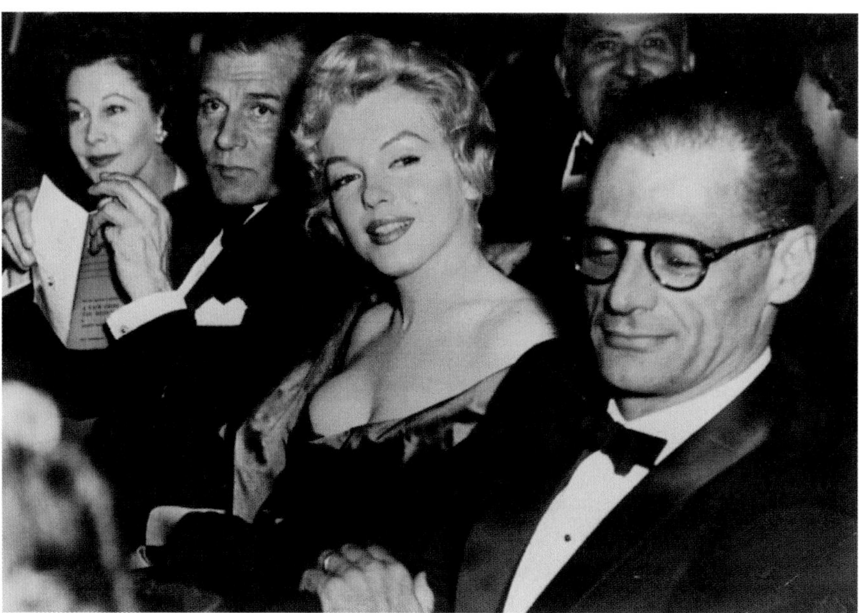

Fig.1 *Vivien Leigh, Laurence Olivier, Marilyn Monroe and Arthur Miller*, 1956
Unknown photographer for *Associated Press*
Gelatin silver print, 150 × 213mm
National Portrait Gallery, London

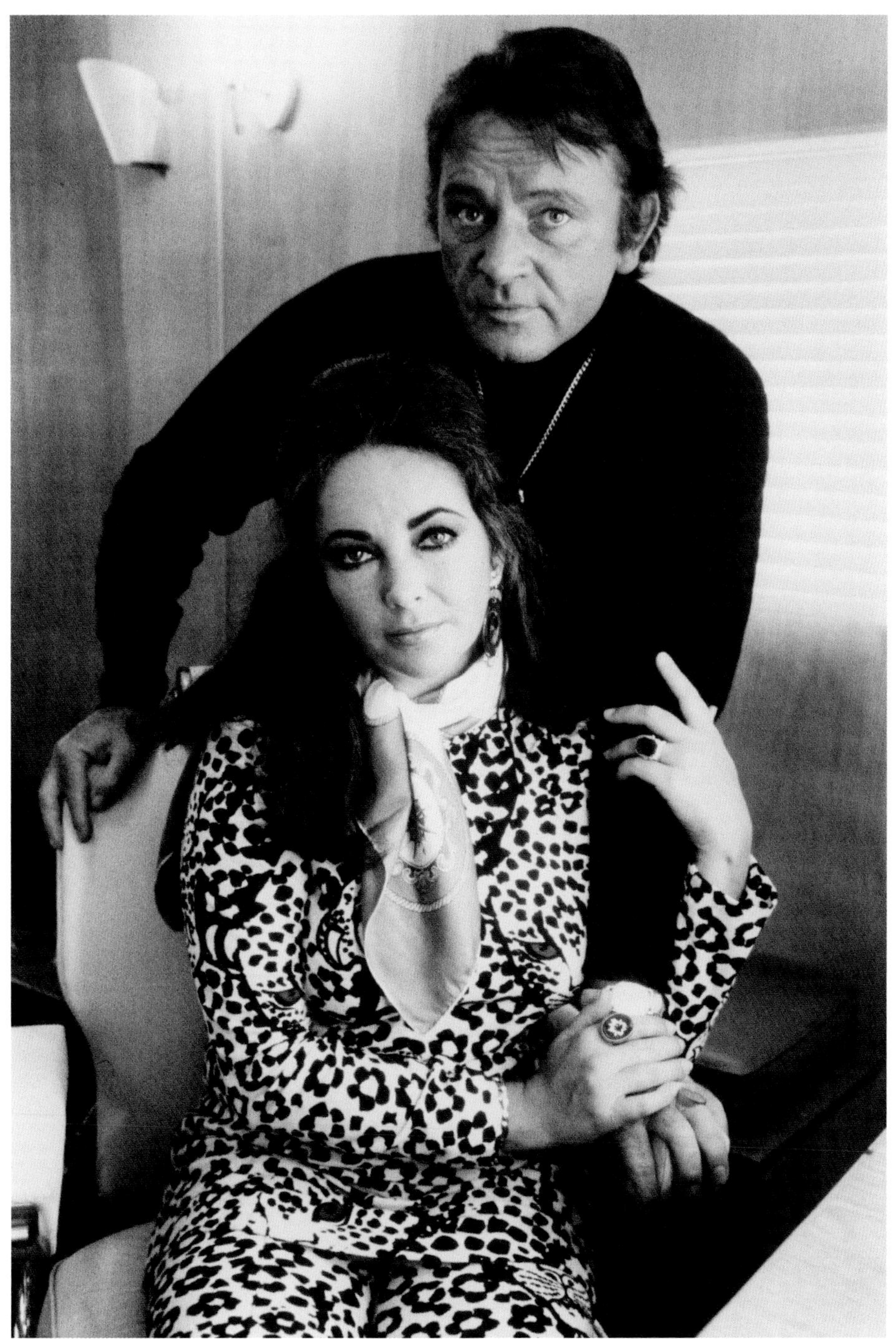

Fig.2 *Richard Burton and Dame Elizabeth Taylor*, 1971
Terry O'Neill
Gelatin silver print, 478 × 317mm
National Portrait Gallery, London

of Miller's plays (fig.1), have been the life-blood of the popular press from the early days of illustrated newspapers and magazines.

The short duration of many modern relationships and speculation and news over the real-life drama of extramarital affairs added a frisson of scandal and excitement to the latest film industry gossip. Film stars Richard Burton and Elizabeth Taylor met on the set of the 1962 film *Cleopatra*. Sharing their first kiss on film, the moment continued even after the director had called 'cut'. They went on to have a turbulent relationship, marrying and divorcing twice. Here, they are captured by Terry O'Neill, one of the most prolific celebrity photographers of the 1970s (fig.2).

The 1960s and 1970s also witnessed the rise of supermodels. Some of the most striking fashion images of the period emerged from collaborations between models and photographers who were also lovers. These include the 'original' supermodel Jean Shrimpton and photographer David Bailey, and, more recently, Kate Moss. Moss was an unknown 18-year-old when she was photographed by her boyfriend Mario Sorrenti in a remarkable series of images that capture all the rawness and intensity of first love and youthful desire (fig.3). They were later used in the Calvin Klein advertising campaign which launched Moss to global stardom.

In the 1970s rock stars inherited the iconic status of Hollywood legends, with photographs of the likes of Mick and Bianca Jagger supporting their fame and promoting their whirlwind romance (see pp.204–6). The subject matter continues to be addressed by leading photographers. Juergen Teller's photograph of David and Victoria Beckham, for example, captures an unusually intimate and quiet moment in a high-profile couple's relationship (fig.4). In the days when they were awaiting the birth of their first child and planning their wedding, Teller shows them lying on the floor of the hallway of the Malmaison Hotel, Manchester, with a heavily pregnant Victoria laying her head on David's shoulder. In 2016, Victoria noted Teller's candid approach to the shoot: 'it just felt like David and I were spending the day together and there happened to be a photographer there'.[1] Afterwards, one of the images hung in the couple's Manchester apartment.

Similarly, royal romance has fascinated the public for centuries and photographic images of royal couples including Queen Elizabeth II and Prince Philip and Prince Charles and Princess Diana have fed this appetite. More recently, Alexi Lubomirski's photographs of the engagement (fig.5) and wedding (fig.6) of the Duke and Duchess of Sussex were instantly shared around the world in print and online. In the age of social media, the interaction between photography, celebrity, love and intimacy is more relevant than ever.

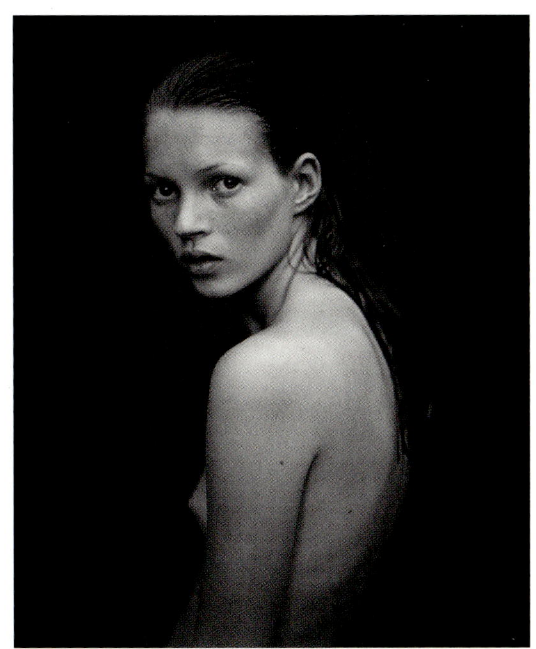

Fig.3 *Kate Moss*, 1993
Mario Sorrenti
Inkjet print, 1000 × 850mm
National Portrait Gallery, London

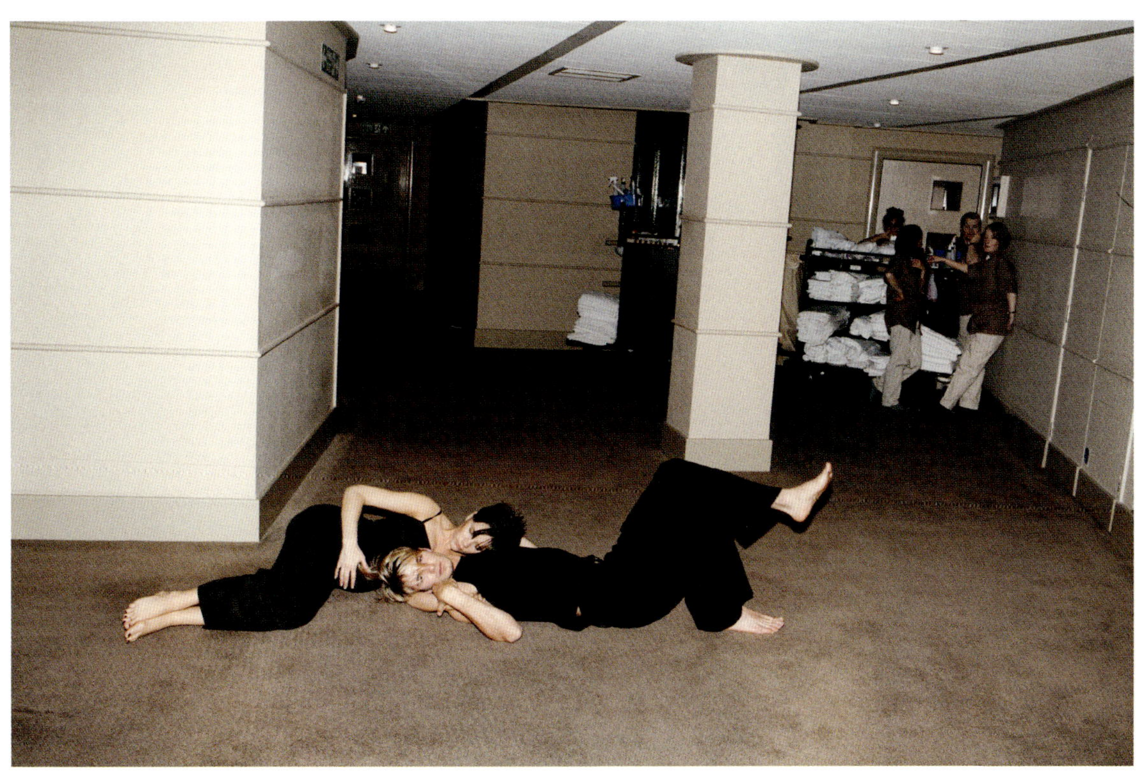

Fig.4 *David and Victoria, Manchester 1998, No.3*, 1998
Juergen Teller
Chromogenic print, 880 × 1280mm
National Portrait Gallery, London

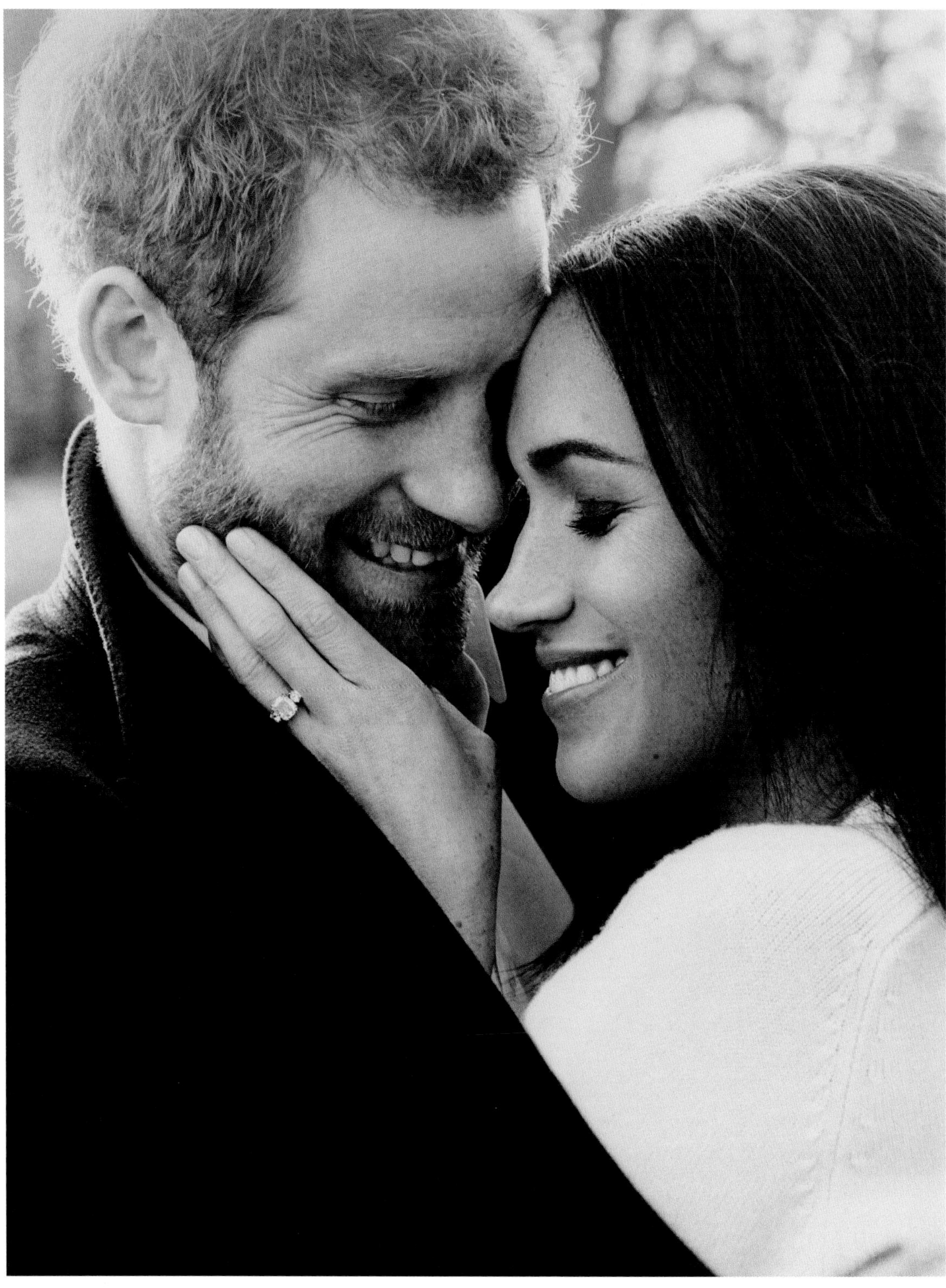

Fig.5 *Prince Harry and Meghan Markle (pose for one of two official engagement photos at Frogmore House), Windsor*, 21 December 2017
Alexi Lubomirski
Gelatin silver print, 575 × 430mm
National Portrait Gallery, London

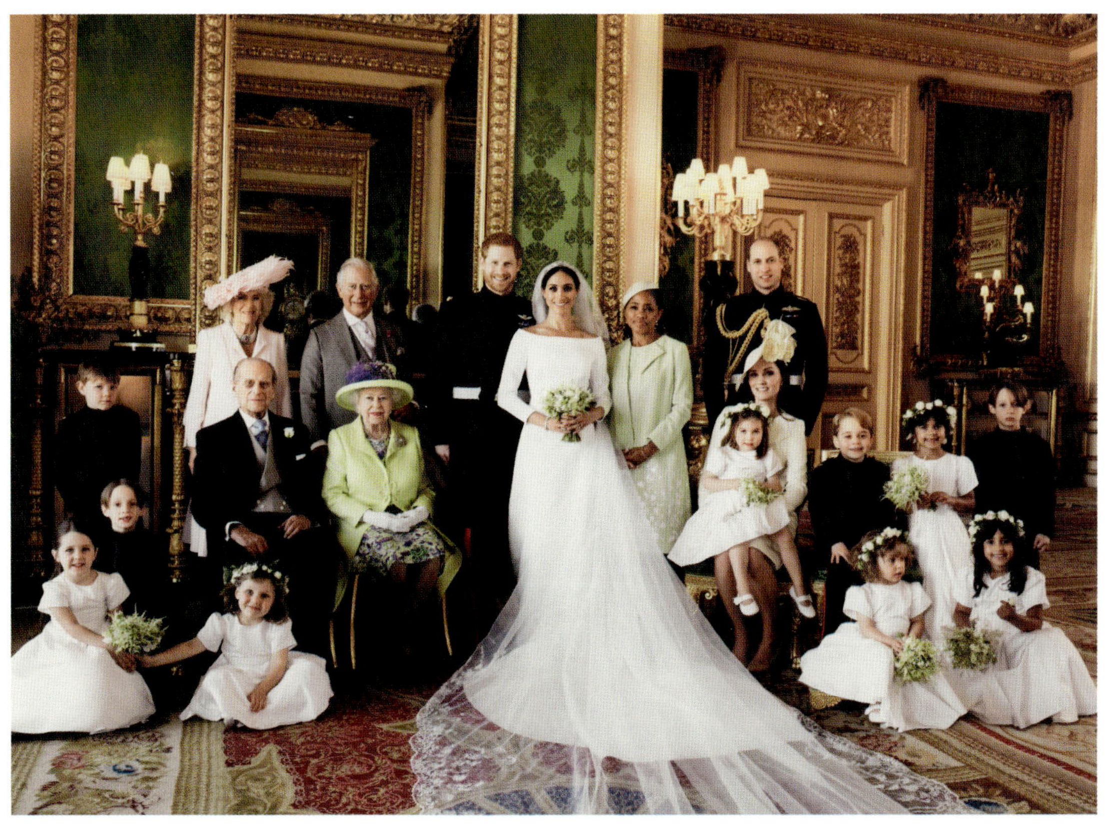

Fig.6 *Meghan, Duchess of Sussex and Prince Harry, Duke of Sussex and Family*, 19 May 2018
Alexi Lubomirski
Inkjet print, 420 × 560mm
National Portrait Gallery, London

SIMON CALLOW

Vivien Leigh & Laurence Olivier

In what is loosely called show business, it is rarer than one might expect for passion and professional careers to coincide. There are many long-established theatrical marriages and partnerships, to be sure, but great passions which find their way onto the marquees and the billboards are rare. The love affair of Laurence Olivier and Vivien Leigh (fig.1) was one such, equal in intensity and just as controversial as that of Richard Burton and Elizabeth Taylor thirty years later.

When they met, in 1935, they were both on the brink of extraordinary careers: that year she had caused a considerable stir in an English adaptation of Sternheim's play *The Mask of Virtue*, which had led to her being contracted by the great film producer Alexander Korda, while Olivier had created a sensation as the hero of the First World War play *Journey's End*. He then appeared as Victor Prynne in the original production of Noël Coward's *Private Lives* in 1930 and finally, in the year he and she met, as a disturbingly sexy Mercutio (alternating with John Gielgud as Romeo), his first stab at a classical play in London. Both of them were noted for their physical beauty and sexual charisma: she was possessed of exquisite natural looks which somehow combined the elements of her background, Anglo-Indian and Armenian. The photographer Cecil Beaton, in his first session with her, described her as 'like a Persian gazelle in the dark studio forest'. Olivier, less naturally beautiful, had turned himself into a matinee idol, dashing, athletic and chiselled. Both were married to other people.

Fig.1 *Laurence Olivier and Vivien Leigh*, 1937
Unknown photographer
Gelatin silver print, 241 x 189mm
National Portrait Gallery, London

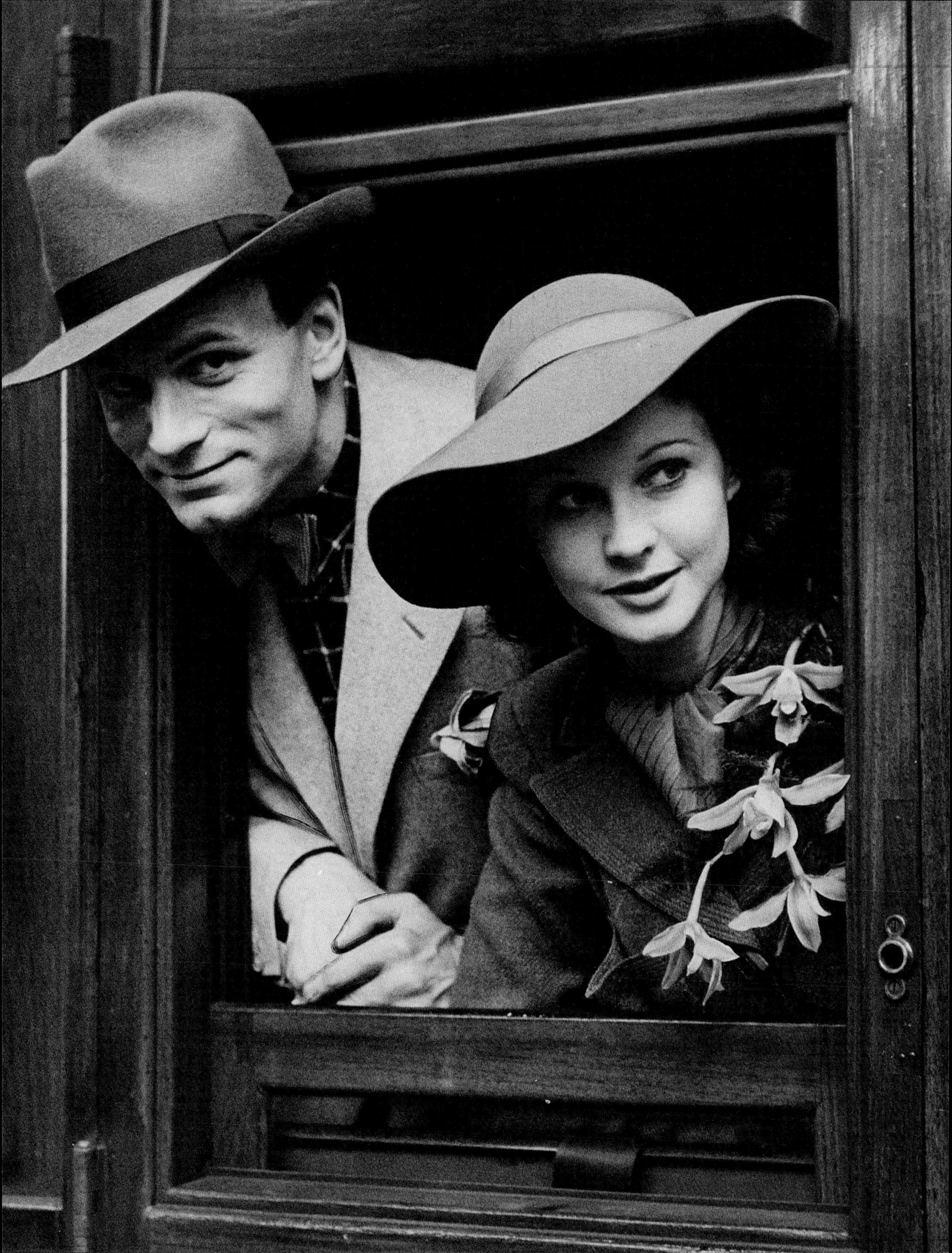

Starting slowly, their relationship quickened into overwhelming and finally irresistible desire. 'I couldn't help myself with Vivien,' said Olivier. 'No man could. I hated myself for cheating on Jill, but then I had cheated before, but this was something different. This wasn't just out of lust. This was love that I really didn't ask for but was drawn into.' In Leigh's case, it was more conscious: when she had first seen Olivier onstage in *Theatre Royal*, the year before they met, she had turned to her best friend and whispered: 'He's the man I'm going to marry.' In 1937, they were cast opposite each other in *Fire Over England*, which its producer Alexander Korda had consciously conceived of as a star vehicle for her, and the relationship became all-consuming, unmistakably so in the finished film. The development of this overwhelming passion coincided with Olivier's wife, the actress Jill Esmond, giving birth to their only child, Tarquin; a week after the boy was born, Olivier decided to end the marriage. Thereafter, he and Leigh lived together discreetly, until their respective spouses agreed to divorce.

In 1937, Olivier played Hamlet at the Old Vic, opposite Leigh's Ophelia (fig.2); neither scored great hits in their respective roles, but the public flocked to the production; later, it was invited to play at Elsinore, and it was there, among the ramparts of the ancient Danish castle, that Olivier had the first intimation of his lover's manic depression, something of which her very closest friends had been aware for some time. From now on, the relationship between them would be underpinned by sudden and devastating eruptions of her condition, which took the form of wild outbursts of energy, savage and often physical assaults on him and a sexual voraciousness towards other men. When the attacks subsided, she would return to her witty, demure self, with no memory of what had happened (fig.3).

They were together for nearly twenty-five years, from 1940 to 1960 as man and wife, installed in their baronial mansion in the lavishly reconstructed Augustinian abbey of Notley in Buckinghamshire. Despite Leigh's regular collapses into mental disturbance, they kept up a gruelling pace of work, frequently appearing together in the great roles of the canon; he often directed her during this time, notably in *A Streetcar Named Desire* (1949), and they maintained the arduous round of public appearances expected of 'the Royal Couple' of British theatre (fig.4). Both had affairs, she most passionately with the Australian actor Peter Finch, but she never wanted or expected their marriage to end; he, however, withdrew more and more into other relationships, finally, in 1958, meeting in Joan Plowright the woman he saw as his future, at exactly the time that he was repositioning himself both as an actor and as the director-elect of the new National Theatre.

The press obsession with the Leigh–Olivier relationship, which had always been intense, reached fever pitch with the breakdown of their marriage; Leigh behaved with notable dignity and despite great heaviness of heart and devastating electric shock treatments for her condition, she continued working, giving a number of remarkable performances on film and stage. John Merrivale, kind and deeply considerate, became her partner,

Fig.2 *Laurence Olivier and Vivien Leigh in Hamlet*, 1937
Unknown photographer
Postcard, 188 × 237mm
National Portrait Gallery, London

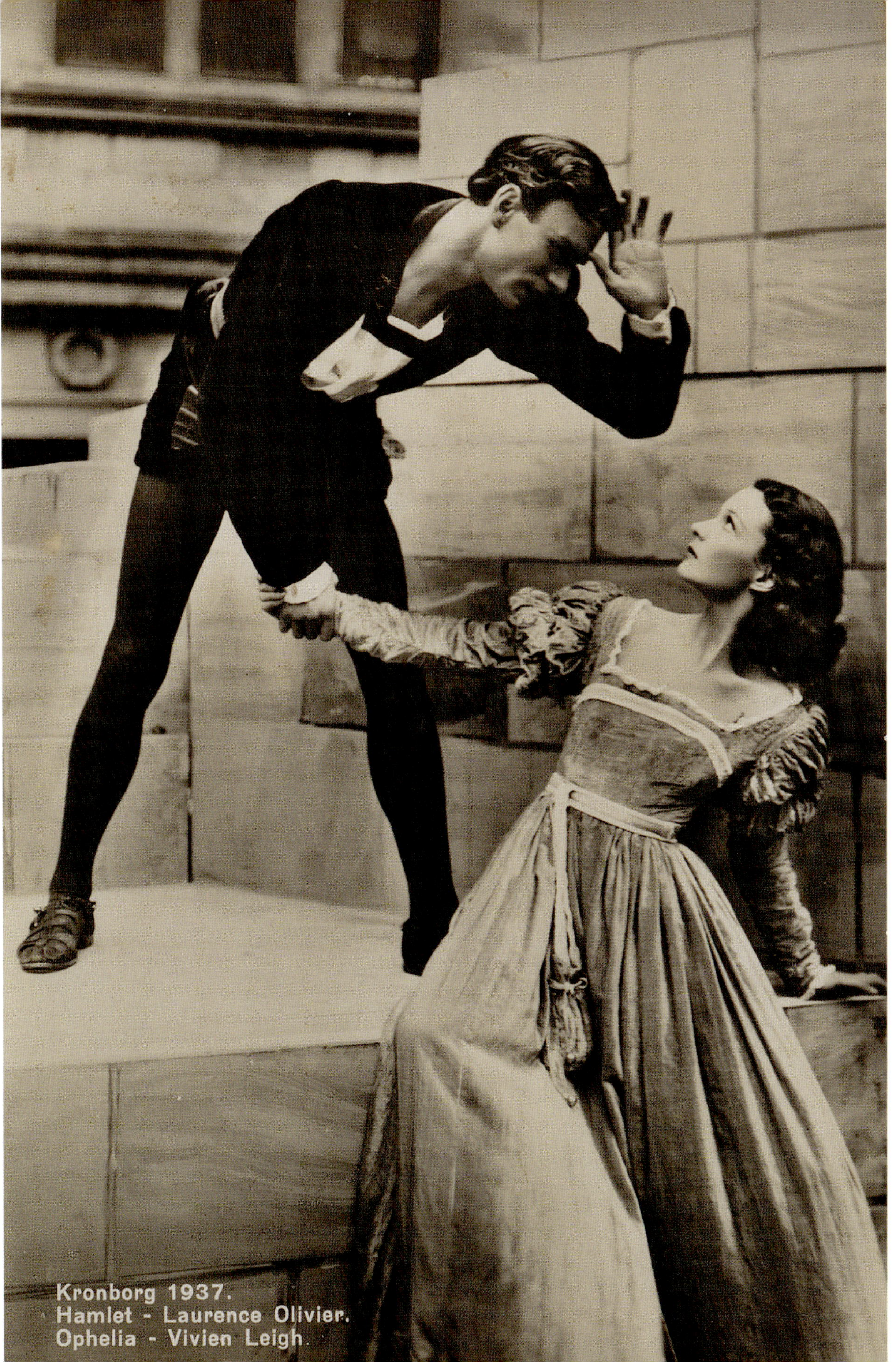
Kronborg 1937.
Hamlet - Laurence Olivier.
Ophelia - Vivien Leigh.

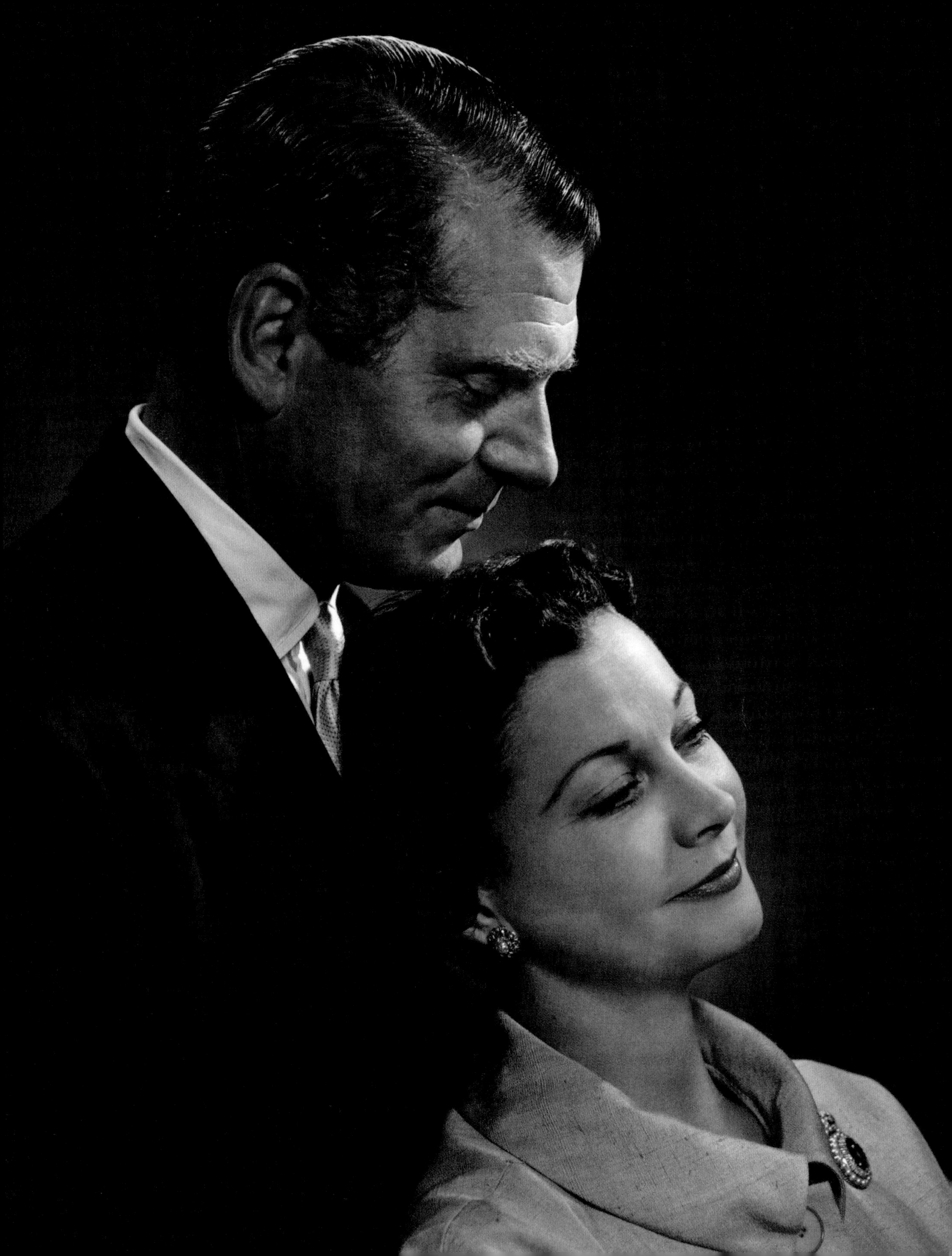

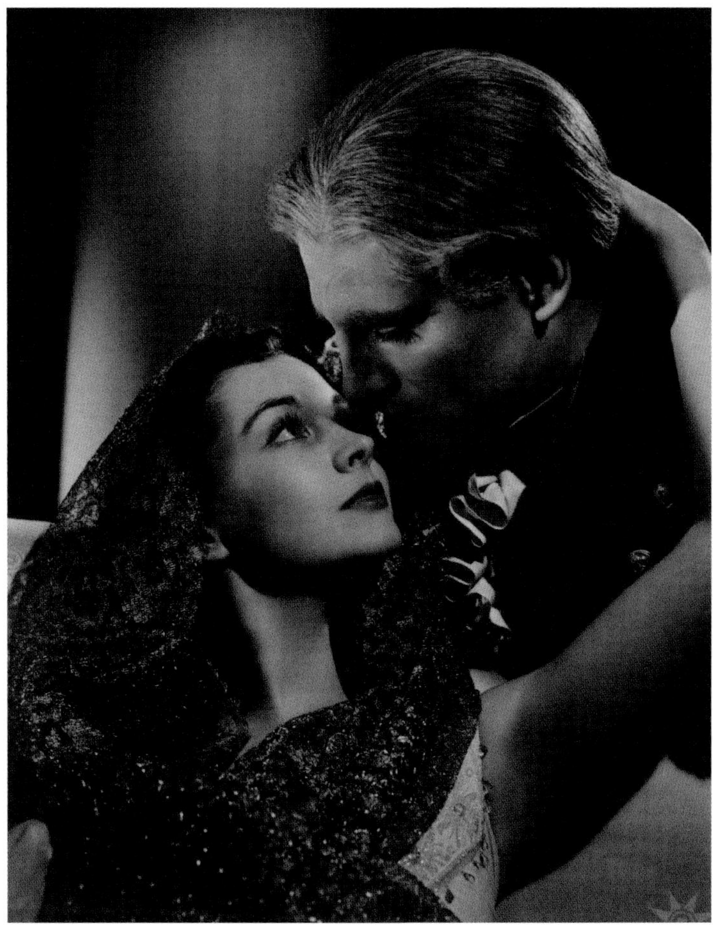

OPPOSITE
Fig.3 *Laurence Olivier and Vivien Leigh*, 1954
Yousuf Karsh
Gelatin silver print, 240 × 190mm
National Portrait Gallery, London

ABOVE
Fig.4 *Vivien Leigh and Laurence Olivier in That Hamilton Woman*, 1941
Robert Coburn
Modern gelatin silver print, 230 × 180mm
National Portrait Gallery, London

though she continued to style herself Vivien Leigh Olivier. Olivier's new life at the head of the National Theatre and as the father of a new young family brought him to ever greater heights of admiration and acclaim. He and Leigh remained in touch, intermittently. Her sudden death from tuberculosis in 1967, at the age of fifty-three, shook him to the core: himself in the throes of treatment for cancer, the moment he heard what had happened, he went to see her dead body, overcome with what he called 'grievous anguish'. After helping Jack Merrivale to make the funeral arrangements, 'I stood and prayed,' he said, 'for forgiveness for all the evils that had sprung up between us.' Like everything else in their love affair, the end was on an epic scale.

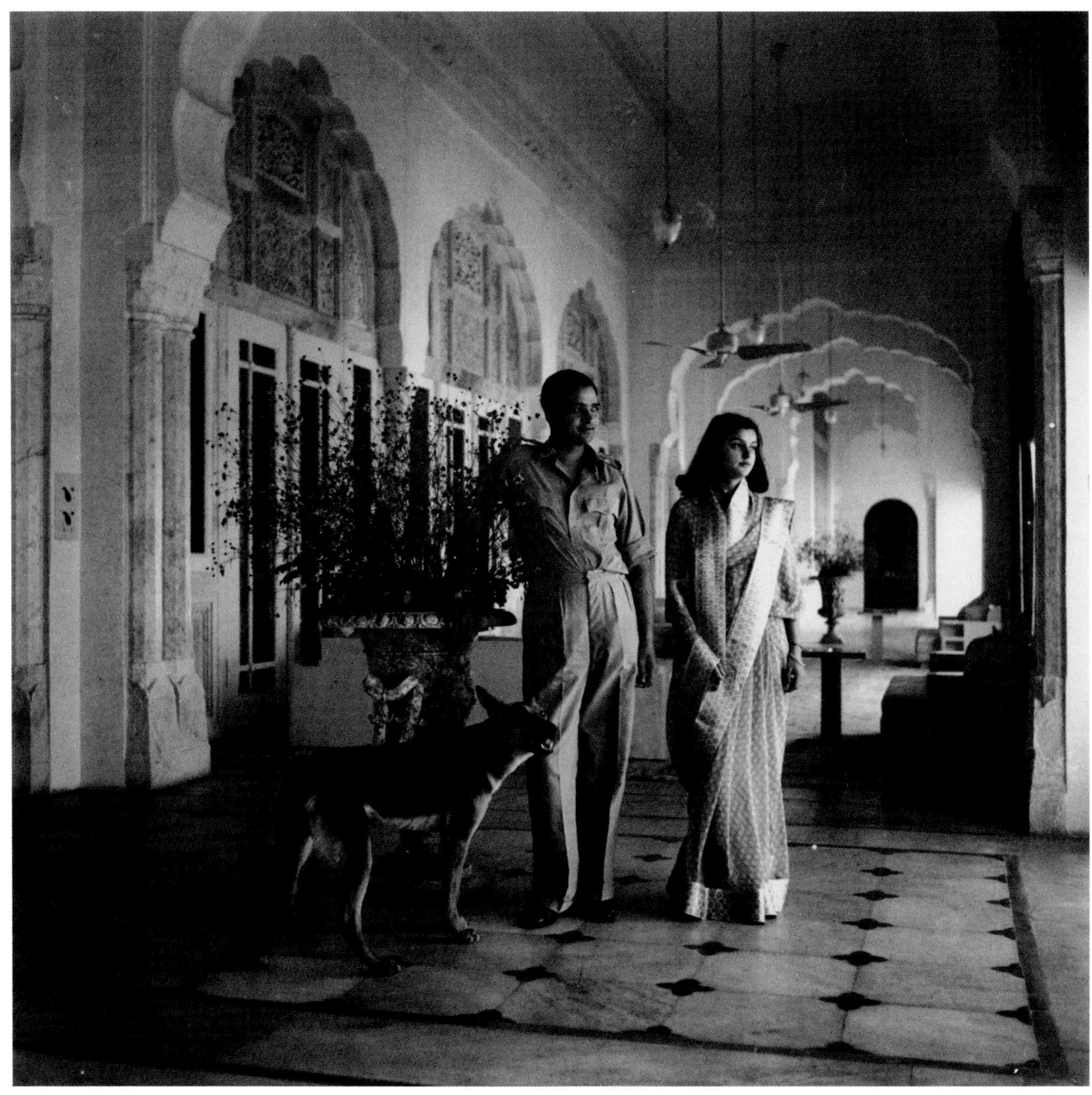

Fig.1 *Sawai Man Singh II, Maharaja of Jaipur and Gayatri Devi, Rajmata of Jaipur*, 1944
Cecil Beaton
Modern gelatin silver print, 254 × 252mm
National Portrait Gallery, London

CLARE FREESTONE

Maharani Gayatri Devi, Rajmata of Jaipur & Sawai Man Singh II, Maharaja of Jaipur

Born in London, Gayatri Devi, Princess of Cooch Behar, became the Maharani of Jaipur on her marriage to Maharaja Sawai Man Singh II in 1940, in what, at the time, was reputed to be the most lavish wedding in history. When Devi was twelve years old she became enamoured with the most glamorous young man in India. The handsome 21-year-old Maharaja enjoyed universal popularity enriched by his 'charm, his possessions and his feats on horseback' (fig.2).[1]

The Maharaja of Jaipur, who had been adopted by Madho Singh II, succeeded to the throne in 1922 when he was just eleven. On meeting Devi he had two wives from the royal family of Jodhpur – polygamy was not uncommon among Indian rulers – but this did not prevent him from becoming entranced by the beautiful and strong-willed princess. Devi was at the Monkey Club finishing school in London when Singh began a secret liaison with her, having to navigate her chaperons to see her. Taking Devi for a drive through Hyde Park, he stumbled through a marriage proposal:

> you are sixteen now, but I have to plan ahead for an event like that and make all sorts of arrangements, so I'd like to know if you want to marry me ... remember I play polo and ride and fly and I may have a horrible accident; still will you marry me?[2]

The answer was yes. Their unofficial engagement caused a sensation, not only would their marriage go against the tradition of parental decree, the Cooch Behar family feared that Devi was condemning herself to a life in a traditional state of *purdah*. She came from a line of strong women. Her grandmother Maharani Chimnabai of Baroda was a spokesperson for the emancipation of

Indian women while her mother, Indira Devi, had refused an arranged marriage, having fallen in love with the younger brother of her suitor.

Gayatri Devi, however, shared the Maharaja's passion for adventure and in the event, their marriage was a great success. The elegant couple enjoyed a charmed lifestyle but were required to embrace modernity at a time when independence and internationalism were replacing tradition and colonialism.

> We went to Calcutta for December and January, to Bombay or Delhi for special (polo) tournaments, to other princely states, and to England in the summer. In any of those places my own life as Jai's wife was filled with fun, excitement, with parties and excursions, and while I understood that there was no good reason why so many people thought of him simply as a polo-playing glamour-boy ... I also began to learn that his real life was in Jaipur and that he cared most deeply about the welfare and just government of his subjects.[3]

In wartime India, Cecil Beaton was contracted by the British Ministry of Information to send back a report celebrating the Empire. He described Jaipur as 'a coral coloured dream town'.[4] Beaton's photographs of the Maharani launched her reputation as one of the most beautiful women in the world (fig.3). In the grounds of the Rambagh Palace, Beaton also captured the harmonious partnership of the royal couple (fig.1) who had set about improving the infrastructure and public institutions of Jaipur, Devi promoting education for girls and Singh a new model army, prompting the city to become the capital of Rajasthan following India's independence in 1947.

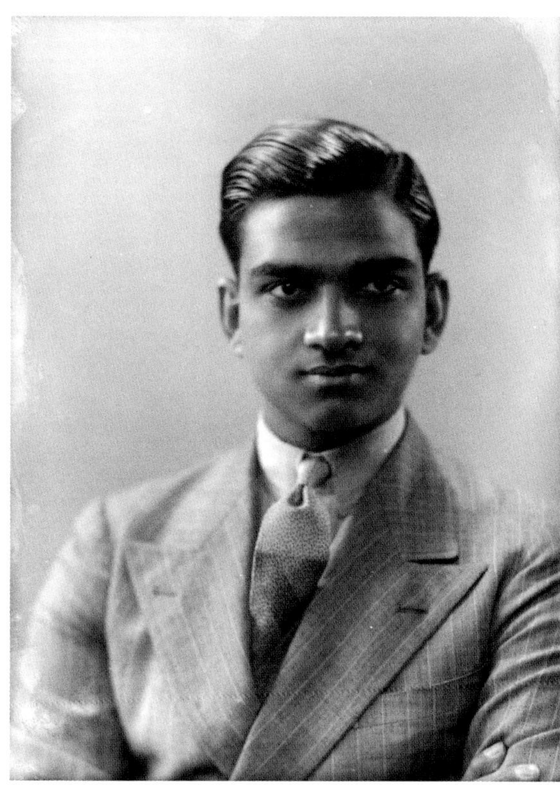

Fig.2 *Sawai Man Singh II, Maharaja of Jaipur*, 21 April 1933
Bassano Ltd
Half-plate glass negative
National Portrait Gallery, London

In 1962, with the royal family's prestige and power in decline, Devi stood as a candidate for the conservative Swatantra Party, with popular appeal underpinning her landslide victory. In 1970 the Indian government introduced a bill to abolish the princely order and the couple flew to England where Singh died suddenly while playing a polo match. Devi described her loss as irreconcilable, but in time continued her active life. She was re-elected in 1971, before standing down following a period of imprisonment for allegedly breaking tax laws. Following the conversion of the Rambagh Palace into a luxury hotel, she spent winters in Lily Pool, the Jaipur dower house which had been built under the direction of her beloved husband.

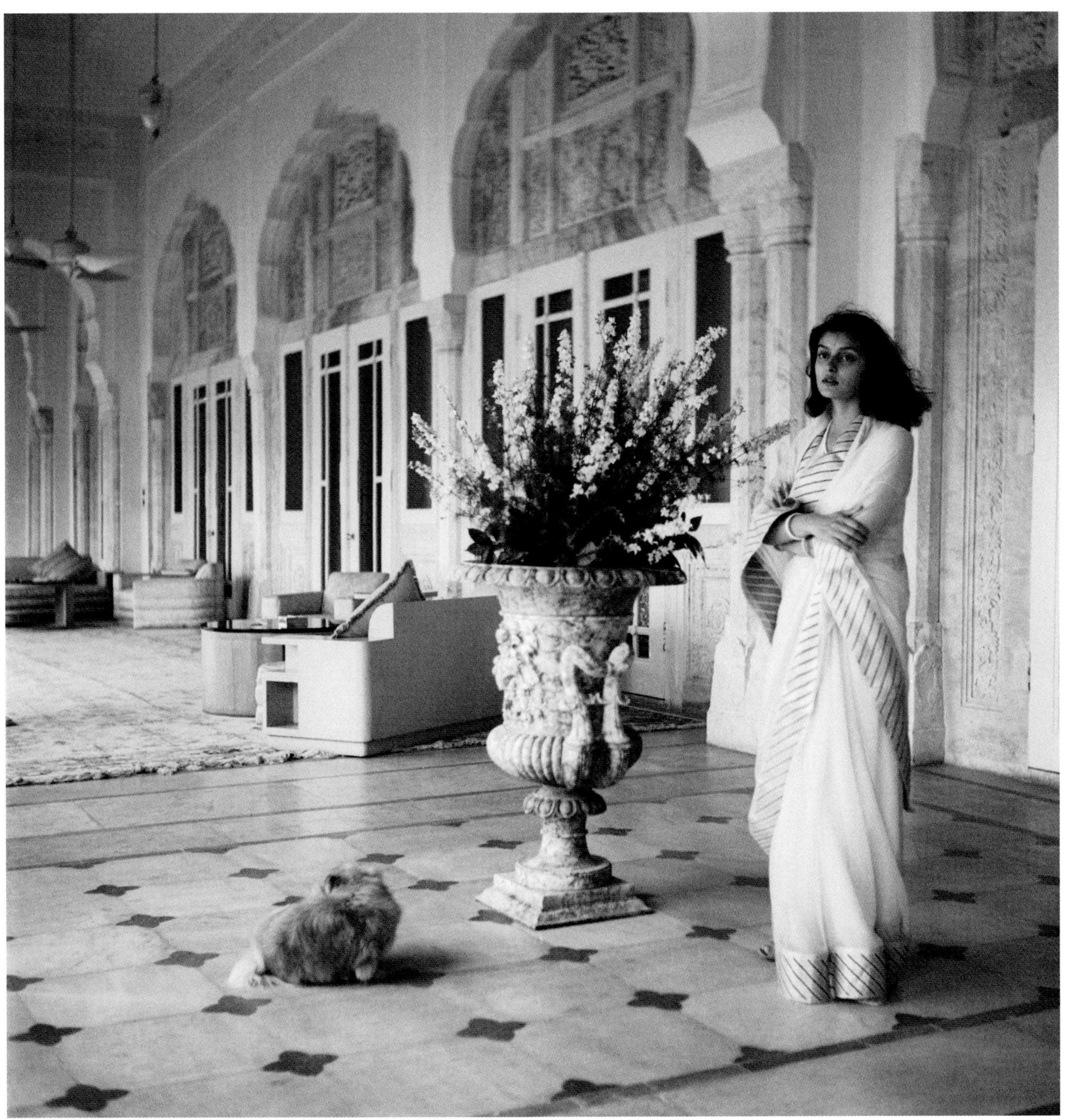

Fig.3 *Gayatri Devi, Maharani of Jaipur*, 1945
Cecil Beaton
Whole-plate nitrate negative
Imperial War Museum, London

SABINA JASKOT-GILL

Mick Jagger & Bianca Jagger

& Jerry Hall

At the age of sixteen Bianca Pérez-Mora Macías received a scholarship to study political science at the Paris Institut d'Études Politiques. Arriving from Nicaragua into a fashionable world of glittering diplomatic parties, she embarked on relationships with actor Michael Caine and record executive Eddie Barclay. Bianca was introduced to the lead singer of the self-styled 'greatest rock and roll band in the world' in 1970, at a party following a Rolling Stones concert in Paris. For Bianca, the meeting was a 'bolt of lightning', finding Mick 'shy, vulnerable, human – the opposite of everything I had ever imagined'.[1]

Mick Jagger had experienced a meteoric rise to fame with the Rolling Stones, a British band that epitomised the life of sex, drugs and rock and roll. As the swaggering, charismatic frontman, Mick became as famous for his showmanship on the stage as his outrageous behaviour off it. Relationships with model Christine Shrimpton, musician Marianne Faithfull and Anita Pallenberg, the partner of his bandmate Keith Richards, earned Mick a reputation as a lothario, and he was expecting a child with actress Marsha Hunt when he first set eyes on his future wife, Bianca.

Nine months later, on 12 May 1971, Mick and Bianca were married in Saint-Tropez, France, with Bianca four months pregnant with their daughter, Jade. The wedding was almost over before it began, with Mick horrified to find the town hall besieged by paparazzi, such was the draw of music's most glamorous couple. A brief civil ceremony was followed by a Catholic service at Chapelle Sainte-Anne, where the bride walked down the aisle to music from the movie *Love Story*, establishing her reputation as a fashion icon by wearing a white Yves Saint-Laurent suit.

Mick's relationships were avidly documented

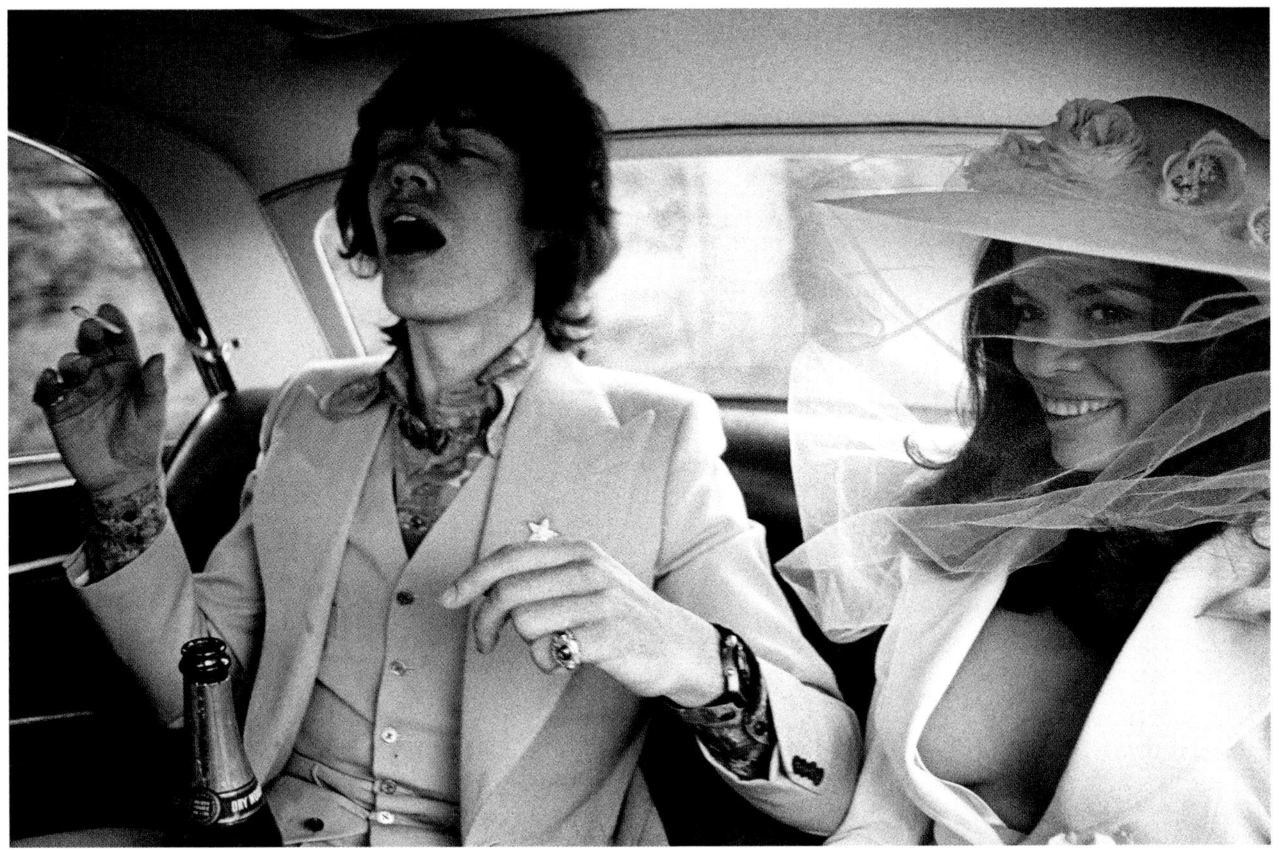

Fig.1 *Mick Jagger and Bianca Jagger*, May 1971
Patrick Lichfield
Inkjet print, 1054 × 1562mm
National Portrait Gallery, London

by celebrity photographers, and Patrick Lichfield was sent by *Associated Newspapers* to cover the wedding. Lichfield's aristocratic background (a first cousin once removed of Queen Elizabeth II), and ability to glamorise the beautiful and the famous, made him a celebrity in his own right, and it was a measure of his social credentials that he was asked to give the bride away that day. Taken from the front seat of the Jaggers' Bentley, Lichfield's snapshot captures an intimate moment between the newlyweds, allowing a tantalising and rarely seen glimpse into the lives of rock royalty (fig.1).

Rock's glamour couple reigned over a period of high decadence in the 1970s. Bianca was known for her impeccable style, and became a fixture in New York's hedonistic Studio 54 set. Photographs of Bianca celebrating her birthday in the club sitting on a white horse appeared in newspapers around the world.

Marriage did little to tame Mick's sexual appetite, and alleged liaisons with men and women abounded. Bianca is reported to have torn her husband's clothes, and even threatened him with a gun during one jealous frenzy, but she appeared philosophical during a candid interview in 1975: 'I don't expect Mick to just pray to God while on tour ... Yes, it bothers me but it is the way to keep our marriage alive ... reuniting is like falling in love all over again'.[2] During these years, Bianca herself was associated with actors Elliott Gould and Ryan O'Neal. Mick's romance with Texan model Jerry Hall proved the final straw, and Bianca filed for divorce in 1978, though she admitted poignantly, 'My marriage ended on my wedding day.'[3]

Jerry was a sought-after model, engaged to Roxy Music singer Bryan Ferry, when she met the Rolling Stone at a dinner party in 1977. The ensuing romance proved to be Mick's longest relationship, lasting twenty-three years. During this time, the couple 'lived life in a goldfish bowl', Jerry noting they were followed by photographers wherever they went.[4]

Perhaps the couple's most iconic portrait was taken by the fashion photographer Norman Parkinson. Jerry frequently collaborated with 'Parks', whom she first met on a 1975 *Vogue* shoot in Jamaica, and his alluring images helped elevate Jerry to supermodel status. Parkinson photographed Jerry and Mick in the bedroom of their London home, in various stages of undress, with Jerry decked in glittering jewels throughout, capturing the gaudy excess of the era (fig.2). A naked portrait of the two was intended for Jerry and Mick alone, but Jerry deemed it 'too good not to share'.[5]

Though she admitted to finding groupies 'irritating',[6] Jerry had her own way of ensuring a successful relationship:

> Be a maid in the living room, a chef in
> the kitchen, and a whore in the bedroom.
> So long as I have a maid and a cook,
> I'll do the rest myself.[7]

Mick still indulged himself with women (he once claimed to have slept with more than four thousand), but Jerry knew how to take revenge; a brief relationship with the wealthy horse breeder Robert Sangster left Mick humiliated.

Hall and Jagger were married in a Hindu ceremony on the Indonesian island of Bali in 1990, but rivals for Mick's affection in this period included the supermodel Carla Bruni, actresses Uma Thurman and Angelina Jolie, and model Luciana Morad, with whom he fathered a child in 1999. News of the pregnancy was a step too far for Jerry, who filed for divorce, only for their wedding to be deemed invalid by a British court. After a relationship spanning more than two decades, the couple remain on good terms, holidaying together with their children. Jerry concluded, 'I think we're more comfortable with each other than we've been in years, now that we know it's over.'[8]

Fig.2 *Mick Jagger and Jerry Hall*, July 1981
Norman Parkinson
Gelatin silver print, 394 × 291mm
National Portrait Gallery, London

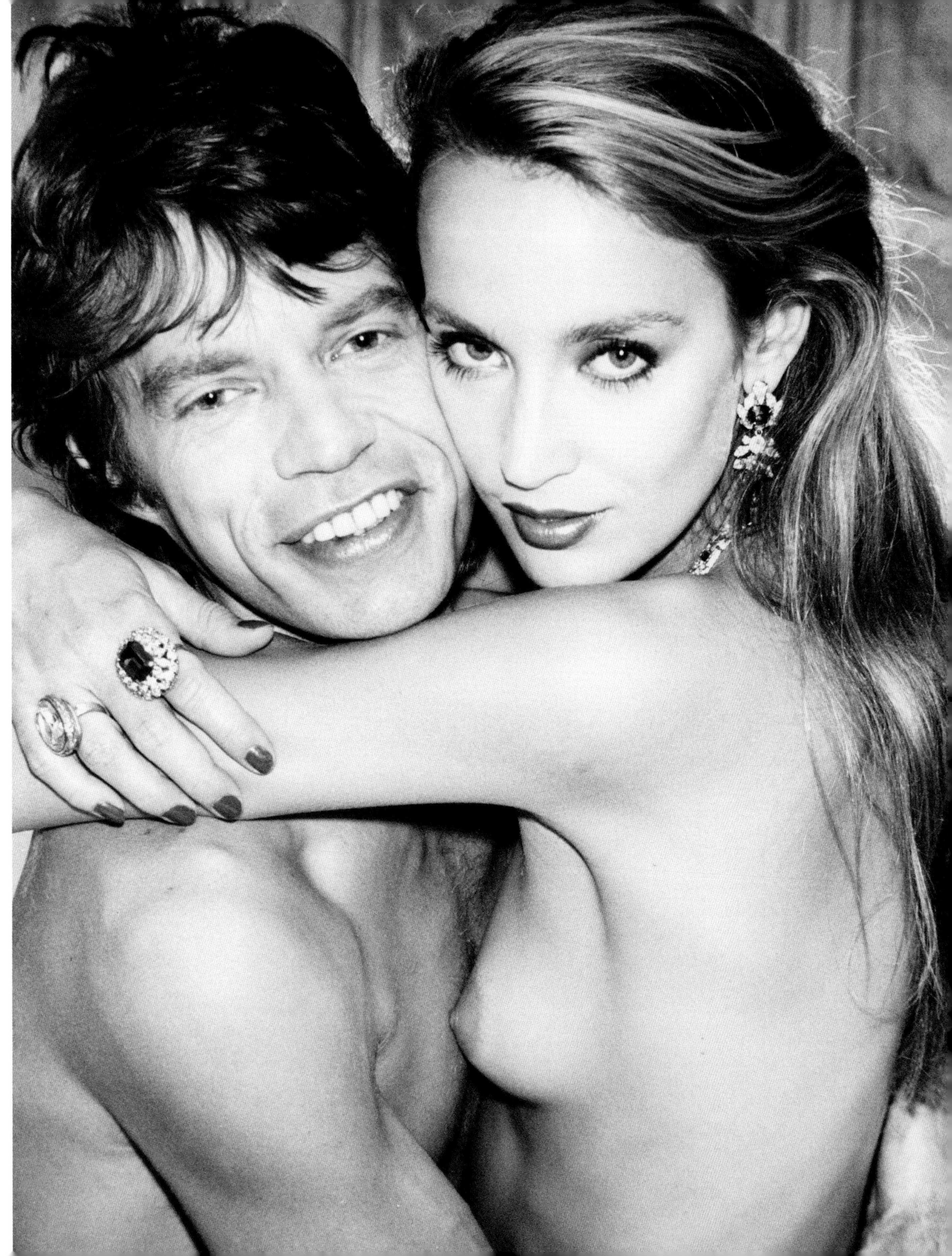

HELENA CUSS

Charles, Prince of Wales & Diana, Princess of Wales

From the outset of her relationship with Prince Charles in 1980 the British press focused its lens on Lady Diana Spencer. A photograph in the National Portrait Gallery Collection provides an illuminating snapshot of their involvement in the early stages of the romance (fig.1). An 18-year-old Diana is hurrying down a London street and looking back over her shoulder, surrounded by paparazzi. Her eyes are wide, although a hint of a smile seems to play about her mouth. Evidently, the British press and its readers already considered her public property even though in May 1980 her involvement with the prince was only a speculation. Although Charles and Diana first met in 1977, it was not until meeting again in July 1980 that the first sparks of romance were ignited. Charles was struck by her directly-expressed sympathy for the recent death of his uncle Lord Mountbatten, with whom he had been very close. According to Diana, they met just eleven more times before becoming engaged on 6 February 1981.

The official engagement photograph, taken by Lord Snowdon, presented the couple in a relaxed embrace and confirmed the news that the public and royal establishment had longed for: that the heir to the throne, dubbed in the press as 'the world's most eligible bachelor', had finally found a suitable woman with whom to settle down. Furthermore, she was considerably younger than him, with an untarnished reputation and 'English rose' beauty that was universally appealing. In a pre-wedding televised interview, Charles was sanguine about the endless fascination with their relationship, noting that 'knowing for years that there are cameras poking at you from every quarter and recording every twitch you make, you can get used to it to a certain extent' adding presciently, 'If you don't try to work out in your own mind some method for

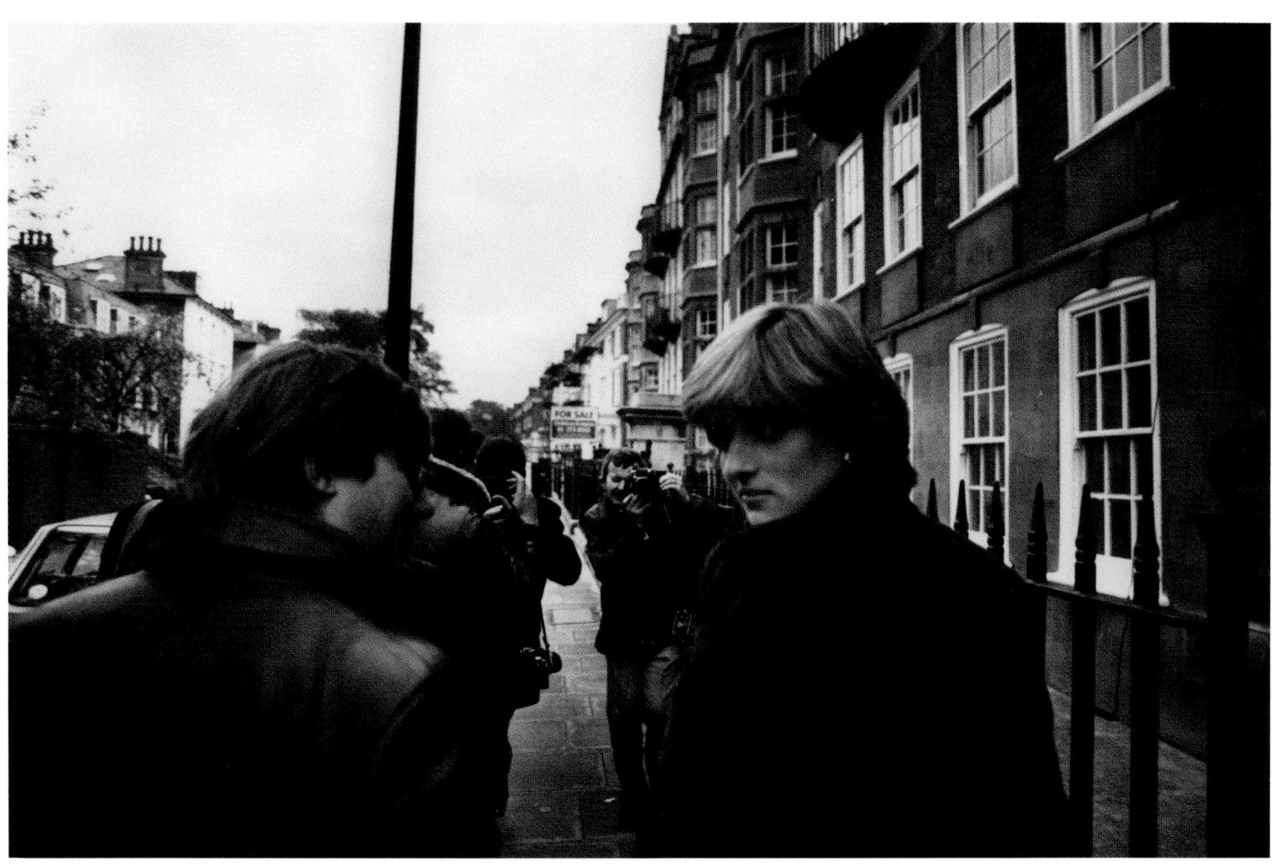

Fig.1 *Lady Diana Spencer*, 13 May 1980
Ian Tyas for Keystone Press Agency Ltd
Gelatin silver print, 151 × 226mm
National Portrait Gallery, London

existing and surviving this kind of thing you would go mad.'[1]

Public enthusiasm and anticipation were heightened as the July wedding approached. The now-iconic images of Diana stepping out of the carriage in a cloud of billowing ivory silk, demure beneath her veil, were broadcast to a global audience of an estimated 750 million viewers. It was the first royal wedding ever televised. The official wedding photographs taken by Patrick Lichfield (fig.2) illustrated the Archbishop of Canterbury's address earlier in the ceremony, in which he declared: 'Here is the stuff of which fairy tales are made. The prince and the princess on their wedding day.'[2] Even Diana herself inhabited the romantic role cast for her, recalling that as she floated down the aisle, she was 'so in love ... I couldn't take my eyes off him. I just absolutely thought I was the luckiest girl in the world and he was going to look after me.'[3] However, the media circus of their wedding was a double edged-sword: Diana described the scene of thousands upon thousands of happy, cheering people being 'so humbling' and 'just wonderful'; but by the time they had reached the wedding breakfast Diana later recalled, the newlyweds were too exhausted to even speak to each other.

As the young royal couple settled into married life, Diana rapidly gained public popularity, partly because of her gift for connecting with people and partly by her rapidly growing status as a fashion icon. This was reflected in the daily newspaper front covers and headlines reporting on the outfits she wore on public visits and at glamorous evening events with Charles. As she settled into her public role she won admiration with her visits to hospitals and charities in which she unself-consciously chatted and held hands with the homeless and those afflicted by AIDS and leprosy, diseases which were much stigmatised at the time. In the early years of their marriage there were moments of happiness and intimacy, especially around the birth of Prince William in 1982 and Prince Harry in 1984. Charles decided that in order to create a sense of home, they should have a permanent residence at Kensington Palace, but he struggled to live up to this paradigm of domesticity.

Despite an ITV documentary capturing the young family's home life in 1986, the news coverage of their relationship was becoming increasingly negative, and their popularity waned as the press began to chronicle the marriage's breakdown. In February 1992 they travelled to India, and a photo appeared of Diana sitting alone at the Taj Mahal, that famous monument to love, a visit from which Charles abstained (fig.3). The press characteristically seized upon this as alleged evidence of the marriage's collapse and the separation of Charles and Diana was formally announced by the Prime Minister in December. In the aftermath of their split both parties tried to tell their side of the story through the medium of television. In 1994 Charles gave an interview to Jonathan Dimbleby in an attempt to rebuild his public reputation; the following year Diana gave a revealing interview to Martin Bashir, in which she spoke out against the royal establishment and about Camilla Parker Bowles' role in the marriage's breakdown, with the famous words, 'there were three of us in this marriage.'

Following their divorce, Diana re-branded herself as a confident, independent woman

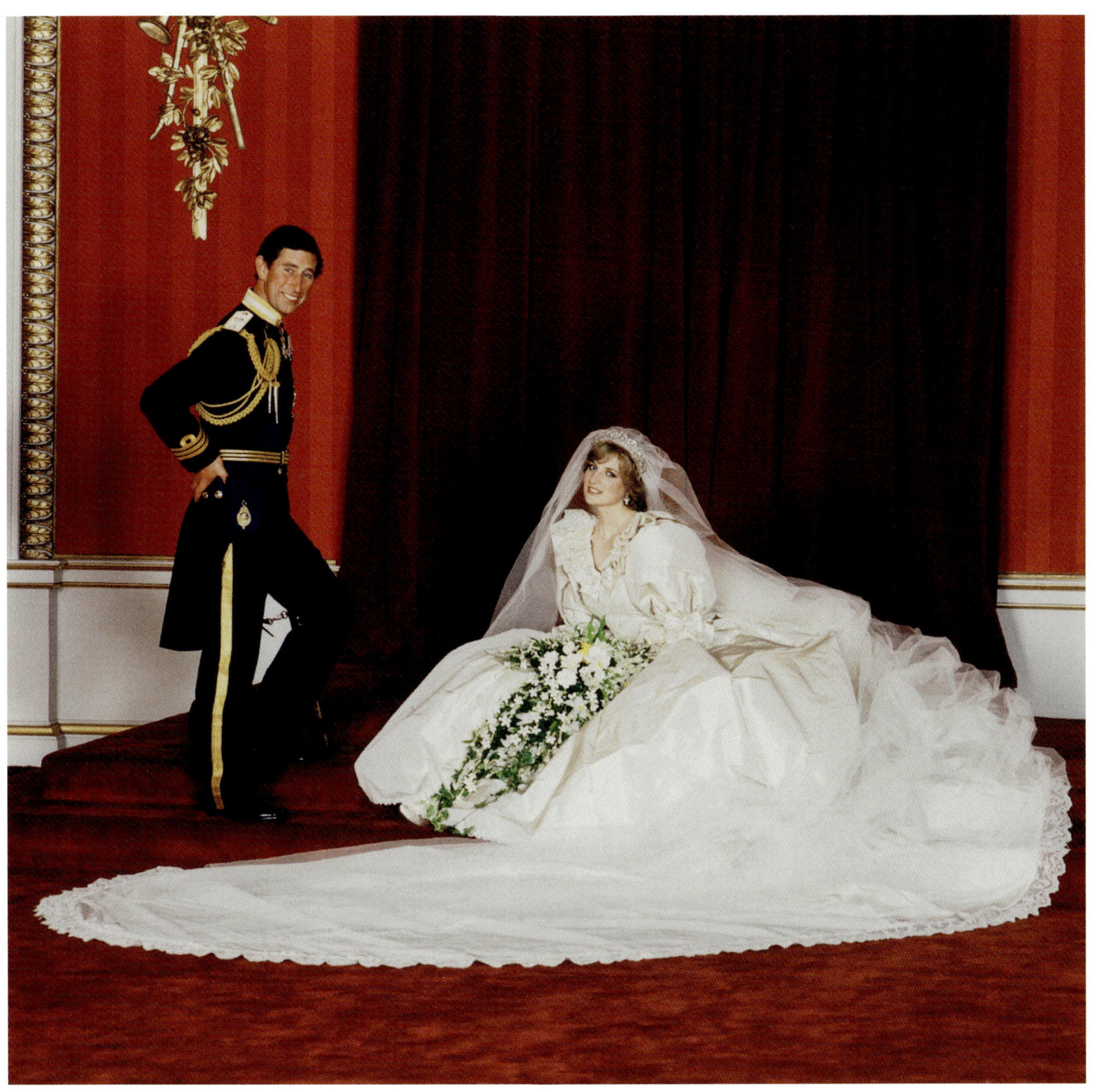

Fig.2 *Prince Charles and Diana, Princess of Wales*, July 1981
Patrick Lichfield
Inkjet print, 304 × 304mm
National Portrait Gallery, London

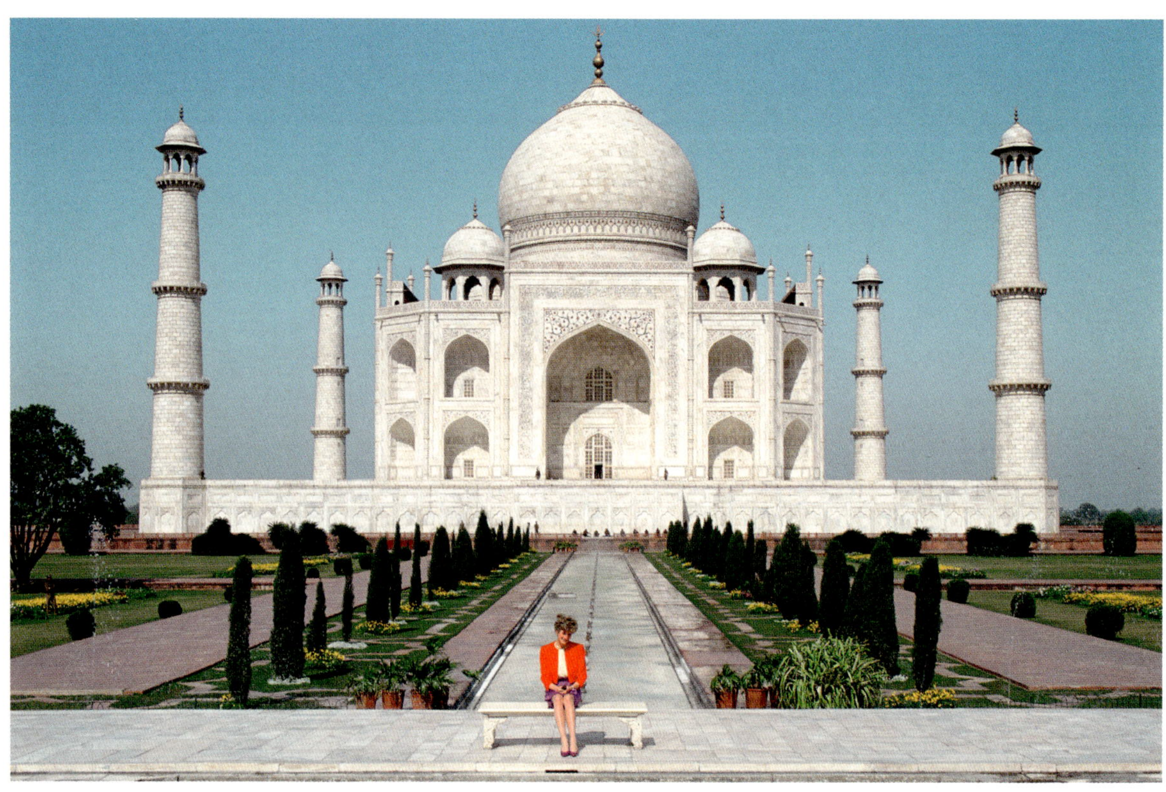

Fig.3 *Diana at the Taj Mahal, India*, 11 February 1992
Tim Graham / Getty Images

through her humanitarian work, and with glamorous photo shoots by celebrity photographers such as Mario Testino and David Bailey. Her role as an enduringly affectionate mother was captured in playful photographs taken for official Christmas cards (fig.4). Now lacking the protection of royal status she tried to participate in a more sophisticated interaction with the press, hoping to regain some influence over the depiction of her private life. Tragically, this backfired: she died in a car accident while trying to evade paparazzi photographers in Paris on 31 August 1997. In the aftermath, Charles sought to protect their sons from the media's glare as much as possible. However, as the 2011 and 2018 weddings of William and Harry testified, public appetite for royal romance and glamour remains unabated in the twenty-first century.

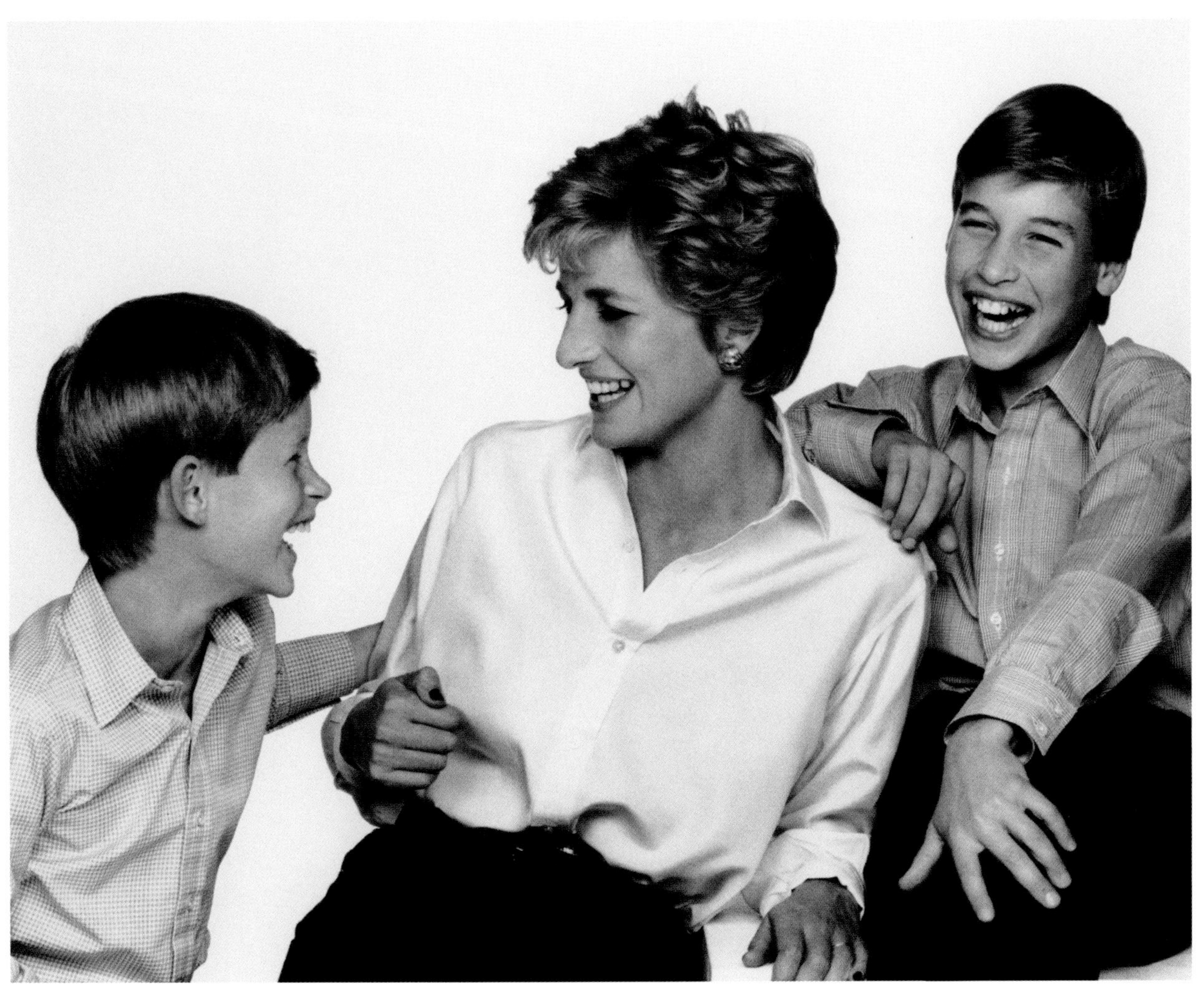

Fig.4 *Diana, Princess of Wales with her Sons*, 1994
John Swannell
Inkjet print, 394 × 482mm
National Portrait Gallery, London

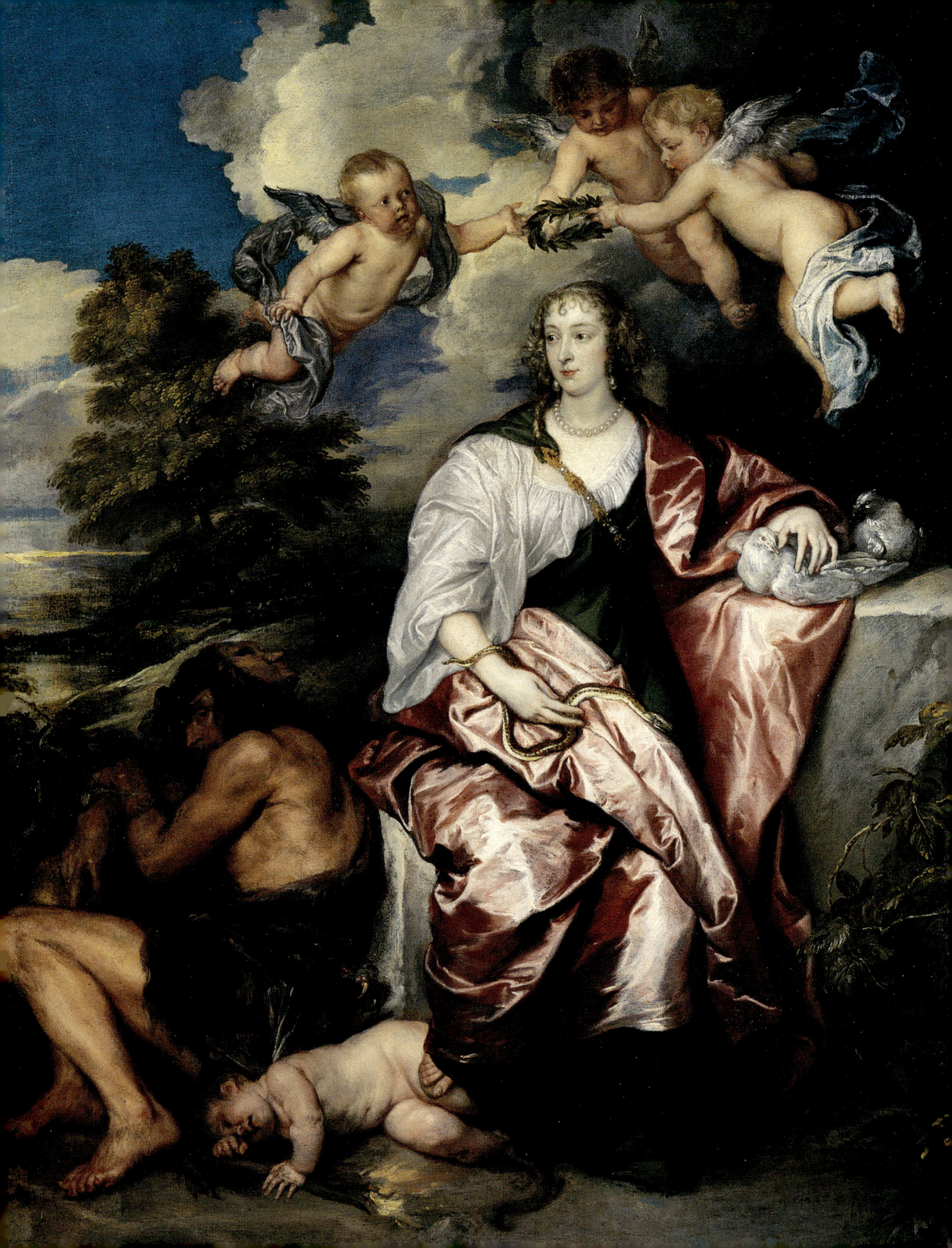

NOTES

PORTRAITS AS LOVE OBJECTS

1 Walter Ralegh, 'Fortune Hath Taken Thee Away, My Mistress', reproduced in Gordon Braden, *Sixteenth-century Poetry: An Annotated Anthology* (John Wiley & Sons: New Jersey, 2005) p.337
2 Jacques Ferrand, *Erotomania: Or A Treatise Discoursing of the Essence, Symptomes, Treatments, Prognosticks and Cure of the Love or Erotique Melancholy* (Edward Forest: Oxford, 1640), title page
3 David Cressy, *Birth, Marriage and Death Ritual, Religion and the Life-Cycle in Tudor and Stuart England* (Oxford University Press: Oxford, 1997) pp.285–97
4 *The Book of Common Prayer, 1559: The Elizabethan Book of Common Prayer*, ed. John E. Booty (University of Virginia Press: Charlottesville and London, 2005), p.290
5 Ginger Frost, *Living in Sin, Cohabiting as Husband and Wife in Nineteenth-Century England* (Manchester University Press: Manchester, 2008) pp.171–4
6 Ibid., pp.3–10
7 Jane Hamlett, *Material Relations: Domestic Interiors and Middle-class Families in England 1850–1910* (Manchester University Press: Manchester, 2010) p.75; on companionate marriage, see Lawrence Stone, *The Family, Sex and Marriage in England 1500–1800* (Penguin: London, 1990) part 4; and Randolph Trumbuch, *The Rise of the Egalitarian Family: Aristocratic Kinship and Domestic Relations in Eighteenth Century England* (Academic Press Inc.: Massachusetts, 1978) pp.97–117
8 Simon May, *Love: A History* (Yale University Press: New Haven, London, 2011) pp.1–2
9 Sally Holloway, *The Game of Love in Georgian England: Courtship, Emotions, and Material Culture* (Oxford University Press: Oxford, 2019) chap.2
10 Judith Schneid Lewis, *In the Family Way, Childbearing in the British Aristocracy 1760–1860* (Rutgers University Press: New Jersey, 1986) p.19 and Hamlett, *Material Relations*, p.74
11 The phrase is derived from the title of a popular narrative poem by Coventry Patmore, published between 1854 and 1862
12 Lynda Nead, *Myths of Sexuality: Representations of Women in Victorian Britain* (Wiley Blackwell: Oxford, 1990) pp.12–47; Leonore Davidoff and Catherine Hall, *Family Fortunes: Men and Women of the English Middle Class 1780–1850* (Routledge: London, 2002) pp.149–92; Eleanor Gordon and Gwyneth Nair, *Public Lives: Women, Family and Society in Victorian Britain* (Yale University Press: New Haven, London, 2003) pp.1–8
13 Catherine Hoffman, *Concepts of Identity: Historical and Contemporary Images and Portraits of Self and Family* (Harper Collins: New York, 1996) p.103; Stephen Kern, *The Culture of Love: Victorians to Moderns* (Harvard University Press: Cambridge MA, London, 1992) pp.24–5; May, *Love: A History*, pp.xii; Claire Langhamer, *The English in Love: The Intimate Story of an Emotional Revolution* (Oxford University Press: Oxford, 2013)
14 Clare Barlow, 'Introduction', in *Queer British Art, 1861–1967* (Tate Publishing: London, 2017), p.15
15 Reproduced in Henry Savage (ed.), *The Love Letters of Henry VIII* (Allan Wingate: London, 1949) pp.27–8
16 'Biblioteca Apostolica Vaticana, Vat. Lat. 3731A fol.5', reproduced in Susan Doran (ed.), *Henry VIII Man and Monarch* (British Library: London, 2009) p.115
17 Peter Rushton, 'The Testament of Gifts: Marriage Tokens and Disputed Contracts in North-East England, 1560–1630' in *Folk Life* (vol.24, 1985–6) pp.25–31; Marcia Pointon, '"Surrounded with Brilliants": Miniature Portraits in Eighteenth-Century England', *The Art Bulletin* (vol.83, no.1, March 2001) p.5; Catherine Richardson, '"As my whole trust is in him": Jewellery and the Quality of Early Modern Relationships' in Bella Mirabella (ed.), *Ornamentalism: The Art of Renaissance Accessories* (University of Michigan Press: Ann Arbor, 2011) pp.190–5; Angela Hesson and Lisa Beaven, 'Objects of Love' in *Love: Art of Emotion 1400–1800* (National Gallery of Victoria: Melbourne, 2017) p.124; Holloway, *The Game of Love*, pp.69–92
18 Eric Ives considers Anne's gift of the jewel as indicating her willingness to marry Henry. See *The Life and Death of Anne Boleyn* (Blackwell: Oxford, Victoria, 2004) pp.87–8
19 Ann Rosalins Jones and Peter Stallybrass, 'Busks, Bodices, Bodies' in Bella Mirabella (ed.), *Ornamentalism*, pp.85–101; Sarah Anne Bendall, 'To Write a Distick upon It: Busks and the Language of Courtship and Sexual Desire in Sixteenth and Seventeenth-Century England' in *Gender & History* (vol.26, no. 2, August 2014) pp.199–222
20 W. Ruskin Butterfield, 'Concerning Decorated Stay Busks', *The Connoisseur* (vol.15, 1919), pp.74–80; Holloway, *The Game of Love*, p.79
21 Bendall, 'To Write a Distick upon It', p.201
22 For rhymes about memory, see Butterfield, p.80
23 Some stay busks featuring portraits of men do survive. Two nineteenth-century American scrimshaw examples were sold at Christie's New York, 16–17 January 2003, lots, 149, 150 and other examples are cited by Bendall, pp.205, 210
24 See Rushton, 'The Testament of Gifts'

25 See Bridget Millimore, 'Love Tokens: Engraved Coins, Emotions and the Poor 1700–1856' (PhD thesis, University of Brighton: Brighton, 2015); Sally Holloway, 'Romantic Love in Words and Objects during Courtship and Adultery *c.*1730–1800' (PhD thesis, Royal Holloway, University of London: Egham, 2013) pp.83–4; Jennine Hurl-Eamon, 'Love Tokens: Objects as Memory for Plebeian Women in Early Modern England' in *Early Modern Women* (vol.6, Fall 2011), pp.181–6

26 Holloway, 'Romantic Love', p.84; Michele Field and Timothy Millet, *Convict Love Tokens: The Leaden Hearts the Convicts Left Behind* (Wakefield Press: Cambridge, MA, 1998)

27 For an example of a token with a loop, see http://love-tokens.nma.gov.au/tokens/2008.0039.0101 [accessed 18.01.20]

28 Millett, *Convict Love Tokens*, pp.12, 24–5

29 Although until the nineteenth century arranged marriages were common in Britain, romantic love was considered to be an important element of marital relationships from the Middle Ages. See Alan MacFarlane, *Marriage and Love in England: Modes of Reproduction* (Basil Blackwell: Oxford, 1987) pp.174–208

30 Arianne Burnette, Joan Carlile, Oxford Dictionary of National Biography (c.1606–79), 2004, https://doi.org/10.1093/ref:odnb/4681 [accessed 17.01.19]; Moore, Flis and Vanke, The Paston Treasure (Yale University Press: New Haven, London) pp.486–7

31 John Whitefoot, 'Some minutes for the life of Sir Thomas Browne' in *Posthumous Works of the Learned Sir Thomas Browne* (London, 1712) p.xxxii

32 Victoria Kahn, '"The Duty to Love": Passion and Obligation in Early Modern Political Theory' in *Representations* (No.68, Autumn, 1999) pp.84–107; Victoria Kahn, *Wayward Contracts: The Crisis of Political Obligation in England 1640–1674* (Princeton University Press: New Jersey, 2016) pp.174–84; Angela McShane, 'Subjects and Objects: Material Expressions of Love and Loyalty in Seventeenth-Century England' in *Journal of British Studies* (vol.48, no.4, October 2009) pp.871–86; Chris King, 'Domestic Buildings: Understanding houses and society' in *The Routledge Handbook of Material Culture in Early Modern Europe* (Routledge: London, 2016) p.117; David Smith discusses this in relation to Dutch portraiture in *Masks of Wedlock: Seventeenth-century Dutch marriage portraiture* (UMI Research Press: Michigan, 1982) pp.10–12, 25

33 Hesson and Beaven, 'Objects of Love', pp.160–2

34 Andrew Wilton, *The Swagger Portrait: Grand Manner Portraiture in Britain from Van Dyck to Augustus John* (Tate Publishing, London, 1992) p.148; Judy Egerton, *The British School* (Yale University Press: New Haven, London, 2016) p.122

35 Egerton, *The British School*, p.123

36 Margaret Homans, 'Victoria's Sovereign Obedience', in Carol Christ and John Jordan, *Victorian Literature and the Victorian Visual Imagination* (University of California Press: Los Angeles, London) pp.169–96, especially p.180 on Mayall's photographs of Victoria and Albert.

37 National Portrait Gallery Archive, Registered Packet 7020

38 National Portrait Gallery Archive, Registered Packet 6583

39 National Portrait Gallery, 'An Interview with Neil and Glenys Kinnock' at https://www.npg.org.uk/collections/search/portrait/mw56971/Neil-Kinnock-Glenys-Kinnock [accessed 18.09.19]

40 Leon Battista Alberti, *On Painting* in Joanna Woodall, *Portraiture: Facing the Subject* (Manchester University Press, Manchester, 1997) p.8; Francisco de Hollanda, *Four Dialogues on Painting* (Oxford University Press, Oxford, 1928) pp.25–6

41 Donald W. Foster, '"Against the perjured falsehood of your tongues": Frances Howard on the Course of Love' in *The Encyclopedia of English Renaissance Literature* (John Wiley & Sons: New Jersey, 2017) p.90

42 It has been suggested that she was also the author of a pamphlet in defence of women against misogyny, Ester hath hang's Haman. See Foster, '"Against the perjured falsehood of your tongues...", pp.72–103

43 Wilson, *The History of Great Britain*, p.258

44 See pp.146–9 on Venetia and Kenelm Digby

45 Ralph M. Wardle, *Mary Wollstonecraft A Critical Biography* (University of Kansas Press, Kansas, 1951) p.307

46 Quoted in Ford K Brown, *The Life of William Godwin* (J.M. Dent, London, 1926) p.372

47 James Curl, *The Victorian Celebration of Death* (Sutton Publishing: Stroud, 2004); Esther Schor, *Bearing the Dead: The British Culture of Mourning from the Enlightenment to Victoria* (Princeton University Press: New Jersey, 1994); Lou Taylor, *Mourning Dress* (Routledge Revivals: London, 2010); and Deborah Lutz, *Relics of Death in Victorian Literature and Culture* (Cambridge University Press: Cambridge, 2015)

48 Queen Victoria, journal entry, 10 February 1840 at http://www.queenvictoriasjournals.org/search/browseByDate.do [accessed 28.02.19]

49 Jonathan Marsden, *Victoria & Albert: Art & Love* (The Royal Collection: London, 2010) p.12

50 Helen Rappaport, *A Magnificent Obsession: Victoria, Albert, and the Death That Changed the British Monarchy*, (Griffin: New York, 2013) p.122

51 Lutz, *Relics of Death*, p.55
52 Samuel Johnson, 'On Painting: Portraits Defended', *The Idler* (vol.45, 24 February 1758), reprinted in *The Works of Samuel Johnson*, ed. A Murphy, vol.1 (George Dearborn: New York, 1837) p.399

OBSESSED WITH THE MUSE

1 Collection: British Library Add. MS. 22950 f.41
2 Quoted in Wilton, *The Swagger Portrait*, p.86
3 Quoted in Terence Pepper and Helen Trompeteler, *Audrey Hepburn, Portraits of an Icon* (National Portrait Gallery: London, 2015) p.54
4 Quoted in Bruce Bernard, Derek Birdsall, *Lucian Freud* (Random House: London, 1996) p.19

Ellen Terry & George Frederic Watts

1 Divorce Proceedings, 13 Mar. 1877, High Court of Justice, Probate, Divorce and Admiralty Division, as quoted in David Loshak, 'G.F. Watts and Ellen Terry,' in the *Burlington Magazine*, vol. 105, Nov. 1963), p.483
2 K. Preston, *Letters from Graham Robertson* (Hamish Hamilton: London, 1953) p.316

The Bloomsbury Group

1 Peter and Leni Gillman, *The Wildest Dream: Mallory, his Life and Conflicting Passions* (Headline: London, 2000) p.97
2 Virginia Woolf, *The Letters of Virginia Woolf*, in (ed.) Anne Olivier Bell vol.4, 1929–1932 (Harcourt Brace: San Diego, 1980) p.200
3 See Anne Chisholm (ed.) *Carrington's Letters: Her Art, Her Loves, Her Friendships* (Vintage Digital: London, 2017)
4 Margaret Irwin, *Fire Down Below* (Heinemann: London, 1928) p.109

Lucian Freud & Caroline, Lady Blackwood

1 Lucian Freud, 'Some Thoughts on Painting', *Encounter* (July 1954), pp.23–4
2 Caroline Blackwood, *Lucian Freud: Early Works* (Robert Miller Gallery: New York, 1993), p.16
3 Caroline Blackwood, 'Francis Bacon (1909–1992)' *New York Review of Books*, (24 September 1992)
4 Stephen M. L. Aronson, 'Sophisticated Lady', *Town & Country*, (September 1993) p.148
5 Cecil Beaton, *The Strenuous Years: Diaries, 1948–55* (London: Weidenfeld & Nicolson, 1973) pp.133–4
6 William Feaver, *The Lives of Lucian Freud: Youth* (Bloomsbury: London, 2019),p.407
7 Daniel Farson, 'A Freudian Lunch in Mayfair', *Sacred Monsters* (Bloomsbury: London, 1988), p.179
8 Quoted in Nancy Schonenberger, *Dangerous Muse: The Life of Lady Caroline Blackwood* (Knopf Doubleday Publishing Group: London, 2012), p.209
9 Blackwood, *Freud: Early Works*, p.13

LITERARY LOVE

1 Letter from Joseph Severn to George Scharf, 21 December [1859?] in the National Portrait Gallery Archive.
2 Lady Sydney Morgan, *Lady Morgan's Memoirs, Autobiography, Diaries and Correspondence* in W.H. Allen, (vol. II, 1862) p.202. The attribution is now doubted, but is part of Lamb's mythology. See Paul Douglass, *Lady Caroline Lamb: A Biography* (Palgrave Macmillan: London and NY, 2004) p.104
3 Letter from Byron to Lady Caroline Lamb, estimated April 1812 in *British Library Journal*, 2:1, p.116

Mary Shelley & Percy Bysshe Shelley

1 Letter from Mary Godwin to Percy Bysshe Shelley, 25 October 1814, MS Shelley, chapter 1, 129v–130r, (Bodleian Library, Oxford, 1814)

Elizabeth Barrett Browning & Robert Browning

1 Marjorie Stone, 'Elizabeth Barrett Browning' in *Oxford Dictionary of National Biography*, (4 October 2008), https://doi.org/10.1093/ref.odnb/3711 [accessed: 06.09.19]
2 Clyde de L. Ryais, 'Robert Browning', *Oxford Dictionary of National Biography*, (25 May 2006) https://doi.org/10.1093/ref.odnb/3714 [accessed 06.09.19]
3 Cited in Julia Markus, *Dared and Done: The Marriage of Elizabeth Barrett and Robert Browning* (Bloomsbury: London, 1997) p.80
4 Clyde de L. Ryais, 'Robert Browning', *Oxford Dictionary of National Biography*

Ted Hughes & Sylvia Plath

1 *The Journals of Sylvia Plath, 1950–1962*, (ed.) Karen V.Kukil (Faber and Faber: London, 2000) p.212
2 Ted Hughes, 'A Pink Wool Knitted Dress', in *Birthday Letters* (ISIS: Oxford, 1999) p.32
3 Ted Hughes, 'Drawing', in *Birthday Letters* (ISIS: Oxford, 1999) p.43
4 Sylvia Plath, 'Daddy', in *Ariel* (Faber and Faber: London, 1967) p.56
5 Sylvia Plath, 'The Edge', in *Ariel* (Faber and Faber: London, 1967) p.85

Alice B. Toklas & Gertrude Stein

1 Alice B. Toklas, *What is Remembered: An Autobiography with Special Reference to Gertrude Stein* (Michael Joseph: London, 1963) p.23

A SHARED STUDIO

1 Maria Cosway, letter to Sir William Cosway, 1830, National Art Library (MS Eng. L. 961–1953, fol.1v)
2 Marylebone Parish Church, London
3 BBC Radio 4, 'Living sculptures: At home with Gilbert & George,' *Front Row*, 23 September 2017, https://www.bbc.co.uk/programmes/articles/22ywTtt7WhmgzJt5Z4N942h/living-sculptures-at-home-with-gilbert-george [accessed 14.10.19]

Mary Beale & Charles Beale

1 Mary Beale, *Discourse on Friendship*, 1667, British Library, (MS Harley 6828 ff.510–23) quoted in Tabitha Barber, *Mary Beale: Portrait of a Seventeenth-Century Painter, her Family and her Studio* (Geffrye Museum: London, 1999) p.30
2 Charles Beale, Letter 104, Bodleian Library (MS Rawlinson) quoted in Barber, *Mary Beale*, p.13
3 Charles Beale, notebook, 7 August 1677, MS Rawlinson. 80 572, Bodleian Library, Oxford; quoted in Christopher Reeve, 'Mary Beale', *Oxford Dictionary of National Biography* (4 October 2008), https://www.oxforddnb.com/view/10.1093/ref:odnb/9780198614128.001.0001/odnb-9780198614128-e-1803
4 Samuel Woodforde, diary, 2 December 1664, MS Eng. misc. f. 381, Bodleian Library, Oxford; quoted in Reeve, *op. cit.*

Lee Miller & Man Ray

1 Antony Penrose, *The Lives of Lee Miller* (Thames and Hudson: London, 1985) p.29
2 Ibid. p.37
3 Neil Baldwin, *Man Ray. American Artist* (Da Capo Press: New York, 2001) pp.15–16
4 Man Ray, *Self Portrait* (Penguin: London, 2012) p.170; reprised Penrose, *Lee Miller*, p.25
5 Ibid.
6 Ibid.
7 Penrose, *Lee Miller*, p.22
8 Baldwin, *Man Ray*, p.99
9 Mark Haworth-Booth, *The Art of Lee Miller* (V&A Publications: London, 2007) p.22; Baldwin, *Man Ray*, p.155
10 Whitney Chadwick, *Women Artists and the Surrealist Movement* (Thames and Hudson: London,1985) p.39; Penrose, *Lee Miller*, p.25
11 Ibid, p.30
12 Ibid, pp.30–1

Barbara Hepworth & Ben Nicholson

1 Barbara Hepworth in *Barbara Hepworth: Carvings and Drawings*, introduction by Herbert Read (Lund Humphries: London, 1952) quoted in Charles Harrison, *English Art and Modernism 1900–1939* (Yale University Press: New Haven, London, 1981) p.265
2 Herbert Read, 'A Nest of Gentle Artists' in *Apollo* (September 1962) pp.536–40
3 Ben Nicholson, letter to Helen Sutherland, 3 May 1932 quoted in *Hepworth Nicholson Sculpture and Painting in the 1930s*, exh. cat. (Hazlitt Holland-Hibbert: London, 2019) p.5
4 Adrian Stokes in *The Spectator*, 1933, quoted in Charles Harrison, *English Art and Modernism 1900–39*, (Yale University Press: New Haven, London, 1994) p.230

Mervyn Peake & Maeve Gilmore

1 Quoted in G. Peter Winnington, *Mervyn Peake: The Man and His Art* (Peter Owen Publishers: London, 2006) p.49
2 Maeve Gilmore, *A World Away: A Memoir of Mervyn Peake* (Gollancz: London, 1970)
3 Maeve Gilmore, Mervyn Peake, *Titus Awakes: The Lost Book of Gormenghast* (Random House: London, 2011) p.265

David Garrick & Eva Maria Garrick

1 Letter from Horace Walpole to George Montagu, 18 May 1749, *Yale Edition of the Correspondence of Horace Walpole*, 48 vols, ed. W.S. Lewis (Yale University Press: New Haven, London, 1937–83) vol.IX p.81
2 MS found among David Garrick's papers on his death, quoted in Philip H. Highfill, Kalman A. Burnim, et al (ed.), *A Biographical Dictionary of Actors, Actresses, Musicians, Dancers ... and Other Stage Personnel in London 1600–1800* (Southern Illinois University Press: Carbondale and Edwardsville, 1978, vol.6, p.20
3 William Roberts, *Memoirs of the Life and Correspondence of Mrs Hannah More*, vol.1 (Harper and Brothers: New York, 1834) p.96

Dame Millicent Garrett Fawcett & Henry Fawcett

1 Lawrence Goldman, 'Henry Fawcett' in *Oxford Dictionary of National Biography* (25 May 2006) https://www.oxforddnb.com/view/10.1093/ref:odnb/9780198614128.001.0001/odnb-9780198614128-e-9218 [accessed 04.09.19]
2 Mary Bennett, *Ford Madox Brown: A Catalogue Raisonné*, 2 vols (Yale University Press: London and New Haven, 2010) vol.2, p.398
3 Leslie Stephen, *Life of Henry Fawcett* (Smith, Elder & Co.: London, 1885) p.127
4 Janet Howarth, 'Dame Millicent Garrett Fawcett' in *Oxford Dictionary of National Biography*, https://www.oxforddnb.com/view/10.1093/ref:odnb/9780198614128.001.0001/odnb-9780198614128-e-33096?docPos=1&mediaType=Article [accessed 04.09.19], citing NUWSS typescript, Manchester Central Library, M50/2/10/20
5 Bennett, *Ford Madox Brown: A Catalogue Raisonné*, vol.2, p.399

Charles Shannon & Charles Ricketts

1 Jacques-Emile Blanche, *Portraits of a Lifetime: The Late Victorian Era; the Edwardian Pageant 1870–1914* (J.M. Dent: London, 1937) p.166
2 Letters from Charles Ricketts to Michael Field, 16 and 30 November 1898, quoted in Joseph Darracott, *The World of Charles Ricketts* (Methuen: London, 1980) pp.22–3
3 J.G.P. Delaney, *Charles Ricketts: A Biography* (Oxford University Press: Oxford, 1990) p.220

John Maynard Keynes & Lydia Lopokova

1 Cited by Robert Skidelsky in *John Maynard Keynes: A Biography. Vol. 1, Hopes Betrayed (1883–1920)* (MacMillan: London, 1992) pp.352–3
2 Cited by Robert Skidelsky in *John Maynard Keynes: A Biography. Vol. 2, The Economist as Saviour (1920–1937)* (MacMillan: London, 1992) p.93
3 All quotes from their letters in this paragraph come from Polly Hill and Richard Keynes (eds), *Lydia and Maynard: Letters between Lydia Lopokova and John Maynard Keynes.* (Andre Deutsch: London, 1989)
4 Ibid.
5 Cited by Milo Keynes in *Lydia Lopokova* (Weidenfeld and Nicolson: London, *c.*1983) pp.1–2

SCANDAL & TRAGEDY

1 James Melville, *J. Melville of Halhill, Memoirs of his Own Life* (The Bannatyne Club: Edinburgh, 1827) p.122
2 Richard Polwhele, *The Unsex'd Females: A Poem Addressed to the Author of the Pursuits of Literature* (W.M. Cobbett: London, 1798), p.13

Sir Kenelm Digby & Venetia, Lady Digby

1 Susan J. Barnes, Nora De Poorter, Oliver Millar and Horst Vey, *Van Dyck: A Complete Catalogue of the Paintings* (Yale University Press for the Paul Mellon Centre for Studies in British Art: New Haven, London, 2004) p.506
2 Michael Foster, 'Sir Kenelm Digby', *Oxford Dictionary of National Biography* (Oxford University Press: Oxford, 2004)
3 National Archive, PRO, PROB 11/325, f.130

Emma Hamilton & Admiral Lord Nelson

1 Emma Hamilton to Horatio Nelson, 8 September 1798, BL Add MSS 34989 ff.4–7. See Kate Williams, *England's Mistress* (Hutchinson: London, 2006) p.206
2 Letter from Lord Spencer to Horatio Nelson, 9 May 1800, in Sir Nicholas Harris, *Dispatches and Letters of Vice Admiral Lord Horatio Nelson* (Henry Colburn: London, 1845), vol.4, p.242; see Williams, *England's Mistress,* p.233
3 Letter from Horatio Nelson to Emma Hamilton, January 1800, Private Collection; see Williams, *England's Mistress,* p.232

Oscar Wilde & Lord Alfred Douglas

1 Oscar Wilde to Lord Alfred Douglas, March 1893, in Merlin Holland and Rupert Hart-Davis, *The Complete Letters of Oscar Wilde* (Henry Holt & Company: New York, 2000) p.559
2 Colm Tóibín, *Mad, Bad, Dangerous to Know: The Fathers of Wilde, Yeats and Joyce* (Penguin: London, 2018) p.59
3 Lord Alfred Douglas to Marquess of Queensberry, June 1894, cited in Richard Ellmann, *Oscar Wilde* (Penguin: London, 1988), p.396
4 Ellmann, *Oscar Wilde,* p.541
5 Oscar Wilde to Robert Ross, 21 September 1897, in Holland and Hart-Davis, *Complete Letters,* p.943

Edward VIII & Wallis Simpson

1 Brian MacArthur, *The Penguin Book of Twentieth-Century Speeches* (Viking: London, 1992) p.156
2 Cecil Beaton, *The Wandering Years: Diaries: 1922–1939* (Weidenfeld and Nicolson: London, 1961) p.311
3 Greg King, *The Duchess of Windsor* (Citadel Press: New York, 1999) p.388

John Lennon & Yoko Ono

1 Maureen Cleave, 'How Does a Beatle Live? John Lennon Lives Like This', *London Evening Standard* (4 March 1966)
2 'The Real John Lennon', interview with Barbara Graustark, *Newsweek* (29 September 1980)

3 David Sheff and G. Barry Golson (eds), *Last Interview: All We Are Saying, John Lennon and Yoko Ono* (Sidgwick & Jackson: London, 2000) p.208
4 Graustark, *Newsweek* (29 September 1980)
5 John Lennon, interview, Amsterdam Hilton, 25 March 1969 in Barry Miles, *The Beatles Diary. Volume 1: The Beatles Years* (Omnibus Press: London, 2001) p.337
6 John Lennon, interview with Dave Sholin, 8 December 1980 (broadcast 14 December 1980, RKO Radio Network), *Lennon on Lennon: Conversations with John Lennon*, ed. Jeff Burger (Omnibus Press: London, 2017) p.412
7 Yoko Ono, interview, *Telegraph* (27 March 2012)
8 John Lennon, interview with Scott Muni, 13 February 1975 (broadcast live, WNEW-FM, New York), *Lennon on Lennon*, p.374
9 Annie Leibovitz and Sharon DeLano (ed.), *Annie Leibovitz at work* (Jonathan Cape: London, 2008) p.46
10 Ibid.

LOVE AGAINST THE ODDS

1 'Letter from Lady Mary Wortley Montagu' in *London Magazine or the Gentleman's Monthly Intelligencer*, (vol. 36, January 1767) p.348
2 Jessie Coleridge-Taylor, *A Memory Sketch or Personal Reminiscences of my Husband, Genius and Musician, S. Coleridge-Taylor* (John Crowther: Bognor Regis, 1943) pp.20–21
3 Ibid., p.27

Sir William Temple & Dorothy, Lady Temple

1 Letter from Dorothy Osborne to William Temple, 4 February 1654 in *Wayfarer's Library* (J.M Dent & Sons: London, 1914)

Sarah Forbes Bonetta & James Pinson Labulo Davies

1 Queen Victoria's Diaries, Princess Beatrice's copies, 9 November 1850 (Windsor Castle, vol. 30, Royal Archives) pp.165–7
2 Frederick Edwyn Forbes, Dahomey and the Dahomans; Being the Journals of Two Missions to the King of Dahomey, and Residence at his Capital, in the Year 1849 and 1850 (Longman: London, 1851) p.81
3 Letter to Mrs Schoen on 16 March 1861, quoted in Walter Dean Myers, An African Princess (Walker Books: London, 1999) p.106
4 Letter to Mrs Schoen, 7 April 1880, Royal Edinburgh Hotel, Funchal, Madeira, quoted in Myers, *African Princess* p.106

LOVE & THE LENS

1 'The Inside Story: Victoria Beckham's Juergen Teller Vogue Shoot', *Vogue*, September 2016, https://www.vogue.co.uk/article/victoria-beckham-juergen-teller-vogue-shoot [accessed 14.10.19]

Maharani Gayatri Devi, Rajmata of Jaipur & Sawai Man Singh II, Maharaja of Jaipur

1 Rosita Forbes quoted in Gayatri Devi and Santha Rama Rao, *A Princess Remembers: Memoirs of the Maharani of Jaipur* (Rupa Publications: New Dehli, 1995) p.99
2 Ibid., p.120
3 Ibid., p.184
4 Cecil Beaton, *The Years Between: Diaries 1939–44* (Weidenfeld & Nicholson: London, 1965)

Mick Jagger & Bianca Jagger & Jerry Hall

1 Jim Jerome, 'The Jaggers', *People Weekly* (9 June 1975)
2 Ibid.
3 Bianca Jagger, interview, *New York Daily News* (1986)
4 Jerry Hall, *Jerry Hall: My Life in Pictures* (Quadrille: London, 2010) p.145
5 Nicola Roberts, 'Norman Parkinson: legend behind a lens', *Financial Times* (29 March 2013)
6 Jerry Hall, *Hall: My Life in Pictures* p.150
7 Christopher Anderson, *Mick: the Wild Life and Mad Genius of Jagger* (Robson: London, 2012) p.186
8 Ibid., p.253

Charles, Prince of Wales & Diana, Princess of Wales

1 Interview by Andrew Gardner and Angela Rippon, 28 July 1981. In 'Diana: in her own words', Channel 4/ National Geographic documentary 2017 [accessed on Netflix 29.08.19]
2 K.D. Reynolds, 'Diana [née Lady Diana Frances Spencer], princess of Wales (1961–1997)', *Oxford Dictionary of National Biography*, https://www.oxforddnb.com/view/10.1093/ref:odnb/9780198614128.001.0001/odnb-9780198614128-e-68348#odnb-9780198614128-e-68348-div1-d60882e202 [accessed 29/08/19]
3 From 'Diana: in her own words'

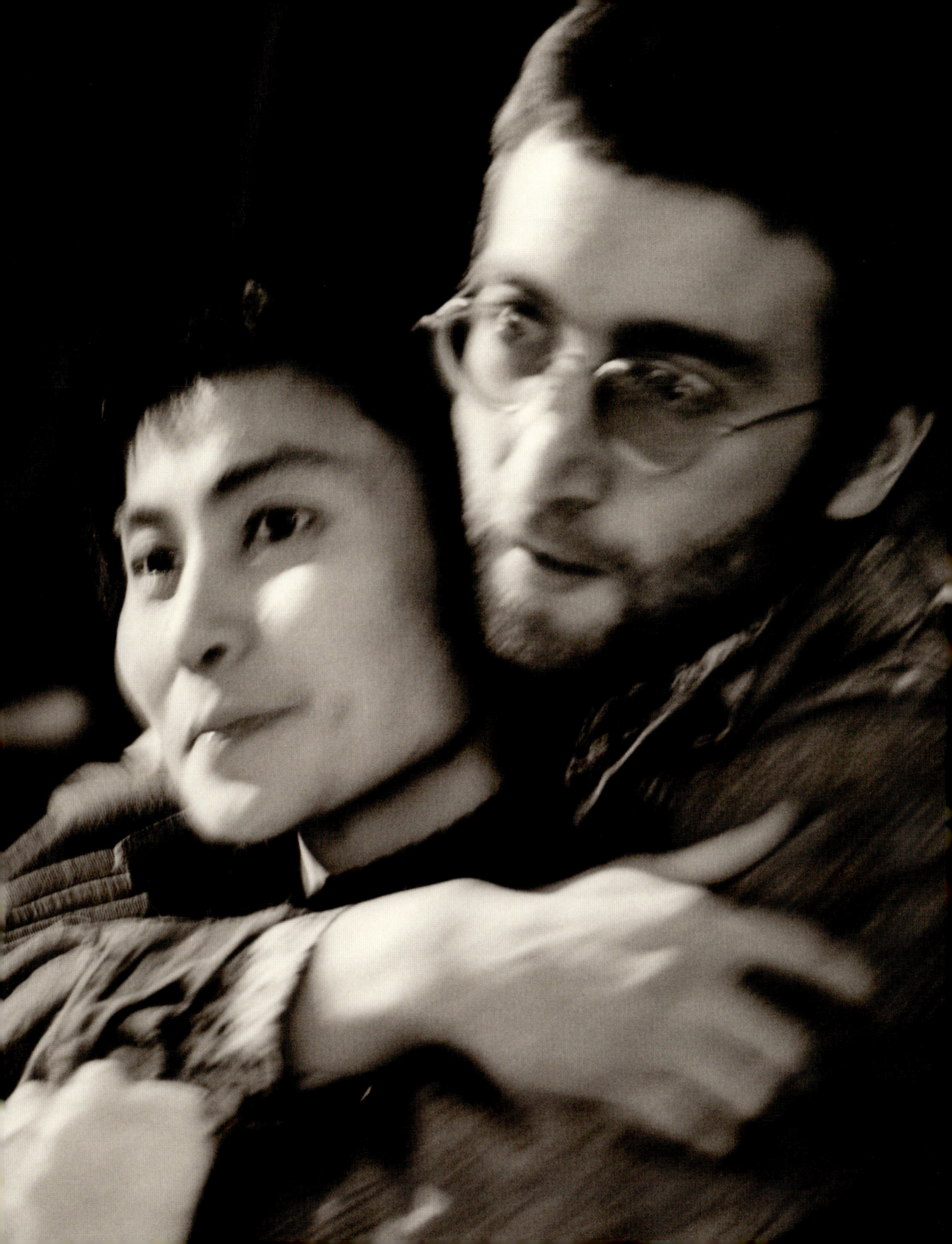

FURTHER READING

Ellen Terry & George Frederic Watts

Wilfred Blunt, *England's Michelangelo: A Biography of George Frederic Watts* (Hamish Hamilton: London, 1975)

Elizabeth Heath, 'Choosing by G.F. Watts' in *Later Victorian Portraits Catalogue* (National Portrait Gallery: London, https://www.npg.org.uk/research/programmes/late-victorian-catalogue, accessed: 11.02.20)

The Bloomsbury Group

Anne Chisholm (ed.) *Carrington's Letters Her Art, Her Loves, Her Friendships* (Vintage Digital: London, 2017)

Peter and Leni Gillman, *The Wildest Dream: Mallory, his Life and Conflicting Passions* (Headline: London, 2000)

Brenda Helt and Madelyn Detloff (eds), *Queer Bloomsbury* (Edinburgh University Press: Edinburgh, 2016)

Christopher Reed, *Bloomsbury Rooms: Modernism, Subculture, and Domesticity* (Yale University Press: New Haven and London, 2004)

Frances Spalding, *The Bloomsbury Group* (National Portrait Gallery: London, 2005)

Virginia Woolf, *The Letters of Virginia Woolf*, (vol.4, 1929–1932) in (ed.) Anne Olivier Bell (Harcourt Brace: San Diego, 1980)

Lucian Freud & Caroline, Lady Blackwood

Caroline Blackwood, *Lucian Freud: Early Works* (Robert Miller Gallery: New York, 1993)

William Feaver, *The Lives of Lucian Freud: Youth* (Bloomsbury: London, 2019)

Lucian Freud, 'Some Thoughts on Painting', *Encounter* (July 1954)

Nancy Schonenberger, *Dangerous Muse: The Life of Lady Caroline Blackwood* (Knopf Doubleday Publishing Group: London, 2012

Mary Shelley & Percy Bysshe Shelley

Richard Holmes, *Shelley: The Pursuit* (NYRB Classics: New York, 2003)

Fiona Sampson, *In Search of Mary Shelley: The Girl Who Wrote Frankenstein* (Profile Books: London, 2018)

Elizabeth Barrett Browning & Robert Browning

R.B. Browning, *The Letters of Robert Browning and Elizabeth Barrett Browning 1845–1846*, vol.1 (Project Gutenberg: eBook, 2005)

Clyde de L. Ryais, 'Robert Browning', *Oxford Dictionary of National Biography*, 25 May 2006 (Accessed: 6 September 2019, https://doi.org/10.1093/ref.odnb/3714)

Marjorie Stone, 'Elizabeth Barrett Browning' *in Oxford Dictionary of National Biography*, (4 October 2008), https://doi.org/10.1093/ref.odnb/3711

Ted Hughes & Sylvia Plath

Ted Hughes, *Birthday Letters* (ISIS: Oxford, 1999)

Sylvia Plath, *Ariel* (Faber and Faber: London, 1967)

The Journals of Sylvia Plath, 1950–1962, edited by Karen V. Kukil (Faber and Faber: London, 2000)

Alice B. Toklas & Gertrude Stein

Cecil Beaton, *Cecil Beaton's Diaries: The Wandering Years 1922–1939* (Weidenfeld & Nicolson: London, 1961)

Wanda W. Corn & Tirza Latimer, *Seeing Gertrude Stein: Five Stories* (University of California Press: Berkeley, 2011)

Diana Souhami, *Gertrude and Alice* (Pandora Press, Harper Collins: London, 1991)

Mary Beale & Charles Beale

Tabitha Barber, *Mary Beale: Portrait of a Seventeenth-Century Painter, her Family and her Studio* (Geffrye Museum: London, 1999)

Christopher Reeve, 'Mary Beale', *Oxford Dictionary of National Biography* (4 October 2008), https://www.oxforddnb.com/view/10.1093/ref:odnb/9780198614128.001.0001/odnb-9780198614128-e-1803.

Lee Miller & Man Ray

Jane Alison and Coralie Malissard (eds.), *Modern Couples. Art, Intimacy and the Avant-garde* (Prestel Publishing: London, 2018)

Sam Bardaouil, *Surrealism in Egypt: Modernism and the Art and Liberty Group* (London; New York: I.B. Tauris, 2013).

Terence Pepper, (ed.), *Man Ray. Portraits* (National Portrait Gallery: London, 2013)

Barbara Hepworth & Ben Nicholson

Sophie Bowness, *Barbara Hepworth: The Sculptor in the Studio* (Tate Publishing: London, 2017)

Norbert Lynton, *Ben Nicholson* (Phaidon Press: London, 1998)

Mervyn Peake & Maeve Gilmore

Alison Eldred, Sebastian Peake, G. Peter Winnington, *Mervyn Peake: The Man and His Art* (Peter Owen Publishers: London, 2006)

Maeve Gilmore, *A World Away: A Memoir of Mervyn Peake* (Gollancz: London, 1970)

Malcolm Yorke, *Mervyn Peake: My Eyes Mint Gold* (Overlook Press: New York, 2002)

David Garrick & Eva Maria Garrick

Ian McIntyre, *Garrick* (Penguin: London, 1999)

Dame Millicent Garrett Fawcett & Henry Fawcett

Mary Bennett, Ford Madox Brown: *A Catalogue Raisonné,* 2 vols (Yale University Press: London and New Haven, 2010)

Lawrence Goldman, (ed.) *The Blind Victorian: Henry Fawcett & British Liberalism* (Cambridge University Press: Cambridge, 1989)

Leslie Stephen, *Life of Henry Fawcett* (Cambridge University Press: Cambridge, 1885)

Charles Shannon & Charles Ricketts

Matt Cook, *Queer Domesticities: Homosexuality and Home Life in Twentieth-Century London* (Palgrave Macmillan: Basingstoke, 2014)

Joseph Darracott, *The World of Charles Ricketts* (Methuen: London, 1980)

J.G.P. Delaney, *Charles Ricketts: A Biography* (Oxford University Press: Oxford, 1990)

John Maynard Keynes & Lydia Lopokova

Polly Hill and Richard Keynes (eds), *Lydia and Maynard: Letters between Lydia Lopokova and John Maynard Keynes* (André Deutsch: London, 1989)

Judith Mackrell, *Bloomsbury Ballerina: Lydia Lopokova, Imperial Dancer and Mrs John Maynard Keynes* (Phoenix: London, 2013)

Robert Skidelsky, *John Maynard Keynes: a biography* (3 volumes) (MacMillan: London, 1992–2000)

Sir Kenelm Digby & Venetia, Lady Digby

Ann Sumner (ed.), *Death, Passion and Politics* (Dulwich Picture Gallery: London, 1995)

Joe Moshenska, *A Stain in the Blood: The Remarkable Voyage of Sir Kenelm Digby* (William Heinemann: New York, 2016)

Edward VIII & Wallis Simpson

Anne Sebba, *That Woman: The Life of Wallis Simpson, Duchess of Windsor* (Weidenfeld & Nicolson: London, 2011)

Philip Ziegler, *King Edward VIII: The Official Biography* (Alfred A. Knopf: New York, 1991)

John Lennon & Yoko Ono

Jeff Burger (ed.), *Lennon on Lennon: Conversations with John Lennon* (Omnibus Press: London, 2017)

David Sheff and G. Barry Golson (ed.), *Last Interview: All We Are Saying, John Lennon and Yoko Ono* (Sidgwick & Jackson: London, 2000)

Sir William Temple & Dorothy, Lady Temple

Jane Dunn, *Read my Heart: Dorothy Osborne and Sir William Temple, A Love Story in the Age of Revolution* (HarperPress: London, 2009)

Carrie A Hintz, *An Audience of One: Dorothy Osborne's letters to Sir William Temple 1652 –1654* (University of Toronto Press: Toronto, 2005)

Kenneth Parker, *Dorothy Osborne: Letters to Sir William Temple, 1652–54: Observations on Love, Literature Politics and Religion,* 2nd ed, (Ashgate: Aldershot, 2002)

Sarah Forbes Bonetta & James Pinson Labulo Davies

Walter Dean Myers, *An African Princess* (Walker Books: London, 1999)

Jan Marsh, *Black Victorians: Black People in British Art 1800–1900* (Lund Humphries, Manchester City Art Gallery: London, Manchester, 2005)

Maharani Gayatri Devi, Rajmata of Jaipur & Sawai Man Singh II, Maharaja of Jaipur

Cecil Beaton, *Indian Album* (B.T. Batsford: London, 1945)

Gayatri Devi, *A Princess Remembers: The Memoirs of the Maharani of Jaipur* (Rupa Publications: New Delhi, 1995)

Mick Jagger & Bianca Jagger & Jerry Hall

Jerry Hall, *Jerry Hall: My Life in Pictures* (Quadrille: London, 2010)

Mark Paytress, *The Rolling Stones: Off the Record* (Omnibus: London, 2003)

Charles, Prince of Wales & Diana, Princess of Wales

Andrew Morton, *Diana: Her True Story – In her Own Words* (Chivers Press: Bath, 1998)

K.D. Reynolds, 'Diana [née Lady Diana Frances Spencer], princess of Wales (1961–1997)', *Oxford Dictionary of National Biography,* https://www.oxforddnb.com/view/10.1093/ref:odnb/9780198614128.001.0001/odnb-9780198614128-e-68348#odnb-9780198614128-e-68348-div1-d60882e202

'Diana: in her own words', Channel 4/National Geographic documentary 2017

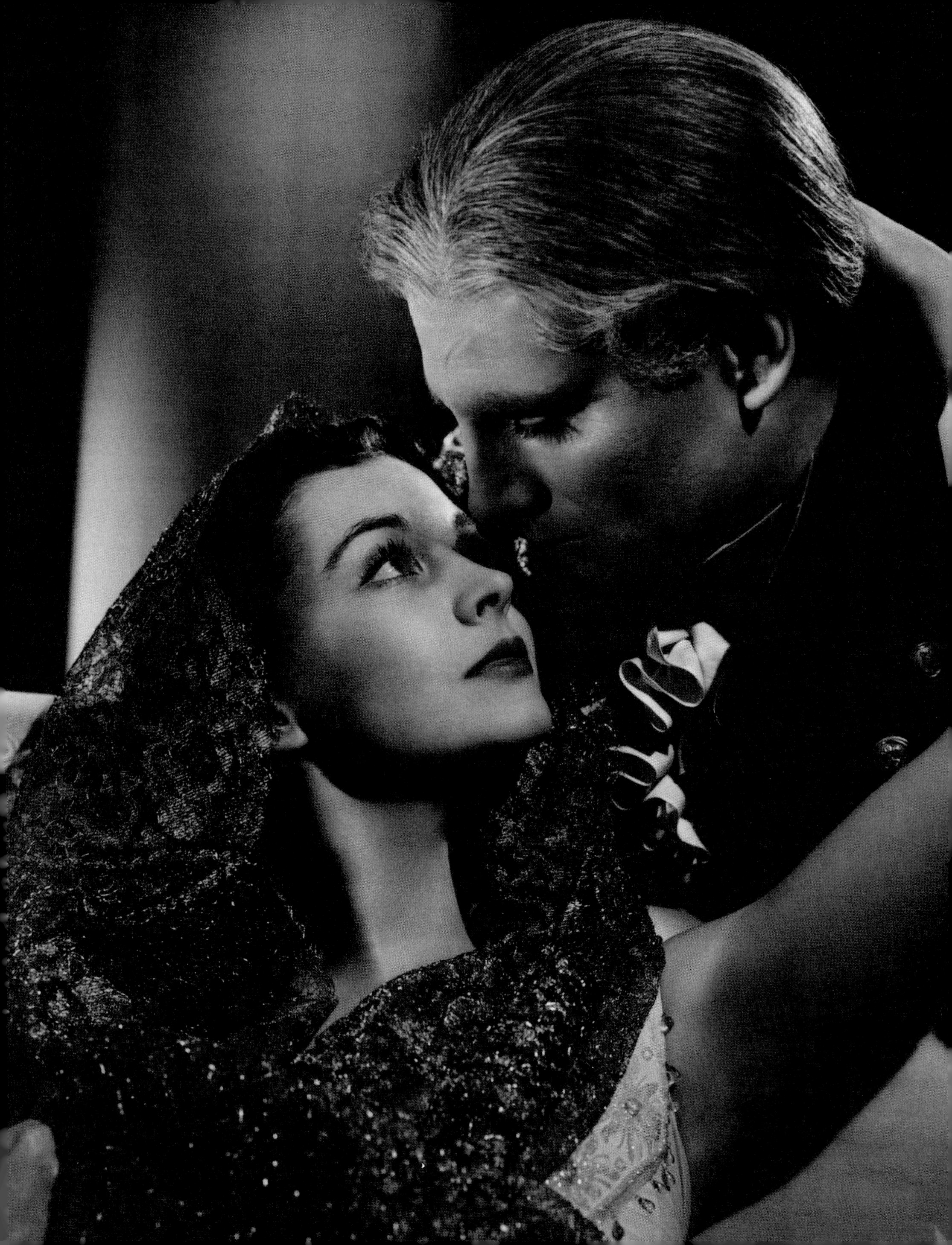

NATIONAL PORTRAIT GALLERY, LONDON

This book was inspired by the Gallery's international touring exhibition *Love Stories*. We are most grateful to Louise Stewart, the lead curator of the *Love Stories* exhibition and to Lucy Peltz for her role as co-editor and co-curator, and to all the Gallery's curators for their contributions and expertise. We would also like to thank our contributors to this book including Simon Callow, Marina Warner, Kate Williams, and Peter Funnell. Thanks are also due to John H. Bryan and Jenny Saunt at Crabtree Farm for providing access to the wonderful collections there.

We would particularly like to thank the directors and staff of our initial partner museums, in particular Karen Quinlan at the National Portrait Gallery of Australia, and Christoph Heinrich at the Denver Art Museum. Their collaboration, enthusiasm and commitment to the exhibition were instrumental to its realisation.

At the National Portrait Gallery, our thanks also go to Sarah Tinsley, Director of Programmes and Partnerships; Melanie Pilbrow, Head of International Programmes; Ted McDonald-Toone, International Partnerships Manager; and Imogen Haines, International Projects Manager. Thanks are also due to Amelia Collins, Kara Green, Anna Starling, Mark Lynch and Ruth Müller-Wirth for their work on this book and to Katie Andrews, Tanya Bentley, Helena Cuss, Jan Marsh and all the staff who have contributed to realising the exhibition and the present volume.

Nicholas Cullinan
Director
National Portrait Gallery, London

NATIONAL PORTRAIT GALLERY, AUSTRALIA

The National Portrait Gallery of Australia acknowledges the support of the Australian Government International Exhibitions Insurance program, and the financial support of the ACT Government's Major Event Fund in bringing Love Stories *to the National Portrait Gallery.*

The National Portrait Gallery of Australia is delighted to collaborate with our esteemed partner institution as the exclusive Australian venue for the exhibition *Love Stories*. Love's infinite iterations through the centuries are brought to light through the artworks in the show and in this book, emphasising portraiture's powerful capacity to engage – as a genre affecting, instructive and exhilarating in equal measure.

With the richness of the *Love Stories* artworks assured, it's the alignment of our institutions' missions that binds the collaboration. The National Portrait Gallery, London emphasises portraiture's role in promoting the men and women who have made and are making British history and culture. It's a *raison d'être* in lockstep with the beat of our own institutional heart, and the passionate work of our team here in Canberra: we're also enmeshed with an evolving national narrative, and the cast of characters of noteworthy Australians we feature is wide-ranging – from leaders, thinkers and pariahs; villains to vaudevillians; those we variously desire or denounce; and, of course, a cavalcade of lovers of all stripes.

We welcome *Love Stories* to our walls, and commend this book both as superb accompaniment, and – as a tome of love's multiple, intoxicating manifestations in portraiture – a beguiling volume in perpetuity.

Karen Quinlan AM
Director
National Portrait Gallery of Australia

DENVER ART MUSEUM

The Denver Art Museum is pleased to bring the National Portrait Gallery's *Love Stories* to the United States. This celebration of a universal theme reveals the myriad ways in which love and relationships have inspired and encouraged creativity across time.

The project team included Jennifer R. Henneman, Lauren Thompson, Meg Erickson, Sarah Cucinella-McDaniel, Lori Iliff and Jill Desmond. The presentation of this exhibition in Denver would not have been possible without the creative contributions of the extended Denver Art Museum team.

Christoph Heinrich
Frederick and Jan May Director
Denver Art Museum

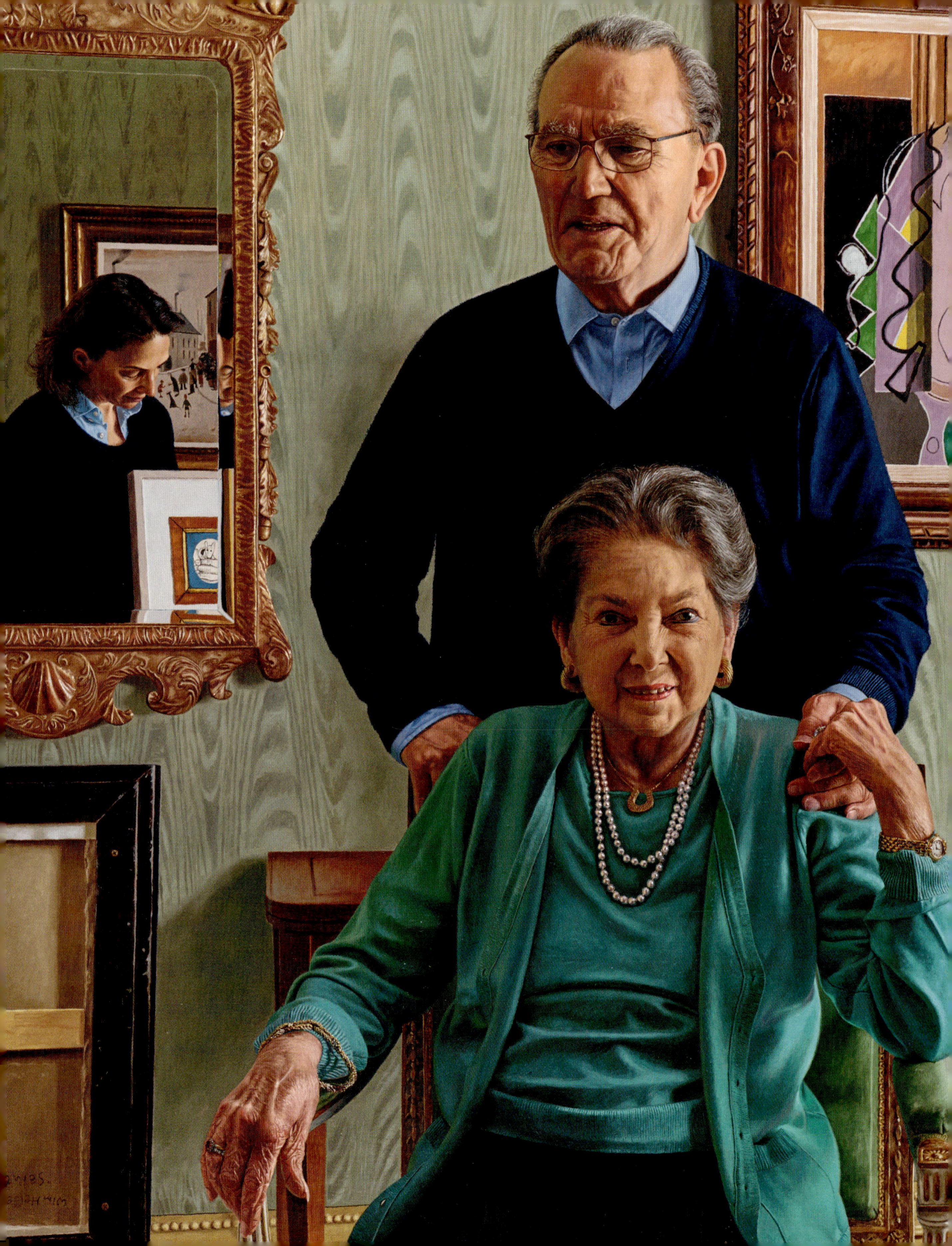

CREDITS

Unless otherwise stated, all illustrations are © National Portrait Gallery, London (NPG). Every effort has been made to contact holders of copyright material, and any omissions will be corrected in future editions if the publisher is notified in writing. The publisher would like to thank the following for permissions to reproduce works for which they hold copyright:

p.3 NPG, purchased 1998 © Estate of Mildred E. Eldridge; p.6–7 NPG, © Graham Hughes; p.9 © Courtesy National Gallery of Art, Washington; p.11 (l) NPG, Purchased with help from the National Heritage Memorial Fund, the Art Fund, Lord Harris of Peckham, L.L. Brownrigg, the Portrait Fund, Sir Harry Djanogly, the Headley Trust, the Eva & Hans K. Rausing Trust, The Pidem Fund, Mr O. Damgaard-Nielsen, Sir David and Lady Scholey and numerous Gallery visitors and supporters, 2006; p.11 (r) NPG, Purchased with help from the Art Fund, the National Heritage Memorial Fund and the Dame Helen Gardner, Bequest, 1992; p.12 The Syndics of the Fitzwilliam Museum, University of Cambridge. Bought,1920, Image © Fitzwilliam Museum, Cambridge; p.18 © Bryan Collection, USA; p.19 © National Museum of Australia / CC BY-SA 4.0; p.21 © Courtesy of the Mercers' Company, London; p.23 The National Gallery, London. Bought with a contribution from The Art Fund (Sir Robert Witt Fund), 1954 © The National Gallery, London / Scala, Florence; p.24 (l) NPG, Given by W.M. Campbell Smyth, 1935; p.24 (r) NPG, Acquired Jonathan Ruffer, 1976; p.25 NPG, Purchased with help from the Art Fund and Sir Simon Robertson KT, 2016; p.26 (t) NPG, Given by Mrs Mary Behrend, 1973; p.26 (b) NPG, © Graham Hughes; p.29 (l) Gift of the Thomas Gilcrease Foundation, 1955, © Gilcrease Museum; p.30 Royal Collection Trust / © Her Majesty Queen Elizabeth II 2020 / Bridgeman Images; p.32 NPG, Accepted in lieu of tax by H.M. Government and allocated to the Gallery, 1975; p.35 (r) NPG, Given by Henry Witte Martin, 1861; p.36 NPG, Purchased with help from the National Heritage Memorial Fund, through the Art Fund (with a contribution from the Wolfson Foundation), Camelot Group plc, David and Catharine Alexander, David Wilson, E.A. Whitehead, Glyn Hopkin and numerous other supporters of a public appeal including members of the Chelsea Arts Club, 2005; p.37 (l) NPG, Given by Adrian Woodhouse, 2006, © Adrian Woodhouse; p.37 (r) NPG, purchased, 2016, © estate of Jack Cardiff / www.jackcardiffportraits.com; p.38 (l) NPG, Given by David Ball, 2015, © Estate of Angus McBean; p.38 (r) Purchased, 2008, © Estate of Angus McBean; p.39 (t) NPG, Given by Mark Haworth-Booth, 2009, © Estate of Bruce Bernard, courtesy of Virgina Verran; p.39 (b) NPG, Commissioned; made possible by J.P. Morgan through the Fund for New Commissions, 2004, © Sam Taylor-Wood; p.41 NPG, Accepted in lieu of tax by H.M. Government and allocated to the Gallery, 1975; p.42 © Eastnor Castle Collection, Herefordshire; p.45 NPG, Given by Barbara Strachey (Hultin, later Halpern), 1999; p.47 NPG, Accepted in lieu of tax by H.M. Government and allocated to the Gallery, 1985; p.48 (l) NPG, © Man Ray 2015 Trust / ADAGP, Paris and DACS, London; p.48 (r) NPG, Bequeathed by Nigel Nicolson, 2005; p.49, NPG. © Estate of Duncan Grant. All rights reserved, DACS 2020; p.51 NPG, Bequeathed by Frances Catherine Partridge (née Marshall), 2004; p.52 Arts Council Collection, Southbank Centre, London, © The Lucian Freud Archive / Bridgeman Images; p.54 NPG, Given by Terence Pepper, 2013, © reserved; p.55 NPG, Accepted in lieu of tax by H.M. Government and allocated to the Gallery, 2016, © The Lucian Freud Archive / Bridgeman Images; p.56–57 NPG, © reserved / Estate of Harry Patrick Ogden; p.59 NPG, Given by S. Smith Travers, 1859; p.61 NPG, Given by Lady Helen Lett (née Browne), 1946; p.63 NPG, © Estate of Mildred E. Eldridge; p.65 (t) NPG, Bequeathed by the sitter's daughter-in-law, Jane, Lady Shelley, 1899; p.65 (b) NPG, bequeathed by the sitter's daughter-in-law, Jane, Lady Shelley, 1899; p.66 (t) NPG, Bequeathed by Jane, Lady Shelley, 1899; p.66 (b)NPG, Bequeathed by Jane, Lady Shelley, 1899; p.69 NPG, Given by Mrs Richard Fuller, 1943; p.70 NPG, Given by Florence L. Barclay (Florence Louisa Barclay (née Charlesworth)), 1921; p.71 NPG, Given by Florence L. Barclay (Florence Louisa Barclay (née Charlesworth)), 1921; p.73 NPG, © reserved / Estate of Harry Patrick Ogden; p.74 NPG, Purchased with help from Mrs T.S. Eliot, the Art Fund, and Roy Davids, 2005, © estate of Sylvia Plath / Faber & Faber Ltd; p.75 NPG, Given by Rosalie Thorne McKenna Foundation, 2011, © Rosalie Thorne McKenna Foundation; Courtesy Center for Creative Photography, University of Arizona Foundation; p.77 NPG, Accepted in lieu of tax by H.M. Government and allocated to the Gallery, 1991, © The Cecil Beaton Studio Archive; p.78 NPG, Accepted in lieu of tax by H.M. Government and allocated to the Gallery, 1991, © The Cecil Beaton Studio Archive; p.79 NPG, Accepted in lieu of tax by H.M. Government and allocated to the Gallery, 1991, © The Cecil Beaton Studio Archive; p.80–1 NPG, © Angela Verren Taunt. All rights reserved, DACS 2020; p.83 (t) NPG, Given by Georgiana Margaretta Zornlin, 1870; p.85 NPG, Purchased with help from the Art Fund, 2007; p.87 NPG, © Gilbert & George; p.89 The Geffrye Museum of the Home, London, © Photo: The Geffrye Museum of the Home, London / Bridgeman Images; p.92 © St Edmundsbury Heritage Service, Suffolk; p.95 (l) Scottish National Gallery Of Modern Art, Image: National Galleries of Scotland © Succession Picasso / DACS, London 2020; p.95 (r) Lee Miller Archives, © Lee Miller Archives, England 2020. All rights reserved. www.leemiller.co.uk; p.97 (tl) NPG, Given by Terence Pepper, 2012, © Man Ray 2015 Trust / ADAGP, Paris and DACS, London; p.97 (m) NPG, Given by Terence Pepper, 2013, © Man Ray 2015 Trust / ADAGP, Paris and DACS,

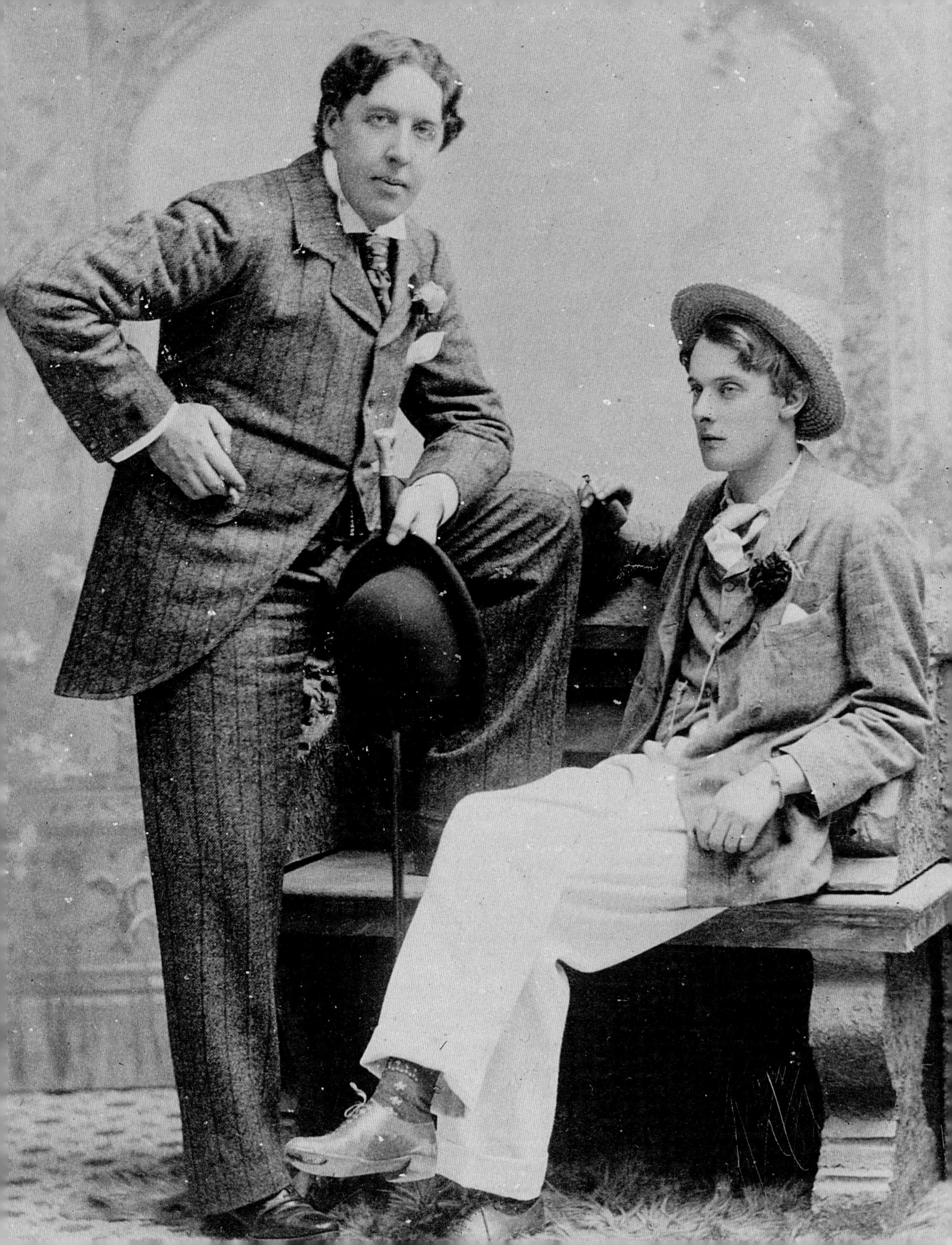

London and © Lee Miller Archives, England 2019. All rights reserved. leemiller.co.uk; p.97 (bl) NPG, Given by Terence Pepper, 2012, © Man Ray 2015 Trust / ADAGP, Paris and DACS, London; p.98 NPG, Given by Terence Pepper, 2012, © Man Ray 2015 Trust / ADAGP, Paris and DACS, London; p.99 Lee Miller Archives, © Lee Miller Archives, England 2020. All rights reserved. www.leemiller.co.uk; p.100 NPG, Given by Chris Beetles Fine Photographs, 2013, © Lee Miller Archives, England 2019. All rights reserved. leemiller.co.uk; p.101 The Roland Penrose Collection, England, © Man Ray 2015 Trust / ADAGP, Paris and DACS, London. Image courtesy of The Penrose Collection; p.103 NPG, © Angela Verren Taunt. All rights reserved, DACS 2020; p.104 NPG, Bequeathed by Dr Priaulx Rainier, 1987, © Bowness; p.107 NPG, Given by Robert Moller in memory of Savile and Marjorie Moller, 2018, Reproduced by permission of Peters Fraser & Dunlop (www.petersfraserdunlop.com) on behalf of the Estate of Mervyn Peake; p.108 NPG, Lent by the estate of Mervyn Peake, 1986, With kind permission of the Mervyn Peake estate; on loan to the National Portrait Gallery, London; p.110–1 NPG, Bequeathed by Sir Charles Wentworth Dilke, 2nd Bt, 1911; p.113 (l) NPG, Accepted in lieu of tax by H.M. Government and allocated to the Gallery, 1980; p.113 (r) NPG, Accepted in lieu of tax by H.M. Government and allocated to the Gallery, 1980; p.114 NPG, Purchased with help from the National Heritage Memorial Fund, 1985; p.115 NPG, Commissioned as part of the First Prize, 1992 BP Portrait Award, 1993; p.116 NPG, Given by British Museum, 1995; p.117 NPG, Given by IPC Newspapers Limited, 1971, © Science & Society Picture Library / National Portrait Gallery, London; p.121 Royal Collection Trust / © Her Majesty Queen Elizabeth II 2020 / Bridgeman Images; p.123 NPG, Bequeathed by Sir Charles Wentworth Dilke, 2nd Bt, 1911; p.124 © The Women's Library, LSE, London; p.125 Courtesy of Gillian Wearing. Photo by Greater London Authority / Caroline Teo; p.127 The Syndics of the Fitzwilliam Museum, Cambridge. Bequeathed by Dr Eric George Millar, DLitt, 1966, © The Estate of Edmund Dulac. All rights reserved. DACS 2020. Image © Fitzwilliam Museum, Cambridge; p.128–9 NPG, given by the Art Fund, 1942; p.133 NPG, Given by King's College: Cambridge: UK, 1983 © The Estate of John David Roberts. Reproduced with the permission of the William Roberts Society; p.134 © Lebrecht Music & Arts / Alamy; p.139 Private Collection / © The Lucian Freud Archive / Bridgeman Images; p.140–1 NPG, Given by Camera Press: London: UK, 2007, Photograph by Tom Blau, Camera Press, London; p.143 (t) NPG, Purchased with help from the Art Fund, the Pilgrim Trust, H.M. Government and an anonymous donor, 1961; p.145, Harvard Law School Library, Harvard University; p.147 Dulwich Picture Gallery, London. Bourgeois Bequest, 1811, Photo: Dulwich Picture Gallery, London, UK / Bridgeman Images; p.148 NPG, Purchased with help from the Pilgrim Trust, 1984; p.152 NPG, Transferred from Tate Gallery, 1957; p.153 (l) NPG, Purchased with help from the Friends of the National Libraries and the Pilgrim Trust, 1966; p.160, 163 © Victoria and Albert Museum, London; p.163–5 NPG, Given by the photographer's sister, Susan Morton, 1976; p.167 NPG, Given by the photographer, Annie Leibovitz, 1995, © Annie Leibovitz; p.168 NPG, Given by John Morton Morris, 2015, © estate of John Lennon; p.169 NPG, Given by Terence Pepper, 2014, © Getty Images; p.170 NPG, Given by Camera Press: London: UK, 2007, Photograph by Tom Blau, Camera Press, London; p.171 NPG, Given by Herb Schmitz, 1994, © Herb Schmitz; p.174 Government Art Collection, London, Image © Crown Copyright, Government Art Collection, London; p.176 NPG, Given by Ernest E. Leggatt; p.177 NPG, Given by Terence Pepper, 2010, © E.O. Hoppé Estate Collection / Curatorial Assistance; pp.186–7 NPG, Given by Thomas Patrick John Anson, 5th Earl of Lichfield, 2003 in conjunction with the exhibition 'Lichfield: the early years 1962–1982', © Lichfield; p.188 NPG, © Associated Press / Shutterstock; p.189 NPG, Given by Terry O'Neill, 2003, © Terry O'Neill / Iconic Images; p.191 (t) NPG, Purchased with help from the proceeds of the 150th anniversary gala, 2007, © Mario Sorrenti / Art Partner; p.191(b) NPG, Given by Juergen Teller, 2016, © Juergen Teller; pp.192–3 NPG, © Alexi Lubomirski; p.195 NPG, Acquired Daily Herald, 1980; p.197 NPG, Bequeathed by the estate of Stan Smith, 2013; p.198 NPG, Given by the photographer, Yousuf Karsh, 1991, Photograph by Yousuf Karsh, Camera Press, London; p.199 NPG, Given by John Kobal Foundation, 2013, © Robert Coburn for Alexander Korda Films, Inc.; p.200 NPG, purchased, 2004 in conjunction with Beaton: Portraits exhibition, © IWM 2020; p.202 NPG, Given by Bassano & Vandyk Studios, 1974; p.203 Imperial War Museum, London, © IWM 2020; p.205 NPG, Given by Thomas Patrick John Anson, 5th Earl of Lichfield, 2003 in conjunction with the exhibition 'Lichfield: the early years 1962–1982', © Lichfield; p.207 NPG, Given by Norman Parkinson, 1981 in conjunction with the NPG exhibition 'Norman Parkinson: 50 Years of Portraits and Fashion', © Norman Parkinson Archive / Iconic Images; p.209 NPG, Given by Getty Images, Hulton Archive, 2007, © Getty Images; p.211 NPG, Given by Thomas Patrick John Anson, 5th Earl of Lichfield, 2003 in conjunction with the exhibition 'Lichfield: the early years 1962–1982'; © Lichfield, p.212 Getty Images, © Tim Graham / Getty Images; p.213 NPG, Given by the photographer, John Swannell, 1998, © John Swannell / Iconic Images; p.214 NPG, Purchased with help from the Pilgrim Trust, 1984; p.221 NPG, Given by Herb Schmitz, 1994, © Herb Schmitz.

Published in Great Britain
by National Portrait Gallery Publications
National Portrait Gallery
St Martin's Place
London WC2H 0HE

Published to accompany the exhibition:
Love Stories

This exhibition is organised by the:
National Portrait Gallery, London
and will tour to the following venues:
National Portrait Gallery, Australia and
Denver Art Museum

Every purchase supports the National
Portrait Gallery, London. For a complete
catalogue of current publications, please
visit our website at www.npg.org/publications

ISBN 978-1-85514-703-4

A catalogue record for this book
is available from the British Library

10 9 8 7 6 5 4 3 2 1

Director of Commercial: Anna Starling
Publishing Manager: Kara Green
Editor: Amelia Collins
Assistant Editor: Tijana Todorinovic
Picture Researcher: Mark Lynch
Production Manager: Ruth Müller-Wirth
Proofreader: Alison Effeny

Design: Raymonde Watkins

Printed in Italy by Printer Trento
Reproductions by DL Imaging

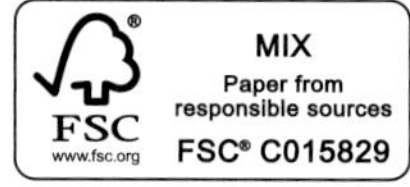